Collins

second edition

SOCIOLOGY AS
FOR OCR

Stephen Moore   Dave Aiken   Steve Chapman   Peter Langley

INTRODUCTION

Features of the textbook

The book is divided into chapters that match the OCR AS-level topics. Each chapter containsa number of features designed to help you with learning,revision and exam-preparation.

Getting you thinking

The opening activity draws on your existing knowledge and experiences to lead in to some of the main issues of the topic. The questions are usually open and, although suitable for individual work, may be more effectively used in discussion in pairs or small groups, where experiences and ideas can be shared.

OCR specification table

At the start of each chapter, a clearly laid out table shows how the topics in that chapter cover the OCR AS-level specification.

OCR specification		Coverage
The formation of culture		
Key concepts	• norms, values, status, culture and roles	Covered in Topic 1
Types of culture, how they are formed and how they may change over time	• high culture, popular culture, subculture, cultural diversity, multiculturalism, consumer culture and global culture	Covered in Topic 1
The process of socialization		
The process of socialization including	• the nature versus nurture debate, primary socialization, secondary socialization, and formal and informal social control.	Covered in Topic 2
Agents of socialization including	• the family, education (e.g. hidden curriculum), the mass media (e.g. consumerism), religion, the peer group and the workplace.	Covered in Topic 2
The role of socialization in the creation of identities		
Definitions of identity and how it relates to both culture and socialization		Covered in Topics 3, 4, 5 & 6
The creation and reinforcement of particular identities	• gender, femininities and masculinities; social-class: upper, middle-class and working-class; ethnicity and hybridisation; and age; old age, middle age and youth.	Covered in Topics 3, 4, 5 & 6

Key terms

These are simple definitions of important terms and concepts used in each topic, linked to the context in which the word or phrase occurs. Most key terms are sociological, but some of the more difficult but essential vocabulary is also included. Each key term is printed in **bold type** the first time it appears in the main text.

Key terms

Anglo-Saxon a White speaker of English as a first language.

Caste the Hindu system of organizing society into hereditary classes based on religious purity.

Celtic relating to Wales, Scotland and Ireland.

Collectivist group-orientated.

Dual identity hybrid identity, e.g. combination of British and Asian identity.

Ethnicity ethnic distinctiveness.

Hyper-male exaggerating masculine characteristics.

Multicultural lots of different cultures living side by side.

Activities

At the end of each topic, there are two types of activity that will help you take your learning further:

- Research ideas – Suggestions for small-scale research which could be used for class or homework activities.

- Web tasks – Activities using the worldwide web to develop your understanding and analysis skills. This feature also serves to identify some of the key websites for each topic.

Chapter summary

Each chapter ends with a summary in the form of a 'mind map' that provides an attractive visual overview of the whole chapter using key headings. This clearly shows how the topics fit together and is useful for revision.

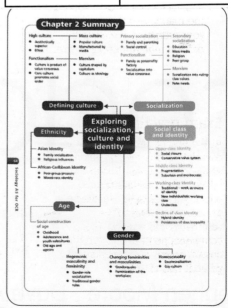

Focus on research activities

A recent piece of interesting and relevant research is summarized, followed by questions that ncourage you to evaluate the methods used as well as the conclusions drawn.

Methods in action activities

These appear in Chapter 3: they are similar to the Focus on research activities in Chapters 1 to 7, but concentrate on the research methods used in the piece of research described.

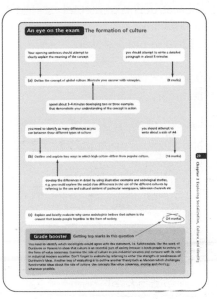

An eye on the exam

OCR-style exam questions with some helpful hints and Grade Booster advice to help you get top marks. Use these to assess your progress, as well as to provide regular exam practice.

Exam practice

At the end of each chapter is a complete exam-style question of the type you will find in the relevant OCR AS-level exam paper. A candidate's 'answer' is provided, together with comments and a mark. The comments point out where the answer scores good marks and when it fails to score.

Methods in action

George Davey Smith et al. (2003)
The health of ethnic minorities: a meta-study

George Davey Smith and his colleagues were concerned that there was relatively little information on the health of ethnic minorities in Great Britain. They therefore conducted a **meta-study** to try to provide an overall picture of health care. They looked at data from a range of surveys including official publications, small-scale surveys and earlier sociological studies. Putting all of this together, they provided a picture of standards of health for different ethnic groups in Britain, taking into account the impact of social class. In order to do this, they also had to review a wide range of theoretical and methodological books and articles. The study therefore includes secondary research based upon both theoretical and statistical studies, from government as well as academic sources.

They found that, overall, the health standards of ethnic minorities in Britain were worse than those of the general population, and that these differences were most apparent in childhood and old age. They found that most previous studies tended to explain any differences in health between ethnic minorities and the majority population in terms of cultural, dietary or genetic differences. However, they concluded that ethnicity by itself does not explain these differences. They suggest instead that differences in health are closely linked to social class and income.

Davey Smith, G., Chaturvedi, N., Harding, S., Nazroo, J. and Williams, R. (2003) *Health Inequalities: Lifecourse approaches*, Bristol: Policy Press

1 Why did the researchers use a meta-study?
2 How did the use of secondary sources allow them to reach different conclusions from earlier research?

Check your understanding

These comprise a set of basic comprehension questions – all answers can be found in the preceding text.

Focus on research

Simon Charlesworth (2000)
Deadman's Town

Charlesworth takes a phenomenological approach to working-class experience on an extremely deprived council estate in Rotherham. 'Phenomenological' means looking at a social phenomenon from the perspective of those experiencing it, usually in their own words. Charlesworth's account of the experience of long-term unemployment in one of Britain's poorest and bleakest towns (known by locals as 'Deadman's Town') puts working-class people's interpretations at the heart of the study.

Charlesworth found that working-class identity was still a very strong feeling among the poor in Rotherham, although it had been adapted to cope with the conditions of exclusion, hardship and humiliation that are a normal part of everyday life. From the outside, and particularly from a middle-class perspective, the everyday culture of working-class people on this estate might seem narrow and irresponsible. Charlesworth notes that people on the estate do not seem proud of their heritage nor are they positive about their futures. Instead, they indulge in behaviour – heavy drinking, drug use, stealing, etc. – that brings them criticism as 'chavs' or as a deadbeat idle underclass. However, the reality, says Charlesworth, is that their response is a rational one to the economic decay of their area.

Charlesworth, S. (2000) *A Phenomenology of Working Class Experience*, Cambridge: Cambridge University Press

1 How do you think Charlesworth gathered the information for this study?
2 How was working-class identity interpreted and expressed by people living on this council estate in Rotherham?

Check your understanding

1 Identify three differences between 'sex' and 'gender'.
2 Explain, using examples, what is meant by 'hegemonic' masculinity and femininity.
3 Explain why the family is the most important agency of gender-role socialization.
4 How do mass media representations of masculinity and femininity reinforce traditional stereotypes about men and women?
5 How have economic and social changes contributed to the emergence of new types of femininity and masculinity?
6 How have sexual identities evolved over the last 50 years?

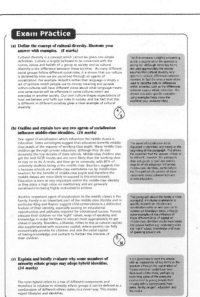

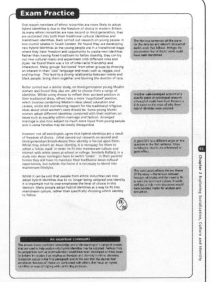

CONTENTS

Sociology AS for OCR

Introduction:
Sociological perspectives

Consensus, culture and identity

Getting you thinking

1 Can Barley's description of the typical suburban home be applied to your general experience of home?

2 Do you think this description is typical of most homes in the UK?

3 Barley is describing a very ordered and structured world. What do you think is the reason for all this order and predictability? Where does it come from?

Examining the homes in a typical English suburb, Nigel Barley noticed how similar they were in their organization. Most had front gardens kept in good order with flowerbeds and so on. However, he observed that people very rarely sat in these or used them for family activities such as barbecues. This was the function of back gardens, although people maintained their privacy through the use of hedges and fences. Rooms on the ground floor were generally regarded as public rooms – some had best front rooms used only for entertaining at the weekend. Kitchens were used to prepare and eat meals. Most had a sitting room in which the television was kept and this was the focus of most family activity, especially entertaining guests. The most private rooms were the toilets. Visitors would seek permission to use these. Upstairs bedrooms, too, were generally regarded as private because these were associated with intimate activities. Consequently, family members knocked on doors before entering. Bedrooms were also individually furnished and decorated so that it was not difficult to identify which family members occupied them.

Adapted from Billington, R. *et al.* (1998)
Exploring Self and Society,
Basingstoke: Macmillan, pp. 38–9

We learn from an early age to see our status as wrapped up with our home, and to see a happy family and home as important goals. In other words, there exists a great deal of agreement in society about how we ought to organize our daily lives. Sociologists refer to this agreement among members of society as **consensus**. This consensus means that we have a good idea of how we should behave in most situations. It also means that we can anticipate pretty accurately how other people are going to behave, just as we can guess the layout of their house or flat. Some sociologists see this order and predictability as the key to understanding society. If this order did not exist – if we were always confused and uncertain about our own and others' values and behaviour – then, they believe, chaos and anarchy would be the result. This theory of society is known as **functionalism** or consensus theory.

Functionalism

Functionalism is a **structuralist theory**. This means that it sees the individual as less important than the **social structure** or organization of society. It is a 'top-down' theory that looks at society rather than the individuals within it. Society is more important because the individual is produced by society. People are the product of all the social influences on them: their family, friends, educational and religious background, their experiences at work, in leisure, and their exposure to the media. All of these influences make them what they are. They are born into society, play their role in it and then die. But their deaths do not mean the end of society. Society continues long after they are gone.

Social order

Functionalists study the role of different parts of society – social institutions – in bringing about the patterns of shared and stable behaviour that they refer to as **social order**. They might study, for example, how families teach children the difference between right and wrong, or how education provides people with the skills and qualifications needed in the world of work. For functionalists, society is a complex system made up of parts that all work together to keep the whole system going. The economic system (work), the political system, family and kinship, and the cultural system (education, mass media, religion and youth culture) all have their part to play in maintaining a stable society from generation to generation.

A major function of social institutions is to socialize every individual into a system of norms and values that will guide their future behaviour and thinking. People need to be taught the core values of their society and to internalize them, so that they become shared and 'taken for granted'. The end result of this process is **value consensus** – members of society agree on what counts as important values and standards of behaviour. Such consensus produces a sense of **social solidarity**, i.e. we feel part of a community that has something in common. We feel a sense of common **identity**.

Another important foundation stone of social order in modern societies is the specialized division of labour. This refers to the organization of jobs and skills in a society. All members of society are dependent upon this division of labour, which supplies a vast and invisible army of workers to maintain the standard of living we take for granted. For example, hundreds of unskilled and skilled manual workers, professionals and managers are involved in supplying us with essential services such as electricity, gas, water, sewage systems, transport, food in supermarkets, and so on. The fact that you are able to sit in a classroom and read this book is also the product of hundreds of workers you will never see or meet. For example, someone has decided that your area needs a school or college, somebody has hired a caretaker to open and maintain the building, cleaners to clean, secretaries to run the office, teachers to teach and managers to decide to put on AS Sociology. The presence of this book in front of you required an author, editors, proofreaders, graphic designers, picture researchers, illustrators, a publisher, printers, people involved in the production of paper and ink, lorry drivers to transport the finished product to warehouses and bookshops, and someone behind the counter or a computer to sell it on to schools, teachers and students. Note, too, that you are already part of this division of labour. Without students, educational institutions would be pointless. The list of people we are dependent upon is endless. Think about how your life would change if all electricity workers were abducted by aliens overnight!

The specialized division of labour, therefore, is crucial because without it, society would soon descend into chaos. Consequently, another function of **social institutions** is to prepare young people to take their place in the division of labour by transmitting the idea that education, qualifications, working hard and a career are all worthwhile things. This ensures that young people will eventually come to replace workers who have retired or died, and so social order is maintained.

Figure 1.1 Understanding functionalism

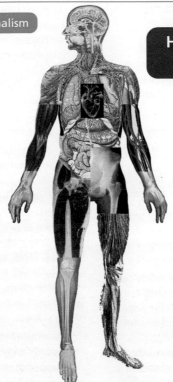

How is society like a human body?

Functionalism looks at society as though it were a living thing like a human being.

The body

Every part of the body has a function which helps to keep it alive and healthy.

- The human body grows and develops.

- All of the parts of the body link together into one big system.

- The body fights disease.

Society

Every part of society helps to keep society going – for example, the family helps by bringing up the next generation.

- Societies gradually develop and change.

- All of the parts of society work together and depend on each other – they are interdependent.

- Society has mechanisms to deal with problems when they occur, such as the police and the legal system.

Talcott Parsons

Talcott Parsons (1902–79) was a key functionalist thinker. He argued that socialization is the key to understanding human behaviour patterns. The role of social institutions, such as the family, education, religion and the media, is to ensure the passing on, or reproduction, of socially acceptable patterns of behaviour. Social institutions do this in a number of ways:

- They socialize people into key values of society, such as the importance of nuclear family life, achievement, respect for authority and hierarchy, and so on. The result is that most members of our society share common values and norms of behaviour (value consensus), and so we can predict how people are going to behave in the vast majority of social situations. The family, education and the mass media are primarily responsible for this function.
- Social institutions give some values and norms a sacred quality, so that they become powerful formal and informal moral codes governing social behaviour. These moral codes underpin our definitions of criminal, deviant and immoral behaviour. An example of a formal moral code is 'do not steal', because it is embodied in the law, while examples of more informal moral codes are 'do not lie' or 'do not commit adultery'. The social institutions of religion and the law are primarily responsible for the transmission of these codes, although media reporting of crime and deviance also contributes by reminding members of society about what counts as normality and deviance, and publicizing the punishments handed out to those who indulge in behaviour that lies outside the consensus.
- They encourage social solidarity (a sense of community) and **social integration** (a sense of belonging). For example, the teaching of history is an important means of achieving this goal, because it reminds members of society about their shared culture.

So, our behaviour is controlled by the rules of the society into which we are born. The result is that we don't have to be told that what we are doing is socially unacceptable. We will probably feel inhibited from indulging in deviant behaviour in the first place because we are so successfully immersed in the common values of society by our experience of socialization.

Identity

Identity is the way we feel about ourselves, which is partly shaped by how others view us. People's identity as fathers, mothers and children, for example, is controlled by a value consensus. This defines and therefore largely determines what roles each status has to adopt if it is to fit successfully into society. In other words, there is a clear set of expectations about what makes a 'good' mother or father, son or daughter. For example, people defined as

'normal' parents will engage in socially approved behaviour – they will protect their children from harm rather than neglect them or inflict excessive physical punishment on them; they will give them unconditional love; they will support them economically, and so on. Note that these expectations may change according to gender – hence the commonly held belief that working mothers, rather than working fathers, may be a cause of psychological damage in children. Functionalists point out that our experience of socialization and social control ensures that most of us will attempt to live up to these social and cultural expectations without question.

Criticisms of functionalism

Functionalism is far less popular in sociology today than it was in the 1950s. Part of its decline in popularity is probably linked to the problems it had attempting to explain all the diversity and conflict that existed in society from the 1960s onwards. Criticism of its core ideas has therefore been widespread:

- Functionalism has been criticized for overemphasizing consensus and order, and failing to explain the social conflicts that characterize the modern world. We see clear differences in behaviour all around us every day, and there may be clear cultural differences present in the same society. For example, behaviours on which most of society might have been agreed 50 years ago, such as women with young children going out to work, cohabitation, abortion or homosexuality (which were all regarded as wrong), now attract a range of differing opinions. Some functionalists have attempted to explain this by reference to subculture. This can be defined as a way of life subscribed to by a significant minority who may share some general values and norms with the larger culture, but who may be in opposition to others. For example, in a multicultural society like the UK, some minority ethnic groups may retain very traditional ideas about women's roles, marriage, homosexuality, etc.
- Functionalism has also been accused of ignoring the freedom of choice enjoyed by individuals. People choose what to do – they do what makes sense to them. Their behaviour and ideas are not imposed on them by structural factors beyond their control. In this sense, functionalism may present 'an oversocialized' picture of human beings.
- There may also be problems in the way functionalists view socialization as a positive process that never fails. If this were the case, then delinquency, child abuse and illegal drug-taking would not be the social problems they are.
- Finally, functionalism has been accused by Marxists of ignoring the fact that power is not equally distributed in society. Some groups have more wealth and power than others and may be able to impose their norms and values on less powerful groups. The next few topics focus on this process.

Key terms

Consensus a general agreement.

Functionalism a sociological perspective that focuses on understanding how the different parts of society work together to keep it running smoothly.

Identity the way we feel about ourselves.

Social institution a part of society, such as education or the family.

Social integration a sense of belonging to society.

Social order patterns of shared and predictable behaviour.

Social solidarity a sense of community.

Social structure an alternative term for the social organization of society.

Structuralist theory a theory that believes that human behaviour is influenced by the organization of society.

Value, or moral, consensus an agreement among a majority of members of society that something is good and worthwhile.

Check your understanding

1   Using your own words, explain what is meant by 'value consensus'.

2   What are the key values of society according to Parsons, and what agencies are mainly responsible for their transmission?

3   What agencies are responsible for turning key values into powerful moral codes that guide our most basic behaviour?

4   Why do social agencies such as the law and the media need to regulate our behaviour?

5   How might the teaching of British history encourage a sense of community and integration in British schools?

Activities

Exploring social institutions

Read the following text and then answer the questions on the right.

Durkheim believed that the function of social institutions was to promote and maintain social order and social solidarity. He regarded the family as the most important institution because it links the individual to society. Romantic love and marriage provide society with an orderly means of reproduction, while the family unit provides physical and economic support for children during the early years of dependence. Most importantly, the family is the primary agent of socialization – children learn society's essential ideas and values, the accepted ways of behaving and the social roles (such as feminine and masculine roles) required for adult life. Education, too, develops both the values and skills required for children to take their place eventually as working adults in the specialized division of labour. The discipline structure and secondary socialization that occurs in schools also function to maintain consensus, as most people accept that a future of work and a career are the norm. Finally, religious beliefs provide people with moral guidelines and practices which socially integrate people into a common identity and community.

1   Explain what is meant by 'the specialized division of labour'.   (2 marks)

2   Identify two functions of religion.
                                                                (4 marks)

3   Identify three examples which suggest that socialization is not as successful as functionalists claim.   (6 marks)

4   Identify and briefly explain two reasons why functionalists might be criticized for overemphasizing consensus and order.
                                                                (8 marks)

Research idea

Interview a sample of males and females of different ages about what they see as important. You could ask them about issues such as love, marriage, how family life should be organized, how children should be brought up, what they regard as deviant, their religious beliefs and so on. However, remember to explain the aims of this research to your participants and gain their informed consent.

Web.task

Search for the website 'Dead Sociologists' Society'. Use it to find out about the ideas of the founding father of functionalism, Emile Durkheim.

Conflict, culture and identity

Sociology AS for OCR

Getting you thinking

Imagine that everybody in the British economy was to march past you in an hour-long parade, and that the marchers are organised by income, with the poor at the front and the rich at the back. Now imagine that the height of the people marching by is proportional to their income, so a person with average income will be average height, a person earning half the average income will be half the average height, and so on.

What would this parade look like? Most of us would picture a parade where people slowly but steadily got taller. We'd be wrong. As the parade begins, the first marchers are really tiny. For five minutes or so, you are peering down at people just inches high – single mothers, the disabled, the elderly and the unemployed. Ten minutes in, the full-time labour force has arrived: to begin with, mainly unskilled manual and clerical workers, standing about waist-high to the observers. At this point things start to get dull, because there are an incredible number of these very small people. The minutes pass, and pass, and they just keep on coming. It is only in the last 20 minutes of the parade that you are able to look anyone in the eye – and then, only for a fleeting moment because, suddenly, heights begin to surge

upward at a madly accelerating rate. Doctors, lawyers, and senior civil servants 20 feet tall speed by. Moments later, bankers and stockbrokers peer down from 50 feet, 100 feet, 500 feet. And then in the last seconds you see the unimaginably huge giants: the great untaxed. The very soles of their shoes are hundreds of feet thick. Most of them are businessmen, owners of companies, film stars, and a few members of the Royal Family. Robbie Williams and Prince Charles are over a mile high. Britain's richest man is the last in the parade – he measures over four miles high.

Adapted from Johann Hari, *The Independent*, 25 June 2007

1 **What does this parade tell us about the way income is divided in the UK?**

2 **Give examples of how long it took for people on different incomes to appear in the parade.**

3 **Does the parade surprise you in any way? Is Britain more, or less, unequal than you thought?**

Lots of students have part-time jobs. Perhaps you have. If so, you sell your time and your ability to work to an employer who, in return, gives you money. But is this a fair exchange? Think about why they employ you. It's not to do you a favour, but because they benefit: the work you do is worth more to them than the amount they pay you. They would benefit even more if they paid you less for the same work or got you to do more work for the same pay.

Of course, it would be better for you if you were paid more for the same work or worked less for the same pay. To put it another way, what is good for your boss is bad for you, and vice versa. There's a very basic conflict of interest between you and your employer. This conflict occurs not because you are unreasonable or your boss is money-grabbing. It occurs simply because the system works that way.

Marxism

This is the starting point for **Marxism**, a sociological perspective based on the ideas of Karl Marx (1818–83). For Marxists, the system we live in (which he called **capitalism**) divides everyone up into two basic classes: bosses and workers. Marx called the bosses the **bourgeoisie** or ruling class (because they controlled society), and the workers he called the **proletariat** or working class. The ruling class benefit in every way from how society operates, while the workers get far less than they deserve.

Like functionalism, Marxism is a structuralist theory – that is, it sees the individual as less important than the social structure of society. In particular, Marxism sees the economic organization of societies as responsible for the behaviour of individuals. This is because Marxism claims that individuals are the products of the class relationships that characterize economic life.

Society is based on an exploitative and unequal relationship between two economic classes. The bourgeoisie are the economically dominant class (the ruling class) who own the **means of production** (machinery, factories, land, etc.). The working class, on the other hand, own only their ability to work. They sell this to the bourgeoisie in return for a wage. However, the relationship between these two classes is unequal and based on conflict because the bourgeoisie aim to extract the maximum labour from workers at the lowest possible cost.

According to Marxists, the result is that the bourgeoisie exploit the labour of the working class. The difference between the value of the goods and services produced by the worker and the wages paid is pocketed by the capitalist class and lies at the heart of the vast profits made by many employers. These profits fuel the great inequalities in wealth and income between the ruling class and the working class. For example, according to HM Revenue and Customs, in 2003, 71 per cent of all financial wealth in the UK was owned by just 10 per cent of the population. Even if we add property ownership to financial wealth, the least wealthy 50 per cent of the population only own about 7 per cent of all wealth in the UK in 2003. These figures are also likely to be underestimates, because people generally do not declare the full sum of their wealth to the tax authorities – for instance, they may keep wealth abroad.

If society is so unfair, why do the working class go along with it? Why aren't there riots, strikes and political rebellion? Why does society actually appear quite stable, with most people seemingly content with their position?

Ideology

Marxists argue that the working class rarely challenge capitalism because those who control the economy also control the family, education, media, religion – in fact, all the cultural institutions that are responsible for socializing individuals. Louis Althusser (1971) argued that the function of these cultural institutions is to maintain and **legitimate** class inequality. The family, education, the mass media and religion pass off ruling-class norms and values as 'normal' and 'natural'. Marxists refer to these ruling-class ideas as **ideology**.

Marxists argue that socialization is an ideological process in that its main aim is to transmit the ruling-class idea that capitalist society is **meritocratic** – that is, if you work hard enough, you can get on – despite the fact that the evidence rarely supports this view. This ideological device is so successful that the majority of the working class are convinced that their position in society is deserved. In other words, they are persuaded to accept their lot and may even be convinced that capitalism has provided them with a decent standard of living.

Marxists argue that capitalist ideology shapes the way of life of a society – its culture. A good example of this, say Marxists, is the way that the mass media convince us through advertising and popular culture – television, cinema, pop music, tabloid newspapers, etc. – that our priority should be to buy more and more material goods (see Figure 1.2 below). We want to be rich so that we can buy more consumer goods, and, somehow, this will make us happy. What is more, while we are all watching soap operas and reading the latest celebrity gossip, we fail to notice the inequalities and exploitation which are the norm in the capitalist system.

This means that most of us are unaware of our 'real' identity as exploited and oppressed workers. We experience what Marxists describe as **false class consciousness**. Eventually though, Marxists believe, we will learn the real truth of our situation and rebel against the capitalist system.

Criticisms of Marxism

- The notion of 'false class consciousness' has been undermined by surveys such as those conducted by Marshall *et al.* (1988), and the government in the form of the British Social Attitudes survey (Jowell *et al.* 1995). The British Social Attitudes survey found that 69 per cent of people thought their opportunities were influenced by their social class 'a great deal' or 'quite a lot'. Marshall argued that over 70 per cent of his survey sample believed that social class was an inevitable feature of British society and over 50 per cent felt that class conflict existed in the UK between a ruling class that monopolized economic and political power and a

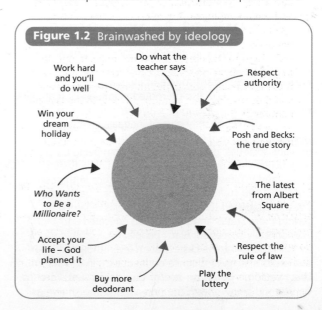

Figure 1.2 Brainwashed by ideology

lower class that could do little to change its position. Marshall noted that most people were aware of social injustices, especially relating to inequalities in the distribution of wealth and income, but felt there was little they could do practically to bring about more equality. However, in support of the concept of ideology, Charlesworth's (2000) study of working-class people in Rotherham blames the educational system for this indifference and cynicism. He argues that the working-class experience of education results in them devaluing themselves and restricting their ambitions to 'being disappointed' in life.

- Like functionalism, Marxism has been accused of ignoring the freedom of choice enjoyed by individuals. People choose what to do and think – they are not 'brainwashed' by ideology. In this sense, Marxism too may present an 'oversocialized' picture of human beings.
- This criticism is not true of all Marxists. Some have argued that **oppositional subcultures** can exist within the capitalist system. For example, Hall and Jefferson (1993) argued that youth subcultures are often a means by which young people can express dissatisfaction with the capitalist system. They argued that the value systems, dress codes and behaviour of groups such as mods, skinheads and punks are a form of symbolic and temporary resistance to society. Their resistance is symbolic in that their behaviour often shocks society, but temporary in that they eventually become passive adults.
- Marxism may put too much emphasis on conflict. After all, despite all its inequalities, capitalism has managed to improve most people's standard of living. Marxism also neglects the common interests that employers and workers may have. If workers work well, then the business does well and employers can afford to increase wages.
- Marxism, in general, has been criticized for claiming that all cultural activity is geared to class or economic interests. Consequently, Marxists neglect the fact that culture may reflect religious, **patriarchal**, nationalistic and ethnic interests.

The work of Max Weber

Another sociologist who took a conflict perspective was Max Weber (1864–1920). He agreed with Marx that social class was an important source of inequality but argued that inequality could also be rooted in influences that have nothing to do with economics. Weber claimed that 'status differences' were at the heart of inequality – class was only one form of status. For example, Weber pointed out that in many societies, power is acquired from being born into a particular tribe or ethnic group. Inequality between Blacks and Whites in apartheid South Africa in the period 1950 to 1990 stemmed from status rather than social class, in that even the poorest White was regarded as having more status and power than educated and economically successful Black people.

In Hindu India, the caste system (even though illegal) still exerts a strong influence on inequality. In this system, every person is born into one of four closed status groups or, situated below these, the non-caste group known as 'untouchables'. This system of status differences is based upon religious purity – the better the life you lead, the more likely you will be reborn (reincarnated) as a member of a higher caste. Meanwhile, you cannot work your way out of your caste, your job is determined by it and you must marry within it.

Feminism

Feminists argue that another important status difference and source of inequality and conflict is gender. They point out that the UK is a patriarchal society – that is, men generally have more power and prestige than women across a range of social institutions. Women generally have less economic power than men. In 2006, women working full time earned on average 17 per cent less than men working full time and they were more likely to be in poverty. Natasha Walter, in *The New Feminism* (1999), claimed that women do not enjoy equality of access to jobs, especially the top jobs in the city. Males still monopolize professional and managerial positions – for example, in 2006, only 17 per cent of directors and chief executives of major organisations, 8 per cent of top judges and 7 per cent of surgeons were women. Moreover, women are still expected to be predominantly responsible for the upkeep of the home and childrearing – surveys continue to indicate that family life is not yet characterized by equality between the sexes in terms of household labour.

Feminists believe that sexual discrimination is still a problem today and Walter argues that women still need to achieve financial, educational, domestic and legal equality with men. Liberal feminists are optimistic that this will eventually happen. They believe that there has been a steady improvement in the position of women, as old-fashioned attitudes break down, more girls do well in education and more women have successful careers.

Other types of feminists are not so hopeful. Marxist-feminists argue that patriarchy suits the capitalist system as well as men, because women are unpaid domestic labourers who service the male labour force, making them fit and healthy for work, and who produce and rear the future workforce. True equality between the sexes can only occur when the capitalist system is dismantled.

Radical feminists believe that the patriarchal oppression and exploitation of women is built into every aspect of the way society is organized. In particular, the family is identified as the social institution in which patriarchy is rooted. Radical feminists argue that, through gender-role socialization, women are socialized into accepting female subordination and into seeing motherhood as their main goal in life. Moreover, radical feminists argue that men aggressively exercise their physical, economic and cultural power to dominate women in all areas of social life, and particularly in personal relationships, such as marriage, domestic labour, childcare and sex. All men benefit from this inequality – there are no good guys!

Key terms

Bourgeoisie (or **capitalists**) the owners of businesses, and the dominant class in capitalist societies.

Capitalism an economic system associated with modern societies, based on private ownership of businesses.

False class consciousness the state of not being aware of our true identity as exploited workers.

Feminism a set of ideas that suggest that women are oppressed and exploited by men.

Ideology the norms and values that justify the capitalist system.

Legitimate make something appear fair and reasonable.

Marxism a sociological perspective based on the writings of Karl Marx. It believes that societies are unequal and unfair.

Means of production the land, factories, machines, science and technology, and labour power required to produce goods.

Meritocratic based on ability and effort.

Oppositional subcultures social groups whose value systems and behaviour challenge the dominant capitalist value system.

Patriarchal dominated by males.

Proletariat the working class in capitalist societies.

Check your understanding

1   What is the relationship between the bourgeoisie and the proletariat?

2   What is the function of ideology?

3   Describe two important criticisms of Marxism.

4   What is the purpose of socialization according to Marxists?

5   How do youth subcultures challenge capitalism?

6   What other sources of inequality exist, apart from social class, according to Weber and feminist sociologists?

Activities

Exploring capitalist values

Marxists believe that social institutions such as the education system, the media, the legal system and religion are agents of capitalism that transmit ruling-class ideology. For example, the education system socializes the working class into believing that their educational failure is due to lack of ability and effort, when, in reality, the capitalist system deliberately fails them so that they will continue to be factory workers. Television socializes the working class into believing that consensus is the norm and that serious protest about the way society is organized is 'extremist'. The law socializes the working class into believing that the law is on their side when, in reality, it mainly supports and enforces the values and institutions of the capitalist ruling class. Finally, Marxists argue that religions are also ideological because they convince some working-class people that their poverty is the product of sin and moral weakness, and that they should seek solutions in the form of salvation and spirituality.

1   Explain what is meant by the term 'ideology'.   (2 marks)

2   Identify the two basic classes that characterize capitalist societies.
                                                                  (4 marks)

3   Identify three ways in which the working class are socialized into accepting inequality.   (6 marks)

4   Identify and briefly describe two trends or patterns that suggest that the UK is a society characterized by economic inequality.   (8 marks)

Research idea

Conduct a small survey to see how aware people are of (a) their social class and (b) inequalities in income and wealth in the UK.

Web.tasks

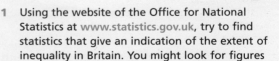

1   Using the website of the Office for National Statistics at www.statistics.gov.uk, try to find statistics that give an indication of the extent of inequality in Britain. You might look for figures on income, wealth, education and health.

2   Search for the website 'Dead Sociologists' Society'. Use it to find out about the ideas of Karl Marx

Social action, culture and identity

Getting you thinking

DRIVING LICENCE   A030019

1 Surname
   PAYNE MR
2 Other names
   JAMES   Town of birth
3 Date of birth   Worcester
   24 03 1990
4 Permanent Address
   14 Roseacre Drive
   Worcester WR8 9LA
5 Issued by DVLA SWANSEA

6 Valid from   Valid until
   17 09 2007   23 03 2060
7 No
   PAYN 785288 B87VU

Signature
   James Payne

EUROPEAN UNION
UNITED KINGDOM OF GREAT BRITAIN AND NORTHERN IRELAND
DIEU ET MON DROIT
PASSPORT

I have known Rachael for four years. She is a mature young woman who takes her responsibilities seriously. Consequently, she has a conscientious and industrious approach to her academic studies and can be trusted to work independently and with initiative. She also works well as a member of a team and is well liked and respected by both her peers and teachers. I have no doubt that you will find Rachael to be a thoroughly honest and reliable person. I was always impressed by her enthusiasm, persistence, motivation and ability to work under pressure. I have no hesitation in recommending her to your institution.

My mother loves me.
I feel good.
I feel good because she loves me.

I am good because I feel good
I feel good because I am good
My mother loves me because I am good.

My mother does not love me.
I feel bad.
I feel bad because she does not love me
I am bad because I feel bad
I feel bad because I am bad
I am bad because she does not love me
She does not love me because I am bad.

R.D. Laing (1970) *Knots*,
Harmondsworth: Penguin

1   What do these documents tell us about a person? What do they not tell us?

2   What does the reference tell us about Rachael's identity? What doesn't it tell us?

3   What does the poem tell us about this person's identity?

4   How does the self-identity apparent in the poem contrast with the picture of the individual in the reference?

Official documents tell us about the identity we present to the world – our date and place of birth, age, nationality, address, marital status and so on. References, like the example on the left, give us some insight into **social identity** – how well we perform our social roles, such as our jobs. However, poems, like the one on the left, can tell us about the way we see ourselves – our **self-identity** – and how this is often the result of how we interpret other people's reactions to us.

Think about a small child. Children try out different sorts of behaviour and then watch how the people important to them (significant others) react. By doing this, they learn what is acceptable and unacceptable behaviour. This assists the development of their conscience, which modifies and regulates future behaviour – children remember whether they were rewarded or punished for particular types of behaviour and usually choose to avoid those activities that previously resulted in disapproval. Parents further contribute to this interactive process by encouraging children to imitate socially approved adult behaviour, such as good manners, gendered dress codes and so on.

Social action theory

What has just been described is the view of **social action** or **interactionist** sociologists. They reject the structuralist assumption that social behaviour is determined, constrained and even made predictable by the organization of society. They see people as having a much more positive and active role in shaping social life. If structuralist theory is a 'top-down' theory, then social action theory is 'bottom-up', as it starts with people rather than society.

Social action theorists reject the view that people's behaviour is the product of external forces over which they have little control. Most people do not feel themselves to be puppets of society. Rather, as Chris Brown (1979) notes:

>> *they feel they are living their own lives, making their own decisions and engaging, for the most part, in voluntary behaviour. There may be things they have to do which they resent, but resentment is, of course, tangible evidence of an independent self, forced to comply, but unwillingly and under protest.>>*

However, although we operate as individuals, we are aware of other people around us. Social action theorists argue that the attitudes and actions of those other people influence the way we think and behave – that society is the product of people coming together in social groups and trying to make sense of their own and each other's behaviour.

People are able to work out what is happening in any given situation because they bring a set of **interpretations** to every interaction and use them to make sense of social behaviour. In particular, we apply meanings to symbolic behaviour. For example, gestures are symbols – putting up two fingers in a V-sign may be interpreted as insulting, because it has an obscene meaning. When we are interacting with others, we are constantly on the lookout for symbols, because these give us clues as to how the other person is interpreting our behaviour – for instance, if they are

smiling, we might interpret this as social approval, and if they maintain prolonged, intense eye contact, we might interpret this as a 'come-on'.

Our experience of this 'symbolic interaction' means we acquire a stock of knowledge about what is appropriate behaviour in particular situations. We learn that particular contexts demand particular social responses. For example, I might interpret drinking and dancing at a party as appropriate, yet the same behaviour at a funeral as inappropriate. It is likely that other people will share my interpretations and so it is unlikely that the behaviour described would occur at the funeral.

Socialization and identity

Socialization involves learning a stock of shared interpretations and meanings for most given social interactions. Families, for example, teach us how to interact with and interpret the actions of others; education brings us into contact with a greater range of social groups and teaches us how to interpret social action in a broader range of social contexts. The result of such socialization is that children acquire an identity.

Social action theorists suggest that identity has three components:

1 Personal identity refers to aspects of individuality that identify people as unique and distinct from others. These include personal name, nickname, signature, photograph, address, National Insurance number, etc.
2 Social identity refers to the personality characteristics and qualities that particular cultures associate with certain social roles or groups. For example, in our culture, mothers are supposed to be loving, nurturing and selfless; therefore, women who are mothers will attempt to live up to this description and hence acquire that social identity. As children grow up, they too will acquire a range of social identities, such as brother, sister, best friend, student. Socialization and interaction with others will make it clear to them what our culture expects of these roles in terms of obligations, duties and behaviour.
3 The individual has a **subjective** (internal) sense of their own uniqueness and identity. Sociologists call this the 'self'. It is partly the product of what others think is expected of a person's social identity. For example, a mother may see herself as a good mother because she achieves society's standards in that respect. However, 'self' is also the product of how the individual interprets their experience and life history. For example, some women may have, in their own mind, serious misgivings about their role as mother. The self, then, is the link between what society expects from a particular role and the individual's interpretation of whether they are living up to that role successfully.

The concept of self has been explored extensively by social action sociologists. Some have suggested that the self has two components – the 'I' and the 'me'. The 'I' is the private inner self, whereas the 'me' is the social self that participates in everyday interaction. When a person plays a social role as a teacher or student, it is the 'me' that is in action. The 'me' is shaped by the reactions of others – that is, we act in ways that we think are socially desirable.

However, the 'I' supplies the confidence or self-esteem to play the role successfully.

Goffman (1959) argues that interaction is essentially about successful role-playing. He suggests that we are all social actors engaged in the drama of everyday life. Stage directions are symbolized by the social and cultural context in which the action takes place. For example, the classroom as a stage symbolizes particular rules that must be followed if the interaction is to be successful, e.g. students sit at desks while teachers can move around the room freely. Sometimes the script is already in place, so for instance, we adhere to cultural rules about greeting people – 'Good morning, how are you?' – although often the script has to be improvised. Goffman argues that the public or social identity we present to the world is often simply a performance designed to create a particular impression. This makes sense if we think about how we behave in particular contexts or company. For example, your behaviour in front of your grandparents is likely to be very different compared with your behaviour in front of friends. Therefore, you have a catalogue of different identities you can adopt.

Goffman invents a number of concepts that he claims people as social actors use in everyday action to assist in the management of other people's impression of them. Some people will use 'front' to manage an interaction. This refers to items of physical or body equipment that a social actor uses to enhance their performance – for example, teachers who want to convey authority may wear formal clothing to distance themselves from students. Another concept is 'region' – the classroom is the front region where the teacher 'performs', while the staffroom is where they relax and become another person, such as the colleague or friend.

Labelling theory

Labelling theory is closely linked to the social action approach and helps us to understand how some parts of society may be responsible for socializing some people into identities that may have negative consequences. Take education as an example. Interactionists believe that the social identity of pupils may be dependent on how they interact with teachers. If teachers act in such a way that pupils feel negatively labelled – as 'lazy' or 'thick', for example – then this will seriously affect their behaviour and progress.

Howard Becker (1963) pointed out that labels often have the power of a **master status**. For example, the master status of 'criminal' can override all other statuses, such as father, son or husband. In other words, deviant labels can radically alter a person's social identity. For example, someone labelled as 'criminal' may be discriminated against and find it difficult to get employment, make new friends and be accepted into their community. They may end up seeking others with similar identities and values, and form deviant subcultures. A **self-fulfilling prophecy** is the result, as the reaction to the label makes it come true.

Think about how the experience of streaming or setting may affect the self-esteem of a pupil. How do pupils who are placed in low streams or sets feel? They may well accept a view of themselves as 'failures' and stop trying – after all, what's the point if you're 'thick'? Or what if a pupil feels labelled as a 'troublemaker' because they are Black? The negative label may be internalized (accepted) and a self-fulfilling prophecy may occur. The self sees itself as a 'failure' or as 'deviant' and reacts accordingly. The label becomes true (see Figure 1.2).

Goffman (1961) illustrated the power of such labelling in his ethnographic study of inmates in a mental hospital in the USA. Goffman refers to such hospitals as 'total institutions' because they attempt to shape all aspects of their inmates lives, e.g. by organizing their routine. Goffman argues that total institutions deliberately break down a person's sense of self through a process he calls 'mortification' – they are stripped, given a common uniform to wear and referred to by a serial number. In other words, the institution sets about destroying individuality. The institution then attempts to rebuild the self in its own collective image. However, Goffman notes

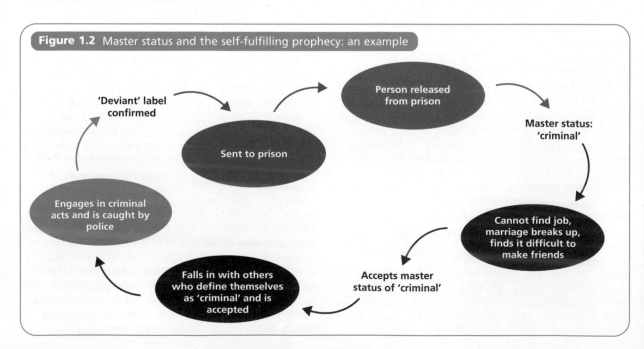

Figure 1.2 Master status and the self-fulfilling prophecy: an example

that the inmates he studied reacted in various ways to this process. Some conformed to the institution's demands; some even became institutionalized – they became so completely dependent on the institution that they could no longer survive in the outside world. Some, however, hung on to their individuality by giving the impression that they were conforming, while others openly opposed the system. What Goffman's work indicates is that the self and self-esteem can be very resilient and that labelling does not always have to be such a destructive process. Those who have been labelled can actually resist the definitions of the powerful.

Body image

Recent studies in a social action context have focused on how we interpret our bodies. It is argued that the way people view themselves and others is shaped by the dominant cultural ideas and images about ageing, body shape, weight and beauty that we see in media products such as magazines, advertisements, television and films. It is argued by feminist commentators that British culture sees the slim or thin female form as the ideal, with the result that young girls are socialized into seeing the slim figure as a source of status and success, while 'too much' weight is unattractive and socially inadequate. It is suggested that eating disorders, such as anorexia and bulimia, may be the outcome of these dominant cultural ideas, as female identity is often bound up with how women perceive their bodies. Research on female eating disorders suggests that those with the disorders often have low self-esteem and often subscribe to distorted images about their weight and attractiveness. A survey of 25 000 women aged 17 to 34 conducted by Radio 1's *NewsBeat* in 2006 found that 51 per cent would have surgery to improve their looks and a third of size 12 women thought they were overweight. Furthermore, almost half the sample said they had skipped a meal to lose weight, while 8 per cent had made themselves sick. More than half of girls aged 12 to 16 felt that their body image either stopped them from getting a boyfriend or from relaxing in a relationship.

Disability

Social action studies of disability by sociologists such as Colin Barnes and Tom Shakespeare are very critical of official and medical definitions of disability. As Shakespeare and Watson (1997) note, disabled people are defined by society and social institutions such as the mass media as 'that group of people whose bodies do not work; or who look or act differently; or who cannot do

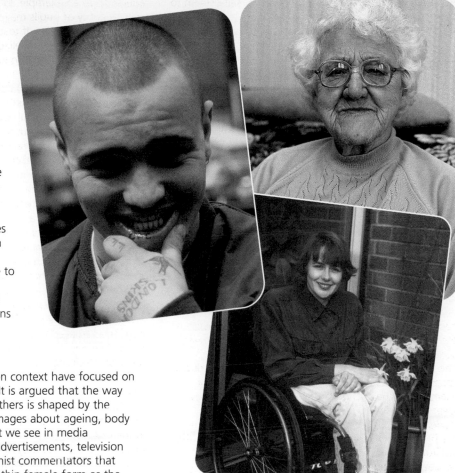

Suggest how labelling might affect the lives and the identities of the people in these photographs.

productive work'. In other words, the disabled are defined as abnormal or deviant by society, and disability is something to be avoided at all costs. Furthermore, Shakespeare and Watson argue that medical approaches to disability consider any negative self-identity held by disabled people to be exclusively the product of their physical impairment and 'focus on the need for adjustment, mourning, and coming to terms with loss'.

In contrast, social action theory advocates a social model of disability which suggests that disabled people are actually 'disabled by society' – by social attitudes based on prejudicial stereotypes and by social policy which assumes that physical impairment results in dependency. Social action theory argues that we learn our social identity through the process of socialization and this forms the basis of how we see ourselves and, most importantly, how we think we are seen by others. It is argued that if disabled people are constantly subjected to the view that they are dependent, weak, abnormal and have little status, the disabled individual may actually take on a 'disabled identity' in order to interact successfully with doctors, social workers, the general public and so on. The prophecy of dependency and weakness is fulfilled as the disabled person lives up to social expectations and is not encouraged to be an independent person. Social policy also contributes to this process by failing to provide the disabled with practical facilities, such as wheelchair access to buildings and public transport, that would enable them to lead a normal life.

Shyness

A recent symbolic interactionist study focused on shyness. Scott (2003) carried out in-depth interviews with 16 'shy' individuals in the South Wales area who volunteered after responding to an advertisement. She also set up a website about 'shyness and society' that included an email distribution list. Over a period of nine months, a virtual community composed of 42 individuals was created which exchanged ideas and discussed online the social aspects of shyness.

Scott found evidence of the notion of an 'I' and a 'me', in that shyness was often experienced as a conflict between a desire to be part of a social scene and the fear of being negatively judged or criticized. The shy 'I' was often beset by feelings of 'anxiety, uncertainty and inhibition', while the shy 'me' was concerned about how other people would view them – that is, they were afraid of making a fool of themselves or not fitting in. Many participants felt plagued by 'what if' feelings, such as 'what if they don't like me?'. Scott's sample often felt shy in particular social contexts in which the reactions of others were perceived as important. Scott notes that shyness is often seen as a 'deviant' activity, although society is likely to interpret it as 'normal' in particular social groups, e.g. among girls. She argues that there is a lot of moral pressure put on shy people to overcome their 'problem' through the use self-help books, miracle drugs and shyness clinics.

Criticisms of social action theory

Social action theories have been criticized because they tend to be very vague in explaining who is responsible for defining acceptable norms of behaviour. They do not explain who is responsible for making the rules that so-called deviant groups break. In this sense, they fail to explore the origin of power and neglect potential sources, such as social class, gender and ethnicity. For example, Marxists argue that the capitalist ruling class define how social institutions such as education and the law operate. In other words, social action theories tend to be descriptive rather than explanatory.

Focus on research

Anne Becker (2003)
Eating disorders in Fiji

Anne Becker (2003) carried out a study to evaluate the impact of the introduction of Western television in the 1990s on Fijian adolescent girls. Traditionally, Fijian society favoured robust appetites and plump body shapes among women, and eating disorders were rare. However, the study found that subjects living in a house with a TV set were three times more likely to show symptoms of eating disorders. Dieting, too, became common among the study population, with 74 per cent reporting that they felt 'too big or fat'. Analysis of interview data found that 77 per cent of girls strongly admired TV characters, and wanted to copy them by changing behaviour, clothing or hairstyle, or through reshaping their body.

Adapted from Becker, A. *et al.* (2003) 'Binge eating and binge eating disorder in a small-scale, indigenous society: the view from Fiji', published online in Wiley InterScience (www.interscience.wiley.com)

1 What was the main cause of the appearance of eating disorders in Fiji in your view?

2 How did Fijians view the female body before the introduction of television?

3 Identify three ways in which Fijian girls' identity has been negatively influenced by Western media imagery.

Check your understanding

1 How is society formed, according to social action theorists?

2 From an interactionist perspective, what is the function of socialization?

3 What is meant by 'social identity'?

4 Explain the meaning of 'self'.

5 What causes a 'self-fulfilling prophecy'?

6 What is the result of deviant labels becoming master statuses?

Key terms

Interpretations the meanings that we attach to particular objects or situations, e.g. we usually interpret classrooms as learning environments and act accordingly.

Labelling theory the idea that categorizing or stereotyping individuals or groups can seriously affect their behaviour. Used especially in the fields of education and deviance.

Master status a label or status that can override all others (e.g. criminal, child abuser).

Self-identity refers to how we see ourselves, usually in reaction to how we think others see us.

Self-fulfilling prophecy a prediction that makes itself become true.

Social action theory or **interactionism** a sociological perspective that focuses on the ways in which people give meaning to their own and others' actions.

Social identity refers to how society sees us, in terms of whether we live up to the cultural expectations attached to the social roles we play.

Subjective personal, based on your own view.

Activities

Exploring social institutions

Individuals, like actors, are performing for an audience. Speech, acts and gestures all require someone else to be watching or listening. Our identities, therefore, are the product of how we present ourselves and how others perceive us. For example, you have to persuade your tutor that you have seriously adopted the identity and role of student. Your tutor may respond by according you an 'ideal' student label or identity. If you fail to convince, you may be labelled as a 'deviant' student, i.e. as idle or troublesome. This 'deviant' label is a 'master status' which overshadows other aspects of identity. Often, people who are considered deviant in one respect are assumed to be deviant in other respects. For example, other teachers may judge you negatively in staffroom discussions.

Those labelled as 'deviants' often experience stigma – people behaving differently towards them. In reaction, those labelled may pursue a deviant career by adopting a lifestyle which confirms their deviant status. In other words, a self-fulfilling prophecy results.

Adapted from Woodward, K. (ed.) (2000) *Questioning Identity: Gender, Class, Nation,* London: Routledge, pp. 14–15

1 Explain what is meant by the term 'self-fulfilling prophecy'. (2 marks)

2 Identify two aspects of your own identity. (4 marks)

3 Identify three possible consequences of being labelled by an institution, such as a school, the police or a mental hospital. (6 marks)

4 Identify and briefly describe two criticisms of the concept of 'labelling'. (8 marks)

Research ideas

1 Observe an everyday situation involving interaction between people. It could be in a library, at a bus stop, in a common room or a pub.

– What is going on?

– Does everyone share the same interpretation of the situation?

– How do people try to manage the impression they give of themselves?

2 Find two groups of students: one group who have experience of being placed in a high stream, and one group who have experience of being placed in a low stream. Give a questionnaire to, or interview, each group in order to find out how streaming affected their self-image, motivation and progress. Compare the responses of the two samples.

Web.task

Visit the following websites on shyness and write a brief report detailing how shyness may affect a person's self-esteem and identity:

● The Royal College of Psychiatrists – find information about 'Shyness and Social Phobia' in the section on Mental Health Information. www.rcpsych.ac.uk

● The Shyness Institute, a major shyness research centre at www.shyness.com/shyness-institute.html

● The Shyness Home Page detailing the work of the American sociologists, L. Henderson and P.G. Zimbardo, at www.shyness.com

TOPIC 4

Postmodernism

Getting you thinking

Try to imagine the life ahead for the woman from the 1930s in the photograph above.

1   What sort of family life do you think she would have had?

2   Might she have had paid employment? What problems might she have faced in pursuing a career?

3   What about the roles played by her and her husband?

Now think about the future for the young woman of today.

4   What sort of family life do you think she is likely to have?

5   Is she likely to have paid employment?

6   What about her relationship with her husband?

You may well have found it fairly straightforward to plot out the future for the young woman of 70 years ago. Attempting the same task for a woman today is much more difficult. Maybe she will choose not to marry or live in a family. Maybe she won't have children. Alternatively, she could devote her life to a family, but then again she might decide to focus on following a career – or she could do both. The choices appear endless. Being a woman today seems much more flexible and uncertain – and less predictable – than in the past.

Sociologists have watched recent social changes with great interest. Some have reached the conclusion that society has experienced such major upheavals that the old ways of explaining it just won't work any more. They believe that we are entering a new sort of society, which they refer

to as the postmodern world or **postmodernity**. But before we can consider this, we need to head back to the beginnings of sociology.

Have you ever wondered why sociology came about? History tells us that sociology developed in order to explain the rapid social changes associated with **industrialization** and **urbanization** during the 19th century. Lives changed so drastically during this period that, not surprisingly, people began to look for theories and explanations that would help make sense of the bewildering changes taking place. Families left the rural communities where they had lived for centuries, to find work in the new cities. They had to adjust to a different lifestyle, different work, different bosses and different kinds of relationships with family and community.

On the whole, early sociologists approved of these changes and the kind of society they created – now commonly referred to as **modernity** or the modern world. They set out to document the key features of what they saw as an exciting new order.

The nature of the modern world

Sociologists have identified four major characteristics of the modern world:

1 *Industrialization* – Production is industrial and economic relationships are capitalist. Factories produce goods, bosses own factories, and workers sell their labour to bosses. Social class is therefore the basic source of difference and identity in modern societies.
2 *Urbanization* – Early modernity was associated with great population movement to the cities, known as urbanization. Twentieth-century theories of modernity tended to celebrate the bright lights and innovation of the city while ridiculing rural culture as living in the past.
3 *Centralized government* – Government is characterized by a **bureaucratic** state that takes a great deal of responsibility both for the economy and for the welfare of its citizens.
4 *Rational, scientific thinking* – What really made modern society stand apart from premodern societies was the revolution in the way people thought about the world. Before industrialization, tradition, religion and superstition had provided the basis for views of the world. The modern world adopted a new way of thinking, shaped by science and reason.

New ideas and theories (referred to by postmodernists as '**big stories**' or **meta-narratives**) competed with each other to explain this constantly changing modern world and these theories frequently called for more social progress. Some of these theories were political (e.g. socialism), while others were cultural (e.g. the ideas of feminism). To paraphrase Marx, one of the leading modernist thinkers, their job was not just to explain the world – the point was to change it.

Sociology and the modern world

Sociologists were caught up in this excitement about modernity, and attempted to create scientific theories that would explain the transition from the traditional to the modern. One of the founding fathers of sociology, Auguste Comte, believed that sociology was the science of society. This **positivist** view argued that sociological research based upon scientific **rationality** could rid the world of social problems such as crime.

Marx, too, celebrated modernity, despite his criticism of its economic relationships, because he believed that science had given people the power to change the world. Sociological theories such as functionalism and Marxism, therefore, also developed into meta-narratives as they attempted to provide us with knowledge or 'truth' about the nature of modernity.

The postmodern world

In the past 20 years or so, some sociologists have identified trends and developments which, they claim, show that modernity is fragmenting or dissolving. They argue that it is being replaced by a postmodern world in which many sociological ideas and concepts are becoming irrelevant.

Characteristics of postmodernity have been identified in aspects of work, culture, identity, globalization and knowledge.

Work

The nature of work and economic life has changed. Work is no longer dominated by mass factory production in which thousands of people work alongside each other. Work today is mainly located within the **service sector**, and is dominated either by jobs that mainly involve the processing of information (e.g. the financial sector), or by jobs that involve the servicing of **consumption** (e.g. working in a shop).

Our ideas about work have also changed. People today are less likely to expect a job for life, and are more willing to accept a range of flexible working practices, such as part-time work, working from home and job-sharing.

Culture

As our society has grown wealthier, so the media and other cultural industries – such as fashion, film, advertising and music – have become increasingly central to how we organize our lives. It is suggested that we are a 'media-saturated' society in which media advice is available on how we can 'make over' our homes, gardens, partners and even ourselves. Look, for example, at the lifestyle magazines ranged on the shelves of bookshops and newsagents, advising you on skin care, body size and shape, hair colour and type, fitness, cosmetic surgery and so on. What these trends tell us is that consumption is now a central defining feature in our lives.

Postmodern culture is also about mixing and matching seemingly contradictory styles. For example, think about the way in which different music from different times and different styles is 'sampled', with musical phrases from one recording being used in another recording.

Identity

Our identities are now likely to be influenced by mainstream popular culture which celebrates **diversity**, consumerism and choice. In other words, the old 'me' was about where I came from in terms of my family and class background, the area I lived in and so on. The new postmodern 'me', however, is about designer labels, being seen in the right places, the car I drive, listening to the right music and buying the right clothes. Style has become more important than substance. As Steve Taylor (1999) argues, society has been transformed into:

>> *something resembling an endless shopping mall where people now have much greater choice about how they look, what they consume and what they believe in.* >>

Globalization

The global expansion of **transnational companies** – such as McDonald's, Sony, Coca-Cola and Nike – and the global marketing of cultural forms – such as cinema, music and computer games – have contributed to this emphasis on consumption. Such globalization has resulted in symbols that are recognized and consumed across the world. Images of Britney Spears and Michael Jackson are as likely to be found adorning the walls of a village hut in the interior of New Guinea as they are a bedroom wall in Croydon. Brands like Nike and Coca-Cola use global events like the World Cup and the Olympic Games to beam themselves into millions of homes across the world.

It is therefore no wonder that this global culture is seen to be challenging the importance of national and local cultures, and challenging **nationalism** as a source of identity. Information technology and electronic communication, such as email and the internet, have also been seen as part of this process.

Knowledge

In the postmodern world, people no longer have any faith in great truths. In particular, people have become sceptical, even cynical, about the power of science to change the world, because many of the world's problems have been brought about by technology. In the political world, ideologies such as **socialism** – which claimed they were the best way of transforming the world – have been discredited in many people's eyes, with the collapse of communism in Eastern Europe. Postmodernists insist that truth is both unattainable and irrelevant in the postmodern world. Instead, they stress the **relativity** of knowledge, ideas and lifestyles, such that many different yet equally authentic values are possible.

Postmodernism and sociology

Steve Taylor argues that these developments have three main consequences for sociology:

1 Most sociology is concerned with explaining the nature and organization of modern societies and social institutions. However, the key relationships that underpin such societies – class, family, gender – are no longer relevant.

2 Sociologists can no longer claim to produce expert knowledge about society, because in postmodern societies, relativity and uncertainty have replaced absolute judgements about what is or should be. As Swingewood (2000) argues, in postmodern societies 'knowledge is always incomplete, there are no universal standards, only differences and **ambiguity**'. The big sociological stories, such as functionalism and Marxism, have become redundant, because 'knowledge' is now judged in terms of its usefulness rather than its claim to be a universal 'truth'.

3 Sociologists can no longer make judgements or claim that they know what is best for societies. Sociology is only one set of ideas competing with others. All have something relevant to offer. If people want to listen to sociologists and act upon their findings, it is up to them. It is equally relevant not to do so.

Endless choice in the postmodern world

IF DISSATISFIED WITH ANY PRODUCT SIMPLY RETURN IT AND EXCHANGE IT FOR ANOTHER.

Criticisms of postmodernism

Critics of postmodernism suggest that it is guilty of making too much of recent social changes. Evidence suggests that aspects of the postmodernist argument – especially the decline of social class, ethnicity and nationalism as sources of identity – are exaggerated. For example, surveys indicate that people still see social class as a strong influence in their lives, and use aspects of it to judge their success and status and that of others. There is no doubting that consumption has increased in importance, especially among young people, but it is pointed out that consumption does not exist in a vacuum. The nature of your consumption – what and how much you consume – still very much depends upon your income, which is generally determined by your occupation and social class. Similarly, our ability to make choices is still also constrained by our gender and ethnicity, because of the influence of patriarchy and institutional racism.

Check your understanding

1 **What term is used by postmodernists to describe theories of society?**

2 **What was the role of sociology, according to Auguste Comte?**

3 **Identify two social changes that have led some sociologists to argue that we are entering a postmodern world.**

4 **How do the media contribute to our sense of identity?**

5 **What is the relationship between globalization and postmodernism?**

6 **How did the collapse of communism in Eastern Europe contribute to people's cynicism about meta-narratives?**

7 **What is the role of the internet in postmodern society?**

Key terms

Ambiguity the state of being open to a range of interpretations – the meaning is not clear.

Bureaucratic based on rules and procedures.

Consumption the use of goods and services, especially as part of forming an identity.

Diversity variety.

Industrialization the transformation of societies from being agricultural to industrial, that took place in the 18th and 19th centuries.

Meta-narratives or **'big stories'** the postmodernist term for theories like Marxism and functionalism, which aim to explain how societies work.

Modernity period of time starting with the industrial revolution, associated with industrial production, urban living, rational thinking and strong central government.

Nationalism belief system or political view that stresses shared geographical location, history and culture.

Positivism the view that sociological research based upon scientific principles could rid the world of social problems such as crime.

Postmodernity term used by postmodernists to describe the contemporary period, which is characterized by uncertainty, media-saturation and globalization.

Rationality actions decided by logical thought.

Relativity the idea that no one example of something (e.g. political view, sociological theory, lifestyle, moral) is better than any other.

Service sector a group of economic activities loosely organized around finance, retail and personal care.

Socialism a political belief system based on the idea of collective ownership and equal rights for all.

Transnational companies companies that produce and market goods on a global scale.

Urbanization the trend towards living in towns and cities rather than in rural areas.

Activities

Exploring postmodernism

Although there are many strands to 'postmodernism', the basic idea is that individual freedom has combined with increased geographical mobility, better communication and a media-saturated society to create a world in which 'consumers' select elements of culture from a global cafeteria. Economies based on the production and distribution of things have been superseded by economies based on the production and distribution of ideas and images. We are now bombarded with a mass of different media images, which has led to greater individual choice in terms of personal style, tastes and beliefs so that it makes little sense to talk of a mass of people being shaped by influences such as social class.

An obvious illustration can be found in the matter of accents. Before the 1970s, there was a clear link in British society between certain accents and social status. British broadcasters, particularly on the BBC, spoke in the accents of the upper classes. It used to be possible to guess the political party of a politician by accent. Conservative party politicians spoke like members of the Royal Family, whereas Labour politicians spoke in the regional accent of the working class. Such typing is now vastly more difficult. Well-educated, middle-class children listen to 'gangsta rap' and other musical styles associated with the Black poor of the inner cities and borrow not only vocabulary and accent, but also dress and posture styles.

In politics, it is no longer possible to 'read off' people's preferences from their social class. Instead, we find a variety of consciously created interest groups: radical student movements, environment movements, animal rights campaigns, gay rights groups and women's groups.

Adapted from Bruce, S. (1999) *Sociology: A Very Short Introduction*, Oxford University Press

1 Explain what is meant by a 'media-saturated society'. (2 marks)

2 Identify two sources of identity in modern societies. (4 marks)

3 Identify three characteristics of postmodern society. (6 marks)

4 Identify and briefly describe two ways in which postmodernism may challenge sociological thought. (8 marks)

Research idea

Interview a sample of 16 to 19 year olds about their expectations of the future (jobs, relationships, family, etc.). To what extent are they uncertain or clear about their future?

Web.task

Use the world wide web to search for information on:

● postmodernism – find out about its influence on art, architecture and literature
● Jean Baudrillard, a key postmodern thinker.

Chapter 1 Summary

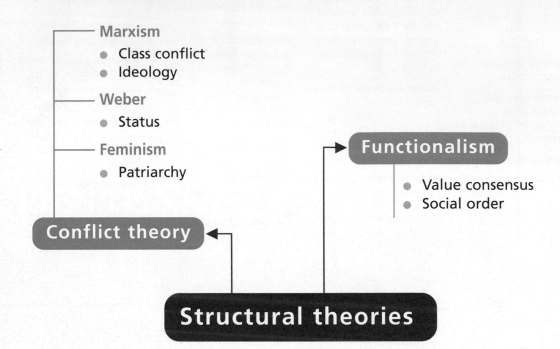

Marxism
- Class conflict
- Ideology

Weber
- Status

Feminism
- Patriarchy

Conflict theory

Functionalism
- Value consensus
- Social order

Structural theories

Social action theory or interactionism
- Interpretations
- Labelling

Postmodernism

Modernity
- Industrialization
- Urbanization
- Centralized government
- Rational thinking

Postmodernity
- Consumption
- 'Mix and match' culture
- Multiple identities
- Globalization
- Relativity of knowledge

Exploring Socialization, Culture and Identity

OCR specification

		Coverage
The formation of culture		
Key concepts	• norms, values, status, culture and roles	Covered in Topic 1
Types of culture, how they are formed and how they may change over time	• high culture, popular culture, subculture, cultural diversity, multiculturalism, consumer culture and global culture	Covered in Topic 1
The process of socialization		
The process of socialization including	• the nature versus nurture debate, primary socialization, secondary socialization, and, formal and informal social controls.	Covered in Topic 2
Agents of socialization including	• the family, education (e.g. hidden curriculum), the mass media (e.g. consumerism), religion, the peer group and the workplace.	Covered in Topic 2
The role of socialization in the creation of identities		
Definitions of identity and how it relates to both culture and socialization		Covered in Topics 3, 4, 5 & 6
The creation and reinforcement of particular identities	• gender; femininities and masculinities, social-class; upper, middle-class and working-class, ethnicity and hybridisation, and age; old age, middle-age and youth.	Covered in Topics 3, 4, 5 & 6

TOPIC 1

The formation of culture

Getting you thinking

Feral children

Feral or 'wild' children are those who, for whatever reason, are not brought up by humans. One famous example of feral children is that of two infant girls, Kamala and Amala, who were lost in the jungle in India in about 1918. The girls had been found living with wolves, in a cave-like den. The older girl was 6 or 7 years old and the other, who died a year later, perhaps a year younger.

Kamala, one of the 'wolf children', being taught to accept food and drink by hand

When captured, the girls were like animals. They were naked and ran in a sort of stooped crouch. They were afraid of artificial light. They were afraid of humans and kept a good distance. They did not display any characteristically human qualities. For example, they did not use tools of any kind, not even a stick. They did not know how to make a shelter. They did not walk upright. They did not laugh. They did not sing. They did not show any affection or attraction or curiosity towards humans. But what is especially striking is that the girls used no language. They used no noises or gestures to communicate. They didn't point at things or directions, or nod their head in agreement or disagreement. They preferred to eat with the dogs in the compound, who seemed to accept them. They ate by pushing their faces into the food, the way dogs do, and they drank by lapping from a bowl.

Adapted from Singh, J.A. and Zingg, R.N. (1942)
Wolf Children and the Feral Man, New York: Harper

Shirbit culture

The Shirbit culture believes that the human body is ugly and that its natural tendency is to feebleness and disease. The Shirbit therefore indulge in rituals and ceremonies designed to avoid this, and consequently every household has a shrine devoted to the body. The rituals associated with the shrine are private and secret. Adults never discuss the rituals and children are told only enough for them to be successfully initiated. The focal point of the shrine is a box built into the wall in which are kept charms and magical potions for the face and body. These are obtained from the medicine men who write down the ingredients in an ancient and secret language which is only understood by the herbalist who prepares the potion. These potions are kept in the charm-box for many years. Beneath the charm-box is a small font. Every day, twice a day, every member of the family enters the shrine room in succession and bows his or her head before the charm-box, mingles different sorts of holy water in the font and proceeds with a brief rite of ablution.

The Shirbit have an almost pathological horror of and fascination with the mouth, the condition of which is believed to have a supernatural influence on all social relationships. Were it not for the rituals of the mouth, they believe their teeth would fall out, their friends would desert them and their lovers would reject them. Finally, men and women indulge in barbaric acts of self-mutilation. Men engage in a daily body ritual of scraping and lacerating their faces with a sharp instrument, while women bake their heads in a small oven once a month.

Based on Levine, R. (1956) 'Body language of the Nacirema',
American Anthropologist, 58

1. Make a list of the things that the feral girls could not do and compare them with what you were capable of at the age of 6 or 7 years.

2. In your opinion, what skills were the feral girls likely to have that you lack?

3. What does the first extract tell us about the behaviour of human beings?

4. What aspects of Shirbit cultural behaviour seem alien to you?

5. In what ways might Shirbit behaviour be thought to resemble British culture?

Defining culture

What would you be like if all human influences were removed from your life? Tragic stories of **feral children**, such as that described on the left, show us very clearly that being human is about contact with other people. Without that contact we are reduced to basic and **instinctive** behaviour. But when humans work together – as they usually do – they create **cultures** that are complex, fascinating and utterly different. Our own culture always appears to be the most 'normal', while other cultures may seem strange, different and even inferior in some cases (a view known as **ethnocentrism**). Did you notice that the odd culture of the 'Shirbit' (described on the left) was actually a description of 'British' behaviour, especially our obsession with cleanliness, as it might appear to someone from a very different culture? ('Shirbit' is an anagram of 'British'.)

The idea of 'culture' is very important for sociologists. Culture is commonly defined as the way of life of a social group. More specifically, the term refers to 'patterns of belief, **values**, attitudes, expectations, ways of thinking, feeling and so on' which people use to make sense of their social worlds (Billington *et al.* 1998). Culture also consists of **customs** and rituals, **norms** of behaviour, **statuses** and **roles**, language, symbols, art and material goods – the entire way in which a **society** expresses itself.

The formation of culture

Culture is made up of several different elements, including values, norms, customs, statuses and roles.

Values

Values are widely accepted beliefs that something is worthwhile and desirable. For example, most societies place a high value on human life – although during wartime this value may be suspended. Other examples of British values include fair play, democracy, free speech, achievement, tolerance, wealth, property, romantic love, marriage and family life.

Norms

Norms are specific rules of behaviour that relate to specific social situations. They govern all aspects of human behaviour. For example, norms govern the way we prepare and eat food, our toilet behaviour and so on. Norms also govern how we are supposed to behave according to our gender – that is, there are rules governing what counts as masculine or feminine behaviour. These norms have changed in recent years – for example, only 40 years ago, women with young babies going out to work or wearing trousers to work would have met with social disapproval.

Customs

Customs are traditional and regular norms of behaviour associated with specific social situations, events and anniversaries which are often accompanied by rituals and ceremonies. For example, in Britain many people practise the custom of celebrating Bonfire Night on November 5th, and this usually involves the ritual of burning a Guy Fawkes effigy and setting off fireworks. It is also the social custom to mourn for the dead at funerals, and this usually involves an elaborate set of ritualistic norms and a ceremony. For example, it is generally expected that people wear black at funerals in Britain. Turning up in a pink tuxedo would be regarded as **deviant**, or norm-breaking, behaviour.

Statuses

All members of society are given a social position or status by their culture. Sociologists distinguish between 'ascribed' statuses and 'achieved' statuses. Ascribed statuses are fixed at birth, usually by inheritance or biology. For example, gender and race are fixed characteristics (which may result in women and ethnic minorities occupying low-status roles in some societies). Achieved statuses are those over which individuals have control. In Western societies, such status is normally attained through education, jobs and sometimes marriage.

Roles

Society expects those of a certain status to behave in a particular way. A set of norms is imposed on the status. These are collectively known as a role. For example, the role of 'doctor' is accompanied by cultural expectations about patient confidentiality and professional behaviour.

Different types of culture

High culture

This is a culture which is mainly subscribed to by the powerful and wealthy elite, i.e. the upper class. It is generally seen by its supporters as superior to other types of culture, particularly popular culture, because it is claimed that it can only be appreciated if people have a particular type of education or outlook that knows good taste, and which values creativity, artistic expression, critical discussion and serious philosophical issues.

High culture usually involves the appreciation of art, sculpture, classical music, opera, ballet, the plays of Shakespeare and other classic playwrights, poetry and 'great' or classic literature such as Austen, Dickens etc. Supporters of high culture believe these activities are culturally special and more worthy because they represent the nation's cultural heritage. It is argued that they should be set apart from the banality of everyday life. This is why society invests millions of pounds in institutions such as museums and art galleries, and in subsidising the arts. Newspapers, magazines and television treat these pursuits with reverence in terms of the time and space devoted to them, e.g. Sky even has a channel, i.e. Sky Arts devoted to the pursuit of high culture.

High culture is often sponsored by the government as good for intellectual and creative development, and consequently is encouraged through aspects of state schooling, e.g. studying Shakespeare. The study of high culture is usually a normal part of the curriculum in private schools.

The institutions which focus on high culture are usually establishment organizations, e.g. the Royal Opera House, the Royal Ballet etc which reinforces their sense of importance and high status. Finally, following high cultural pursuits can be a very expensive business and consequently some high cultural pursuits are often out of the reach of ordinary people.

Popular culture

Popular or mass culture is mainly associated with the entertainment culture – television, cinema, pop music, popular literature, newspapers, magazines etc – enjoyed by the majority of the population. Most popular culture is manufactured mainly by media conglomerates in order to make a profit.

Most popular culture is within reach of ordinary people and consequently forms a major part of their leisure activities. Some sociologists, notably post-modernists, see popular culture as a very positive development because it increases the choices available to people in terms of their identities and lifestyles. It has opened up all sorts of possibilities in terms of our consumption of material goods and how we live our lives in terms of how we want to look and behave. Popular culture in this sense has contributed to society becoming more diverse and complex.

However, not all sociologists agree that popular culture has a positive effect on society. The Marxist sociologists, Clarke and Critcher (1995) argue that we are not free to make choices because our consumption of popular culture is shaped and manipulated by advertising and global corporations.

Other sociologists see popular culture as an inferior and superficial candyfloss culture that has resulted in the dumbing down of intelligence, creativity, critical thinking etc.

Some sociologists have argued that this type of culture is manufactured for mass consumption rather than created for its own sake and, consequently, has little or no artistic merit compared with the products of high culture. Moreover, it is suggested that popular culture is harmful because it discourages critical thought. Others suggest that it is a corrupting influence on young people because celebrity culture, in particular, provides them with deviant and dubious role models.

However, in recent years, popular culture is being increasingly combined with high culture. In the world of classical music and opera, for example, the cross-over success of singers such as Charlotte Church and classical instrumentalists such as Vanessa Mae and Nigel Kennedy have blurred the boundaries between high and popular culture.

Consumer culture

Consumer culture is the product of the increasing emphasis on the consumption of goods and services that has developed over the past thirty years. If we examine the economy of the UK, we can see that it is still in the process of evolving from a manufacturing economy to a service economy. Increasingly factories producing goods such as cars and televisions are less important than companies that produce services such as banking, insurance, hotels, fast food, retail etc in terms of both economic output and numbers employed.

Shopping has become a major leisure pastime in the last ten years and consequently turned the UK into a consumer culture for four major reasons:

● Investment in new shopping experiences such as super-large supermarkets and out-of-town shopping centres which aim to serve regions rather than just the immediate urban areas.
● The take-off of on-line or internet shopping.
● The easy availability of credit cards and loans.
● The increasing importance of **conspicuous consumption** – the buying of particular brands, logos and designer goods in an attempt to gain status and respect from others which has been strongly encouraged by the advertising industry and endorsed by celebrity culture.

Global culture

Only 30 or so years ago, our culture was local and familiar. Travelling abroad was not a common activity; most of the products we consumed were produced in the UK and, although we watched Hollywood films and listened to American singers, there was also a reasonably healthy British entertainment industry focused on pop music and television. Today, however, it can be argued globalization is now a profound influence on how we live our cultural lives. As Marsh and Keating (2006) note:

<<*The British are increasingly a globalized people. We appear willing to travel far and wide. We increasingly eat and drink the foods and beverages that our European or even North American neighbours consume. We drive similar, if not identical cars, albeit on the other side of the road. Moreover, our consumption patterns are increasingly influenced and shaped by the growth of global media and advertising. I can now sit in my hotel room in the USA or Egypt, and watch my favourite Premier League side lose yet again. Our world, that is to say the affluent Western world, is the world of Levi's, a world of Gap, a world of Coca-Cola, McDonald's, H&M, a world of Oil of Ulay.*>>   (p. 431)

Some sociologists, especially postmodernists, argue that this global culture is good for us because it offers us more choice in terms of constructing our identities and lifestyles. Consequently postmodernists argue that our personal identities as well as our cultural identity are now influenced in a positive way by a range of cultures from around the world.

Subcultures and cultural diversity

When societies become larger and more complex, different subcultures may emerge in the same society. Subcultures are social groups that are usually committed to the wider culture that dominates a society. However, they also subscribe to values, norms, customs and lifestyles that are uniquely their own. British society today hosts a range of subcultures and consequently cultural diversity is now the norm. Such diversification takes a number of forms. For example:

● The modern UK is characterised by multiculturalism, a multicultural society. This refers to the fact that about 7 per cent of the British population is made up of ethnic minority people who subscribe to the norms and values of wider British culture whilst remaining committed to aspects of their mother culture such as language, religion and traditional customs and rituals.
● Britain is a class society and consequently different socio-economic groups, e.g. the upper class, the

middle-class and the working-class, have their own sets of values, norms and leisure activities.

- Different regions of Britain – Wales, England, Scotland and Northern Ireland – have their own cultural customs and traditions.
- Since the 1950s, young people have often organised themselves into spectacular youth cultures organised around fashion, music, etc. Some of these have engaged in behaviour in opposition to societal values, e.g. illegal drug use, violence etc.
- Some members of society may subscribe to political subcultures which may be in conflict with societal values, e.g. members of some groups may be committed to environmentalism or feminism and set up squats or communes to live out their counter-cultural values.
- The de-criminalisation of homosexuality and liberalisation of social attitudes has led to the emergence of visible gay and lesbian subcultures and social scenes in most large British cities.

Culture and society

The concept of 'culture' is often used interchangeably with the concept of 'society', but it is important to understand that they do not mean exactly the same thing. Culture forms the connection between the individual and society – it tells the individual how to operate effectively within social institutions such as the family, marriage, education and so on.

Bauman (1990) notes that socialization into culture is about introducing and maintaining social order in society. Individual behaviour that lies outside the cultural norm is perceived as dangerous and worth opposing because it threatens to destabilize society. Consequently, societies develop cultural mechanisms to control and repress such behaviour.

Culture and identity

Culture plays an important role in the construction of our identity. Identity generally refers to our sense of self – this is made up of two components; how we see ourselves and how we think others see and judge us.

Culture and identity are closely related. Culture is what links the individual and their sense of self to society because who we think we are is related to what society – in the shape of cultural values and norms – says we should be like. We are born into particular cultural positions or statuses – we do not choose our social class, gender, ethnic group, age, religion and nationality. However, there is also some choice on our part – that is, we often actively identify with aspects of our culture with regard to particular groups or activities, e.g. a football team, a friendship network, a fashion or trend.

Theoretical perspectives on the formation of culture

Sociobiology

Sociobiologists generally believe that culture is the product of biology or nature. This contrasts with the sociological point of view that culture is the product of social learning or nurture. For example, Morris (1968) argued that biology shapes culture, because sharing culture is based on the in-built or genetic need to continue the life of the social group over time, i.e. to survive.

Most sociologists reject this view. If human behaviour were biologically determined, they argue, we could expect to see little variation in how people behave, whereas human behaviour is actually richly diverse. For example, if we look at other societies, we can see very different values and norms relating to gender roles, marriage, family and bringing up children. Sociologists argue that if human behaviour is influenced by biology at all, it is only at a reflex or physical level, e.g. we feel hungry or need to go to the toilet. However, when you look more closely, you find that even these biological influences are shaped by culture. Cultural values and norms determine what we eat. For example, insects are not popular as a food in Britain, and cannibalism would be regarded with horror. Cultural norms also determine *how* we eat. For example, eating behaviour is accompanied by a set of cultural norms called 'table manners', while the binge eating associated with bulimia is normally conducted in secret because of cultural disapproval. Even *when* we eat are shaped by cultural rules – think, for example, about what time you have 'dinner' or breakfast.

Culture as a system – functionalism

The founder of functionalism, Emile Durkheim (1858–1917) believed that society and culture were more important than the individual. This belief was based on a simple observation: society exists before the individual is born into it and continues relatively undisturbed after the death of the individual.

Durkheim (1893) noted that modern industrial societies are characterized by social order rather than chaos or anarchy. People's behaviour is generally patterned and predictable. Durkheim argued that this was because society's members were united by a **value consensus**, meaning that they shared the same cultural values, goals and norms. Functionalists see culture as the cement that bonds individuals together in the form of society and allows people to interact successfully with each other.

Culture in pre-industrial societies

Durkheim argued that the function of the social institutions that make up society – the family, religion, education, etc. – was to socialize individuals into the value consensus. He noted that in traditional pre-industrial societies, socialization agencies such as religion were extremely powerful cultural influences over individual behaviour. Consequently, in these societies, individual identity was secondary to cultural conformity. In other words, people went along with what society demanded; they rarely spoke out or complained. These societies, therefore, demonstrated high levels of solidarity or social belonging because people felt very similar to each other. Social order was a natural outcome of these processes.

Culture in modern societies

Durkheim notes, however, that industrial societies are much more complex. The social changes that occurred during the 18th and 19th centuries, such as industrialization and urbanization, have the potential to undermine value consensus and cultural conformity because we experience a great deal more choice in our beliefs and actions; we have more opportunity to be individuals. As a result, we become less like each other. This is potentially disruptive, because people may become confused about what values, beliefs, rules, etc., they should live by and come into conflict with each other. Durkheim called this '**anomie**'.

Despite this, Durkheim believed that social order would still be generally maintained (although in a weaker form than previously), because social institutions continue to socialize people into a shared culture – in particular, the cultural goals that achievement, competition and hard work are all important, and that people should be prepared to take their place in the **specialized division of labour**, i.e. the way the economy organizes work. This specialized division of labour reinforces social order because it results in people being dependent upon each other for society's survival and continuation. Jobs do not exist in isolation from each other – teachers need supermarket workers, sewage workers, plumbers, bus drivers, and vice versa.

Criticizing Durkheim

Durkheim has been criticized for exaggerating cultural consensus and hence social order. Social conflict between groups within the same society is generally neglected. Interpetivist sociologists are critical of Durkheim because he sees people as less important than society and culture, i.e. as if their actions and choices are shaped solely by social and cultural forces, and socialization. There is little acknowledgement that people play an active role in shaping culture. However, on the positive side, Durkheim is probably correct to suggest that there is a core culture that is widely shared by a majority of people in a society. The fact that you are sitting reading this text now in pursuit of an A-level in Sociology supports this observation.

Culture as a system – Marxism

Marxism focuses on the economic organization of modern societies, particularly the fact that societies like the UK are **capitalist** societies characterized by class inequalities in wealth, income and power. **Social class** refers to the amount of economic power, i.e. wealth, that social groups have or do not have. Karl Marx (1818–83) saw capitalist societies as characterized by class inequality and conflict. One group – the bourgeoisie – owned and controlled the means of production – the factories, raw materials, investment capital – and exploited the labour power of another group – the proletariat or working class – in order to make even greater wealth.

Culture as ideology

Marx noted that the bourgeoisie, in order to protect their interests, used their wealth to acquire political and cultural power. As Marx and Engels (1974) stated: 'the ideas of the ruling class are in every epoch the ruling ideas, i.e. the class which is the ruling material force of society, is at the same time its ruling intellectual force.' In other words, cultural ideas and values are dominated by ruling-class ideas and values. Marx called this ruling-class culture '**ideology**'. He argued that social institutions such as religion, education, the mass media and even the family, functioned to socialize society's members – especially its working-class members – to accept ruling-class culture and, consequently, to see their own low status and lack of opportunity as 'normal', 'natural' and a product of their own shortcomings. How these agencies do this in practice will be explored further in Topic 2.

Criticizing Marx

Marx's theory may be guilty of overemphasizing social class as the main source of conflict in modern societies. There is evidence that gender, religion, **ethnicity** and **nationalism** may be just as important as causes of inequality. Marxism also assumes that the working class are the passive victims, or puppets, of ruling-class culture and ideology. However, surveys suggest that the working class are aware of inequality and exploitation, but may choose to live with it because of the benefits that capitalism brings in the form of living standards and materialism.

Conclusions

Functionalist and Marxist accounts of culture are probably correct in their assumption that culture is generally shared. On the whole, people get married, live in families, see education as a good thing, vote in elections, follow the Highway Code and respect the law. Shared culture also helps us to make sense of the world. However, both theories are probably guilty of overstating this sharing of culture and, as a result, fail to note that modern societies are now characterized by **cultural diversity**.

The debate about culture is generally focused on three major questions:

1   Is nature responsible for culture, or is culture the product of learning? This will be further explored in Topic 2.
2   Are society and culture integrated into a unified shared whole, or is society characterized by subcultural diversity and possible conflict? This will be explored in greater detail when we examine subcultures based on social class, ethnicity, and age in Topic 3.
3   Are human beings cultural robots passively reacting to the demands of cultural and social forces beyond their control, or are they the masters/mistresses of their own destinies?

Interpretivists are critical of both functionalism and Marxism for ignoring the role of human agency in the construction of culture and identity. They argue that culture is actively created by people via social interaction. They would argue that culture is not static – rather it is constantly evolving, as people interpret the actions of others around them and make their own choices about their behaviour.

Focus on research

Kate Fox (2004)
Watching the English queuing

The English expect each other to observe the rules of queuing and feel highly offended when these rules are violated. However, they lack the confidence or social skills to express their annoyance in a straightforward manner. In England, queue-jumping is regarded as deeply immoral, but the queue-jumper is likely to get away with the offence. Usually, nobody would even think of simply barging to the front of a queue. This is so unthinkable that when it does happen, people assume either that it is a genuine dire emergency or that the person is a foreigner who is unaware of the 'rules'. If you jump a queue in England, you will be subjected to frowns, glares, raised eyebrows and contemptuous looks – accompanied by heavy sighs, pointed coughs, tutting and muttering. However, few English people want to 'cause a scene' or 'make a fuss', and usually direct their comments to each other rather than directly to the offender. They prefer to shame the offender into retreating to the back of the queue.

Adapted from Fox, K. (2004) *Watching the English: The Hidden Rules of English Behaviour*, London: Hodder & Stoughton

1   What sort of research method do you think would produce the most valid data on queuing, and why?

2   What does queuing tell us about how the English interpret conformity and deviance?

Key terms

Aesthetic pleasing, appreciating beauty.

Anomie moral confusion and uncertainty.

Authenticity reflecting reality.

Capitalist economic system based on competition to produce manufactured goods.

Counter-cultural a group or set of ideas that is opposed to the mainstream.

Consumer culture a culture in which shopping – the consumption of material goods – is a major leisure activity.

Conspicuous consumption the consumption of particular logos and designer goods in order to earn status from others.

Cultural diversity differences between groups with regard to beliefs, values, norms, etc.

Culture a way of life of a society.

Customs traditional ways of doing things.

Elitist belief in the superiority of a powerful group.

Ethnicity characteristics associated with particular ethnic group based on factors such as shared race, religion, history and language.

Globalization the influence on British culture of cultural products and activities produced outside the UK.

High culture cultural products and activities that are defined as superior in their creativity to those that make up mass or popular culture.

Identity how the individual sees themselves – influenced, too, by how others see the person.

Ideology a set of ideas that originate with powerful people and function to justify some type of inequality.

Mass culture cultural products that are consumed by large numbers of people.

Multiculturalism a system that promotes the belief that all ethnic groups are of equal status and have the right to maintain their traditions.

Nationalism strong belief and devotion to the concept of a nation, e.g. strong pride in being English.

Norms ways of behaving.

Nurture bringing up or teaching (usually children).

Peer group friendship networks.

Popular culture cultural products such as films, television, pop music, etc., enjoyed by large numbers of people.

Rituals traditional ceremonies, e.g. the State opening of Parliament.

Social class socio-economic status, usually based on job and income.

Socialization the process of teaching and learning culture.

Social roles the norms attached to particular statuses.

Society community bound together by social institutions, culture, etc.

Specialized division of labour the organization of work and jobs in society.

State the government and all its supporting apparatuses, e.g. the armed services.

Subcultures groups that exist within and alongside the wider majority culture.

Value consensus shared agreement on important beliefs/actions.

Values important general beliefs.

Activities

Research idea

Obtain the Review pages from a Sunday broadsheet newspaper such as *The Sunday Times*, *The Sunday Telegraph* or *The Observer*. Work out how many column inches or pages are dedicated to specific cultural activities such as literature (book reviews), films, popular and classical music. Does this evidence suggest that these newspapers distinguish between high culture and popular culture?

Web.tasks

Visit **www.feralchildren.com**

Choose a child and write a report on them detailing how the child differs from children who have experienced normal socialization.

Visit **www.sociology.org.uk** and click on the on-line resource bank, the 'video vault' and access the films on culture and identity, particularly the HSBC adverts. What do these tell us about culture?

Check your understanding

1   What do the stories of feral children tell us about the influence of culture?

2   Identify and explain three of the elements that make up culture.

3   Explain the difference between ascribed and achieved status.

4   How are roles linked to statuses?

5   Give an example to illustrate how popular and high culture can sometimes be combined.

6   Give examples of three ways in which British culture could be said to be 'globalized'.

7   Why is the concept of value consensus important for functionalists?

8   Why is the concept of social class important to Marxists?

9   How do functionalists and Marxists differ in their view of culture?

10 Why are interpretivists critical of both the functionalist and Marxist accounts of culture?

Your opening sentences should attempt to clearly explain the meaning of the concept

you should attempt to write a detailed paragraph in about 5 minutes

(a) Define the concept of global culture. Illustrate your answer with examples.   **(8 marks)**

spend about 3–4 minutes developing two or three examples that demonstrate your understanding of the concept in action

you need to identify as many differences as you can between these different types of culture

you should attempt to write about a side of A4

(b) Outline and explain two ways in which high culture differs from popular culture.   **(16 marks)**

develop the differences in detail by using illustrative examples and sociological studies, e.g. you could explore the social class differences in the use of the different cultures by referring to the use and cultural content of particular newspapers, television channels etc

Popular

(c) Explain and briefly evaluate why some sociologists believe that culture is the cement that bonds people together in the form of society.   (24 marks)

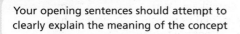

Grade booster Getting top marks in this question

You need to identify which sociologists would agree with this statement, i.e. functionalists. Use the work of Durkheim or Parsons to show that culture is an essential part of society because it binds people to society in the form of value consensus. Examine the role of culture in pre-industrial societies and compare with its role in industrial modern societies. Don't forget to evaluate by referring to either the strengths or weaknesses of Durkheim's ideas. Another way of evaluating is to outline another theory such as Marxism which challenges functionalist ideas about the role of culture. Use concepts like value consensus, anomie and ideology whenever possible.

The process of socialization

Getting you thinking

Ofcom's 2006 survey of young people aged 8 to 15 years and new media in Britain found that:

● 63% of girls and 54% of boys use the internet
● 49% of girls and 36% of boys read newspapers or magazines
● two thirds of the whole sample thought that most or all of what was on the internet was 'true'
● one third thought that 'reality TV' was 'true' most of the time.

Source: Ofcom 2006, quoted in R. Boyle (2007) 'The "now" media generation', *Sociology Review*, 17(1), September 2007

It's a dilemma of modern working parents: finding enough time for their children. Now a major study reveals that parents who fail to do so put their teenagers at risk of problems including drug use and teenage pregnancies. Teenagers who felt emotionally 'connected' to at least one parent were up to a third less likely to show some type of problem behaviour. Professor Blum, the author of the report, said that parents should supervise free time and make themselves available at four key times of the day: early mornings, immediately after school, suppertime and bedtime.

Adapted from G. Hinsliff, 'Peril of the parents who have no time', *The Observer*, 14 April 2002.

1   How might the effectiveness of socialization in the family be undermined by the processes described above?

2   What evidence is there that the mass media may be replacing the family as the main agency of socialization?

The process by which human babies, infants, adolescents and even adults learn behaviour is known as 'socialization'. The primary agency of socialization has always been the family, but – as we can see above – pressures on parenting may be reducing the effectiveness of this particular child-rearing institution. Secondary agencies of socialization, such as the mass media, may be increasing in importance. Some commentators, notably Postman (1982) and Palmer (2007), have expressed anxiety at the quality of the socialization experienced by children viewing television, reading teenage magazines and surfing the internet.

Socialization, culture and subculture

Although the first few years of a person's life are crucial to learning how to behave, it is important to understand that socialization is a life-long process. This is because humans are social animals who live in complex and sophisticated societies based on detailed rules and traditions. For this reason, we have a great deal more to learn than other animals over the course of our lifetime. This learning process is, therefore, a continuous process, which really only ends at death.

For socialization to be effective, it should not be experienced as forced or as an imposition. The individual should not feel that they are being subjected to a form of brainwashing. Such feelings run the risk of rejection, dissent and rebellion. Instead, as Paul Taylor (1997) notes, socialization should be organized in such a way 'that the ways of thinking, behaving and perceiving things that are accepted by culture come to appear normal, natural and inevitable'. As Marsh and Keating (2006) argue, effective socialization should happen to children without them even noticing it.

Stages of socialization – primary socialization

The main agent of primary socialization is the family. The first few years of socialization in the family are crucial to a person's development, having a profound effect upon all later social learning. Close social relationships with other people are essential in order for children to learn to interact and to communicate. These processes allow children to become aware of themselves as 'social beings'. They recognize that they occupy particular social roles, such as son, daughter, brother, sister, etc., and that they are capable of social action that has consequences for others.

As this process develops, they acquire uniquely human skills; they learn that love, sadness and humour are appropriate emotional responses in certain situations, and they acquire the ability to smile, to laugh, to cry, etc. In other words, the socialization process results in children acquiring most of the skills necessary to **empathize** with others. Consequently, the helpless infant becomes a self-aware, competent, skilled and knowledgeable member of society. Children learn to function as good and useful citizens in their community.

Feral children

Feral children are a good example of what happens when a child is denied human contact, interaction and communication. These children have usually grown up with minimal human contact because they have been confined and isolated and, in some cases, been raised by animals. As a result, they have tended to behave like their animal foster parents – walking on all fours, making animal noises, being unable to talk, smile or laugh, biting and being aggressive, eating raw meat, urinating and defecating in public.

Socialization and identity

Baumeister (1986) notes that family socialization provides children with an identity. A very young child has no life apart from its role in the family, and so a child will believe that the family will love and care for it so long as it does what it is supposed to do. Many children successfully learn what they are supposed to do through **imitative play**. Social roles, particularly the significant roles played by parents, provide children with blueprints for action – examples and illustrations of how to behave that they can then copy. Play activities may involve imitating parents by playing 'house' or 'mummies and daddies' – this too encourages empathy, as they gradually learn what it might feel like to be a father or mother.

Socialization and social control

Morgan (1996) suggests that a great deal of socialization is concerned with social control and encouraging **conformity**. This can be illustrated in a number of ways:

- Parents often use **sanctions** to reinforce and reward socially approved behaviour, and to discipline and punish 'naughty', i.e. deviant, behaviour. Positive sanctions might include praise, sweets, and the promise of extra television-viewing or new toys, while negative sanctions include smacking, 'grounding' and especially the threat to withdraw love.
- Sanctions encourage the development of a conscience in the child. It is culturally expected that a child will eventually know the difference between 'good' and 'bad' behaviour, and that guilt will act as a deterrent, preventing deviant behaviour. Socialization is seen to be successful when the child realizes that the costs in terms of parental punishment outweigh the benefits of deviant actions, and so exercises self-control. This is the first step to independent action, i.e. actions not shaped solely by parents.
- Morgan suggests that the function of toilet training is to instil in the child some sense of control over their bodily functions so that the child is accepted into wider society as a 'civilized' being. Similarly, children will be taught 'civilized' norms such as politeness and table manners. At the same time, they will learn to avoid uncivilized behaviours, such as swearing, and vulgar behaviours, such as burping, picking their nose and breaking wind in public.
- Socialization also involves becoming aware of what being a boy or a girl entails. Children internalize cultural expectations with regard to femininity and masculinity, and generally conform to traditional gender roles. Durkin (1995) notes that most children can categorize themselves correctly and consistently as a boy or a girl between the ages of 2 and 3 years of age.

Functionalists and primary socialization

Functionalists such as Parsons see the family as a 'personality factory' – the child is seen as a 'blank slate' at birth and the function of parents, especially the nurturing mother, is to train and mould the passive child in the image of society. The child is to be filled up with the shared cultural values and norms, so that it assumes that cultural values are somehow naturally its own values. This ensures that the child subscribes to value consensus and so feels a strong sense of belonging to society.

Marxism and primary socialization

Marxists are critical of the functionalist view that children are socialized into shared cultural values and norms. Zaretsky (1976), for example, argues that the family is used by the capitalist class to instil values, such as obedience and respect for authority, that are useful to the capitalist ruling class. Such values ensure that individuals can be exploited later in life by the ruling class, because ordinary people will have learnt that power, authority and inequality should be viewed as normal and natural.

Secondary agents of socialization

Sociologists note that, in addition to the family, a range of other social institutions are involved in socialization. These are called the secondary agents of socialization and function to build on what has been learned during primary socialization in order to help the child to take their place in wider society.

The functionalist theory of education as an agent of secondary socialization

Functionalists see education systems as essential in that they transmit shared cultural values, thus producing conformity and **consensus**. Durkheim believed that subjects such as history, language and religious education link the individual to society, past and present, by encouraging a sense of pride in the historical and religious achievements of their nation; this reinforces their sense of belonging to society.

Parsons argued that the main function of education was to act as a social bridge between the family unit and wider society. Education socializes children into important values such as achievement, competition and **individualism** – functionalists see the transmission of these values as essential in preparing young people for the world of work.

The Marxist theory of education as an agent of secondary socialization

In contrast to functionalist theorists, Marxists, such as Althusser (1971), argue that education as an agency of socialization is dominated by a **hidden curriculum** – a ruling-class ideology that encourages conformity and an

unquestioning acceptance of the organization of the capitalist system.

Althusser claimed that few students are allowed to access educational knowledge that challenges the existence of capitalism. It is claimed that when the national curriculum was introduced in 1988, critical subjects such as Sociology, Economics and Politics were deliberately excluded from mainstream education because the ruling class believed that socialization into ideas commonly taught by these subjects might lead to students becoming too critical of capitalist inequality.

Marxists also claim that schools socialize pupils into uncritical acceptance of hierarchy, obedience and failure. In particular, working-class pupils are socialized to see their failure as their own fault and as deserved rather than being caused by capitalism's need for a relatively uneducated manual labour force. In this sense, then, Marxists regard schools as agents of social control.

The functionalist theory of religion as an agent of secondary socialization

According to Durkheim (1912), the major function of religion is to socialize society's members into value consensus by investing certain values with a sacred quality, i.e. by infusing them with religious symbolism and special significance. These values consequently become 'moral codes' – beliefs that society agrees to revere and socialize children into. Such codes socially control our behaviour with regard to crime, sex and obligation to others. The Ten Commandments are a good example of a set of moral codes that have influenced both formal controls, such as the law (e.g. 'thou shalt not kill', 'thou shalt not steal'), as well as informal controls such as moral disapproval (e.g. 'thou shalt not commit adultery').

The Marxist theory of religion as an agent of secondary socialization

Marxists, on the other hand, describe religion as an ideological apparatus that serves to reflect ruling-class ideas and interests. According to Marxists, religion socializes the working class into three sets of false ideas:

- It promotes the idea that material success is a sign of God's favour, whereas poverty is interpreted as caused by wickedness, sin and immorality.
- Religious teachings and the emphasis on blind faith serve to distract the poor and powerless from the true extent of their exploitation by the ruling class.
- Religion makes exploitation, poverty and inequality bearable by promising a reward in the afterlife for those who accept without question their suffering or poverty here and now.

The mass media as an agent of secondary socialization

Many sociologists argue that the mass media – newspapers, magazines, television, films, pop music, computer games, the internet, etc. – comprise the most significant socialization agency today, as far as influence over values and norms (and especially those of young people) are concerned. Many people use the mass media to make sense of the world around them. The media offer a window onto the wider world and provide much of the information required to make sense of events that have a bearing on our everyday lives. The media may also provide us with role models and designs for living, i.e. images and ideas that we use to fashion our identities. It is, therefore, important that all points of view are presented to us in an objective and neutral fashion, because the media may have the power to structure how and what we think.

The Marxist critique of the mass media as an agent of secondary socialization

Marxist sociologists are also critical of the mass media because they argue that it is mainly responsible for mass culture. Sociologists such as Marcuse suggested that popular culture, especially television and advertising, has had a negative effect on culture because, as Marsh and Keating (2006) note, 'popular culture is a false culture devised and packaged by capitalism to keep the masses content' – its function is to encourage 'false needs' (e.g. the acquisition of non-essential consumer goods) and to discourage any serious or critical thought, especially that relating to the inequalities caused by the organization of capitalism.

This theme has been taken up by modern commentators such as Steve Barnett, who argues that media output in the UK that once encouraged a critical outlook, such as quality drama, documentaries and serious news coverage, have gone into decline and are being increasingly replaced with dumbed-down light entertainment – reality shows, soap operas and the like, which focus on transmitting superficial, mindless entertainment (Barnett and Curry 1994). Such critics argue that we are being socialized into not being able to think for ourselves.

In defence of the media, research does indicate that different people interpret media messages in different ways. There is no evidence that audiences passively accept what is being fed to them. Audiences are selective and, at times, critical. The idea that the audience can be manipulated does not recognize the ways in which they actively and critically use the media to enhance their lives and identities.

The peer group

The peer group refers to people of similar status who come into regular contact with each other, either on a social or work-related basis. Peer groups, therefore, include friendship networks, school subcultures and occupational subcultures, i.e. workmates.

Peer groups have a particularly strong influence over adolescent behaviour and attitudes. Teenagers may feel a tension between parental controls and their desire for more responsibility and independence, and so come into conflict with parents. A common site for this conflict may be the teenager's choice of friendships – and especially the choice of boyfriend or girlfriend.

Peer pressure

Adolescents may feel a great deal of peer pressure to fit in with their friends, and this may lead to radical changes in their identity during their teenage years in terms of image and behaviour. Some teenagers may feel that they have to engage in 'deviant' behaviour, such as drug-taking, delinquency and sex, in order to be accepted by their peers. Friendship networks may put considerable pressure on teenagers to conform; they may use negative sanctions such as gossip and bullying to control the behaviour of their fellow adolescents.

Criticisms of the concept of socialization

Many accounts of socialization discuss this process as if it is a relatively straightforward, positive and, hence, unproblematical process. However, not all adults acquire the skills that are required to nurture children towards adulthood; as a result, such poor parenting may, unfortunately, result in neglect or child abuse.

Other commentators suggest that childhood socialization is not as effective today as it was in the past. Postman (1982) suggests that childhood is a much shorter period today compared with 50 years ago and bemoans children's loss of innocence, which he sees as the result of overexposure to sex and violence in the media. Palmer (2007) also notes the negative influence of television and computer games, and argues that parents all too often use these as a substitute for spending quality time interacting with children. Consequently, children today are less likely to be socialized into important moral codes of behaviour. Phillips (1997) argues that children have too many rights today and claims that they have used these to resist parental power, so undermining socialization. She suggests that the antisocial behaviour associated with young people today is a direct result of parents being too content not to take responsibility for their children's upbringing.

Finally, many accounts of socialization portray it as a one-way process – the child being a vessel waiting to be filled up with the wisdom of its parents. However, interpretivist sociologists point out that socialization is a two-way process, and that parenting itself is a learning process.

Formal and informal methods of social control

Once members of society have been socialized into the values, norms and rules of a society, it is important that they abide by what they have learned. Conformity must be policed to make sure that people do not stray from the straight and narrow. Social control mechanisms exist which make sure that people are convinced that it is their interest to continue to conform and that deviance cannot be tolerated. There are essentially two basic methods of social control that back up the socialization process:

● Formal mechanisms of control involve the establishing of formal rules or laws and a system of sanctions or punishments such as prisons or fines for those who break them. Formal agencies of social control such as the police, the courts, prisons, probation officers, social workers and teachers exist to enforce these formal rules.

● Informal methods of control refer to the unwritten guidelines that we learn on a daily basis during the socialization process from our families, friends, teachers, workmates, religions etc. For example, , we learn the difference between right and wrong from our parents, we learn that males and females should behave in socially expected ways from a variety of socialization agencies, we learn to keep confidences from our peer group, we learn that if we work hard our teachers will reward us from schools etc. Generally, we conform to these guidelines because we fear negative societal reaction from our significant others, i.e. people we care about. We want our parents to continue to love us, we want our friends to like us etc. In other words, we want approval and social acceptance rather than disapproval and rejection. Most of us therefore choose not to deviate from mainstream norms and values because we fear being labelled deviant, a problem, unreliable, dishonest etc by who matter to us.

Both socialization and social control are essential social tools in the construction of both culture and identity.

Key terms

Collectivist putting the group interest before your own.

Conformity obeying the rules without question.

Consensus agreement.

Empathy being able to imagine how others feel about something.

Hidden curriculum the invisible ways in which schools encourage conformity.

Imitative play games that involve children copying adults, e.g. playing 'mummies and daddies' or 'doctors and nurses'.

Individualism putting one's own needs and wishes before those of the group or society.

Sanctions punishments and rewards.

Activities

Research idea

Using the contents of this chapter, design a questionnaire that focuses on:

● what parents think are important in bringing about effective primary socialization
● whether parents share the concerns of commentators such as Postman, Palmer and Phillips.

Web.tasks

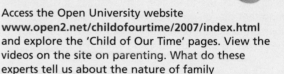

Access the Open University website **www.open2.net/childofourtime/2007/index.html** and explore the 'Child of Our Time' pages. View the videos on the site on parenting. What do these experts tell us about the nature of family socialization?

Check your understanding

1 **Identify six skills that children acquire during primary socialization.**

2 **How do children learn to differentiate between right and wrong during primary socialization?**

3 **What does Parsons mean when he describes the family as a 'personality factory'?**

4 **Why do functionalists and Marxists disagree on the role of education as an agency of secondary socialization?**

5 **Why is the peer group such an important agency of socialization?**

6 **Identify three ways in which socialization might have negative consequences for some children.**

Socialization

your opening sentences should attempt to clearly explain the meaning of the concept

you should attempt to write a detailed paragraph in about 5 minutes

(a) Define the concept of informal social control. Illustrate your answer with examples.　　**(8 marks)**

spend about 3–4 minutes developing two or three examples that demonstrate your understanding of the concept in action

you need to identify the two ways as clearly as you can

develop the ways in detail by using illustrative examples and sociological studies, e.g. you could explore studies that show the peer group replacing the family or studies that show tension between parental controls and peer group pressure.

(b) Outline and explain two ways in which the peer group can influence the identity of young people.　　**(16 marks)**

you should attempt to write about a side of A4

(c) Explain and briefly evaluate why some sociologists argue that primary socialization is not as effective today as it was in the past.　　**(24 marks)**

Grade booster Getting top marks in this question

Begin by defining what is meant by primary socialization and describe the socialization function of the family using the work of Parsons (i.e. families as personality factories), Baumeister and Morgan (socialization as social control). You could contrast an individual socialized by their family into cultural values and norms with a feral child. Don't forget to evaluate by referring to either the strengths or weaknesses of functionalist theories of primary socialization or by outlining the Marxist critique (people are often socialized into ruling class ideology which benefits those who control capitalist society) or the feminist critique (gender role socialization in families ends up confirming women's subordinate position in society). There are also those like Postman and Palmer who believe family socialization does more harm than good. Use concepts like social control, ideology, conformity, sanctions and imitation whenever possible.

Socialization, identity and social class

Getting you thinking

Class rules

A Guardian/ICM poll published in October 2007 shows that Britain remains a nation dominated by class division, with a huge majority certain that their social standing determines the way they are judged. Of those questioned, 89 per cent said they think people are still judged by their class – with almost half saying that it still counts for 'a lot'. Only 8 per cent think that class does not matter at all in shaping the way people are seen.

Despite the collapse of industrial employment, 53 per cent of people consider themselves 'working-class'. Despite huge economic change and the government's efforts to build what it calls an opportunity society, people who think of themselves as 'middle-class' are still in a minority. In 1998, 41 per cent of people thought of themselves as middle-class – exactly the same proportion as today. Only 2 per cent of those who took part in the poll claimed to be 'upper-class'.

Adapted from Glover, J. (2007) 'Class rules', *The Guardian*, 20 October 2007

1   Does this survey suggest that class identity is still important?

2   Why might sociologists be cautious about the findings of surveys like this?

3   How would you define 'working class'?

Defining social class

As we can see from the above exercise, social class can be a difficult concept to define. This is because a person's subjective sense of identity, i.e. what they think they are, may differ from objective attempts to measure the importance of social class.

Objectively, social class refers to the socio-economic status and identity that are attached to a person because of their job. The government categorizes people into one of eight social classes using an occupational scale known as the National Statistics Socio-Economic Classification (NS-SEC). The NS-SEC differentiates between different jobs on the basis of **employment relations** (whether people are employers, self-employed, employees and how much authority they exercise over others) and **market conditions** (how much they earn, their promotion opportunities, job security, etc.). Sociologists have observed that groups of people who share similar socio-economic status also share similar educational backgrounds and experiences, lifestyles and outlooks. There is also evidence that there exist distinct inequalities between social classes in terms of **infant mortality**, life expectancy, the educational achievement of their children and the distribution of wealth and poverty.

It is generally agreed that there are three broad social class identities that exist in the UK today: the upper class, the middle classes and the working class.

Upper-class identity

The upper class is made up of a fairly small number of wealthy **extended families** who are often interconnected by marriage. They tend to share a common background in terms of an elite education at expensive **public schools**, such as Eton College or Harrow, and Oxford and Cambridge universities. Scott (1991) argues that the main purpose of these schools is to mould the ideas and outlooks of their pupils so that they quickly realize their common upper-class interests. In particular, he notes that such schools socialize upper-class pupils into a common culture that promotes the values of conservatism and especially respect for tradition, nationalism, superior breeding and upbringing as well as hostility towards socialist ideals. Moreover, these schools produce '**old-boy**' or '**old school-tie**' networks made up of people who share the same cultural values and assets, and who use these contacts to further each other's adult careers and influence.

There is some evidence that the value system of the upper class differs from that of other social classes. Scott notes that the **conservative** values of tradition and the acceptance of privilege, hierarchy and authority are regarded as particularly important aspects of upper-class identity. Upper-class tastes and activities generally focus on higher cultural pursuits such as classical music, theatre, opera and ballet. Other leisure activities revolve around exclusive social events that provide a distinctive upper-class lifestyle, such as debutantes' balls, hunting, shooting and sports such as polo and rowing.

The upper class, therefore, is a self-selecting and exclusive elite which is closed to outsiders, i.e. this is known as '**social closure**'. This is reinforced by parents encouraging their children to choose partners from other upper-class families and by the practice of sending children away to boarding schools.

The middle classes

The term 'middle classes' is used in a broad way to describe **non-manual** workers. Savage's research (1995) describes four distinct types of middle-class groups and, therefore, identities:

● *Professionals such as doctors and lawyers* – Savage claims that these subscribe to an intellectual identity gained from a long and successful education. He claims that they value **cultural** assets or **capital** such as knowledge, qualifications, achievement, experience of higher education and **altruism** (i.e. they often see themselves as serving a higher purpose – namely, society).
● *Managers* are generally less qualified than professionals and are more likely to have worked their way up in a company, i.e. from the shop or office floor. Savage suggests that this group generally defines its status and identity in terms of its standard of living and leisure pursuits. Managerial middle-class identity is less secure today compared with the past because of factors such as globalization, economic recession, mergers and takeovers.
● Roberts (2001) notes that the *self-employed owners of small businesses* have traditionally been very individualistic. Surveys suggest that they believe that people should be independent and stand on their own two feet rather than rely on the welfare state. They also have great faith in hard work and discipline – believing firmly that success in life is a result of effort and application rather than luck.
● *White-collar or clerical workers* – Clerks and secretaries, for example, have traditionally been seen as having a middle-class identity, despite often being the children of manual workers, because their pay and working conditions were superior to manual workers. However, the introduction of technology such as computers has led to their pay and status going into decline, and it is suggested that they now have more in common with the working class. However, surveys of clerical workers indicate that they still see themselves as middle-class. They rarely mix with manual workers, and spend their leisure time and money in quite different ways.

Despite these differences in material circumstances, sociologists such as Ken Roberts argue that these different groups do share some values. A general middle-class identity, therefore, can be seen to exist which is mainly focused on the home. The middle classes value home ownership – they are more likely than other social groups to have mortgages and to own their own home. They are more likely to live in the suburbs – they are generally a commuting class.

Members of the middle classes generally encourage their children to do well in education. They are keen on private education, although their children also do exceptionally well within the state sector. Middle-class parents often move home to get their children into the catchment area for the best state primary and secondary schools. Their children dominate the top streams of state schools, get the best GCSE results, are more likely to stay on and do A-levels and dominate the university sector (80 per cent of students are from middle-class backgrounds).

The middle classes generally believe in the concept of **meritocracy** – that high position and status can be achieved by ability or effort. It is said that the middle classes are more willing than other social groups to '**defer gratification**' (e.g. financial rewards, pleasure) in the pursuit of education. In other words, they are more willing to make sacrifices whilst qualifications are achieved.

The working classes

The traditional working class

Sociological evidence suggests that those engaged in traditional manual work, especially in industries such as mining and factory work – i.e. the working class – had a very strong sense of their economic or social-class position. This traditional working-class identity was dominant for most of the 20th century and is still very influential in some parts of the UK even today.

Manual workers, probably more than any other group of workers, identified very strongly with each other. This was partly due to the dangerous nature of some manual jobs (such as mining) but was also due to the collective nature of their jobs; for example, factories were often made up of thousands of workers controlled by a minority of supervisors, managers and employers. This led to a strong sense that the world was divided into 'them', i.e. the bosses (capital), who were only interested in exploiting the workers and making profits, and 'us', i.e. the worker on the shop-floor (labour). Consequently, relations between management and labour until the 1980s were often characterized by mistrust and hostility. Many workers belonged to trade unions, which represented workers' interests and engaged in industrial action when it was thought that such interests were being threatened by management.

There is evidence that the traditional working class had a strong political identity and saw the Labour party as representing its natural interests against those of the employers. At general elections until the 1970s, the Labour Party could, therefore, count on the loyal support of about 80 per cent of the working-class electorate. Trade-union support for Labour reinforced this political allegiance.

Such workers also had a strong sense of their class identity because they often lived in close-knit communities made up of extended **kinship** networks. Adult children often lived close to their parents and saw them on a regular basis. **Mutual support** was offered by a range of relatives especially in terms of childcare, financial help and finding work.

The decline of traditional working-class identity

However, more recently, some researchers have claimed that traditional working-class identity is less important today because of the decline in manual work over the last 30 years. The numbers employed in traditional heavy industries such as mining and shipbuilding have fallen rapidly since the 1970s and 1980s. Consequently, manual workers now make up well under half of the total workforce and so the economic basis for class identity and solidarity has weakened.

The new working class

Research has also identified a new sort of working-class identity, mainly found in the South East, which sees work as a means to an end, i.e. a wage, rather than as a source of community, status and identity. This working-class identity tends to be found in the newer types of high-tech manufacturing industries.

This new working class has no heightened sense of class injustice or political loyalty. They believe in individualism (i.e. putting themselves and their immediate families first), rather than collective or community action. They define themselves through their families, their lifestyle and their standard of living, rather than through their work. They vote for whichever political party furthers their individual financial interests.

The underclass

Another type of working-class identity may be held by those who exist at the margins of society. In recent years, a number of commentators, most notably Murray (1994) and Mount (2004), have identified a supposed 'new' form of working-class identity organized around dependency upon state benefits – this is the so-called **urban underclass** allegedly found on run-down council estates and in the depressed inner cities. This group allegedly consists of individuals who are long-term unemployed and single parents, as well as drug addicts, criminals, etc. Murray suggests that the culture and identity of this underclass revolve around being work-shy, feckless, anti-authority, anti-education, immoral and welfare-dependent. It is suggested, too, that the children of the underclass are being socialized by their inadequate parents into a culture of idleness, failure and criminality.

Unemployment, poverty and identity

Not everyone agrees that this so-called deviant underclass exists. Studies of the poor and long-term unemployed carried out by Jordan (1992) suggest that those living in poverty share the same ideas about work and family as everyone else. Surveys also show that the unemployed want to work in order to gain the respect of their loved ones and to regain their dignity. Surveys indicate that unemployment often brings with it negative self-image or identity, shame, guilt, low self-esteem, insecurity and poor mental and physical health. These are not feelings or effects that people choose to have. Surveys clearly show that the long-term

Sociology AS for OCR

Focus on research

Simon Charlesworth (2000) Deadman's Town

Charlesworth takes a phenomenological approach to working-class experience on an extremely deprived council estate in Rotherham. 'Phenomenological' means looking at a social phenomenon from the perspective of those experiencing it, usually in their own words. Charlesworth's account of the experience of long-term unemployment in one of Britain's poorest and bleakest towns (known by locals as 'Deadman's Town') puts working-class people's interpretations at the heart of the study.

Charlesworth found that working-class identity was still a very strong feeling among the poor in Rotherham, although it had been adapted to cope with the conditions of exclusion, hardship and humiliation that are a normal part of everyday life. From the outside, and particularly from a middle-class perspective, the everyday culture of working-class people on this estate might seem narrow and irresponsible. Charlesworth notes that people on the estate do not seem proud of their heritage nor are they positive about their futures. Instead, they indulge in behaviour – heavy drinking, drug use, stealing, etc. – that brings them criticism as 'chavs' or as a deadbeat idle underclass. However, the reality, says Charlesworth, is that their response is a rational one to the economic decay of their area.

Charlesworth, S. (2000) *A Phenomenology of Working Class Experience*, Cambridge: Cambridge University Press

1 How do you think Charlesworth gathered the information for this study?

2 How was working-class identity interpreted and expressed by people living on this council estate in Rotherham?

unemployed want to work in order to gain the respect of their loved ones. Furthermore, most unemployed people do not enjoy a high standard of living. They often lack basics, are in debt and feel guilty because their children go without at crucial times such as birthdays and Christmas.

Jordan also notes that most people do not choose to be unemployed or poor, or to be dependent on welfare benefits. Rather, it is often the fault of global recession, government policies and the fact that capitalist companies find it more profitable to close down factories in the UK and instead exploit workers in the developing world. The unemployed and poor are therefore excluded by society.

Simon Charlesworth's (2000) study of working-class people in Rotherham (see above) suggests that those at the bottom end of the working class are often misunderstood by other social classes because they experience negative self-identity and low self-esteem. He argues that their negative experience of education results in them devaluing themselves, restricting their ambitions to 'being disappointed' in life and hence turning to drink, drugs or antisocial behaviour as a form of compensation.

The decline of social class as a source of identity?

In recent years, some sociologists have argued that class has ceased to be the main factor in creating identity. Postmodernists argue that class identity has fragmented into numerous separate identities – young people, in particular, have more choice today as to how they construct their identity. For example, a young male might experiment with identity by taking ideas from femininity (e.g. make-up, accessories), global culture (e.g. a t-shirt celebrating an American band), a media role model (e.g. copying their hero's hairstyle or attitude) and consumer culture (e.g. wearing designer shades or labelled clothing). It is argued, therefore, that social class as a source of identity is no longer recognized by the young, and **hybrid** identities are increasingly the norm.

However, there is some evidence that postmodern ideas may be exaggerated. Marshall's survey research into how people viewed themselves suggests that the majority of people in the UK still think that social class is a significant source of identity. Members of a range of classes are aware of class differences and are happy to identify themselves using class categories. Furthermore, a Guardian/ICM poll conducted in October 2007 showed that 89 per cent of the sample, including the majority of 18 to 24 year olds who took part believed that social class was still a significant influence on their lives.

Postmodernists also ignore the fact that, for many, consumption – i.e. the ability to buy designer labels and so on – depends on having a job and an income. Poverty is going to limit any desire to pursue a postmodern lifestyle. In other words, consumption – what we buy – depends ultimately on social class.

Key terms

Altruism putting the interests of society and others before self-interest.

Conservative belief in traditional ways of doing things.

Cultural capital positive attitudes towards education, work, etc., based on personal experience; seen to be a middle-class characteristic.

Deferred gratification putting off rewards or pleasure in pursuit of education or training.

Employment relations how much independence and authority a person has in their job.

Extended family family units that include parents and children, as well as relatives such as grandparents, aunts, uncles and so on.

Hybrid a mix of different components.

Infant mortality the number of child deaths at birth and in the first year of life for every 1000 children born.

Kinship relatives.

Market conditions the value of your job in terms of pay, pension, fringe benefits, promotion opportunities, etc.

Meritocracy the idea that achievement is solely the result of intelligence, talent, skill and hard work, rather than inheritance or luck.

Mutual support a system of social, economic and emotional supports, commonly found in traditional working-class communities.

Non-manual jobs that require mental rather than manual labour.

Old-boy network a system of economic and social supports maintained by ex-public-school boys in adulthood.

Old school-tie network see old-boy network above.

Public schools exclusive, elite and expensive private schools, such as Eton College.

Social closure the process by which the upper class maintain wealth and privilege, e.g. by keeping marriage within the class, by sending children to expensive schools.

Underclass a class subculture generally made up of the poor.

Urban living in the city (as opposed to the countryside).

Check your understanding

1. What values does upper class culture socialise its children into?

2. What are the main agencies of upper class socialization?

3. What is 'social closure' and how does the upper class ensure it?

4. Identify four groups that make up the middle classes. How do they differ from one another?

5. What values do most middle-class have in common?

6. What are the main components of traditional working-class identity?

7. What economic and social factors have led to a dramatic fall in the number of traditional manual workers?

8. How do the new working class differ from the traditional working class?

9. Identify the main arguments for and against the idea that a deviant underclass exists in the UK's inner cities.

10. How might Charlesworth's findings be used to criticise the idea of an underclass?

Activities

Research idea

Watch the DVDs of *Brassed Off* and *The Full Monty*. How are the working classes portrayed in these films? How are social and economic changes affecting working-class values and behaviour, according to these films?

Web.tasks

Access the following public school websites – **www.etoncollege.com**, **www.harrowschool.org.uk**, and **www.charterhouse.org.uk**. Compare these schools with the secondary school you attend(ed) – what are the differences in terms of school buildings, history, ethos, rules, ex-pupils, cost and so on?

An eye on the exam — Class identity

your opening sentences should attempt to clearly explain the meaning of the concept

you should attempt to write a detailed paragraph in about 5 minutes

(a) Define the concept of social-class identity. Illustrate your answer with examples. **(8 marks)**

spend about 3–4 minutes developing two or three examples that demonstrate your understanding of the concept in action

you need to identify the two changes in working-class identity as clearly as you can, e.g. new working-class instrumental or privatised identity, underclass, culture of poverty etc

develop the idea of change in detail by using illustrative examples and sociological studies, e.g. you need to begin by considering what has changed – what constituted traditional working-class identity in the first place? What economic and social factors have transformed this identity?

(b) Outline and explain two changes that have occurred in working-class identity over the past thirty years. **(16 marks)**

you should attempt to write about a side of A4

(c) Explain and briefly evaluate the variety of middle-class cultural identities that exist in the contemporary UK.. **(24 marks)**

Grade booster — Getting top marks in this question

Begin by defining what is meant by middle class, i.e. a socio-economic status based on a particular type of job and note that there is no such a thing as an homogeneous middle class. Rather sociologists such as Savage and Roberts suggest that it is fragmented into a number of competing groups, i.e. professionals, managers, the self-employed, white-collar workers etc. There should be some discussion of how these groups differ from each other and from working-class skilled workers. Don't forget to evaluate by referring to those values and norms that these groups might share or the postmodernist idea that social class no longer matters as a source of identity. Use concepts like cultural capital, altruism, meritocracy and deferred gratification whenever possible.

TOPIC 4

Socialization, identity and gender

Getting you thinking

<< A visit to Isabella Mackay's home is like a walk through the pages of *Little Women*. She opens the door wearing a pretty pink blouse, children hiding in her flowing skirt. Isabella has some interesting ideas about motherhood. She says 'I could no more go out to work, abandon my children or disobey my husband than I could grow an extra head. I don't have any of the modern woman's confusion about her role in life. From the day I was born, I knew I was destined to be a wife and mother. By the age of 16, I knew that all I really wanted from life was to get married, have children and make a lovely home. That was my ambition.'

She not only believes that a mother's place is in the home, but that the feminist movement is a 'dangerous cancer and perversion'. The world, she says, would be a better place if the Equal Opportunities Commission was shut down and workplace crèches were scrapped. The rape-within-marriage law should be abolished too. She says 'in the rare event of a wife refusing sex with her husband, he has every right, perhaps even a duty, to take her as gently as possible. Once a woman is married she loses the right to say no to her husband's advances. The female role is a submissive one. The male role is assertive and aggressive.' >>

1 List the stereotypical and non-stereotypical masculine and feminine characteristics that come to mind on first seeing the images above.

2 What aspects of Isabella Mackay's view of femininity do you agree or disagree with?

Gender-role socialization

When examining the source of our identities as males and females, sociologists distinguish between the concepts of '**sex**' and '**gender**'. The term 'sex' refers to the biological differences between males and females, e.g. chromosomes, hormones, menstruation and genitalia. The concept of gender, however, refers to the cultural expectations that society associates with 'masculinity' and 'femininity'. Men and women are expected to conform to expectations about 'masculine' and 'feminine' behaviour. Such expectations are not fixed – they change over time and are often different in other cultures.

Gender expectations are transmitted to the next generation through **gender-role socialization**. Sociologists believe that gender differences between males and females are largely the result of society's expectations. Sociologists therefore argue that masculinity and femininity are **socially constructed** rather than being the product of biology.

Hegemonic definitions of masculinity and femininity

A very traditional set of ideas about how men and women are supposed to behave in the UK has dominated our culture until fairly recently. Connell (2002) refers to these ideas as **hegemonic** masculinity and femininity. This set of ideas has allocated very distinct family roles to men and women. Women were expected to occupy the maternal role and to take on much of the responsibility for housework, whereas men were expected to be the head of the household and the economic breadwinner. A range of characteristics were associated with males and females that were seen to shape their behaviour. For example, females were expected to show emotion and affection openly – it was regarded as perfectly acceptable for females to cry or to kiss, hug and hold hands with each other in public. Men and boys, in contrast, were not expected to show their emotions – rather aggression, rationality and toughness were seen as positive characteristics for males to have.

The family and gender-role socialization

Sociologists note that from an early age, infants and children are trained to conform to social expectations about their gender. Much of this training goes on in the family during primary socialization. Oakley (1982) identifies four processes central to the construction of gender identity:

- **Manipulation** refers to the way in which parents encourage and reward or discourage behaviour on the basis of whether it is appropriate for the child's sex. For example, a mother may encourage her daughter to see her appearance as all important, while a father may encourage a son to take part in sports or discourage him from crying.
- **Canalization** refers to the way in which parents direct children's interests into toys and play activities that are seen as normal for that sex.
- Domestic activities – Daughters may have cultural expectations about their future responsibilities reinforced by mothers insisting they help with housework.
- Verbal appellations – Parents may reinforce cultural expectations by referring to daughters and sons using stereotypical feminine and masculine descriptions such as 'pretty' and 'handsome'.

Gender codes

Gender-role socialization, therefore, involves the learning of gender codes, which generally result in social conformity to expectations about appropriate gender behaviour. These include:

- colour codes – e.g. our parents dress boys in blue and girls in pink
- appearance codes – e.g. we learn what dress, hairstyles, cosmetics and jewellery are appropriate for males and females
- toy codes – e.g. gender-specific toys give us clues about our expected future gender roles, i.e. girls get dolls for mothering whilst boys may receive aggressive or creative toys
- play codes – e.g. boys may be expected to play boisterously whereas girls may be expected to play in more docile or decorous ways
- control codes – e.g. boys and girls are subjected to different types of social control especially when they get to their teenage years, with girls often being interrogated more closely about their social lives, boyfriends, etc., than boys.

Statham (1986) found that by the age of 5, most children have acquired a clear gender identity. They know what gender they belong to and they have a clear idea of what constitutes appropriate behaviour for that gender.

The education system and traditional gender-role socialization

A number of feminist studies of education in the 1970s suggested that females were underachieving because their education was regarded by teachers as less important than that of boys. Females consequently saw the educational aspect of their identity as unimportant and often left school at 16. For example, Sue Sharpe's survey of working-class girls in the early 1970s found that such experiences meant that female identity revolved around 'love, marriage, husbands, children, jobs and careers, more or less in that order' (Sharpe 1994).

The mass media and traditional gender-role socialization

Billington et al. (1998) argue that the mass media has traditionally portrayed masculinity as dominant and femininity as subordinate, so that women were generally represented on television in a narrow range of social roles, whereas men were shown performing the full range of social and occupational roles. Women were rarely shown in high-status occupational roles; rather they tended to be overrepresented in domestic settings – as busy housewives, contented mothers, eager consumers and so on. Women were often presented as sexual objects to be enjoyed by men. The most extreme media version of this is pornography and 'Page 3 girls' in newspapers.

Criticizing gender-role socialization

The idea of gender-role socialization has been criticized on two main counts:

- The experiences of men and women vary greatly. There are huge differences in the experience of socialization because of factors such ethnicity, social class and age. Most accounts of gender socialization ignore these differences. For example, there is evidence that socialization into gender roles in Asian families may be more traditional and hegemonic than that found in other ethnic groups.
- It is assumed that women passively accept the traditional gender identity imposed on them. It neglects the choices that people have in developing an identity and the fact that many women and men resist attempts to make them conform to hegemonic gender stereotypes. This can be illustrated with reference to recent social changes.

Social change and masculine identity in the 21st century

Bob Connell argues that masculinity today is experiencing change. There now exist, in addition to the hegemonic type of masculinity, other alternative types of masculinity:

- Some sociologists suggest that a **'new man'** has emerged in the last ten years who is more in touch with his feminine and emotional feelings and who shares childcare and housework with his female partner. However, others have suggested that this is merely a creation of the advertising industry and that surveys show that although men have increased their

Focus on research

Linda McDowell (2001)
Young men leaving school: White working-class masculinity

Drawing on interviews with 23 young men in Cambridge and Sheffield in the year following the end of their compulsory schooling, this in-depth study

explores young White working-class men and the ways in which they talk about their masculinity.

All the men had been classified as low achievers by their schools and, without exception, they were dismissive of their school experiences and anxious to leave. In both cities, the participants stressed being able to stick up for themselves if need be and to sort out any challenges. In their conversations they were casually sexist, often dismissive or at best tolerant of their female peers.

In their leisure time these young men moved between typical 'laddish' behaviour and more responsible behaviour. Many had a clearly gender-divided social life, going out with their girlfriend on Friday or Saturday but definitely not both. One evening was strictly reserved for going out 'with me mates', usually to play pool or snooker in pubs, or sometimes to go clubbing. Although a small number admitted to drinking too much and to occasional fighting, more commonly they stressed that they were not trouble-makers.

McDowell, L. (2001) *Young Men Leaving School: White working-class masculinity*, York: Joseph Rowntree Foundation

1 How did the men in this study express their masculinity?

2 In what ways might these men be experiencing a crisis of masculinity?

3 How would you criticize this research?

share of domestic and childcare tasks, true equality within the home is still a long way off.

● Mort (1996) has highlighted the emergence of **metrosexual** men – these are heterosexual males who are concerned with image and consequently invest in personal grooming products such as designer label fashion, hair conditioners and skin care products. David Beckham is often cited as a prime example of metrosexual man.

● Homosexuality was **decriminalized** in the 1960s and is becoming part of the mainstream. However, despite greater cultural tolerance, it still generally devalued as a masculine form and is often the subject of negative stereotyping.

Mac an Ghaill (1996) claims that hegemonic masculinity may be experiencing a '**crisis of masculinity**' because of the decline of traditional industries and the resulting unemployment. Work is central to the identity of traditional men, and unemployment can therefore lead to a loss of self-esteem and status as well as a loss of identification with others. Younger males may see their futures as bleak and so view schooling and qualifications as irrelevant to their needs. This may reinforce educational failure as they seek alternative sources of status in activities in which they can stress their masculinity, such as delinquency and gang violence.

However, although masculinity has undergone some change, it would be a mistake to exaggerate these trends. Collier (2002), for example, notes that lads' magazines still objectify women in an explicitly sexual fashion. Some of these magazines, most notably, *Loaded*, *Zoo* and *Nuts*, actively assert traditional notions of masculinity by celebrating 'birds, booze and football'. There is a whole media industry devoted to encouraging women to perfect their figure, make-up and sexual desirability for the benefit of men. The male equivalent of such media does not really exist.

Social change and feminine identity

Today, female achievement at all levels of the examination system outstrips that of males (although a significant number of working-class females continue to underachieve). This success is partly the result of educational initiatives such as Girls Into Science and Technology (GIST), coursework and a national curriculum that aimed to prevent the gender-stereotyping of subject choice. However, the main cause is probably the profound changes that the economy has experienced in the last 25 years. Changes in demand for British goods and the **globalization of the economy** have led to changes in the labour market, particularly a decline in traditional industries such as mining, iron and steel, heavy engineering, etc. (which mainly employed men). Whilst demand for men's jobs fell, there was a corresponding expansion in the **service sector** of the economy, i.e. white-collar and professional jobs in financial and government services, managers of retail outlets in new shopping centres, and so on. Most of these new jobs were aimed at employing women.

Genderquake and feminine identity

It is argued by sociologists such as Wilkinson (1994) and Sharpe (1994) that the increasing participation and success of women in the world of paid work mean that traditional notions of female identity are being abandoned. Helen Wilkinson (1994) argues that there has been a fundamental shift in values and attitudes amongst women aged under 35 compared with their mothers and grandmothers. She argues that this shift is so dramatic that it amounts to a '**genderquake**' and has led to a profound change in the distribution of power between men and women.

Wilkinson argues that the **feminization of the economy and the workplace** has led to a revolution in women's ambitions. Family commitments no longer have priority in women's lives; careers and economic independence are now the defining feature of young women's identity and self-esteem. Younger women and girls are encouraged to think along these lines because they are likely to experience the positive role model of a mother who enjoys a career rather than just a part-time job. Some young women may even choose voluntary childlessness and a career as an alternative to getting married and having children.

Sharpe's study (1994) suggests that young females are becoming more assertive about their rights and are now more likely to rank education and career above marriage and family as priorities in their lives. Moreover, there are signs that women are now more willing to use divorce to escape husbands who insist on their wives playing a subordinate domestic role. Consequently, hegemonic versions of femininity, i.e. being a good mother and housewife – the traditional domestic role – may be becoming less significant in terms of female identity.

Consumption, leisure and feminine identity

Increasing economic independence means that women are now viewed as significant consumers. There are signs that mass-media products are increasingly being targeted at single women. This means that young women today are also likely to see consumption and leisure as key factors in their identity. Such processes have supposedly led to the emergence of 'girl power' and '**ladettes**', who are increasingly adopting male forms of behaviour, such as drinking and smoking heavily, and being sexually aggressive.

Evaluating changes in masculine and feminine identity

A number of evaluative points can be made with regard to the positive changes associated with masculinity and femininity identified in this topic.

- Socialization into gender roles is still very traditional in terms of the ways that families operate, e.g. the toys that parents give children encourage very different futures and particularly encourage girls in the direction of motherhood. Consequently, males are still being brought up to see themselves as superior to girls. There is evidence too that many girls still subscribe to traditional stereotypes about the relationship between the sexes and are happy to subordinate their interests to men as they get older.
- Economic changes may have benefited some women in terms of opening up opportunities to enter the professions and management but men still dominate high status jobs and generally earn more than women. Women are more likely to be working part-time especially if they are mothers. They are likely to experience the dual burden if they work. Furthermore the evidence suggests that the decision to have children still impacts more negatively on the female career than the male career. Connell suggests that all men benefit from a patriarchal dividend in this respect.
- There is still a great deal of pressure from society to become wives and mothers – women who elect to have careers rather than families are seen as deviant and it is

often the case that working mothers are blamed for social problems such as juvenile delinquency or made to feel guilty for working and 'neglecting' their children. Single mums too are often subject to moral panics and blamed for many of society's social problems.
- There are few signs of improvement in terms of how women are portrayed by the mass media. Representations of females still stress their sexual objectification in lads' magazines, tabloid newspapers and pornography. They are judged on the basis of appearance, i.e. weight, shape, size, and general 'sexiness' rather than as individuals with intellects and personality. Some young women according to Wolf and Orbach may internalise a negative self identity because of these images and become anorexic or bulimic. The other major media representation of women stresses their role as mother-housewife through, for example, television advertising.
- Masculinity in ethnic minority cultures tends to be very traditional too, e.g. specific religions such as Islam subscribe to very traditional ideas about women's role in religion, family etc.
- Domestic violence is still a problem and there is evidence that a great number of women are putting up with it and not reporting it.
- The double-standard of sexuality is still very powerful – women are still more likely to be negatively labelled as slut, slag etc if they adopt similar standards of sexual behaviour as men or dress 'inappropriately'.

All in all, although there have undoubtedly been positive changes in the past 30 years for women, we must be aware that these are sometimes exaggerated and women still have a great way to travel before they achieve equal economic, political, social and domestic inequality with men. In the meantime, feminine identity remains a subordinate status compared with masculine status.

Gay subculture

A social phenomena that has challenged traditional notions of both masculinity and femininity has been the emergence of a gay and lesbian subculture in the UK. Homosexuality was **decriminalized** in the 1960s and by the 1970, a distinct gay and lesbian subculture could be seen to have emerged in British culture, particularly in areas such as London, Manchester and Brighton. Furthermore, Gay Pride marches have sought to increase the visibility and social acceptability of gay people. These strategies, aided by the increasing number of celebrities coming out as gay, have undoubtedly made it easier for gay people to lead a normal life today, although it should also be acknowledged that **prejudice** and **discrimination** have not totally disappeared. Male homosexuality is still generally devalued as a masculine form and consequently still subject to negative stereotyping. Homophobic attacks on gay people are still relatively common and suggest that this type of sexuality is not totally accepted by all sections of the community.

Rich (1984) suggests that the emergence of gay and lesbian subcultures is remarkable considering that Western societies tend to be characterized by a fierce '**compulsory heterosexuality**'. Hegemonic masculinity states that 'real men' are not homosexuals. The mass media constantly subject people to heterosexual images through films, television programmes and advertising. Religious organizations criticize homosexuality as sinful, wicked and immoral. Homosexuality is rarely portrayed as a normal or ideal condition.

Key terms

Canalization parental attempts to make sure children play with gender-appropriate toys, etc.

Compulsory heterosexuality the idea that culture automatically socializes its members into heterosexual roles.

Crisis of masculinity the idea that men who have been brought up in traditional ways might feel confused or anxious about the loss of their role as breadwinners, etc.

Decriminalization legalization, no longer criminal.

Discrimination treating someone unfairly because of their sexuality, race, age, etc.

Feminization of the economy/workplace the fact that most available new jobs are for women rather than men.

Gender the behaviour that culture associates with femininity and masculinity.

Genderquake the radical change in attitudes, especially towards education and work, experienced by younger women compared with women of previous generations.

Gender-role socialization the process by which people learn how to act in feminine or masculine ways.

Globalization of the economy the trend towards manufacturing goods more cheaply abroad, e.g. in China, which has contributed to the decline in British industry.

Hegemonic cultural dominance.

Ladettes girls who behave like boys.

Manipulation parental encouragement of gender-appropriate behaviour and disapproval of gender-inappropriate behaviour.

Metrosexual males who spend a lot of time and money on personal grooming.

New Man a caring, sharing male in touch with his own and his female partner's emotions.

Prejudice a preformed opinion, usually an unfavourable one, based on insufficient knowledge, irrational feelings or inaccurate stereotypes.

Service sector that sector of the economy that provides services, e.g. financial or retail services, rather than manufactures goods.

Sex the biological differences between men and women.

Socially constructed produced by society, i.e. manufactured by culture rather than biologically inherited.

Activities

Research idea

Get hold of at least two toy catalogues or catalogues that include toys. Analyse any links between gender and the presentation of the catalogues. Are girls or boys pictured playing with toys? Do the pictures reflect or challenge typical gender roles? Are some toys targeted more at girls and others more at boys? Which are targeted at which? How can you tell?

Web.tasks

1 Visit the web-site **www.theory.org.uk** and click on the link 'Media, Gender and Identity' – this will take you through to a range of resources on femininity and masculinity produced by David Gauntlett and his students, as well as internet links to various sites celebrating masculinity and femininity.

2 Find the website **www.feminist.com**. Access their 'Resources' page and pick an article that relates to some aspect of femininity. What social changes or issues are important to women today according to this website?

Check your understanding

1 Identify three differences between 'sex' and 'gender'.

2 Explain, using examples, what is meant by 'hegemonic' masculinity and femininity.

3 Explain why the family is the most important agency of gender-role socialization.

4 How do mass media representations of masculinity and femininity reinforce traditional stereotypes about men and women?

5 How have economic and social changes contributed to the emergence of new types of femininity and masculinity?

6 How have sexual identities evolved over the last 50 years?

your opening sentences should attempt to clearly explain the meaning of the concept

you should attempt to write a detailed paragraph in about 5 minutes

(a) Define the concept of masculinities. Illustrate your answer with examples. **(8 marks)**

spend about 3–4 minutes developing two or three examples that demonstrate your understanding of the concept in action

you need to begin by defining what is meant by gender-role socialization and then identify two of the ways in which it works in practice in the family

you should attempt to write about a side of A4

(b) Outline and explain two ways in which the family influences gender-role socialization. **(16 marks)**

develop the two aspects of gender-role socialization in the family in detail by using illustrative examples and sociological studies, e.g. you could explore studies, e.g. Ann Oakley that demonstrate parents' use of specific approaches such as canalisation or manipulation, or you could discuss the gender characteristics of children's experiences of toys, play, books etc

(c) Explain and briefly evaluate the view that femininity has undergone dramatic change in the past thirty years. **(24 marks)**

Grade booster Getting top marks in this question

Begin by defining what is traditionally meant by femininity – it is important when discussing 'change' that you have a clear idea of what something was like before, otherwise it is difficult to evaluate the degree of such change. Explain and illustrate how girls were socialized into traditional or hegemonic femininity with reference to the family, education, mass media etc. Outline what changes have allegedly taken place using studies such as Wilkinson and Sharpe. Don't forget to evaluate by referring to evidence relating to pay, top jobs, family roles, mass media representations and domestic violence. Use concepts like patriarchy, glass ceiling, genderquake and feminization of the economy whenever possible.

TOPIC 5

Socialization, identity and ethnicity

Laura Smith: <<There is a story my mother is fond of telling me and it goes like this. When I was three, a little friend of mine pointed at me and said with accusation in her voice: "You're black." My response was one that only a three-year-old could make. Puffing up my chest and probably sticking my nose in the air, I told her firmly: "No, I'm not. I'm pink and brown." It wasn't that being black was a bad thing. It was just that my skin was not literally the colour of my black crayons and so, logically, what she had said was nonsense. Aged seven, I had the dubious distinction of being the only girl with one pink and one brown parent at my north London primary school. Nearly 25 years on, much has changed. Suddenly, mixed-race images are everywhere, projected on posters selling Marks & Spencer's bikinis or sofas for DFS. Mixed-race people have become the acceptable face of ethnic minorities for advertisers and programme makers.

However surveys of mixed-race children tell a different story of racism from both sides. 'You could say you are mixed race and white people will cuss you and black people will cuss you,' said one boy. 'They call you half-breed,' added another girl. Often mixed-race people can find it difficult to find cultural affiliations. They might be rejected by their black side because their skin's too light and their hair's too straight, and rejected by their white side because their skin's too dark and their hair's too frizzy."<<

Adapted from *Absent Voices* by Laura Smith, The Guardian, 6/9/06

Colin Wong: <<My parents arrived in England in the early 1960s from Hong Kong. They settled in rented accommodation in Liverpool working long hours in various poorly paid jobs in local Chinese restaurants and shops. Growing up in a large family was bliss. Being bilingual was the norm; we spoke Cantonese with our parents and English with others. I had a Scouse accent. It was only at secondary school that I began to consider my ethnic identity. Almost overnight, the duality of my life became evident. I attended Anglican schools, yet my home life reflected Buddhism. I celebrated Easter and Christmas yet my family also celebrated Chinese New Year. During my teenage years, it was difficult to decide on my true identity. I felt English, but my adversaries would remind me of my differences to them. I felt Chinese, but I had never been beyond the UK. However, on my first visit to Hong Kong, I felt instantly comfortable with the people, the place, the language and the culture. So who am I? When I complete Ethnic Monitoring Forms, I tick the Chinese box. When I clear Customs at the airport, I walk through the European channel. When I look in the mirror, I do not see a Chinese face or an English face … I just see plain Me.>>

Source: Marsh, I. and Keating, M. (2006) *Sociology: Making Sense of Society*, Harlow: Pearson Education, p. 313

1   **What factors make up the identity of Colin Wong?**

2   **What problems of ethnic identity do Laura Smith and other mixed-race children experience?**

Ethnicity as cultural distinctiveness

If we examine the case study above of Colin Wong, we can see that he has the specific ethnic characteristic of speaking Cantonese. He also shares racial characteristics with Chinese people, i.e. he comes from a Chinese background. Note, though, that this does not mean he subscribes to an exclusively Chinese identity. His ethnic identity is more complex than that. Rather his ethnic identity overlaps with his national identities, as well as his regional identity. Laura Smith's ethnic identity is also problematic because some sections of society are prejudiced and may not be too keen to welcome her as part of their ethnic communities.

Despite these difficulties, sociologists note that significant numbers of people in the UK share an ethnic minority identity, i.e. they recognize that they share cultural characteristics, and that their **ethnicity** is distinctive compared to the majority White and **Anglo-Saxon** culture. These characteristics include:

- *Common descent* – This may be represented by colour or other racial characteristics, e.g. Modood's (1997) research suggests that being Black is an important source of identity for young African-Caribbeans.
- *Geographical origins* – Links with a country of origin are important, and ethnic identity may involve seeing oneself as 'Pakistani' or 'Indian' or 'Irish' or 'Welsh' first and foremost.
- *History* – Members of minority ethnic cultures may share a sense of struggle and oppression, which originates in particular historical contexts, such as slavery, colonialism or persecution. For example, Jewish identity may be partially shaped by events like the Holocaust during the Second World War, while some African-Caribbeans may feel that the fact that they are descendants of slaves is central to their identity.
- *Language* – Members of particular groups may speak the language(s) of their country of origin at home, e.g. older-generation Chinese people may speak in Cantonese, while young British-Pakistani Muslims may talk to each other in a combination of Urdu and English.
- *Religion* – This is the most important influence for some ethnic-minority groups, e.g. some Pakistanis will see themselves first and foremost as Muslim.
- *Traditions and rituals* – These may be religious or cultural, e.g. the Notting Hill Carnival, which is held annually in the UK to celebrate African-Caribbean culture.
- *Racism* – Prejudice and discrimination may be experienced and may take several forms, e.g. name-calling, police harassment, violence, and so on.

Ethnic minorities

In Britain, ethnicity is mainly associated with minority groups from the former British colonies on the Indian subcontinent, in the Caribbean and in Africa. This kind of categorisation is a problem because it emphasises skin colour rather than common cultural characteristics. In doing so it ignores significant white minority ethnic groups resident in the UK, such as Greek Cypriots, Jews, gypsies and Irish people. It also means that differences between minority groups such as Asians and African-Caribbeans, and the majority white population are exaggerated, whilst differences between ethnic minorities such as Bangladeshis and Pakistanis are neglected.

Ethnic identity and racism

The ability of ethnic minorities in Britain to shape their self-identity is also limited by the way in which they are seen and treated by powerful groups. Racial prejudice and discrimination practiced by the majority white group may make it difficult for ethnic minorities to fully express their cultural identity. Discrimination can take a number of different forms.

- There is some evidence of **institutional racism** within the educational system. For example, it is argued that some white teachers are unable to cope with the way African-Caribbean boys express their ethnic identity at school and this is the explanation why these boys are more likely than any other type to be excluded from school.
- Other discriminatory practices have been identified in **policing**. Some commentators have seen the fact that the police stop and search black youth far more than any other ethnic group as a symptom of racism. Evidence suggests that the ethnic identity of African-Caribbean youth may often be based on resentment of such treatment and is consequently anti-authority and anti-police.

Differences between ethnic groups

It is a mistake to assume that there is only one Asian ethnic identity. The Asian community is divided along a number of lines especially country of origin, region within the country of origin and religion. Moreover, even within particular groups, e.g. Sikhs and Hindus, there are differences along caste lines. These divisions too can lead to tension, hostility and even conflict.

Sometimes these differences are very subtle and certainly invisible to many whites. For example, Modood found that Asian ethnic identity is very specific in terms of differences in religion, language, dress codes, jewelry and diet. In his study, a Gujerati Hindu was quoted as saying: 'there is a great deal of difference between a Gujerati and, say, a Punjabi. Their clothing is more expensive. They wear more jewelry. I cannot find many similarities between our cultures'. There may even be subtle differences in the ethnic identity of groups who share the same religion, e.g. between Shia and Sunni Muslims.

Ethnic identity and primary socialization

Singh Ghumann (1999) suggests that the first generation of Asian parents to arrive in the UK in the 1950s and 1960s were concerned to transmit the following key values to their children during primary socialization in the family:

- Children should be obedient, loyal to and respectful of their elders and community around them. Social conformity was demanded.
- Parents were considered to know best the interests of their children regardless of the child's age.
- The choice of marriage partner was thought to be best left to parents.
- Religious training was considered very important because it reinforced respect for family and stressed humility rather than self-pride and assertiveness.
- The role of the mother tongue was seen as crucial in maintaining links between generations. Children therefore tended to be bilingual, and were often able to use both the mother language, e.g. Urdu, Punjabi, Gujerati or Hindi, and English interchangeably.

Many of these family socialization practices are still the norm today. For example, Singh Ghumann (1999) found that Asian families – whether Hindu, Muslim or Sikh – socialize children into a pattern of duty, obligation and loyalty to the extended family community, as well as religious commitment, which, in most cases, they accept. The concept of corporate or family honour (*izzat*) is particularly important in Muslim kinship relations. Consequently, even when they leave home, children will often continue to live near their parents and visit them regularly.

Ethnic identity and arranged marriage

Evidence suggests continuing strong support for arranged marriages across all Asian groups, even among the young. Hennink et al. (1999) found that 75 per cent of Sikh and 85 per cent of Muslim teenage girls expected an arranged marriage. Singh Ghumann (1999) notes that this is the product of successful socialization into a **collectivist** family culture that stresses obedience, loyalty to and respect for elders. Brah (1993) notes that the majority of Asian adolescents felt confident that they would not be forced into a marriage they did not want. Arranged marriage, then, was regarded as a joint undertaking with scope for negotiation. Children were very aware of not letting the family down but expected emotional and psychological support in return. Interestingly, Brah's sample of Asian girls did not see their white peers as advantaged –what they had seen of western romance, marriage and divorce did not convince them that western girls enjoyed greater freedoms.

Asian culture and feminine identity

Studies of domestic labour within Asian families do suggest that women are expected to take responsibility for housework and childcare, although these tasks are not necessarily the exclusive responsibility of the wife or mother. Such tasks are distributed between all women. Single women often share responsibility for looking after younger siblings, nephews, nieces etc according to Brah's study. Brah also found that Asian women were more likely than white women to experience the dual burden of paid and domestic work.

Brah notes too that publicly men are expected to present an image of fearlessness and independence to the outside world and keep close control over female members of the family. For example, for a woman to challenge her husband's or her father's authority in public brings about shame for the male.

However, Brah argues that it is a mistake on the basis of this evidence to dismiss Asian families as patriarchal (i.e. male dominated) institutions. She suggests that this formal and visible subordination to men does not indicate that women do not have any power. Women control the domestic sphere and economic decision-making. They bargain both individually and collectively with men. Husbands cannot afford to ignore the interests and concerns of their wives. Decision-making is therefore largely shared between men and women. In particular, women handle all the private negotiations which precede an arranged marriage. Women play a central role in upholding family honour.

Muslim feminine identity

Muslim families tend to stress the control of females because it is believed the future of the community depends on them becoming wives and mothers and socialising the next generation into key Muslim values.

In Pakistani and Bangladeshi culture men are accorded more freedom because women are perceived as subordinate to men. Moreover reputation and honour is extremely important and consequently so is the reputation of daughters. Many parents may therefore come into conflict with their daughters over issues such as continuing in education and the free-mixing of the sexes especially in westernised contexts. However, the experience of school and college, and the peer relationships established with their white or African-Caribbean peers may result in some Pakistani and Bangladeshi girls challenging the idea that they should play a lesser role in their communities.

Ethnic identity and potential family conflict

Anwar (1981) suggests that the family can be a site of conflict between grandparents, parents and children. The younger generation is seen by the older generation to have mixed with people, i.e. Westerners, who have very different values and attitudes, and this has supposedly resulted in the younger generation believing in values and ideas which their parents regard as alien. This may particularly be the case with regard to young females who wish to continue into further and higher education and pursue professional careers. The older generation might believe these wishes are too ambitious and attempt to restrict females to a more traditional domestic role.

A good example of generational conflict involves dating which is disapproved of by the older Asian generation. However Drury (1991) found that one fifth of girls in her Asian sample were secretly dating boys. Moreover some were going to pubs and drinking alcohol without the knowledge and consent of their parents. Such practices can cause great anguish as the following quote from a Sikh girl indicates.

>> '*I would like to have a boyfriend and I would like to have a love marriage but the consequences are too great. Gossip spreads and you can lose everything. Everyone in the family can be hurt and nobody will want to marry my sister... I think that Sikh boys in England are given too much freedom. They can go out with white girls yet they are expected to marry an innocent Indian girl'.*>>
(Drury, 1991, p.396)

There is also evidence that Asian girls have strong feelings about the freedom given to their male siblings and the fact that they are expected to take on domestic responsibilities, i.e. to help with housework and childcare, when their brothers are not.

Ethnic identity and religion

Religion has a profound influence as an agency of socialization in shaping the ethnic identity of young Asians. Modood (1997) questioned two generations of Asians, African-Caribbeans and Whites about the statement: 'Religion is very important to how I live my life'. He found that those most in favour of religion were the Pakistani and Bangladeshi samples: 82 per cent of the age 50+ sample and 67 per cent of the 16 to 34 year age group valued the importance of Islam in their lives. About one third of young Indians saw their religion as important. The lowest figure was for young Whites – only 5 per cent saw religion as important compared with 18 per cent of young African-Caribbeans.

Modood notes that the centrality of religion in Asian communities – and therefore in shaping their ethnic identity – can be illustrated in the fact that very few Asians marry across religious or **caste** lines, and that most of their children will be socialized into a religious value system. Singh Ghumann notes that the mosque is the centre for the religious, educational and political activities of Muslim communities and these religious institutions often exert a strong influence on the way parents rear and educate their children.

Drury's ethnographic research found that 42% of the Sikh girls in her sample went regularly to the temple whilst 44% said they hardly ever attended. Research by Stopes-Roe and Cochrane (1990) on young Asian people aged 18-21 found that 85% thought the teaching of religion to be very important or important. Interestingly, these ideas seemed to be higher for Pakistani and Bangladeshi youth. However, among Indian youth, religion was less likely to shape their way of life or world view. They were much more likely to challenge the myths and superstitions surrounding their faiths, although many still celebrated traditional rituals and festivals.

Modood (2001) notes that the centrality of religion in Asian communities and therefore in shaping their ethnic identity, can be illustrated in the fact that very few Asians marry across religious or caste lines, and that most of their children will be socialized into a religious value system.

African-Caribbean identity

Modood (1997) found that skin colour is an important source of identity to many young African-Caribbeans. Some African-Caribbean youth stress their Black identity because of their experience of racial prejudice and discrimination from White society. Black pride and power may be celebrated, especially if Black youth perceives itself to be deliberately excluded from jobs or stereotyped by White people – in particular, by symbols of White authority such as teachers and the police.

African–Caribbean identity and peer group pressure

Tony Sewell (1996) argues that peer-group pressure is extremely influential in shaping ethnic identity among disaffected African-Caribbean youth in British inner cities and that this is probably partly responsible for educational underachievement and the high levels of unemployment found in this group.

He argues that African-Caribbean male identity, especially in inner city areas of London, is focused on being a hyper-male and gangsta often as part of highly deviant territorial street gangs based on post-codes. Sewell argues that young black males get involved in these subcultures for three reasons:

- They feel that they do not fit into the dominant mainstream culture which is dominated by whites. They feel rejected by it.
- They become anxious about how they are perceived by society, and especially by their black peers because many live in one-parent families headed by their mothers. They do not have fathers to turn to for advice or guidance.
- They are influenced by media culture, particularly the emphasis on designer labels and the imitation of male role models, e.g. rap stars, in terms of macho attitudes and forms of behaviour.

This culture of hyper-masculinity in which respect is the ultimate goal (and lack of respect the ultimate insult) compensates for their perception that society is loaded against them. The gang is valued as a comfort zone which stresses being ultra-confident and the challenging of authority.

African-Caribbean identity and Religion

There is some evidence that the African-Caribbean community, whether it is the older or younger generation, is more religious than the white community in terms of religious beliefs and practices. Sociological evidence suggests a great involvement by both the younger and older generation in the 'born again' evangelical and gospel Pentecostal and Baptist churches which encourage very informal and spontaneous forms of worship. African-Caribbeans are also attracted by religious sects, particularly the Seventh Day Adventists, Black Muslims and Rastafarianism.

Rastafarianism is particularly popular amongst young Jamaicans in Brixton, Birmingham and Gloucester. This set of beliefs believe that African-Caribbeans are the 'lost tribe of Israel' who were forcibly removed from their spiritual homeland, i.e. Africa by whites via slavery, and forced to live in 'Babylon', i.e. white dominated society. They believe that a Christ-like figure 'Ras Tafari' will one day return and guide them back to the 'promised land', i.e. Ethiopia in Africa. Many young blacks involve themselves in Rastafarianism because of its anti-white beliefs because they felt resentful at racism. The practice of smoking marijuana (which is essential part of Rasta beliefs) is seen to symbolize anti-white authority.

African-Caribbean identity and mass media

Surveys of television, advertising and films indicate that black people are under-represented. When they do appear, the range of roles they play is very limited. Black people are rarely shown as ordinary citizens who just happen to be black. More often they play 'black' roles, i.e. their attitudes and behaviour are heavily determined by their ethnic identity. Some soaps such as EastEnders have included black characters as ordinary members of the community but its main rival on ITV, Coronation Street, has only recently begun to include black characters despite its 40-year history and despite being set in what has long been a multicultural area of Manchester. Research carried out in 2002 by the Broadcasting Standards Commission (BSC) concluded that there needs to be a better representation of minorities both on screen and behind the scenes in decision-making roles.

Akinti (2003) argues that television and newspapers often reflect an inaccurate and superficial view of black life focusing almost exclusively on stereotypical issues such as gun crime, Aids in Africa and black underachievement in schools whilst ignoring the culture and interests of a huge black audience, diverse in interests and age, and their rich contribution to UK society.

Ethnic identity and popular culture

There are a number of media agencies owned and controlled by ethnic minorities themselves. Newspapers, television and especially cinema (Bollywood) and Asian satellite channels can keep minority groups firmly in touch with their countries of origin and cultural norms. Specialist newspapers, magazines and TV and radio channels and programmes all positively contribute to secondary socialization into ethnic identities.

Paul Gilroy (1992) argues that young African-Caribbeans often adopt identities based around influential media role models such as 50 Cent or the So Solid Crew. Gangsta rap and hip-hop, in particular, accessed through MTV and other satellite/cable channels have been powerful influences, and often the adoption of aspects of the gangsta rap lifestyle symbolise opposition to white society. Kellner (1995) agrees and notes that rap music is a means of expressing black identity in what is perceived by African-Caribbeans as a hostile and racist environment.

Mixed-race identity

Recently, sociologists have observed that intermarriage, especially between Whites and African-Caribbeans, has risen considerably. Platt (2009) found that one in 10 children in the UK lives in a mixed-race family. She argues that mixed-race relationships are now so common that some ethnic groups – particularly African-Caribbean and Chinese – are likely to disappear in the UK in the near future. She found that young people are six times more likely to be mixed-race than adults. Tizard and Phoenix (1993) found that 60 per cent of the mixed-race children in their sample were proud of their mixed parentage, but they noted that 'it is still not an easy ride to be of mixed Black and White parentage in our society because of racism from both White and Black populations'.

Hybrid or dual identities

There is some evidence that ethnic identities are evolving and modern hybrid forms are now developing among Britain's younger ethnic-minority citizens. Butler (1995) studied third-generation young Muslim women ('third-generation' means that their parents and grandparents were born in Britain). She found that they choose from a variety of possible identities. Some will choose to reflect their ascribed position through the wearing of traditional dress, while others may take a more 'negotiated' position. This may mean adopting Western ideas about education and careers whilst retaining some respect for traditional religious ideas about the role of women. Some young Islamic women may adopt quite different identities compared with their mothers on issues such as equality, domestic roles, fashion and marriage.

Johal (1998) focused on second- and third-generation British-Asians. He found that they have a **dual identity** in that they inherit an Asian identity and adopt a British one. This results in Asian youth adopting a 'White mask' in order to interact with White peers at school or college, but emphasizing their cultural difference whenever they feel it is necessary. He notes that many British-Asians adopt 'hybrid identities'. They select aspects of British, Asian and global culture relating to fashion, music and food in order to construct their identity. For example, many young British-Asians like Bhangra music – a mixture of Punjabi music married to Western rhythms.

Ghuman suggests that Hindu and Sikh girls use 'compartmentalism' to cope with the twin pressures of parental restriction and racial prejudice. He notes: 'On the one hand, South Asian girls learn to think and behave as obedient and respectful daughters wearing salwar kameez and speaking in Punjabi/Hindi at home. On the other, they

Focus on research

Leon Tikly (2005)
Understanding the Educational Needs of Mixed Heritage Pupils

Tikly carried out qualitative research in the form of semi-structured interviews with 44 teachers and 84 mixed-race or dual-heritage pupils in fourteen schools in six LEAs. He notes that dual- heritage pupils are the fastest growing ethnic minority group in education, making up 2.5% of the school age population and 7.3% of Inner London pupils. However, he notes that their educational attainment is below average and they are more likely than other groups to be excluded from school.

Some mixed-race pupils reported experiencing racism from teachers. Many pupils believed that some teachers 'picked on' or disliked them because of their perceived mixed heritage. Some pupils also reported racism from both their White and Black peers aimed at their mixed heritage in the form of name-calling and exclusion which resulted in low academic aspirations and self esteem and the adoption of rebellious and challenging forms of behaviour.

Tikly's study suggests that mixed heritage children are often alienated by being caught between two worlds in the sense of being neither Black nor White. However, just to confuse matters even further, the police are more likely to see them as Black Caribbean than White, and consequently stop them more than their White peers. These contradictions often result in confusion and negative self-esteem.

Source: DfES Research Brief RB549 – www.dfes.gov.uk/research/

1 How did the children practically respond to the contradictory messages they were picking up about their identity from their experience of the education system?

2 How would you go about criticising the research method used by Tikly?

wear European-style uniform and speak English at school and are engaging and assertive like their English peers'. However, he also notes that some Asian girls have to give up their hope of a career and accept an arranged marriage because of parental pressure. These girls probably re-define their ethnic identity in terms of conforming to their parents' culture by becoming a 'good' wife and mother.

Evaluation: Social change and the continuing influence of tradition

Finally, whilst acknowledging the appearance of new ethnic cultural identities, Modood (2001) notes how important traditional values, customs and rituals still are in shaping ethnic identity today. He points out that nearly all Asians, whether they be Pakistani, Bangladeshi or Indian, can understand a community language and two-thirds use it with other family members younger than themselves.

Studies indicate that the overwhelming majority of young Pakistani and Bangladeshi British people return to the collectivistic value system that underpins their upbringing. Most choose to organise their domestic and personal lives on the basis of the values of obligation, duty, community, honour etc. This is behaviour that is quite distinct from their white peers. Studies suggest that this results from two inter-linked realisations, i.e. that the attractions of English lifestyles do not compensate for a lack of family security and that assimilation into such a culture is pointless because of racism. However, this return involves some modification of their parents' cultural values and norms, especially for females who often now want education and a career.

Moreover, more than half of married 16–34-year-old Pakistanis and Bangladeshis have had their spouse chosen by their parents. He concludes that although there has been some decline in belief in traditional values and practices across the younger generation, this does not mean that the traditional exercises a weak influence.

In fact, he notes that in some cultures, especially Muslim, the traditional is still the main shaper of ethnic identity – Modood notes that Muslim traditional values and practices (i.e. fundamentalism) are experiencing a political and religious revival among Pakistani young men in the early 21st century. These young men are demonstrating a profound opposition to western lifestyles, especially American values, and may express this opposition by resisting white society in a number of ways.

Jacobson (1997) argues that many young Pakistanis are adopting an Islamic identity in terms of diet, dress and everyday routines and practices. She suggests that this is essentially a defensive identity that has developed as a response to racism and social exclusion. Islamic identity compensates for such marginalisation because *it stresses the exclusion of the white excluders by the excluded*. Fairly recently, we saw the 7/7 bombers, young homegrown British Asians expressing their resistance to western lifestyles and actions through terrorism.

Focus on research

Living Apart Together: British Muslims and the Paradox of Multiculturalism (2007)

by Munira Mirza, Abi Senthilkumaran and Zein Ja'far

This research carried out a questionnaire survey in 2007 aimed at a sample of 1000 Muslims and 1000 non-Muslims in Britain in order to find out what constitutes a Muslim identity and how the non-Muslim population perceives that identity.

The research found that the vast majority of Muslims living in Britain practice their religion peacefully and in harmonious cooperation with other religious groups. 87% of Muslims who took part in the survey disagreed with the aims of organizations like al-Qaeda and very few believed in the use of violence to 'Islamicise' society so that it follows the religious codes set down in the Qu'ran – the most holy text of Islam.

However the research did show that there has been a general increase in Muslim perception of their religious and cultural identity among second and third generation Muslims in the UK. Indicators of this include the increased wearing of headscarves among Muslim women, a greater identification with a global Muslim community and a growth in membership of Islamist political and religious associations. There was also an increase in the number of young Muslims going on pilgrimage to the holy city of Mecca. Just over a third of young British Muslims expressed a preference to live under sharia law although the majority of all age groups said they preferred British law. Many young Muslims also expressed anger at British foreign policy towards Muslim countries like Iraq and Afghanistan.

However, the research also found that Muslims are a very culturally and linguistically diverse group who practice their religion in a variety of ways. Many Muslims have adapted comfortably to living in Europe and are very 'westernised' and 'secular', e.g. 70% of Muslim house owners have a normal mortgage despite religious restrictions on paying interest.

The research concludes that it would be a mistake to think that all Muslims think and feel the same about their religion. Muslims in the UK are not an homogeneous group and often do not feel represented by their community 'leaders'.

Source: www.policyexchange.org.uk

1   Why has Muslim identity become more pronounced amongst young British Muslims?

2   How would you use this research to illustrate the view that there is no one single Muslim community or identity?

Regional ethnicities

Some sociologists suggest that people who occupy particular regions of Britain – the English, Scots, Welsh and Irish – also constitute distinct ethnic groups because they have cultural traditions which have been passed down the generations and which are unique to them.

Welsh ethnic identity

Studies of people in Wales see their Welsh ethnic identity as more important than their national identity of British. For example, a Labour Force Survey in 2001 found that 87% of people born in Wales saw themselves as Welsh only. This powerful sense of ethnic identity has been assisted by legislation aimed at protecting the Welsh language and culture especially in the education system. The Welsh language is compulsory in Welsh schools up to year 11 despite the fact that it is only spoken by a minority of the Welsh population.

Language seems to be crucial to Welsh identity. The Labour Force survey found that 89% of Welsh speakers saw themselves as Welsh compared with only 59% of those who did not speak the language. There is a 'Welsh dimension' to all subjects in secondary school. History, for example, partly focuses on Welsh resistance to English occupation. Literature focuses on Welsh poets and novelists. Welsh schools are encouraged to organise their own Eisteddford - a cultural celebration involving Welsh songs, poetry and literature, in addition to celebrating St. David's Day. Welsh identity is also reinforced by two Welsh TV channels as well as strong cultural traditions in fields such as opera and choral singing. Sport in the form of rugby union is an important source of ethnic pride too, especially if this involves beating England.

English ethnic identities?

Some sociologists have attempted to explore whether there is an English ethnic identity. It has been suggested that whilst groups such as the Welsh and Scots have developed a strong sense of ethnic identity underpinned by language, history, education, government and media, English ethnic identity is not so clear cut. As Dencombe (2001) notes:

<<*'English identity tends to be defined by what it is not, rather than what it is; who the English are not, rather than who they are. Those with the strongest sense of English identity are characterised by suspicion of the outsider, the foreigner and those of other races'*>> (p. 20).

Research by Curtice and Heath (2000) suggests that about 17% of the English population which they call 'Little Englanders' stress the importance of their ethnic identity. This group sees their ethnic identity as threatened by immigration and the European Union.

Research also indicates that members of ethnic minority groups born in the UK are less likely than Whites to see themselves as having an English ethnic identity. They are more likely to identify themselves as Afro-Caribbeans, Muslims Sikhs etc. This can particularly be seen in the field of sport. When England play Pakistan, India or the West Indies, young Asians and African-Caribbeans, despite being born in the UK and having British nationality, often identify with and support Pakistan, India and the West Indies, and are often ecstatic if victory over England is achieved. However, they are happy to support England in the football World Cup.

However, there is now some evidence, particularly from Johal, that an increasing number of third-generation young Asians, particularly Indians, are using terms like British-Asians or Indo-British, and even 'Brasian' to describe themselves today as they tap into and are influenced by British culture. However, in Scotland, surveys indicate that young Asians tend to see themselves as Scottish rather than British.

Despite some negative trends, there are positive signs that the old ethnicities may eventually give way to a hybridized ethnicity which combines elements of both the majority and minority ethnic cultures. It is best illustrated with the news that chicken tikka masala, a hybrid of Indian spices and English gravy has now replaced fish and chips as the UK's most popular food. In other words, a new form of ethnicity may be emerging shaped both by the majority ethnic group's values and institutions, and the various other minority cultures that constitute multicultural Britain as well as the increasing influence of global culture.

Key terms

Anglo-Saxon a White speaker of English as a first language.

Caste the Hindu system of organizing society into hereditary classes based on religious purity.

Celtic relating to Wales, Scotland and Ireland.

Collectivist group-orientated.

Dual identity hybrid identity, e.g. combination of British and Asian identity.

Ethnicity ethnic distinctiveness.

Hyper-male exaggerating masculine characteristics.

Multicultural lots of different cultures living side by side.

Check your understanding

1   What seven factors contribute to a person's ethnic identity?

2   What sorts of values and norms are transmitted from generation to generation in the Asian family?

3   How important is religion in acquiring an ethnic identity?

4   What is 'dual' or 'hybrid' identity with regard to both ethnic identity?

5   What sort of inter-generational conflict might arise because of a clash of values between majority and minority cultures?

6   How important is tradition to younger members of ethnic minority groups?

7   What kinds of defensive identities have been adopted by some Muslim youth?

8   In what sense, might dual-heritage or mixed-race children be viewed as a hybrid ethnic identity?

Activities

Research idea

1   List 10 characteristics, images or symbols that constitute English, Welsh, Scottish and Irish identities. Visit the tourist board websites of these countries or look at holiday brochures for clues.

2   Design a questionnaire aimed at measuring young people's attitudes towards family life, education, relationships, friendships, religion and use of media. Distribute it to people from different ethnic groups within your college or community to see whether there are cultural differences in values and norms relating to these issues.

Web.tasks

Find the following websites to get to know more about ethnicity and racism in Britain:

● Play Britkids – it's aimed at students a little younger than you but it's still worth a visit. Find it at: **www.britkid.org**

● Test your knowledge by trying the quiz at the Institute of Race Relations site: **www.irr.org.uk/quiz/index.htm**

● The Institute also has excellent pages about current issues. Head for **www.irr.org.uk/resources/index.htm**

An eye on the exam   Ethnicity

you should attempt to write a detailed paragraph in about 5 minutes

(a) Define the concept of ethnic hybrids. Illustrate your answer with examples.   **(8 marks)**

your opening sentences should attempt to clearly explain the meaning of the concept

spend about 3–4 minutes developing two or three examples that demonstrate your understanding of the concept in action

you need to identify two functions of religion as it relates to different ethnicities

develop the role of religion in the social construction of ethnic identity in detail by using illustrative examples and sociological studies, e.g. you could explore studies, e.g. Mirza or Butler that show the central role religion plays in Muslim identity or studies which demonstrate tension between religious controls and Western influences over factors such as dress, relationships etc

(b) Outline and explain two ways in which religion plays a part in the socialization of people into their ethnic identity.   **(16 marks)**

you should attempt to write about a side of A4

(c) Explain and briefly evaluate the view that ethnic identities are starting to merge in the contemporary UK   **(24 marks)**

Grade booster   Getting top marks in this question

Begin by defining what is meant by 'ethnicity' and therefore ethnic identity. Make sure you show that the UK is characterised by cultural diversity, i.e. a range of ethnic identities, e.g. Whites, African-Caribbeans, Muslims etc. Use sociologists such as Modood and Butler to explain and illustrate how different ethnic groups use agencies such as the family, religion etc to socialise children into their ethnic identities. Don't forget to evaluate by referring to the view that ethnic identities might be evolving towards hybridisation or dual identity. However, evaluation should also focus on how tradition is still a very influential concept in the social construction of identity. Use concepts like multiculturalism, dual identity, compartmentalism and hybrid identity whenever possible.

TOPIC 6

Socialization, identity and age

Getting you thinking

1   **Examine the photographs of the different age groups. List all the positive and negative characteristics that you associate with the identities of people in those age ranges.**

Age and identity

We have seen in previous topics that personal and social identity are shaped by social factors such as social class, gender ethnicity and globalization. However, it is also a fact that the UK segregates its members by age, so that how young or how old people are has a significant influence on their identity. Marsh and Keating (2006, p.358) note that age both enables us and constrains us.

>> *Our age may influence where we shop, what we buy and even how we pay for our goods. Our age may affect the types of books we read, the music we listen to, the television programmes we watch, the leisure activities we engage in. Our everyday lives are shaped by the way our age is understood and expressed in the society we live in.* >>

Biology and age

Biology obviously has some influence on the way that society divides people by age. Babies, infants and children are not physically or psychologically developed enough to perform adult tasks, whilst the ageing process may mean that the elderly may not be as physically or as mentally effective as they were when younger. However, sociologists point out that there are enough cultural differences across different societies and even across subcultural groups within the UK to suggest that age differences – and therefore, identities – are **socially or culturally constructed** rather than just the result of biological differences.

The social and cultural construction of age

This can be illustrated by comparing traditional pre-industrial societies with modern industrial societies such as the UK. In many traditional societies, people often do not have a precise age because births are not registered. People may not even know their birth date and so may not celebrate birthdays. In these traditional societies, people's identities in terms of their age generally go through three major stages:

- *Children* – This age group is regarded as dependent upon older groups for protection and survival.
- *Adults* – Children, usually at puberty, go through a rite of passage or initiation ceremony, in which they are instructed in adult ways. Boys may learn how to be warriors or hunters and have to go through several tests of skill and/or strength. They may also be subjected to physical change and pain, e.g. **circumcision** is common, as is the cutting of the face so that it leaves scars symbolizing manhood. Girls, too, are instructed on sexual matters so that they can become wives and mothers. Some may even undergo female circumcision. Girls can, therefore, be married and be having children shortly after puberty. An important difference between traditional and modern societies is that adolescence – the teenage years – is often not recognized as a distinct period by the former.
- *Elders* – As people get older in tribal societies, they often acquire greater status and power because they are regarded as having greater experience and wisdom than those who are younger. It is often taken for granted that a young man should defer to his elders.

Age and modern industrial societies

In contrast, in modern Western societies such as the UK, the state insist that all births are registered. It is taken for granted that people know their birth dates and that they celebrate birthdays. Bradley (1996) identifies five generational major stages in age identity in the UK. **Generations** are age groups that live through the same historical and social events, and whose common identity and attitudes are cemented by similar experiences of consuming cultural goods such as fashion, music, films, television programmes, etc.

1 Childhood
This is regarded as a special innocent time in which children are supposed to be cosseted and protected by their parents. They are supported in this enterprise by the state, which has introduced laws, e.g. various Children Acts, in order to regulate the quality of parenting. The state has also introduced legislation in order to draw up guidelines for what is acceptable behaviour for children; for example, the state has decided that schooling should be compulsory between the ages of 5 years and 16 years, and that 10 years should be the lowest age that a child can be held responsible for a criminal offence.

The experience of childhood is central to understanding age as a social construct. Some childhood experts, notably Aries (1962), argue that the experience of childhood identity has changed considerably over the last 500 years. Other commentators, such as Postman, argue that the nature of childhood continues to change even today.

2 Adolescence or youth
This is the period between puberty and the achievement of full adult status, i.e. the teenage years. Until the late 1960s, adulthood in the UK was usually celebrated at 21 years, but since the last part of the 20th century, 18 years has become more common – this is the age at which the state confers legal adulthood via being able to vote, to marry or leave home without parental consent, and to sit on a jury.

In the 1950s, **adolescence** or youth was recognized as a unique age group for the first time. Before this period, adolescence was generally regarded as part of adulthood because the majority of youth prior to the Second World War left school in their early teens and started work. They were not recognized as a separate social category because they were generally indistinguishable from their parents in terms of their values, tastes, behaviour, dress, etc. No specific teenage market existed for fashion, cosmetics and mass media such as films and popular music.

The postwar period saw the emergence of a **youth culture** based on specific teenage fashions, hairstyles and tastes in music, such as rock and roll, which the older generation found both shocking and threatening. This culture was the product of an increase in young people's spending power brought about by full employment in the 1950s. **Capitalist entrepreneurs** reacted to this lucrative new market by developing products specifically for youth, such as comics and magazines for teenagers, pop music, radio stations, transistor radios, fashion and cosmetics.

3 Young adulthood
This type of age identity is focused on the period between leaving the parental home and middle age. Pilcher (1996) points out that this age group has rarely been researched and so we have little information about this significant group of people. Jones and Wallace (1992) suggests that modern societies like the UK have private and public 'markers' that signify the beginning of adult status. For example, private markers might include a first sexual encounter or first cigarette, whilst public markers include the right to vote or the granting of a bank loan. Pilcher concludes that adult identity revolves around living with a sexual partner, having children, having a job and maintaining a home. Hockey and James (1993) see it as bound up with having freedom and independence from parents, having control over material resources and having responsibilities.

4 Mid-life
There is some disagreement as to when middle age begins. Brookes-Gunn and Kirsch (1984) set it as low as 35 years, whereas others have suggested it might be as high as 50 years. There are physical indicators of middle age, e.g. greying hair, the appearance of the 'middle-aged spread' and the menopause in women, as well as social indicators, e.g. children leaving home to go to university or having more money for leisure pursuits. There may even be emotional or psychological indicators, i.e. the mid-life crisis.

5 Old age
This period officially and legally begins at 65 years in the UK, when people are expected to retire from paid work and state pensions are paid. Pilcher argues that because of increasing life expectancy and differences in generational attitudes, tastes and behaviour that we should differentiate between the 'young old' (aged 65 to 74), the 'middle-aged old' (aged between 75 and 84 years) and the 'old old' (aged 85+). However, in contrast to traditional societies, the elderly in the UK are not accorded a great deal of respect or status, because work is the major source of status in industrial societies. Loss of work due to retirement can result in a significant decline in self-esteem, social contacts with others and income, as well as a consequent rise in loneliness, poverty, depression and poor health in general.

Age and discrimination

The low status associated with elderly identity in UK society is not helped by the fact that people are often stereotyped and discriminated against because of their age. This is known as **ageism**. Johnson and Bytheway (1993) define it as the 'offensive exercise of power through reference to age' and suggest that it has three integral elements:

- Ageism is often institutionalized in that it is embedded in organizational and legal practices, e.g. people aged over 70 years are excluded from jury service.
- Ageism is often expressed through the stereotypical prejudices that underpin everyday interaction, in that people often assume without question that a person's competency is limited by their age, i.e. they are too old to carry out a particular task.
- Ageism can involve the well-meaning assumption that the very old are vulnerable and depend on younger and fitter adults for care and protection.

There is evidence, therefore, that old age as a stage in the life course is largely negatively perceived. This is reflected in everyday descriptions of elderly people as being 'past it' or 'over the hill' or having 'one foot in the grave'. Pilcher notes that old people are often described in derogatory or condescending ways such as 'old fogey', 'old biddy', 'old bat' or 'sweet little old lady/man'. Pilcher points out that such stereotypes tend to marginalize old people and to label them as inferior.

Ginn and Arber note too that the increasing number of the elderly – in 2002, for the first time people aged 60 years and over formed a larger part of the population than children aged under 16 years – has led to rising fears about the costs to society of the elderly. For example, the rising costs of pensions and of the increased use of health and welfare services have led to media reports portraying the elderly as a 'burden' on taxpayers.

Age identities and socialization

The Family

A study by the Institute for Public Policy Research (IPPR) in 2006 suggested that many adults in the UK were afraid of teenagers. Many adults reported that they had considered moving away from where they lived or that they were afraid to go out at night because of '**paedophobia**' – fear of young people. Furthermore the IPPR research reported that 15 year olds in the UK were more likely than teenagers from other European countries to take drugs, get drunk, to get involved in violence and have sex. The report concluded that the main reason for these trends was the lack of interaction between parents and children after they hit adolescence. For example, in Italy, 93 per cent of teenagers regularly at down to eat a meal with their parents compared with only 64 per cent of teenagers. The report concludes that teenagers who spend quality time with their parents who are less likely to commit anti-social acts.

Another study which cast some doubt on the family experiences of young people in the UK was the Innocenti Report (2007) produced by UNICEF into the well-being of children in 21 of the most economically advanced countries of the world. The UK came out of this exercise particularly badly in that the UK came bottom of the overall ranking for child well-being. In particular, Britain scored poorly on criteria such as behaviours and risks which was based on the percentage of 11,13 and 15 year-olds who reported that their peers were kind and helpful and the percentage of 15 year olds who smoked, had been drunk more than twice, used cannabis, had had sex and used condoms. The number of teenage pregnancies also contributed to the UK's poor rating compared with other countries. Moreover, the UK was also ranked 21st for peer and family relationships, e.g. this criteria included the percentage of children who reported eating the main meal of the day with their parents more than once a week and that parents spent time 'just talking' to them.

Focus on research

Sujata Ray and Ellen Sharp:
Ageism: A benchmark of public attitudes in Britain

This research was a nationally representative sample survey conducted with 1864 people aged 16 and over across Great Britain. The questions were developed through a mixture of thorough literature review and evaluation, workshop development, qualitative testing and quantitative validation. This was followed by in-depth pilot testing of the questionnaire with focus groups. The survey aimed to explore the nature and prevalence of prejudice and discrimination about age and ageing.

The research looked at scientifically robust examples of prejudice but because the researchers felt that few people would be likely to openly admit to being ageist, the researchers analysed more subtle aspects of stereotypes and attitudes to gauge the nature and extent of ageism. The research found that:

- More people (29%) reported suffering age discrimination than any other form.
- From the age of 55 onwards people were nearly twice as likely to have experienced age prejudice than compared with any other form of discrimination.
- Nearly 30% of people believed there is more prejudice against the old than five years ago, and that this will continue to get worse.
- One third of people thought that the demographic shift towards an older society would make life worse in terms of standards of living, security, health, jobs and education.
- One in three respondents said that the over 70s are incompetent and incapable.

Source: *How Ageist is Britain?*, www.ageconcern.org.uk 2005

1   **How does the design of this research contribute to the validity of its findings?**

2   **How might agencies of socialization contribute to ageist attitudes?**

Focus on research

Time trends in parenting and outcomes for young people

Frances Gardner, Stephen Collishaw and Barbara Maughan

The project focused particularly on the relationship between parenting and behaviour problems in teenagers such as lying, stealing, and disobedience in the UK.

The research team used secondary data in the form of statistics collected by the British Household Panel Survey (BHPS) which had collected data on parenting reported by teenagers and their parents and their parents from 1994 onwards, and 'Youth Trends' – a study specifically designed to explore causes of trends in youth mental health. Youth Trends compares a large representative sample of 16 year olds (members of the 1970 British Cohort Study) studied in 1986 with a new representative sample of 700+ 16 year olds studied twenty years later, in 2006.

The study found that parents and teenagers are choosing to spend more quality time together than 25 years ago, with 70% of young people regularly spending time with their mothers in 2006 compared to 62% in 1986. For fathers, the figure had increased from 47% to 52%. Teenagers reported that they enjoyed talking to their parents. Today's parents are also more likely to know where their teenage children are and what they are doing than their 1980s equivalents. The research team concluded that on balance, it was unlikely that youth problem behaviour could not be accounted for by a decline in the general quality of parenting.

However, the study found that today's parents face a different set of challenges compared to 25 years ago. Young people now are reliant on their parents for longer, with higher proportions of 20-24 year olds living with their parents as they remain in education or training. In addition, the development of new technology, such as mobile phones and the Internet, has created new monitoring challenges for parents. It is also possible that parents are increasing monitoring as a reaction to a perceived increase in the risks their children are exposed to.

Source: www.nuffieldfoundation.org.uk

1   What are the strengths and weaknesses of using secondary data for studying the relationships between parents and children?

2   How does this study support the view that families can positively contribute to the identity of teenagers?

Mass media and youth

Many studies of the mass media have focused on how youth is **demonized** by the mass media. Cohen (1980) was the first sociologist to observe how newspapers tend to sensationalize and exaggerate the behaviour of groups of young people in order to create **newsworthiness** and to sell papers. His study described how fights between two sets of youths in 1964 – labelled 'mods' and 'rockers' – produced a '**moral panic**', i.e. social anxiety about young people in general, and '**folk devils**', with young people being blamed for the moral decline of the nation. According to Cohen, this generally illustrates how young people are seen as 'folk devils, i.e. as a 'social problem' by the older generation. Contemporary studies of the mass media's portrayal of teenagers, particularly Thornton (1995) and Savage (2007), suggest that teenagers are more frequently condemned than praised by the mass media.

Griffin (1993) suggests that youth are portrayed as a social problem in three ways. First, they are portrayed as 'dysfunctional' – as not being properly socialized or operating enough self-control. Second, they are seen to be suffering a 'deficit' –they do not achieve enough educationally. Third, they are portrayed as 'deviant' rule breakers. Consequently, Astley suggests government policies about young people are aimed at care and control –to keep young people in their place and in a state of dependency. For example, the government has encouraged the expansion of post-16 education which has resulted in an extension of childhood dependency on parents and the State (e.g. in the form of Educational Maintenance Allowance).

However, studies of young people suggest that the **generation gap** implied by moral panics is exaggerated. There is little evidence that youth identity is significantly different in terms of what young people value compared with their parents. Very few young people have got involved with those youth subcultures defined as deviant by the mass media, such as teddy-boys (1950s), mods and rockers (1960s), skinheads (early 1970s), punks (late 1970s) or ecstasy-using ravers (1980s/1990s). Most young people are generally conformist – they get on well with their parents and place a high value on traditional goals such as getting married, having children and buying a house.

Ageism and the mass media

Ageism is often reflected through mass media representations of youth and old age. Advertising reinforces the view that the appearance of youth is central to looking good and that ageing should be resisted at all costs. As a result, adverts for anti-ageing creams, hair dyes to conceal greyness and cosmetic surgery are common on television and particularly in women's magazines.

Ageism may also be reflected through the underrepresentation of middle-aged and elderly women as news presenters and hosts of light-entertainment shows. Sontag (1978) suggests that there is double standard of ageing especially in television, whereby women are required to be youthful throughout their media careers but men are not. The newscaster, Moira Stuart claimed to be a victim of this type of ageism at the BBC in 2007 when she was 'retired' by the corporation at the age of 58, whilst male counterparts such as David Dimbleby (72 in 2010) and Peter Sissons (68 in 2007) were allowed to carry on beyond retirement age.

The peer group

Some sociologists, most notably Sue Heath (2004), have suggested that friendship networks are becoming increasingly important as agents of socialization in the period known as 'young adulthood'. This period is characterized by movement in and out of a variety of independent living arrangements – for example, a student may move between living in a hall of residence, flat sharing and going home to stay with parents. It is also marked out as the period when a person is likely to be single. Cote (2000) suggests that in young adulthood, peer group or friendship networks eventually become more important than relationships with parents as a source of knowledge about how to live one's life.

Religion

Voas and Crockett (2005) note that surveys of religious belief indicate that young White people are increasingly likely to describe themselves as non-religious. However, young Africans, African-Caribbeans and Asians, especially Muslims are not so indifferent to religion. Surveys generally demonstrate a majority of these groups professing a respect for religious values and in many cases, through dress, diet or behaviour, putting such ideas into practice.

Sociologists have identified a number of reasons why young White people may no longer be socialized into a set of religious values:

● They find religious teaching boring and uncool because they associate it with the older generation and therefore out of touch with the needs of their age-group.
● The liberalisation of attitudes towards Sunday trading in the 1990s has resulted in more leisure options being available for young people which are more attractive than churchgoing. For example, in the past, many young people had no choice but to go to Sunday school.
● Young people may feel peer group pressure not to express religious beliefs because it is regarded as unfashionable. These may exist but may be kept private.
● Religion no longer plays the central role at school or in the family that it did for previous generations. Schools are now more likely to offer a generalised moral and multicultural education and consequently pupils are no longer exposed to the explicitly religious messages of the past.
● Society is less religious than in the past – religious sentiments are no longer common and are less likely to be observed. This is called secularisation. This is not the case in ethnic minority communities where religious observance is much stricter and very much part of family life.

Evidence suggests that the elderly are more likely to be religious for two main reasons. Firstly, they were brought up in a more religious era – when saying grace and prayers mattered, when schools had religious assemblies and when families went to church together. In other words, their socialization into religious values was much more intense. Secondly, some sociologists suggest that people think more about spiritual matters as they get older and approach death.

The workplace

Work is a central part of most people's identity because it gives them status. In Western societies, people categorise themselves and judge other people by the work they do. For example, social class position is largely determined by occupation. Moreover, the lifestyle and life-chances of an individual depend upon the income that is paid for a particular job. Work is also a major source of friendship and community life. It provides people with a strong sense of belonging and often socializes them into community values such as mutual support.

Arber and Ginn (1993) suggest that ageism against the elderly is reinforced and perpetuated by employment practices such as redundancy, unemployment and retirement. For example, it is often the case that workers who are made redundant in their mid-40s experience age barriers in finding new jobs. They have a limited working life because employers are reluctant to invest in training them. Bradley (1996) notes that old people are often seen by employers as less suitable for employment because they are assumed to be 'physically slow, lacking in dynamism and not very adaptable to change although the Employment Equality (Age) Regulations Act which came into force in late 2006, provides protection against age discrimination in employment and education.

Some sociologists have highlighted the negative effect of retirement for the elderly. Retirement often leads to a loss of status, self-respect and purpose. It may also result in social isolation and loneliness as often a person's main social contacts are in the workplace. Furthermore, it can be a time of poverty and debt if a person is relying solely on a state pension.

However, on a more positive note, retirement might have some advantages in that it releases time for the elderly to enjoy new interests, learn new skills or do charity or voluntary work. As Giddens (1999) notes, it allows people to continue growing, learning and exploring. Some will immerse themselves in the family and offer their services in looking after grandchildren. Some retired people take the opportunity to travel or even move abroad.

Giddens refers to the retirement years as the 'third-age' (childhood is the 'first age' and the working years are the 'second age'). He suggests this period is longer than ever before and improved health means that individuals now lead more active and independent lives in this period. However, as we approach death we head into the 'fourth age' in which people become more dependent upon others as their independence is compromised by ill-health and chronic illness or disability.

Age and identity – conclusions

Sociologists argue that age and generation are products of the culture of the society to which we belong. As Marsh and Keating (2006) observe, different cultures attach different cultural meanings and values to different age groups. These shape our behaviour in terms of how we respond to others of the same generation and how we treat people in other age groups. It is also important to note that how particular age groups or generations are treated will often be shaped by influences such as gender, social class and ethnicity. For example, the experience of being an elderly African-Caribbean woman may be quite different to that of a White middle-class elderly man. Evidence for this observation can be found in Topics 3, 4 and 5.

Key terms

Adolescence period from puberty to adulthood, i.e. teenage years.

Ageism discrimination and prejudice on the basis of age.

Capitalist entrepreneurs businessmen and -women.

Circumcision practice of removing foreskin from penis.

Culturally constructed product of culture or society, rather than biology.

Folk devils groups stereotyped by the media as deviants.

Demonized the process of being negatively labelled or stereotyped.

Generation a group of people born within the same historical period who share similar cultural experiences.

Generation gap the notion that teenagers and their parents are in conflict because they hold different sets of values.

Moral panics anxiety felt by members of society about the behaviour of social groups, caused by media sensationalism and exaggeration.

Newsworthiness the process by which a story becomes interesting and sells papers.

Self-fulfilling prophecy predictions about the behaviour of social groups that come true as a result of positive or negative labelling.

Socially constructed product of society or culture, rather than biology.

Youth culture set of values and norms of behaviour relating to fashion, dress, hairstyle, lifestyle, etc., subscribed to by some young people that may be seen as deviant by mainstream culture.

Activities

Research idea

1 How do young people see the elderly? Design a questionnaire which explores the extent and social character of ageism. Use the ageism survey 'How ageist is Britain?', which can be found on **www.ageconcern.org.uk**, as the basis for your questionnaire.

2 Carry out three or four unstructured interviews with elderly people who fall into the categories of young elderly, middle-aged elderly and old elderly. How are their experiences of being elderly similar or different? How do they interpret their situation? Have they experienced ageism? In what shape or form?

Web.tasks

1 Visit the sites **www.ace.org.uk** and **www.cpa.org.uk** How do these sites promote positive images of the elderly?

Visit the web-site **www.campaignforrealbeauty.co.uk** How does this site challenge ageist stereotypes?

Check your understanding

1 How does age identity differ in traditional societies compared with modern industrial societies?

2 How does pre-Second World War youth identity in the UK compare with youth identity in the 1950s?

3 What is 'ageism' and how does it affect the social identity of the elderly?

4 What do studies of teenagers tell us about the relationship between adolescent identity and family life?

5 How do media representations of youth contribute to adolescent identity?

6 Why is the peer group often an important agent of socialization in young adulthood?

7 What reasons have been given for the unpopularity of religion for many young White people?

8 How are older people sometimes discriminated against in the workplace?

Age identity

your opening sentences should attempt to clearly explain the meaning of the concept

you should attempt to write a detailed paragraph in about 5 minutes

(a) Define the concept of youth. Illustrate your answer with examples. **(8 marks)**

spend about 3–4 minutes developing two or three examples that demonstrate your understanding of the concept in action

you need to identify the two ways clearly, it is likely that your main focus will be on the mass media

develop aspects of the media construction of young people as a social problem in detail by using illustrative examples and sociological studies, e.g. you could explore various studies of moral panics and/or youth subcultures, or focus in depth on one specific example of a so-called social problem, e.g. gangs.

(b) Outline and explain two ways in which young people are often seen as a social problem by society. **(16 marks)**

you should attempt to write about a side of A4

(c) Explain and briefly evaluate the view that ageism has a negative effect on the identity of the elderly. **(24 marks)**

Grade booster Getting top marks in this question

Begin by defining what is meant by 'ageism' and therefore elderly identity. Make sure you explain and illustrate how agencies of socialization such as the mass media and the workplace might socialize the population into ageist stereotypes and the effect this stigmatised identity might have on the self esteem of the elderly. Don't forget to evaluate by referring to the positive effects of retirement using the ideas of Giddens and others. Use concepts like labelling, stigmatised identity, institutionalised ageism and self-fulfilling prophecy whenever possible.

Exam Practice

(a) Define the concept of cultural diversity. Illustrate your answer with examples. *(8 marks)*

Cultural diversity is a concept which cannot be given one simple definition. Culture is largely believed to be concerned with the norms, values and beliefs of a group or society and so cultural diversity is the difference between these societies. As many different social groups follow different social roles, it is shown that our culture is dictated by how we are socialized through all agents of socialization. For example Abbott's writes that language is simply a set of symbols which people use to convey meaning and people within cultures will have different views about what language means and some words will be offensive in some cultures which are everyday in another society. Our own culture shapes expectations of how we behave and fulfil our roles in society, and the fact that this is different in different societies gives a clear example of cultural diversity.

The first sentence is slightly concerning as this is exactly what the question is asking for. Although some key terms are used appropriately the answer assumes that cultural diversity only applies to cultural differences between societies. In fact the term is more often used to describe cultural differences *within* societies, such as the differences between various ethnic minorities. The answer also lacks specific examples – using examples helps show the examiner your understanding.

4/8

(b) Outline and explain how any two agents of socialization influence middle-class identities. *(16 marks)*

One agent of socialization which influences the middle classes is education. Some sociologists suggest that education benefits middle-class pupils at the expense of working class pupils. Many middle-class children go through private education, although they do also dominate the top streams of state schools. Middle-class children also get the best GCSE results and are more likely than the working class to stay on to do A levels, and then go to university, with 80% of university students being in the middle class. Bourdieu suggests this is because schools are middle-class institutions run by middle-class teachers for the benefit of middle-class pupils and therefore the middle classes are more likely to succeed in this environment. Education is seen as very important within the middle-class identity as they place a high value on meritocracy and are generally socialized into being highly motivated to achieve.

The agent of socialization to be discussed is identified very clearly at the beginning of the paragraph. This shows the examiner that the answer is likely to be relevant. However, the paragraph does not go on to spell out specific ways in which education influences middle-class identities, particularly in the first part which consists of some statements about achievement and private education.

Another important agent of socialization to the middle classes is the family. Family is an important part of the middle-class identity and in particular King and Raynor suggest child-centeredness is a distinctive feature of their identity, especially passing on educational opportunities and attitudes required for educational success. Parents educate their children on the 'right' values, ways of speaking and knowledge in order for them to interact most appropriately to get ahead in society. Bourdieu, a Marxist, refers to this as cultural capital, also supplemented with economic capital, where parents can fully economically provide for children and also the social capital of having knowledge and contacts to further the interests of their children.

This paragraph about the family is more successful. It includes a reference to specific research on middle-class socialization patterns and goes on to summarize Bourdieu's ideas, although some examples of the influence of these different kinds of capital on middle-class identities would have taken the answer further e.g. explaining what the 'right' values, knowledge and ways of speaking actually are.

11/16

(c) Explain and briefly evaluate why some members of minority ethnic groups may adopt hybrid identities. *(24 marks)*

The term hybrid refers to a mix of different components and therefore in relation to minority ethnic groups it can be defined as a combination of different ethnic styles, in a novel way. This creates mixed lifestyles and identities.

It is a good idea to start the answer with an explanation of key terms in the question although the explanation of 'hybrid identities' could have been developed a little more, perhaps by explaining some of the pressures experienced by young people from minority ethnic backgrounds from peers, family, religion, education and the media.

One reason members of ethnic minorities are more likely to adopt hybrid identities is due to the freedom of choice in modern Britain. As many ethnic minorities are now second or third generation, they are socialized into both their traditional cultural identities and mainstream identities. Back carried out research on young people in two council estates in South London. He found they are developing new hybrid identities as the young people are in a transitional stage where they have freedom and opportunity to create new identities. Rather than having fixed traditions to follow slavishly, they can try out new cultural masks and experiment with different roles and styles. He found there was a lot of inter-racial friendship and interaction. Many groups 'borrowed' from other groups by showing an interest in their 'cool' language and music such as reggae, soul and hip-hop. This lead to a strong relationship between white and black people, bring them together and blurring the division of race.

> The first two sentences set the scene for the detailed and relevant account of Back's work that follows. Perhaps the postmodern feel of Backs' work could have been mentioned.

Butler carried out a similar study, on third-generation young Muslim women and found they also are able to choose from a range of identities. Whilst some choose to reflect their ascribed position in their traditional dress, others take a more 'negotiated' position, which involves combining Western ideas about education and careers, whilst still maintaining respect for the traditional religious ideas about what women's roles should be. Some young Islamic women adopt different identities compared with their mothers on issues such as equality within marriage and fashion. Arranged marriage is also now subject to much more input from young people and in some families may be totally disregarded.

> Another well-developed account of a specific piece of sociological research although it could have been focused a little more on the issue of why these hybrid identities were adopted.

However not all sociologists agree that hybrid identities are a result of freedom of choice. Johal carried out research on second and third-generation British-Asians their identity is forced upon them. Whilst they inherit an Asian identity, it is necessary for them to adopt a 'white mask' in order to fit into mainstream culture and interact with white peers at school or college. Similarly Ballard, in a study into Asian teenagers have to switch 'codes' – in their parents' homes they still have to maintain their traditional Asian cultural expectations, but outside the home it is necessary to blend into mainstream lifestyles.

> A good link to a different angle on the question in the first sentence. More sociological studies are referenced to good effect.

Whilst it can be said that people from ethnic minorities can now adopt hybrid identities due to no longer being assigned one identity, it is important not to over-emphasise the level of choice in this decision. Many people adopt hybrid identities as a way to fit into mainstream culture, rather than specifically choosing which identity to follow.

> This conclusion reflects the key theme of the essay – the tension between freedom of choice and the need to fit in with the dominant culture. It works well but a little more discussion would have boosted marks for analysis and evaluation.

An examiner comments

The answer shows confident knowledge and understanding of a range of studies that are used to help explain why hybrid identities may be adopted. Perhaps links to perspectives such as postmodernism could have been developed as these ideas lie behind the studies that emphasize freedom and diversity in ethnic identities. Evaluation occurs in the final paragraph and in the way that the studies that emphasize freedom of choice are contrasted with others that focus on hybrid identities as ways of coping with conflicting pressures.

Chapter 2 Summary

High culture
- Aesthetically superior
- Elitist

Functionalism
- Culture is product of value consensus
- Core culture promotes social order

Mass culture
- Popular culture
- Manufactured by media

Marxism
- Culture shaped by capitalism
- Culture as ideology

Primary socialization
- Family and parenting
- Social control

Functionalism
- Family as personality factory
- Socialization into value consensus

Secondary socialization
- Education
- Mass media
- Religion
- Peer group

Marxism
- Socialization into ruling-class values
- False needs

Defining culture

Socialization

Exploring socialization, culture and identity

Ethnicity

Asian identity
- Family socialization
- Religious influences

African-Caribbean identity
- Peer-group pressure
- Mixed-race identity

Social class and identity

Upper-class identity
- Social closure
- Conservative value system

Middle-class identity
- Fragmentation
- Suburban and meritocratic

Working-class identity
- Traditional – work as source of identity
- New individualistic working class
- Underclass

Decline of class identity
- Hybrid identity
- Persistence of class inequality

Age

Social construction of age
- Childhood
- Adolescence and youth subcultures
- Old age and ageism

Gender

Hegemonic masculinity and femininity
- Gender-role socialization
- Traditional gender roles

Changing femininities and masculinities
- Genderquake
- Feminization of the workplace

Homosexuality
- Decriminalization
- Gay culture

Sociological methods

OCR specification		Coverage
Exploring the research process		
Stages and issues in the research process	• operationalization • primary data collection methods • secondary data collection methods • sampling • access • ethics • pilot studies • interpretation of data	Primary and secondary data are explained in Topic 1, sampling, ethics and the interpretation of data in Topic 2. Piloting is covered in Topic 3, access in Topic 4 and operationalization in Topic 5.
Key concepts in the research process	• validity • reliability • representativeness • generalisability	These terms are explained in Topic 1.
Exploring the use of quantitative data collection methods		
Quantitative data collection methods	• questionnaires • structured interviews • statistical data (official and non-official) • content analysis	An overview of quantitative data collection is provided in Topic 3. Questionnaires and structured interviews are explained in Topic 5. Statistical data and content analysis are covered in Topic 6.
Key concepts	• patterns • trends • cause and effect • positivism • reliability • objectivity • value freedom • quantitative data analysis	A discussion of patterns, trends and cause and effect, objectivity and value freedom is included in Topic 1. Positivism is covered in Topic 2.
Exploring the use of qualitative data collection methods		
Qualitative data collection methods	• observation • unstructured interviews • semi-structured interviews • personal documents • ethnography • focus groups	Types of observation and ethnography are covered in Topic 4. Qualitative interviews are discussed in Topics 4 and 5. Personal documents are covered in Topic 6.
Key concepts	• meanings and experiences • interpretivism • verstehen • validity • empathy • rapport • qualitative data	Interpretive sociology is discussed in Topic 1. Concepts associated with qualitative data are covered in Topic 3.
Exploring the use of mixed methodology		
Key concepts	• triangulation • methodological pluralism	Mixed methods research is discussed in Topic 2.
Mixed methods data analysis	• fitness for purpose	

TOPIC 1

Researching social life

Getting you thinking

A scene from inside the Big Brother house 2007, as the housemates perform one of the tasks set by Big Brother

Big Brother is a television series in which a group of people are required to live together in a house for a period of several months. During that time all their activities and conversations are monitored. Edited versions are shown to a television audience, which then votes contestants out each week, until the last remaining 'survivor' is declared the winner.

1 Do you think that people who live in the Big Brother household are representative of the country as a whole?

2 Do you think the people in the household act naturally? If not, why do they behave the way they do?

3 Does Big Brother therefore give a 'true' picture of what life would be like if a group of young people lived together? Explain your answer.

4 Do you think that a lot of what goes on is 'edited out' by the producers? What kinds of things are left out? Why?

Sociologists generally try to take a 'sideways' look at social life – seeking to provide insights into the social world that the ordinary person would not normally have. In some ways, this interest in society is shared by journalists and other 'interested observers' of the world, but whereas these people tend to rely heavily on their *common sense* or *personal experience* in exploring society, sociologists reject these as adequate ways of explaining society. Common sense and personal experience, they argue, are usually based on our own limited and **biased** opinions already held, which override our objectivity. In research, bias occurs where the researchers' views affect the research. Instead, sociologists claim that the best way to study society is to conduct research which uncovers patterns that would normally remain hidden. This research is ideally founded on facts rather than opinions. However, the activities of sociologists do not stop at undertaking research – once they have uncovered these patterns, they then seek explanations for the relationships between them. This process of constructing explanations for the social patterns is known as 'theorizing'.

So, research leads – eventually – to theories.

Even that is not the end of it. For once theories exist, other sociologists are influenced by them and will use them as the starting point for their research.

So, research leads to theories, which lead to more research and – yes, you've guessed it – more theories!

What does sociological research set out to do?

Sociological research does three main things: gathers data, makes correlations and suggests or confirms theories.

Gathering data

The first task of research is simply to gather information about the social world. This very basic function is the starting point for any kind of sociological understanding. Knowledge can take the form of statistical information, such as the numbers of marriages and divorces, and sociological 'facts', such as the attitudes of people in society towards marriage as an institution. (This sort of research is conducted by the Office for National Statistics – a government organization which collects data about the UK.) It can also include observations of people in social situations – such as Philippe Bourgois' study of crime and drugs in a New York 'ghetto' (2003) – or people talking about their own lives – Ken Plummer has used this form of biographical research with gay men (1995).

However, we need to be wary about accepting these data at face value. As we shall see later, what is a 'fact' for someone may not be for others, as they may use different theories and methods to interpret the facts. A famous

Figure 5.1 Research and common sense: why common sense is faulty

Common sense	Research
What is common sense ✗ for one person is not common sense for another.	✔ Research is based on evidence.
Common sense derives ✗ from personal experience and people have limited experience.	✔ Research can be conducted in areas where most people have little experience.
Common sense is not ✗ objective.	✔ Research is objective.
Common sense can be ✗ based on false beliefs and information.	✔ Research can be tested.
Common sense is often ✗ based upon memories which may be faulty.	✔ Research can compare memories with other evidence to check their accuracy.

example of this is research on suicide by Durkheim (1897/1952). He collected a large number of statistics and then based his theory of the causes of suicide on these statistics. However, much later, other sociologists looked at exactly the same statistics and produced very different interpretations of these same 'facts'. They argued that the statistics on which Durkheim had based his research were fundamentally flawed. These sociologists said that in only a few cases can we know for certain whether the death was suicide or not, as there are rarely suicide notes. The real research, they argued, was in studying how coroners go about making their decision as to whether or not to classify a death as suicide.

Much effort is made in sociological research to make sure that the data gathered is as clear and accurate as possible, but sociologists always approach any data – whether in the form of statistics, observation or narrative – in a very cautious way.

Establishing correlations

Research can go further than just gathering information. It can help us explore relationships between different elements of society. At its most basic it can be in the form of simple **correlations**. Sociologists describe a correlation as the situation where when one social event occurs, another one tends to do so as well. This is clearer if we use an illustration. Bennett and Holloway (2005) conducted a national research project over a number of years which involved testing the urine of people immediately after they were arrested by the police and being held in police cells. The results of the urine tests demonstrated that the offenders had a very high chance indeed of showing evidence of illegal drug use (as well as alcohol). The statistical results therefore show that there is a correlation between drug use and crime, as when one social event (committing crime) occurs, then another (taking drugs) tends to do so as well.

Cause and effect

The immediate conclusion that most people would draw from this correlation is that drug use causes crime. But this may not be true. It could be argued that people who commit crime are more likely to take drugs – and indeed there is considerable evidence to support this argument (Pudney 2002). We could also argue that people who like to do drugs also like to commit crime. Therefore a completely different social event causes people both to commit crime and do drugs. There is considerable evidence for this explanation too (Hough and Roberts 2004).

Just because statistics demonstrate that two social events tend to occur together – *a correlation* – it does not mean there is actually a **causal relationship**. Identifying and agreeing a causal relationship between social events is often complicated and linked with developing a sociological theory.

Developing theories

The final role of research is to support or disprove a **sociological theory**. (A theory is simply a general explanation of social events.) Researchers gather information and statistics which help sociologists explain why certain social events occur. This often involves providing an explanation for correlations. So, if a correlation exists between drug use and crime, various theories can be developed. One theoretical explanation for heroin users having high rates of burglary is that they need money to pay for their drug habit. An alternative is that burglars have a high income and so are more likely to have a pleasurable lifestyle that involves using drugs. A third theoretical explanation could be that people with unhappy home backgrounds turn to crime and drugs. It was just this sort of problem that Pudney (2002) tackled in a research project on whether young offenders started taking drugs before they committed crimes or after.

Sources and types of data

Data can come from either primary or secondary sources:

- **Primary data** are those collected directly by the researchers themselves. The most common methods of providing primary data are surveys, observational studies, questionnaires, interviews and experiments.
- **Secondary data** are those which are used by sociologists but have been collected by other people. These include official and commercial statistics; radio, internet and TV; historical and official documents; personal letters and diaries.

There are two types of data (see Table 5.1 on next page):

- **Quantitative data** is the term used for statistical charts and tables.
- **Qualitative data** is the term used to describe data in the form of observation or other published or broadcast sources.

Table 5.1 Types of data		
Types of data	**Sources of data**	
	Primary data	*Secondary data*
Qualitative data	Interviews, observations	Historical documents, TV programmes
Quantitative data	Statistical surveys	Official statistics

Evaluating data

When conducting research or reading sociological research reports written by others, sociologists are always very critical of the methods employed and the data used. They know that if the **methodology** is weak, then the research may well be inaccurate. All sociologists are committed to making sure that their research is of the highest quality and achieves what it sets out to do. When sociologists evaluate research, they need to look at its reliability, validity, representativeness, generalizability and objectivity. We will look at each of these in more detail.

Reliability

The very nature of sociology means that it has to use a variety of very different methods, in a range of circumstances, to study people. In these circumstances, it can often be quite difficult to compare one piece of research with another and sociologists accept this. However, what is always expected is that if the same piece of research were repeated by different sociologists, then it should produce the same results. If this is not the case, then we could not rely upon the evidence produced.

Sociologists, therefore, always ask questions about whether or not the research, if repeated, would be likely to produce the same results – the issue of **reliability**. Some methods of research are much more likely to produce results which can be repeated than others. Well-designed questionnaires are probably the method most likely to

produce similar research results each time and are therefore regarded as highly reliable. At the other extreme, when a lone sociologist engages in participant observation (that is, joins a group of people and observes their behaviour), the research is likely to be far less reliable, as the research is affected by the specific circumstances surrounding the group and the relationship of the observer to the group. Overall, quantitative methods tend to be more reliable, qualititative methods less reliable.

Validity

The second crucial factor in evaluating research is the extent to which it is **valid**, i.e. how far it gives a true picture of the subject being studied. In evaluating a piece of research, sociologists will ask whether the methods used were those most likely to get to the truth of the matter. Interestingly, validity and reliability do not always go hand in hand. We saw before that questionnaires are likely to be highly reliable, but this does not necessarily mean that they are valid. For example, when asked about embarrassing subjects, such as sex or criminal activity, people often lie. Therefore, if the study were repeated, the results would be exactly the same, yet they would never be true! Observational studies are usually difficult to repeat and so are fairly unreliable. However, if the observation has been done well, then it may actually be very valid.

Representativeness

The third crucial element in any evaluation is that of **representativeness**. Does the sample of people chosen for the research reflect a typical cross section of the group or society the researcher is interested in gaining information about? If the respondents in the study are not representative, then it is simply not possible to generalize to the whole group or society (see the following point). For example, if sociologists wish to talk about the population as a whole, then the chosen group must be representative of society as a whole. Similarly, if they wish to comment on people who are terminally ill, then the study must be of a representative group from this section of society.

Key terms

Bias where the views of the researchers affect the research.

Causal relationship where there is a relationship between two social events with one causing the other.

Correlation a statistical relationship between two things. It does not necessarily mean that one causes the other. For example, over 70 per cent of burglars drink coffee, but this does not mean that drinking coffee causes someone to commit burglary.

Data the information uncovered by research.

Generalizability if the group sociologists choose to study are representative of the population as a whole, then they will be able to make generalizations about the whole society. If the group is not representative, they will only be able to speak about the particular group studied.

Methodology the process of undertaking research using the appropriate sociological methods

Objectivity or value freedom quality achieved when a

researcher's values do not affect their work.

Primary data information obtained directly by the sociologist.

Qualitative data information from a range of sources which are not statistical, such as observation.

Quantitative data statistical information.

Reliability quality of repeatability: if the same piece of research were repeated by different sociologists, then it should produce the same results.

Representativeness situation where the people sociologists study are a cross section of the group they wish to generalize about.

Secondary data information obtained from sources originally collected by someone other than the sociologist conducting the research.

Sociological theory (or **theorizing**) an explanation of how different parts of society or different events relate to one another.

Validity the extent to which data give a true picture of the subject being studied.

Generalizability

The aim of most (though not all) sociological research is to produce knowledge which can aid us in understanding the behaviour of people in general – not just the specific group being studied. If the knowledge gained from studying the group cannot be **generalized** to all society, then it has limited use. This is why many sociologists are concerned that the people they study are typical or representative of a cross section of the society which they wish to generalize about. Overall, the larger the numbers of people in the study and the more sophisticated the methods used to select these people, the greater the chance of the study being representative.

Objectivity or value freedom

The final key element in ensuring that research is of high standard is the extent to which the researchers have ensured that their own values and beliefs have not had any influence on the design or the carrying out of the research. This is known as **objectivity** or **value freedom**. If sociologists allow their own values to intrude into the research process, then this will seriously weaken the research and certainly impact upon the validity of the research. However, we cannot say that all values should be kept out of research, as this is simply impossible, just that there should never be intentional bias.

Methods in action

Reay et al. (2001)
Choice in higher education

Diane Reay and her colleagues wished to study the choices and views of people entering higher education made by people who were not school leavers from traditional middle-class backgrounds.

The researchers studied people from six different educational institutions. They gave out 502 questionnaires and followed this up with 53 interviews with students and 'a small number of interviews with parents' and others. The study drew upon the 'qualitative' interviews with the 53 students who Reay says were 'not representative of the sample as a whole'. The students were asked to define their ethnicity themselves and the result was that only 23 of the 53 people in the sample defined themselves as being 'White'. One of the interviewees defined himself as 'Irish', rather than any other category such as 'White'.

The students were also classified by the researchers into social-class groupings. The researchers used the registrar-general's five-point scale, but in order to simplify things, did not use one of the categories (III Non-manual).

Reay, D., Davies, J., David, M. and Ball, S.J. (2001) 'Choices of degree or degrees of choice? Class, 'race' and the higher education process', *Sociology*, 35(4)

1 The researchers quantify various elements of the research, but not the 'small number' of interviews. Why not?

2 If the students are not 'representative', how easy is it to generalize?

3 What problems can you identify regarding 'self-definition' of ethnicity?

4 The researchers adopted the reliable Registrar-General categorisation, but chose to leave one grouping out. What implications could this have for their research?

Activities

Research idea

Divide into small groups. Each group should write a short questionnaire consisting of three questions. The questions should aim to collect opinions on:

(a) whether cannabis should be legalized
(b) whether the use of drugs causes crime.

Decide on the wording of your questions and then put them to a sample of six people.

Compare the answers of the different groups. Are they all similar? If they are different, can you think of reasons why? What might this tell us about validity, bias and representativeness?

Web.tasks

Find some of the statistics on drugs and crime. These are available through the Home Office website at www.homeoffice.gov.uk

You will need to select or search for the section on 'Drugs' or 'Drugs and crime'. Give examples of the sort of figures and information provided. Comment on their validity, reliability and representativeness.

Check your understanding

1 Explain the three main aims of sociological research in your own words.

2 Give two reasons why sociological research is more trustworthy than 'common sense'.

3 Explain the difference between a 'correlation' and a 'causal relationship'.

4 What term is used by sociologists for statistical data?

5 Give two examples of:
   (a) primary data
   (b) secondary data.

6 Why is it important for a sociological study to be 'valid'?

TOPIC 2

Choices in research: methods, theories and ethics

Getting you thinking

Karen Sharpe studied the lives of prostitutes by acting as a 'secretary' for them. Read the passage (right) about the aims of her research and then answer the questions that follow.

<< The central objective of my research was to understand why and how women entered the world of prostitution: to discover the motivating factors, the dynamics of the introductory process, and how they learnt the skills, values and codes of conduct of the business. I wanted to explore the importance and impact of prostitution on their lifestyles and to put the 'deviance' of prostitution into context with other aspects of their criminality. I also wanted to discover how the women themselves and their families and friends, subjectively defined, perceived and rationalized their activities. >>

1   Suggest two possible ways of undertaking this. List the advantages of your choices and the disadvantages.

2   This research was conducted by a woman. Do you think it would be possible for a male researcher to have done this? Explain the reasons for your answer.

3   Do you think that there is any point in doing this research? Explain your answer.

4   If during your research you found that one of the women was very unhappy and you knew you could help her, but if you did so it would ruin the research – what would you do?

In the previous topic, we found that objective research and the creation of theories comprise the key elements that distinguish sociology as a distinct academic subject. However, the reality of actually undertaking research and creating theories is complex and full of pitfalls. Several important issues arise:

1   Why do some topics of research occur again and again (e.g. young people and offending), while other issues are rarely explored (e.g. the breaking of ecological rules by multinational companies)? Could it be that the more commonly researched issues are easier or perhaps cheaper or more interesting for sociologists to do? Perhaps more worryingly, is funding less likely to be obtained for research into subject areas that threaten the interests of more powerful groups?

2   If the aim of research is to generate or to confirm theoretical approaches, why do different, conflicting theories continue to exist in sociology? Surely, by now research would have provided enough evidence for one theoretical approach to be seen as correct and deny the claim of others?

3   Sociology seeks to provide objective information about society – but is that possible? After all, sociologists are

people like anyone else, with values, beliefs and prejudices. Can they really put these values to one side? Even if they can, don't they have to take into account when starting their research that their results may well have significant consequences for people's lives? For example, sociological research is largely responsible for the move away from grammar/secondary modern schools to the comprehensive system.

4   The final big issue is the choice of methods. Sociologists have a wide range of methodological approaches to use. These range from questionnaires handed out to thousands of people which are then subjected to statistical analysis, to a sociologist hanging around with young, homeless people simply being part of their lives. Which method is more useful in which circumstances? Are there any implications for the research project in using one method rather than another?

In this topic, we seek some answers to these questions and provide a few signposts to help guide us through the complex issues of ethical and theoretical debates and their relationship to research methods.

The relationship between research and ethics

Research can have a powerful impact on people's lives. It can do so in both harmful and beneficial ways. Therefore, researchers must always think very carefully about the impact of the research and how they ought to behave, so that no harm comes to the subjects of the research or to society in general. These sorts of concerns are generally discussed under the umbrella term **ethical issues**.

Most sociological researchers would agree that there are five areas of ethical concern.

1   Choice of topic

The first ethical issue relates to the decision about what to study. Merely by choosing an area, the researcher might be confirming some people's prejudices about a particular issue. For example, many sociologists are concerned about the extent of research into the 'negative' side of African-Caribbean life, with studies on school failure, lower levels of job success and even the claimed higher rate of criminality. Critics argue that merely by studying this, a continued association is made between race and criminality or race and failure.

2   Choice of group to be studied

One of the trickiest problems that sociologists face is gaining access to study particular groups. The more powerful the group, the less likely it is that the sociologist will manage to obtain agreement to study its members. The result, as you will see, is that the groups most commonly studied by sociologists are the least powerful – so students, petty criminals and less-skilled workers are the staple diet of sociological research. The really powerful evade study. Does sociology have a duty to explore the lives of the powerful?

3   Effects on the people being studied

Research can often have an effect on the people being studied. So, before setting out to do research, sociologists must think carefully about what these effects will be, although it is not always possible to anticipate them.

One of the reasons why sociologists rarely use experiments, for example, is that these may lead to the subjects being harmed by the experiment. In participant observational studies, where the researcher actually joins in with the group being studied (see Topic 4), the researcher can often become an important member of the group and may influence other members to behave in ways they would not normally.

4   Effects on the wider society

It is not only the people being studied who are potentially affected by the research. The families of those being researched may have information given about them that they wish to keep secret. Also, victims of crime may be upset by the information that researchers obtain about the perpetrators, as they may prefer to forget the incident.

5   Issues of legality and immorality

Finally, sociologists may be drawn into situations where they may commit crimes or possibly help in or witness deviant acts. While undertaking research on a prisoner in

the USA, Kenneth Tunnell (1998) discovered that the prisoner had actually taken on the identity of someone else (who was dead), in order to avoid a much longer prison sentence. The prison authorities became suspicious and investigated the prisoner's background. Though Tunnell knew the truth, he felt that he owed the prisoner confidentiality and deliberately lied, stating that he knew nothing about the identity 'theft'. As a result, the prisoner was released many years early.

The relationship between theories and methods

Earlier, we saw that research findings could be used either to generate new sociological theories, or to confirm or challenge existing theories. However, the relationship between research and theory is even more complicated than this. If a sociologist has a particular interest in a theoretical approach, then this may well influence their research methodology. There are three areas in which theory has a strong influence on research.

1   Theory and choice of an area of research

One of the great joys of studying sociology is that the variety of different views and theories generates so many different opinions about society. However, when reading sociological research, you must always be aware that sociologists who hold strong theoretical beliefs about society are bound to study the topics that, in their eyes, are the most important, and to be less interested in other areas.

- **Feminist sociologists** see it as their role to examine the position of women in society, and to uncover the ways in which **patriarchy**, or the power of men, has been used to control and oppress women. Consequently, their choice of research projects will be influenced by this.
- **Marxist or critical sociologists** argue that the most important area of study is the question of how a relatively small group of people exploits the vast majority of the population. They will study issues such as the concentration of power and wealth, and the importance of social class divisions.
- **Functionalist-oriented sociologists** think that society is based on a general consensus of values. They are interested in looking at the ways in which society maintains agreement on values and solves social problems. Therefore, they will look at the role of religion or schools in passing on values.

2   Theory and techniques of study

Various theories may point to different areas of interest, but theories also nudge sociologists into different ways of studying society. Theories in sociology usually fall into two camps – **top-down** and **bottom-up** theories.

Top-down approaches

Top-down approaches, such as functionalism and Marxism, say that the best way to understand society is to view it as a real 'thing' which exists above and beyond us all as individuals. It shapes our lives and provides us with the social world in which we live. Our role is generally to conform. These sorts of theoretical approaches emphasize that any research ought to bear this in mind and that the researcher should be looking for general patterns of behaviour – which individuals may not even be aware of.

The favoured research methods used by these sociologists tend to be those that generate sets of statistics (such as questionnaires), known as **quantitative methods** (see Topic 3). Sociologists sympathetic to the use of these more 'scientific' methods are sometimes known as **positivists**.

Bottom-up approaches

Bottom-up approaches, such as interactionism (see Chapter 1, p. xx), stress that the only way to understand society is to look at the world through the eyes of individuals, as it is the activities and beliefs of individuals that make up the social world. Research must start at 'the bottom' and work upwards. The sorts of research methods favoured by those who advocate this approach (known as **interpretive sociologists**) tend to be those that allow the researcher to see the world from the same perspective as those being studied (known as **qualitative methods**). An example is participant observation (see p. xxx).

Triangulation and mixed methods research

Although one group of sociologists is largely in favour of using quantitative methods and others prefer qualitative methods, in practice both groups will dip into the 'other side's' methods if they think it will be useful. Mixed methods research is sometimes referred to as **methodological pluralism**. From this viewpoint, all methods have their advantages and disadvantages so using a combination provides a broad and balanced picture of the aspect of social life being researched. One particular approach to mixed methods research is known as

triangulation. This involves the use of different methods to check data.

So, quantitative researchers may well back up their work by including some observation or some in-depth, unstructured interviewing, whilst qualitative researchers may well engage in some structured interviewing or draw upon secondary sources.

3 The interpretation of research findings

The final impact of theory on research comes when interpreting the research findings. The research is completed and the results are all there in the computer. How does the researcher make sense of the results? This will depend, of course, on what they are looking for, and that, in turn, depends upon what theoretical approach the researcher sympathizes with. This is very different from bias or personal values – rather, it is a matter of choosing which results are most important, and this will always depend upon what best fits the theoretical framework of the researcher. A feminist researcher will be keen to understand the position of women; the Marxist will be looking for signs of class struggle; the functionalist will be looking at the key indicators to prove that a set of common beliefs exists.

The relationship between practical issues and research

So far we have looked at the ethical and theoretical issues which have an important influence on the research process. As you can see, these are quite difficult 'abstract' issues, which sometimes seem far removed from the reality of everyday life. However, just as important are a range of very down-to-earth influences on the research process.

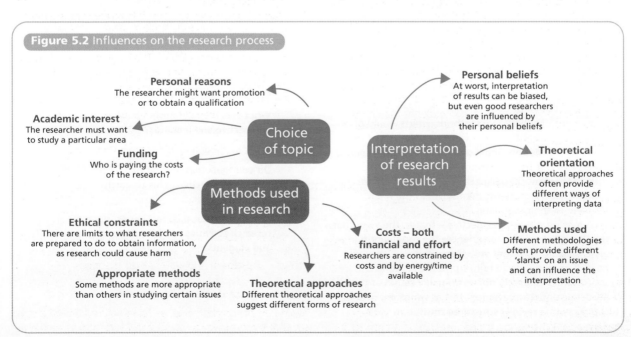

Figure 5.2 Influences on the research process

Personal reasons
The researcher might want promotion or to obtain a qualification

Academic interest
The researcher must want to study a particular area

Funding
Who is paying the costs of the research?

Choice of topic

Ethical constraints
There are limits to what researchers are prepared to do to obtain information, as research could cause harm

Methods used in research

Appropriate methods
Some methods are more appropriate than others in studying certain issues

Theoretical approaches
Different theoretical approaches suggest different forms of research

Personal beliefs
At worst, interpretation of results can be biased, but even good researchers are influenced by their personal beliefs

Interpretation of research results

Theoretical orientation
Theoretical approaches often provide different ways of interpreting data

Costs – both financial and effort
Researchers are constrained by costs and by energy/time available

Methods used
Different methodologies often provide different 'slants' on an issue and can influence the interpretation

Methods in action

Mac an Ghaill (1998)
Ethnographic studies in educational research

In *Young, Gifted and Black*, Mairtin Mac an Ghaill carried out two ethnographic studies in inner-city educational institutions in which he worked. The first study looks at the relations between White teachers and two groups of antischool male students – the Asian Warriors and the African-Caribbean Rasta Heads – and the second study looks at a group of black female students, of African-Caribbean and Asian parentage, called the Black Sisters.

Why study this subject?

Originally, Mac an Ghaill wanted to study Irish school students for his PhD, but no university supervisor was available to do so. He was advised to study students of African-Caribbean origin instead and agreed to do so. He then began his study of (male) Asian Warriors and the African-Caribbean Rasta Heads.

Similarly, his later study of ethnic-minority females was also not planned. As Mac an Ghaill puts it: 'I had not intended to carry out a study of black female students. In fact it would be more accurate to say that they chose me.' Mac an Ghaill was teaching sociology at the time in a sixth-form college and, because he was seen to be on the side of the students, the Black Sisters were happy to talk to him about their views of racism.

The relationship between theory and method

Mac an Ghaill started his research by accepting the then current sociological explanation for the underachievement in school of young people of African-Caribbean origin, namely that there were cultural differences with the dominant White culture. Initially, therefore, he wanted to research the problem of young African-Caribbean students as trapped between two cultures.

Because Mac an Ghaill wanted to understand the nature of the cultural differences, he decided to use participant observational methods, which would give him a close insight into the values and beliefs of the students. As Mac an Ghaill says: 'Intensive participant observation of the antischool Rasta Heads led me to shift my theoretical perspective, identifying racism rather than the students themselves as the main problem in their schooling.

Adopting a Black perspective – that is, the view that the Black community experiences the social world in a systematically different way from Whites – was vital here. It enabled me to reinterpret the students' subcultural responses, not as primarily causal of their academic underachievement but as symptoms of their coping with a racially structured institution.'

Although he used participant observational methods, he also collected a range of quantitative information, including data on school absences, lateness, suspensions, the ethnic composition of students in academic/non-academic teaching groups and examination results. As the study developed, he used this material, linking it with what the students told him, to provide a deeper understanding of the students' perspectives.

Objectivity

During the research, Mac an Ghaill became friendly with the students, as he puts it: 'Over the research periods the Rasta Heads, the Warriors and the Black Sisters visited my home regularly. The experience of talking, eating, dancing and listening to music together helped to break down the potential social barriers of the teacher– researcher role that may have been assigned to me and my seeing them as students with the accompanying status perception.'

Mac an Ghaill does not claim to be value free in his research, and states that he was committed to helping the students to overcome the racially based barriers they faced in life.

Practical issues and research

Mac an Ghaill was able to gain entry into the research because he was a teacher in both educational institutions over the period of research. Beyond that, his sympathy and support for the students convinced them that he was a trustworthy person who was 'on their side'. Mac an Ghaill also lived in the area and was recognized as a local. However, there was always tension between his role as a teacher and that of a friend and researcher of the young people. He found that in the staff room he became the defender of the ethnic-minority students and a critic of the institutional racism he believed existed in the school and wider society. This position sometimes caused conflict with other members of staff.

Mac an Ghaill, M. (1998) *Young, Gifted and Black: Student-teacher relations in the schooling of black youth*, Milton Keynes: Open University Press

1   What factors influenced the choice of subject Mac an Ghaill studied?

2   What was the relationship between theoretical perspective and methods?

3   What methodology did Mac an Ghaill use?

4   Do you think that Mac an Ghaill found it difficult to remain objective in his research? Give reasons for your answer.

5   How did 'practical issues' impact upon his research activities and his relationship with staff and students?

Funding

All research has to be paid for by someone and those who pay for research have a reason for doing so. These funding organizations may vary from those who wish to extend knowledge about society and to improve the quality of life (such as the Joseph Rowntree Foundation), to private companies wanting to sell more products or services (such as market research organizations). Despite the differences between the funding organizations, each has an aim that constrains the research choices and activities of sociologists.

Probably the largest funder of sociological research in Britain is the government, which pays for a wide range of research into areas such as transport, health, crime and housing. However, anyone conducting research for the government signs a contract that restricts what they can say and publish about their findings.

Academic specialism

Sociologists at university specialize in particular areas within sociology – for example, some will only study the family and others only health issues. Clearly, the research they will wish to undertake will be within their specialism.

Personal reasons

Sociologists, like everyone else, want to have successful careers, be promoted and become respected. Research choices are often influenced by these desires. If there are various areas of research to choose from, the ambitious sociologist chooses that one that may lead to promotion.

Fitness for purpose

The methods used in a study are usually dictated by its aims - whichever methods most suit the purpose of the research are selected. Generally, if a large number of people need to be studied, then the sociologist will use questionnaires or structured interviews. If a few people need to be studied in depth, then some form of semi-structured interviewing or observation is usually employed.

Activities

Research idea

Look in your school or college library for resources about drugs and alcohol. Who published the material? Can you suggest reasons why they published the material? Could this affect the content of the material in any way?

Web.tasks

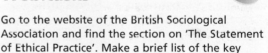

Go to the website of the British Sociological Association and find the section on 'The Statement of Ethical Practice'. Make a brief list of the key elements.
Do you think they are all necessary?
How could 'informed consent' cause problems for studying young people or deviant groups?

Key terms

Bottom-up theories (generally called 'micro' or 'interpretive' approaches) sociological theories that analyse society by studying the ways in which individuals interpret the world.

Ethical Issues moral concerns about the benefits and potential harm of research to the people being researched, to researchers themselves and to society.

Feminist sociology an approach within sociology that concerns itself with studying the way in which women are oppressed by men.

Fitness for purpose choosing the methods that are most suitable for fulfilling the aims of the study.

Functionalism an approach within sociology that stresses that society is based on a general agreement of values.

Interpretive sociology an approach favouring the use of qualitative methods, such as participant observation, that allow the researcher to see the world from the same perspective as those being studied.

Marxist or critical sociology an approach within sociology

that stresses the exploitation of the majority of the population by a small and powerful 'ruling class'.

Methodological pluralism term used to describe the use of mixed methods (quantitative and qualitative) in research.

Patriarchy the oppression of women by men.

Positivism the view that sociology should try to use more 'scientific' approaches and methods, such as questionnaires and official statistics.

Qualitative methods methods, such as participant observation, that produce primarily written data and allow the researcher to see things from the same perspective as those being studied.

Quantitative methods methods, such as questionnaires, that produce primarily statistical data.

Top-down theories (often called 'macro' or 'structural' approaches) sociological theories that believe it is important to look at society as a whole when studying it.

Triangulation the combining of methods so that data can be cross-checked.

Check your understanding

1   Name the three main aims that sociological researchers set out to achieve.

2   Explain in your own words what is meant by the term 'ethical issues'.

3   Illustrate how ethical issues may emerge in:

   (a)   the choice of topic to be studied

   (b)   the effects on the people being studied.

4   How can a theoretical approach influence:

   (a)   the area of study?

   (b)   the methodological techniques chosen?

5   Give two examples that show the influence of practical issues on the nature of research.

Quantitative methods of research

Getting you thinking

Young men most likely to binge drink

In Great Britain, men aged 16–24 are the most likely to binge drink (consume twice the recommended daily amount of 3 to 4 units of alcohol for men). In 2005, 30 per cent had done so on at least one day in the previous week, a slightly higher proportion than among the 25–44 age group at 25 per cent. Among women aged 16–24, 22 per cent had consumed twice the recommended daily amount on at least one day during the preceding week, twice the proportion of those in the 25–44 age group, (who were the next most likely age group to have consumed at least twice the recommended daily level).

Source: *Health Statistics Quarterly*

Every year a survey called the Health Related Behaviour Questionnaire takes place. Young people are asked about their experiences of a range of health issues. According to the latest, conducted in 2002:

- Up to 21 per cent of 10- to 11-year-olds had consumed an alcoholic drink during the previous week.
- 19 per cent of 15-year-old males drank more than 11 units of alcohol in the previous week.
- Up to 65 per cent of young people will have smoked by Year 10.
- About one in four pupils in Year 10 have tried at least one illegal drug.
- Up to 8 per cent of 12- to 13-year olds have taken cannabis.

Adapted from: Schools Health Education Unit (2003), *Young people in 2002*, Exeter: SHEU

1. How can anyone make the above claims? For example, did they ask every school student in Britain? If they didn't, how is it possible to arrive at these figures?

2. Do you believe these figures. Why?

3. How honestly do you think pupils will answer these questions?

4. On what sort of questions do you think people would lie? Why?

5. Do you think that males and females might lie over different sorts of questions? Give examples.

Sociologists choose different methods of research depending upon what method seems most appropriate in the circumstances, and the resources available to them. The approach covered in this topic is quantitative research. This stresses the importance of gathering statistical information that can be checked and tested. Quantitative research usually involves one or more of the following:

- **surveys**
- **experiments**
- **comparative research**
- **case studies**.

Quantitative research methods are most often chosen by sociologists who believe that sociology should attempt to be similar to the natural sciences in the way it researches. Sociologists who prefer the natural sciences model of

research argue that the closest they can get to scientific research is if they use highly advanced statistical methods, which can, they argue, factually prove the relationship between different social events. Therefore, statistical analyses have demonstrated beyond doubt that social class, ethnicity and gender are all directly related to educational success. This approach to sociological research is known as **positivism**.

Positivists reject qualitative research, which is based on the principle that people construct the social world through their perceptions of what is real or true. Positivists argue that only through obtaining verifiable and objective information about the social world can knowledge be generated.

Surveys

A social survey involves obtaining information in a standardized manner from a large group of people. Surveys usually obtain this information through questionnaires or, less often, through interviews. The information is then analysed using statistical techniques. There are three possible aims of social surveys. They can be used to:

- find out 'facts' about the population – e.g. how many people have access to the internet
- uncover differences in beliefs, values and behaviour – e.g. whether young people have a more positive view of the internet than older people
- test 'a hypothesis' – e.g. that women are less confident in using the internet than men.

A good example of a survey is the British Crime Survey, which takes place every two years and asks people about their experience of crime. This survey has helped sociologists gain a fuller understanding of patterns of crime. We now know a lot more about issues such as people's fear of crime, the factors affecting the reporting of crime and the likelihood of different social groups becoming victims of crime.

Before a full social survey is carried out, it is usual for a researcher to carry out a **pilot survey**. This is a small-scale version of the full survey, which is intended to:

- help evaluate the usefulness of the larger survey
- test the quality and the accuracy of the questions
- test the accuracy of the sample
- find out if there are any unforeseen problems.

Sampling

It is usually impossible for sociologists to study the entire population, on the grounds of cost and practicality. Instead, they have to find a way of studying a smaller proportion of the population whose views will exactly mirror the views of the whole population.

Random sampling

This is based on the idea that, by choosing randomly, each person has an equal chance of being selected and so those chosen are likely to be a cross section of the population. A simple random sample involves selecting names randomly from a list, known as a **sampling frame**. If the sampling frame is inaccurate, this can lead to great errors in the final findings. Therefore, it needs to be a true reflection of the sort of people whom the researcher wishes to study. Examples of commonly used sampling frames are electoral registers (lists of people entitled to vote, which are publicly available) or the Postcode Address File (see Methods in action below).

Methods in action

The Health Survey for England

The Health Survey for England (HSE) is part of a programme of surveys commissioned by the Information Centre for health and social care, and has been carried out regularly since 1994; they have become increasingly broader over time. The study provides information on changing health trends and risk factors linked to certain health conditions.

Sampling

The most recent survey, the HSE 2005, included a general population sample of adults and children, representative of the whole population at both national and regional level. In total, 7200 addresses were randomly selected in 720 postcode sectors.

At each address, everyone in them was eligible for inclusion in the survey. However, where there were three or more children aged 0–15 in a household, two of the children were selected at random.

As the 2005 survey was focusing on older people, a booster sample of people aged 65 and over was selected which consisted of 11 520 addresses in the same 720 postcode sectors as the main sample.

Interviews were held with 7630 adults aged 16 and over, and 1852 children from the general population. The boost sample resulted in an additional 2673 adults aged 65 and over, and 1142 children aged 2 to 15 being interviewed.

Response rate: 89 per cent of adults in the general households agreed to be interviewed, and 97 per cent of older people chosen agreed.

Interview and questionnaire

The survey used a mixture of interviews and self-completed questionnaires. The interview included questions on core topics such as general health, alcohol consumption, smoking, and fruit and vegetable consumption. Older informants were also asked about use of health, dental and social care services, cardiovascular disease (CVD), chronic diseases and quality of care, disabilities and falls.

Craig, R. and Mindell, J. (eds) (2007) *Health Survey for England 2005. The health of older people: Summary of key findings*, Joint Health Surveys Unit
www.ic.nhs.uk/webfiles/publications/hseolder/HSESummary.pdf

1   What sampling frame was used in this research?

2   How many households were chosen in (a) the main sample and (b) the booster sample? How can this number of households represent the views of the British population?

3   Why did they use a 'booster sample'?

4   Why do you think they obtained such a high response rate (a typical response rate is lower than 60 per cent)?

5   What problems do you think might occur when interviewing older people?

However, a simple random sample does not guarantee a representative sample – you may, for instance, select too many young people, too many males or too many from some other group. For this reason, many sociologists break down their list of names into separate categories (for example, males and females) and then select from those lists.

Experiments

Experiments are very commonly used in the natural sciences (e.g. physics and chemistry). An experiment is basically research in which all the variables are closely controlled, so that the effect of changing one or more of the variables can be understood. Experiments are widely used in psychology, but much less so in sociology. There are several reasons for this:

- It is impossible to recreate normal life in the artificial environment of an experiment.
- There are many ethical problems in performing experiments on people.
- There is the possibility of the experimenter effect, where the awareness of being in an experiment affects the behaviour of the participants.

Occasionally, sociologists use **field experiments**, where a form of experiment is undertaken in the community. Rosenhan (1982) sent 'normal' people to psychiatric institutions in the USA in the late 1960s to see how they were treated by the staff. (Rather worryingly, the staff treated ordinary behaviour in institutions as evidence of insanity!)

Comparative research

The sociological version of an experiment is the **comparative method**. When a sociologist is interested in explaining a particular issue, one way of doing so is by comparing differences across groups or societies, or across one society over time. By comparing the different social variables in the different societies and their effects upon the issue being studied, it is sometimes possible to identify a particular social practice or value which is the key factor in determining that issue. Emile Durkheim (1897/1952) used the comparative method in his classic study of the different levels of suicide in societies, concluding that specific cultural differences motivated people to commit suicide. In order to arrive at this conclusion, Durkheim collected official statistics from a number of different countries and then compared the different levels of suicide, linking them to cultural differences, including religion and family relationships, which varied across the different countries.

Case studies

A case study is a detailed study of one particular group or organization. Instead of searching out a wide range of people via sampling, the researcher focuses on one group. The resulting studies are usually extremely detailed and provide a depth of information not normally available. However, there is always the problem that this intense scrutiny may miss wider issues by its very concentration. An example of a case study is Grieshaber's work (1997), where she conducted case studies of how families ate their meals, and the rules that the parents and their children negotiated.

Key terms

Case study a highly detailed study of one or two social situations or groups.

Comparative method a comparison across countries or cultures; sociology's version of an experiment.

Cross-sectional survey (also known as **social survey** or **snapshot survey**) a survey conducted at one time with no attempt to follow up the people surveyed over a longer time.

Experiment a highly controlled situation where the researchers try to isolate the influence of each variable. Rarely used in sociology.

Field experiment an experiment undertaken in the community rather than in a controlled environment.

Longitudinal survey a survey carried out over a considerable number of years on the same group of people.

Pilot survey a small-scale survey carried out before the main one, to iron out any problems.

Positivism the belief that the methods of the natural sciences are best suited to the study of society. Positivists prefer, wherever possible, to use statistics.

Random sampling where a representative sample of the population is chosen by entirely random methods.

Representative a sample is representative if it is an accurate cross section of the whole population being studied.

Sampling frame a list used as the source for a random sample.

Survey a large-scale piece of quantitative research aiming to make general statements about a particular population.

Activities

Research idea

1 Work out the proportions needed in your sample if you were to do a quota sample of your school or college.

2 Conduct a small survey to discover the patterns of alcohol use in your college. Ask males and females how much they drink per week on average and when they drink. Construct charts to demonstrate the patterns that emerge. What explanations could you suggest? You will need to work out your statistics based on alcohol units, and to do this, you should go to: www.at-bristol.org.uk/Alcoholandyou /Facts/units.html

Web.tasks

1 Go to the website 'School Surveys' at www.schoolsurveys.co.uk, where you can organize your own online survey. You will need to get your teacher to register first.

2 Go to www.nextstepsstudy.org.uk/who-is-the-study-for.asp

Find out all you can about 'Next Steps'.

Check your understanding

1   What do we mean by 'quantitative research'?

2   Explain in your own words the importance of sampling.

3   Why are random samples not always representative?

4   Why do sociologists rarely use experiments?

5   What is a case study?

6   Give one example of a research project that has used the comparative method.

An eye on the exam   Quantitative methods of data collection

JOINED-UP TEXTING: THE ROLE OF MOBILE PHONES IN YOUNG PEOPLE'S LIVES

Helen Haste (2005)

The aims of this study were to:
- consider how young people use their phones to communicate
- investigate forms of communication and other new technologies
- investigate how mobile phones reflect style and identity
- discover age, sex and locational differences in mobile phone etiquette and use.

A random sample of 200 schools and colleges was selected from a mixture of geographical areas. Letters were sent to the headteachers and principals and, as a result, a sample of 25 institutions was selected.

The survey consisted of a self-completion questionnaire. The interviewer arranged a suitable time and place for the questionnaire to be completed so they could be present. Teachers were also present during the administration of the questionnaires in order to deal with issues of discipline. Each participating school received a donation of £100.

The questionnaire consisted of a sequence of closed questions from which respondents could pick appropriate answers and tick their choices. It covered more information than merely mobile phone use and referred to computer access as well as gaming machines and satellite or cable televisions. It also included questions referring to all the various uses of mobile phone technology such as cameras, moving video, gaming and recording of notes. There were questions about the economics of phone ownership in terms of who and how much is paid for the technology.

The survey found that the mobile phone has become essential to the lives of young people. Teenage social life is often centred around the peer group and mobile phones allow young people to influence and keep track of each other in more ways than ever before. But it is not only the peer group that is sustained through the mobile phone, there is also an impact on family relationships. Teenagers can be given more freedom to be independent of their parents, whilst at the same time avoid being isolated from them.

Adapted from Blundell, J. and Griffiths, J. (2008) *Sociology since 2000*. Lewes: Connect Publications
Haste, H. (2005) *Joined-Up Texting: The Role of Mobile Phones in Young People's Lives*
Nestle Social Research Programme, Report No. 3

Using the extract above and your own sociological knowledge, explain and evaluate why social surveys might be used to investigate young people's use of mobile phones.

(52 marks)

Grade booster   Getting top marks in this question

Show the examiner that you know the meaning of the term 'social survey' at the start of your answer. Take each aim of the study in turn and explain why a social survey might be an appropriate method for finding out about them. Don't forget to evaluate both the positive and negative points of the study. Use the terms reliability, validity, representativeness and generalisability to illustrate the points you make.

Qualitative methods of research

Getting you thinking

The extract on the right is from a research project which studies the lives and attitudes of door staff ('bouncers') working in night clubs. The researcher narrating the story is a student who has got a job as a bouncer as part of the research project.

<< It's Friday evening outside a club in a city centre ... one young woman has shouted an insult at another, the recipient of which has turned on her heel and begun to walk away. The first young woman continues to throw insults until the retreating young woman seemingly has a change of heart, turns, picks up an empty lager bottle from the street and hits the first young woman in the face with it.

A hush descends on the busy street. It isn't funny any more. Nobody is laughing; in fact there was a palpable 'Oh!' sound emitted from the spectators, mixed with the sound of thick glass crashing into tender flesh and bone. The injured young woman has her hand pressed to her mouth – she isn't screaming or crying, but instantly it is possible to tell that she is badly injured.

I snap out of my shocked state when I see Paul (bouncer and colleague) putting his arm around her back to support her unsteady steps ... After some gentle coaxing, the woman releases her grip on the wound ... blood spurts all over Paul's shirt. Her upper lip is split entirely, right up to her right nostril. It's a wide gash and through the resulting hole it becomes apparent that the woman has also lost at least three teeth. Blood is everywhere. Paul's shirt now appears tie-dyed red with blood.

Later when a policeman calls to take a statement, he informs me that I may be called as a witness in any resulting court case. When I ask how the young woman is, he informs me that 'She lost four teeth, 28 stitches to the upper lip, the usual bruising and swelling ... Shame really. Pretty girl.' Turns out she's only 15. >>

Source: Winlow, S., Hobbs, D., Lister, S. and Hadfield, P. (2001) 'Get ready to duck: bouncers and the realities of ethnographic research on violent groups', *British Journal of Criminology*, 41, pp. 536–48

1   What is your immediate reaction to the story?

2   Why do you think the girl was attacked by her friend?

3   Have you ever seen a fight outside a club at night? What happened? What did the doorstaff do?

4   Why do you think the researcher chose to get a job as a bouncer in order to study their lives? Could you think of a better way?

Have you ever watched a sporting event on television and heard the commentator saying what a fantastic atmosphere there is? Yet, at home, you remain outside it. You know there is a fantastic atmosphere, you hear the roar of the crowd, yet you are not part of it. For the people actually in the stadium, the experience of the occasion is quite different. The heat, the closeness of thousands of others, the noise and the emotional highs and lows of the actual event, all combine to give a totally different sense of what is happening.

Some sociologists 'stay at home' to do their research. They may use questionnaires, interviews and surveys to obtain a clear, overall view. On the other hand, there are sociologists who are more interested in experiencing the emotions and sense of actually being there. These sociologists set out to immerse themselves in the lifestyle of the group they wish to study.

Because this form of research is less interested in statistics to prove its point (that is, quantitative research), and more interested in the qualities of social life, it is sometimes known as **qualitative research**. Qualitative approaches are based on the belief that it is not appropriate or possible to measure and categorize the social world accurately – all that is possible is to observe and describe what is happening and offer possible explanations. The aim of ethnographic research is to get close to the people being studied so that the researcher can experience the social world in the same ways. If this is successful, then **verstehen** – an **empathic** understanding, can be achieved.

There are three common forms of qualitative research:

- observational studies
- informal interviews
- focus groups.

In this topic we will concentrate on observational studies, as many of the issues surrounding asking questions and discussion are covered in the following topic. However, we should remember that, strictly speaking, qualitative research can include a wide variety of other approaches, such as video and audio recording of activities, interviews, analysis of the internet, or even non-statistical analysis of books, magazines and journals.

Although there is still some debate, the general consensus is that qualitative research is a naturalistic, interpretative approach concerned with understanding the meanings which people attach to actions, decisions, beliefs, values, etc., within their social world; it is also about understanding the mental mapping process that respondents use to make sense of and interpret the world around them (Ritchie and Lewis 2003).

The most common form of qualitative research consists of observational studies in which a particular group of people is closely observed and their activities noted. The belief is that, by exploring the lives of people in detail, insights may be gained that can be applied to the understanding of society in general. Observational studies derive from **ethnography**, which is the term used to describe the work of anthropologists who study simple, small-scale societies by living with the (usually tribal) people and observing their daily lives.

Observational research

Observational research is a general term that covers a range of different research techniques. Observational studies vary in two main ways (see Fig. 5.3 below):

1. the extent to which the researcher joins in the activities of the group – the researcher may decide to be a participant or not. The choice is between **participant observation** and **non-participant observation**
2. whether the researcher is honest and tells the group about the research, or prefers to pretend to be one of the group. The choice is between **overt** and **covert** research.

Participant observation

The most common form of observational study is participant observation, where the researcher joins the group being studied.

The advantages of participant observation

- *Experience* – Participant observation allows the researcher to join the group fully and see things through the eyes (and actions) of the people in the

---

Figure 5.3 Types of observational research

COVERT

Laud Humphries (1975) studied homosexual activity in public toilets. He pretended to be a gay voyeur.

Amy Flowers (1998) got a job as a telephone sex line worker and studied the way that the women learned to mask their feelings and emotions when talking to clients. Neither employees nor managers knew about her research.

NON-PARTICIPANT

PARTICIPANT

Heidi Safia Mirza and Diane Reay (2000) studied two African-Caribbean 'supplementary' schools, run by the African-Caribbean-origin community for their children. The researchers attended and observed the classes (as well as using in-depth interviews).

Stephen Lyng (1990) studied 'high risk' groups (sky divers and motorcyclists) to find out why they did it. Lyng never hid the fact he was an academic but joined in all the dangerous activities.

OVERT

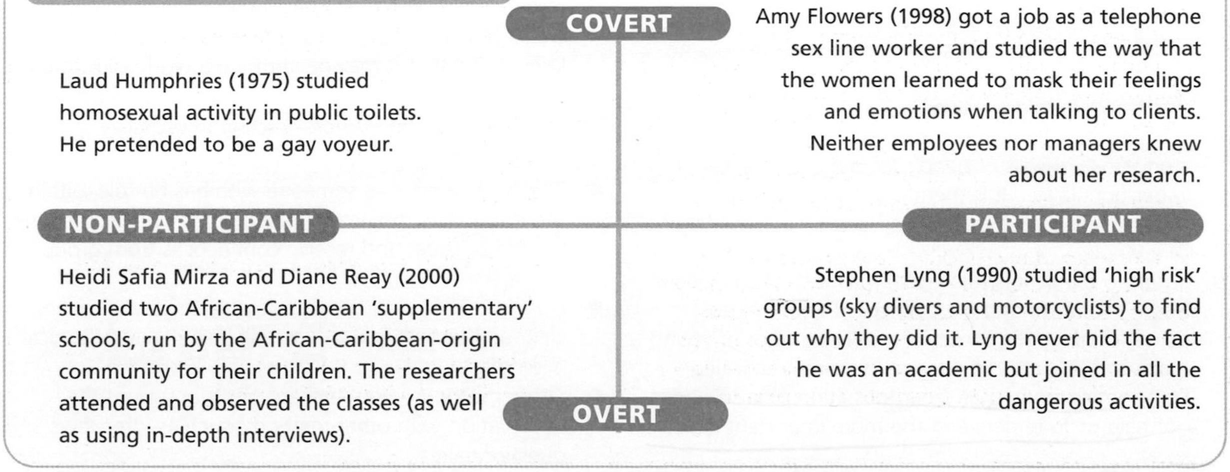

group. The researcher is placed in exactly the same situation as the group under study, fully experiencing what is happening. This results in the researcher seeing social life from the same perspective as the group.

- *Generating new ideas* – Often this can lead to completely new insights and generate new theoretical ideas, unlike traditional research, which undertakes the study in order to explore an existing theory or hypothesis.
- *Getting the truth* – One of the problems with questionnaires, and to a lesser extent with interviews, is that the respondent can lie. Participant observation prevents this because the researcher can see the person in action – it may also help them understand why the person would lie in a questionnaire or interview.
- *Digging deep* – Participant observation can create a close bond between the researcher and the group under study, and individuals in the group may be prepared to confide in the researcher on issues and views that would normally remain hidden.
- *Dynamic* – Questionnaires and interviews are 'static': they are only able to gain an understanding of a person's behaviour or attitudes at the precise moment of the interview. Participant observation takes place over a period of time and allows an understanding of how changes in attitudes and behaviour take place.
- *Reaching into difficult areas* – Participant observation is normally used to obtain research information on hard-to-reach groups, such as religious sects and young offenders.

The disadvantages of participant observation

- *Bias* – The main problem lies with bias, as the observer can be drawn into the group and start to see things through their eyes. This may blind the observer to the insights that would otherwise be available.
- *Influence of the researcher* – The presence of the researcher may make the group act less naturally as they are aware of being studied. Of course, this is less likely to happen if the researcher is operating covertly.
- *Ethics* – If the researcher is studying a group engaged in deviant behaviour, then there is a moral issue of how far the researcher should be drawn into the activities of the group – particularly if these activities are immoral or illegal.
- *Proof* – Critics have pointed out that there is no way of knowing objectively whether the findings of participant observation are actually true or not, since there is no possibility of replicating the research. In other words, the results may lack reliability.
- *Too specific* – Participant observation is usually used to study small groups of people who are not typical of the wider population. It is therefore difficult to claim that the findings can be generalized across the population as a whole.
- *Studying the powerless* – Finally, almost all participant observational studies are concerned with the least powerful groups in society – typically groups of young males or females who engage in deviant activities. Some critics argue that the information obtained does not help us to understand the more important issues in society.

Non-participant observation

Some researchers prefer to withdraw from participation and merely observe.

Advantages of non-participant observation

- *Bias* – As the researcher is less likely to be drawn into the group, the researchers' views are also less likely to be biased.
- *Influencing the group* – As the researcher is not making any decisions or joining in activities, the group may be less influenced than in participant observation.

Disadvantages of non-participant observation

- *Superficial* – The whole point of participant observation is to be a member of the group and experience life as the group experiences it. Merely observing leaves the researcher on the outside and may limit understanding.
- *Altering behaviour* – People may well act differently if they know they are being watched.

Covert and overt methods

Observational research is usually carried out amongst deviant groups or other groups who are unusual in some way, such as religious cults. Usually, these groups will not be very welcoming to a researcher. Before researchers begin their work, therefore, they must decide whether they wish to conduct the research in a covert or overt way.

The advantages of covert research

- *Forbidden fruit* – Researchers can enter forbidden areas, be fully accepted and trusted, and immerse themselves totally in the group being studied. This can generate a real sense of understanding of the views of the group.
- *Normal behaviour* – The group will continue to act naturally, unaware that they are being studied.

The disadvantages of covert research

- *Danger* – If the researcher's true role is uncovered, it may place the researcher in danger.
- *Ethical dilemmas* – First, there is the issue that it is wrong to study a group without telling them. Second, if the group engages in illegal or immoral activities, the researchers may have to engage in these activities as well. They may then find themselves in possession of knowledge that it may be immoral to withhold from the authorities.

The advantages of overt observation

- *The confidante* – As someone who has no role within the group, the researcher may be in the position of the trusted outsider and receive confidences from group members.
- *Honest* – The researcher is also able to play an open, clear and honest role, which will help minimize ethical dilemmas.
- *Other methods* – Researchers can supplement their observation with other methods, such as interviews and questionnaires.

The disadvantage of overt observation

● *Outsider* – There will be many situations where only a trusted insider will be let into the secrets. Anyone else, even a sympathetic observer, will be excluded.

Doing ethnographic research

The process of doing ethnographic research involves solving some key problems.

Joining the group

Observational studies usually involve groups of people on the margins of society, and the first problem is actually to contact and join the group. The sociologist has to find a place where the group goes and a situation in which they would accept the researcher. Shane Blackman (1997) studied a group of young homeless people, whom he met at an advice centre for young people. Sometimes sociologists make use of **gatekeepers** – members of the group who help the sociologist become accepted and introduce them to new people and situations. Andy Bennett (2004) describes how his route 'into' the local hip hop scene in Newcastle was facilitated by a local breakdancer who also worked as an instructor at a community dance project. Through this contact, he gained access to, or learned of, key figures in the scene. He would accompany the gatekeeper and a number of his dance students and other friends to around a dozen weekly hip hop nights held in a bar.

Methods in action

Dympna Devine (2003)
Observational research with primary-school children

Devine studied primary school pupils in three schools in Ireland: one was in a working-class area, another in a slightly more mixed area and the third in an affluent area. She mainly used 'extended observation' of the classroom and the playground, although she also used a range of other qualitative methods, including interviews and children's drawings and diaries. The interviews were friendly and informal and developed out of her observations.

The observational work was done by her joining classes and sitting in the room with them. In order to demonstrate that she was not a teacher or an adult in charge, she sat on a low chair at a desk, the same as the children. Furthermore, she was careful never to take the role of teacher by trying to impose any discipline or reporting any misbehaving. According to Devine, she was thus able to gain their trust. During school breaks, Devine usually went into the playground with the children and not to the staffroom. When she did go into the staffroom, it was not as another adult, but as an outsider and she tended to listen to the conversations of the teachers about the pupils. All this allowed her to build up a picture, from the children's perspective, of life in a primary school.

According to Devine, her conclusions are that what children want most from schooling is 'to be taught clearly, to be treated fairly and to be taken seriously by adults in school'. Devine suggests that the power in primary schools is too much in the hands of adults and teachers, and that children are unable to put their views across in such a way as to change things.

Devine, D. (2003) *Children, Power and Schooling,* Stoke on Trent: Trentham Books

1 Why can this research be best described as qualitative?

2 Of the four types of observational techniques we discuss in this topic, which do you think are used here?

3 How did Devine obtain the children's trust?

4 Devine claims to provide the perspective of the children. Do you think this is possible? Explain your answer.

5 Could this work claim to be generalizable? Explain your answer.

6 What other way of finding out about the views of young children could you use?

Acceptance by the group

There are often barriers of age, ethnicity and gender to overcome if the group are to accept the researcher. Moore (2004) researched young people 'hanging around'. He was initially unable to gain full acceptance because of his age. He overcame this by using young, female researchers.

Recording information

When researchers are actually hanging around with a group, it is difficult to make notes – particularly if engaged in covert research. Even if the group members are aware of the research, someone constantly making notes would disrupt normal activity and, of course, the researcher would also be unable to pay full attention to what was going on. In participant observational studies, therefore, researchers generally use a **field diary**. This is simply a detailed record of what happened, which the researcher writes up as often as possible. However, the research diary can also be a real weakness of the research.

Research diaries

Ethnographic researchers do not keep regular hours. Their observation may well go on into the night. It can be difficult to write up a diary each evening. Therefore, there is plenty of time to forget things and to distort them. Most observational studies include quotes, yet as it is impossible to remember the exact words, the quotes reflect what the researcher thinks the people said. This may be inaccurate.

Maintaining objectivity

In observational research, it is hard to remain objective. Close contact with the group under study means that feelings almost always emerge. In the introduction to Bourgois' (2003) study of crack cocaine dealers, he comments on how these dealers are his friends and how much he owes to the 'comments, corrections and discussions' provided by one particular dealer.

Influencing the situation

The more involved the researcher is with the people being studied, the greater the chance of influencing what happens. Stephen Lyng (1990) joined a group of males who engaged in 'edgework' – that is, putting their lives at risk through skydiving and (illegal) road motorcycle racing.

Lyng became so entangled in this style of life that he actually helped encourage others into life-risking behaviour.

Informal interviews

We discuss interviewing techniques in some detail in Topic 5, but it is worth stressing that informal interviewing is a very important part of qualitative research. The aim of informal interviews is to try to focus on a particular issue with one person and to guide them into explaining how they perceive that issue. It is better to view such an interview as a sort of 'controlled conversation'. Qualitative interviews tend to use '**open questions**', which allow the respondent to talk in some depth, choosing their own words and rely for their validity on a **rapport**, or friendly and trusting relationship, being established between the interviewer and respondent..

Usually, the conversations are recorded (with the respondent's permission) and the sociologist later listens again to the interview and makes notes. If a large number of interviews are conducted, sociologists tend to use special software which analyses conversations and collects words or themes which recur.

The advantage of qualitative interviews is that they allow a person to talk in depth about their views and it is often possible to get a real sense of a person's understanding of a situation. Often, new ideas are generated which the researcher had not previously thought of.

The disadvantage is that qualitative interviews do not lend themselves to statistical analysis and so it is difficult to generalize from them.

Focus groups

Focus groups are one of the more common types of research now used in sociology. These groups consist of a group of people who are gathered together by the researcher and asked to discuss a particular issue. In many ways, focus groups can be seen as a group informal interview. The researcher leads with an introduction and then allows the group to discuss the particular issue. The role of the researcher is simply to ensure that the discussion does not drift too far away from the desired research topic.

Focus groups can be very useful in providing insights into complex problems, although the researcher must be very careful not to 'lead' the group into any particular direction.

Key terms

Covert observation where the sociologist does not admit to being a researcher.

Empathic being able to put yourself in the position of others.

Ethnography describes the work of anthropologists who study simple, small-scale societies by living with the people and observing their daily lives. The term has been used by sociologists to describe modern-day observational studies.

Field diary a detailed record of events, conversations and thoughts kept by participant observers, written up as often as possible.

Gatekeeper person who can allow a researcher access to an individual, group or event.

Non-participant observation where the sociologist simply observes the group but does not seek to join in their activities.

Open questions allow respondents to express themselves fully.

Participant observation where the sociologist joins a group of people and studies their behaviour.

Qualitative research a general term for approaches to research that are less interested in collecting statistical data, and more interested in observing and interpreting the ways in which people behave.

Overt observation where the sociologist is open about the research role.

Rapport a friendly and effective relationship based on mutual trust.

Verstehen understanding of other people's meanings and actions based on the ability of the researcher to put themselves in the same position.

Check your understanding

1   What forms of observational studies are there?

2   What advantages does observational research have over quantitative methods?

3   Identify three problems associated with participant observation.

4   Suggest two examples of research where it would be possible to justify covert observation.

5   Suggest two examples of research situations where observational methods would be appropriate.

6   Suggest two examples of research situations where it might be more appropriate to undertake a survey.

Activities

Research idea

1   Carry out these two pieces of observation:
   ● Go to your local library. Spend one hour watching how people behave. Write down as accurate a description as you can.
   ● Then spend an evening at home 'observing' your family. Write down as accurate a description of home behaviour that evening as you can.

2   Which study is likely to be more biased? Why? Does this make it any less accurate? Are you able to get greater depth studying your family? Why? Do you think it would make a difference if you operated in a covert rather than an overt way with your family?

Web.tasks
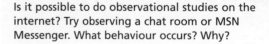

Is it possible to do observational studies on the internet? Try observing a chat room or MSN Messenger. What behaviour occurs? Why?

Chapter 3 Exploring Socialisation, Culture and Identity

GOTH: IDENTITY, STYLE AND SUBCULTURE

Paul Hodkinson

Paul Hodkinson investigated the Goth subculture in the 1980s. His research was ethnographic, using a variety of mainly qualitative methods including participant observation and semi-structured interviews, although he also used a mutiple-choice questionnaire.

As part of his research, Hodkinson attended Goth events around the country, describing himself as a 'critical insider'. He was an 'enthusiastic participant in the Goth scene' from the early 1990s and this allowed him easier access to Goths and their culture. However, he had to, remember to be 'critical' as well as an 'insider'; he had to step back to assess his role and his findings.

In addition to participant observation, Hodkinson conducted semi-structured interviews with 72 individuals. Among those interviewed were DJs, event promoters, fanzine editors and band members. The interviews were face to face except for four conducted by post and five by e-mail. Hodkinson was able to use his status as an insider to make the respondents feel at ease and allow the interviews to take the form of open, flowing conversation.

The questionnaire was given to a sample of 112 people at the Whitby Gothic Weekend in October 1997. As well as asking about occupation, ethnicity, relationships and children, Hodkinson asked about what they liked about the Whitby Gothic Weekend, their attendance at Goth events, the most important aspects of the Goth scene and where they bought music, clothes and accessories.

Adapted from Blundell, J. and Griffiths, J. (2008) *Sociology since 2000*. Lewes: Connect Publications

Hodkinson, P. (2002) *Goth: Identity, Style and Subculture*. Oxford: Berg

Using the extract above and your own sociological knowledge, explain and evaluate the use of qualitative methods to investigate the Goth subculture.

(52 marks)

Grade booster Getting top marks in this question

There are some key terms near the start of the extract that you will need to explain: ethnographic, qualitative methods, participant observation and semi-structured interviews. It is a good idea to link the choice of qualitative methods to an interpretive approach and to the idea of 'verstehen'. Go through each qualitative method used in turn and explain the reasons for Hodkinson's choice. You will also need to evaluate his approach overall and his use of individual methods. An interesting area for discussion is the issue of access and the role of 'critical insider'. The concepts of validity, reliability, representativeness and generalisability will help your evaluation, as will some knowledge of the alternative positivist approach.

TOPIC 5

Asking questions: questionnaires and interviews

Getting you thinking

Are you a top scorer in the friendship game, or someone your mates could do without? Take our quiz to find out.

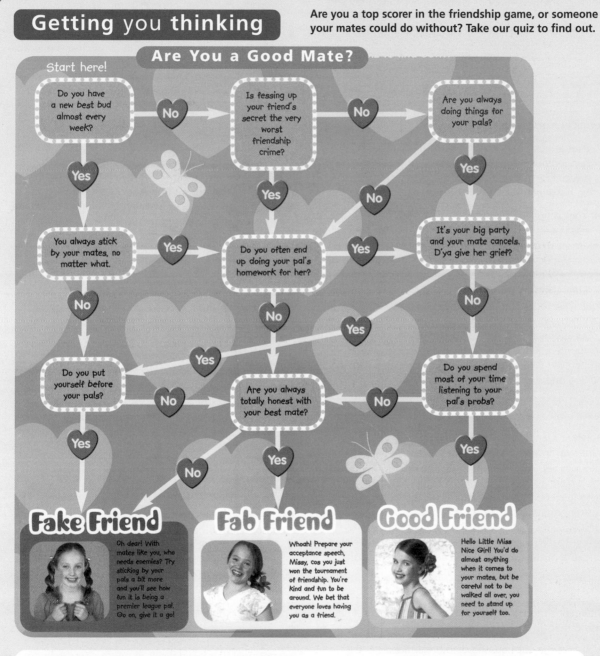

Are You a Good Mate?

Start here!

Do you have a new best bud almost every week? — No → Is fessing up your friend's secret the very worst friendship crime? — No → Are you always doing things for your pals?

You always stick by your mates, no matter what. — Yes → Do you often end up doing your pal's homework for her? — Yes → It's your big party and your mate cancels. D'ya give her grief?

Do you put yourself before your pals? — No → Are you always totally honest with your best mate? — No → Do you spend most of your time listening to your pal's probs?

Fake Friend
Oh dear! With mates like you, who needs enemies? Try sticking by your pals a bit more and you'll see how fun it is being a premier league pal. Go on, give it a go!

Fab Friend
Whoah! Prepare your acceptance speech, Missy, cos you just won the tournament of friendship. You're kind and fun to be around. We bet that everyone loves having you as a friend.

Good Friend
Hello Little Miss Nice Girl! You'd do almost anything when it comes to your mates, but be careful not to be walked all over, you need to stand up for yourself too.

1 Complete this questionnaire from *Go Girl* magazine to find whether or not you are a 'good mate'.

2 Do you think the conclusion about your strengths and weaknesses as a friend is justified? Explain your answer.

3 Do you think people will answer all the questions honestly? Explain your answer.

4 How good a questionnaire do you think this is? Why?

The most obvious way of finding out something is to ask questions. It is not surprising, then, to find that one of the most common methods of research used by sociologists is just to ask people questions about their attitudes and actions.

Sociologists ask questions in two main ways:

1 asking the questions face to face – the interview
2 writing the questions down and handing them to someone to complete – the questionnaire.

Which of the two methods is chosen depends upon which way of asking questions seems to fit the circumstances best – and has the best chance of gaining the information required.

Questionnaires

Questionnaires are used for reaching:

● a large number of people, since the forms can just be handed out
● a widely dispersed group of people, as they can simply be posted out.

Self-completion questionnaires are also less time-consuming for researchers than interviewing, as they do not require the researcher to go and talk to people face to face.

Anonymous questionnaires are also very useful if the researcher wishes to ask embarrassing questions about such things as sexual activities or illegal acts. People are more likely to tell the truth if they can do so anonymously than if they have to face an interviewer.

Questionnaires – particularly **closed** questionnaires – are a favourite method used by positivist sociologists, as they can be used in large numbers and the answers can be codified and subjected to statistical tests.

Types of questionnaires

There are many different types of questionnaire. They vary in the way in which they expect the person to answer the questions set. At one extreme are closed questionnaires, which have a series of questions with a choice of answers – all the respondent has to do is tick the box next to the most appropriate answer. At the other extreme are **open** questionnaires that seek the respondent's opinion by leaving space for their response. Some questionnaires contain a mixture of both open and closed questions.

The essence of a good questionnaire

When constructing a questionnaire, the sociologist has to ensure that:

● it asks the right questions to unearth exactly the information wanted
● the questions are asked in a clear and simple manner that can be understood by the people completing the questionnaire
● it is as short as possible, since people usually cannot be bothered to spend a long time completing questionnaires.

Issues in undertaking questionnaires

● Unfortunately, many people cannot be bothered to reply to questionnaires – that is, unless there is some benefit to them, such as the chance to win a prize. This is a serious drawback of questionnaires in research.
● A low **response rate** (the proportion of people who reply) makes a survey useless, as you do not know if the small number of replies is representative of all who were sent the questionnaire. Those who reply might have strong opinions on an issue, for example, whereas the majority may have much less firm convictions. Without an adequate number of replies, you will never know.
● It is difficult to go into depth in a questionnaire, because the questions need to be as clear and simple as possible.
● You can never be sure that the correct person answers. If you mail a questionnaire to one member of a household, how do you know that that person answers it?
● You can never be sure that the person who replies to the questionnaire interprets the questions in the way that the researcher intended, so their replies might actually mean something different from what the researcher believes they mean.
● Lying is also a danger. People may simply not tell the truth when answering questionnaires. There is little that the researcher can do, apart from putting in 'check questions' – questions that ask for the same information, but are phrased differently.

Interviews

An interview can either be a series of questions asked directly by the researcher to the respondent or it can be conducted as a discussion. Sociologists generally use interviews:

● if the subject of enquiry is complex, and a questionnaire would not allow the researcher to probe deeply
● when they want to compare their observations with the replies given by the respondents, to see if they appear true or not.

Advantages of interviews

● The interviewer can help explain questions to the respondent if necessary.
● Researchers are also sure that they are getting information from the right person.
● They can be organized virtually on the spot and so can be done immediately – as opposed to preparing a questionnaire, finding a sampling frame and posting the questionnaires out.
● There is a much higher response rate with interviews than with questionnaires, as the process is more personal and it is difficult to refuse a researcher when approached politely.

Types of interviews

Interviews fall between two extremes: **structured** and **unstructured**. At their most structured, they can be very tightly organized, with the interviewer simply reading out questions from a prepared questionnaire. At the other extreme they can be unstructured, where the interviewer simply has a basic area for discussion and asks any questions that seem relevant. Interviews that fall between the two extremes are known as 'semi-structured' interviews.

There are also individual and group interviews. Most people assume that an interview is between just two people, but in sociological research a group of people may get together to discuss an issue, rather than simply giving an answer to a question. Group interviews are commonly used where the researcher wants to explore the dynamics of the group, believing that a 'truer' picture emerges when the group are all together, creating a 'group dynamic'. An example of this is Mairtin Mac an Ghaill's *The Making of Men: Masculinities, Sexualities and Schooling* (1994), in which a group of gay students discuss their experiences of school.

Issues in undertaking interviews

Influencing the replies

Interviews are a form of conversation between people and, as in any conversation, likes and dislikes emerge. The problem is to ensure that the interviewer does not influence the replies provided by the respondent in any way – known as **interviewer bias**. For example, respondents may want to please the interviewer and so give the replies they think the interviewer wants. Influences that can affect the outcome of the interview include manner of speech, ethnic origin, sex or personal habits.

Lying

There is no reason why people should tell the truth to researchers, and this is particularly true when a sensitive issue is being researched. When questioned about sexual activities or numbers of friends, for example, people may exaggerate in order to impress the interviewer.

Interview reliability

The aim of the research process is to conduct enough interviews for the researcher to be able to make an accurate generalization. However, if interviews are actually different from each other as a result of the interaction, then it is wrong to make generalizations.

Recording the information

Unstructured interviews are generally recorded and usually require **transcribing** (writing up), which is time-consuming. Tizard and Hughes (1991) recorded interviews with students to find out how they went about learning – every hour of interview took 17 hours to transcribe and check! However, writing down the replies at the time is slow and can disrupt the flow of an interview.

Operationalizing concepts

Ideas that are discussed in sociology, such as 'sexual deviance', 'educational failure', or 'ill health', are all pretty vague when you spend a few moments thinking about

them. Take educational failure – does this mean not having A levels? Perhaps it means having 'low' grades at GCSE (whatever the concept 'low grades' means)? Or only having one or two GCSEs? You can see that a concept as apparently simple as 'educational failure' is actually capable of having different meanings to different people.

However, concepts such as educational failure or ill health are used all the time in sociological research, so sociologists have had to find a way around this problem when they ask people questions about the concepts. For example, if you were to ask somebody if they 'suffered from ill health', the reply would depend upon the individual definition of ill health and different people might (in fact we know they *do*) use very different definitions of ill health.

In research, we need to use concepts such as sexual deviance, educational failure and ill health, but in a way which is valid and reliable (see p. 166). By this, we mean that the concepts are accurately measured (valid), and that each time we use them, we are sure that every respondent understands the concept in the same way (reliable).

When concepts are used in research, sociologists say that they are **operationalizing** them. So, if there is a piece of research to find out the levels of ill health amongst retired people, the concept 'ill health' will need to be operationalized. The problem when operationalizing a concept is how to ensure that it is accurately and reliably measured.

Indicators

The answer is that sociologists use **indicators**. An indicator is something 'concrete' that stands in for the abstract concept, but which people can understand and sociologists can actually measure. Let us return to the example of 'ill health'. It is possible to ask people the following:

- whether they suffer from any specific diseases or any long-term disability
- whether they are receiving any specific medication
- how frequently they have attended a GP surgery or clinic in the last year.

Problems with indicators

An indicator then, is a short cut sociologists use to measure an abstract concept. Unfortunately, short cuts in any academic area of study bring problems. We need to remember that what is actually being measured are the *indicators,* not *the actual concept.* This may not be a problem if the indicators are a perfect reflection of the original concept, but this is rarely the case. Let's go back to ill health. One question used is how often people have visited the GP surgery in the last year. However, this does not necessarily tell us about *levels* of health, it may just tell us that some people tend to visit the GP (whether they need to or not) more than others. Someone might be very ill but refuse to visit a GP. For example, there is considerable evidence that older people visit GPs less often than their medical conditions warrant.

Furthermore, it is not the actual number of visits that could be considered important, but the reasons why they went. A younger person may be seeing a GP for contraceptive advice, while an older person may be concerned about a heart condition.

Coding

Using clear indicators in research allows answers to be **coded** – that is broken down into simple, distinct answers that can be counted. The researchers can simply add up the numbers of people replying to each category of indicator and then make statements such as '82 per cent of people have seen a doctor on their own behalf in 2002' (Department of Health 2003).

Questions and values

Both questionnaires and interviews share the problem of the values of the researcher creeping into the questions asked. Two problems are particularly important – using leading questions and using loaded words:

- *Leading questions*: Researchers write or ask questions that suggest what the appropriate answer is, e.g. 'Wouldn't you agree that …?'

Methods in action

Stephen Frosh et al. (2002) Asking boys questions

Stephen Frosh wanted to find out how boys in the early years of secondary school came to an idea of what masculinity means to them and how this impacts upon their behaviour and their learning. Frosh undertook two main types of qualitative research: group interviews/focus groups and informal interviews. In total, 78 boys were interviewed.

Each interviewer was given a list of topics and possible questions which guided them through the interview. This is a perfect example of qualitative, semi-structured interviewing methods. All the answers were recorded and then transcribed, and the researchers looked for the key themes that emerged.

General self-description
- Could you tell me three things you think are important about yourself?

Ethnicity
- What ethnic group do you think you belong to?
- Do you see some boys as belonging to a different ethnic group to you? How would you describe their background? Do you go around with boys from this/these backgrounds? Why/why not? Do you do the same things with them as boys from your 'own' ethnic background?
- Can you imagine having a girlfriend from a different ethnic group?
- Do you think boys are treated differently because of where their parents come from? Is your ethnic background important to you? What difference does it make being a boy from this background? Are you pleased you are from this background?
- Have you ever thought you'd not like to be?
- Are there things you dislike about boys from other ethnic and cultural backgrounds?
- Are there things you admire about boys from other ethnic and cultural backgrounds?

Sources: Frosh, S., Phoenix, A. and Pattman, R. (2002) *Young Masculinities: Understanding Boys in Contemporary Society,* Basingstoke: Palgrave Macmillan; Youth Lifetime Leisure Survey, Home Office, www.data-archive.ac.uk/doc/4345/mrdoc/pdf/a4345uab.pdf

Youth Lifetime Leisure Survey

The following questions were taken from a quantitative study into bullying by young people. It was part of a Home Office national survey and was completed by 4800 people between the ages of 12 and 30.

2.2 BULLYING

Would you say that students are bullied by other students …

a   a lot   b   a little   c   or not at all?

In the last 12 MONTHS, have you been bullied by other students?

a   Yes   b   No

If yes … how often has this happened in the last 12 months?

a   Every day   e   Once a month
b   A few times a week   f   Less often than this
c   Once or twice a week   g   It varies
d   Once every two weeks

In the last 12 months, have other students made you give them money or your personal possessions?

a   Yes   b   No

1   Compare the questions in the two extracts

2   What are the advantages and disadvantages of each type of questioning?

3   Which type of questioning do you think is more time consuming? Why?

4   Which type of questioning do you think is likely to lead to greater reliability? Explain your answer.

5   Which type of questioning do you think is likely to lead to greater validity? Explain your answer.

6   Considering only the second set of questions on ethnicity, do you think that there might be different answers if the questions were asked by:

   (a)   females rather than males?

   (b)   African-Caribbean-origin researchers rather than White researchers?

   Explain your answer.

7   Explain how bias might possibly creep into this form of research interview?

- *Loaded words and phrases*: Researchers use particular forms of language that either indicate a viewpoint or will generate a particular positive or negative response – for example, 'termination of pregnancy' (a positive view) or 'abortion' (a negative view); 'gay' or 'homosexual'.

Interviews and scientific methods

Interviews are used by all kinds of sociologists. The more structured the interviews, the more likely they are to be used in a quantitative way to produce statistics. The more unstructured the interviews (including group interviews), the more likely they are to be of use to interpretive sociologists.

Issues of validity and reliability

Validity

Questions asked should actually produce the information required. This is a crucial issue in sociological research and is known as the issue of **validity** (i.e. getting at the truth). The type of questions asked in the questionnaire or interview must allow the respondent to give a true and accurate reply.

Reliability

The researcher must ensure not only that the design of the question gets to the truth of the matter, but also that it does so consistently. If the question means different things to different people, or can be interpreted differently, then the research is not reliable. **Reliability**, then, refers to the fact that all completed questionnaires and interviews can be accurately compared.

Check your understanding

1 What are the three elements of a good questionnaire?

2 Why are response rates so important?

3 In what situations is it better to use self-completion questionnaires rather than interviews?

4 When would it be more appropriate to use open questions? Give an example of an open question.

5 Explain the difference between structured, semi-structured, unstructured and group interviews.

6 What do we mean by 'transcribing'?

7 What do we mean when we talk about 'loaded questions' and 'leading questions'? Illustrate your answer with an example of each and show how the problem could be overcome by writing a 'correct' example of the same questions.

Activities

Research idea

Working with a partner of the opposite sex, draft guide questions for an unstructured interview with young men about their attitudes to sex. Each partner should then conduct three of these interviews.

Discuss the different ways interviewees responded. Are the young men more honest and open with a male or female interviewer or is there no difference? Do you think that one of the interviewers obtained more valid results? If so, what reasons can you suggest for this?

Web.tasks

1 Go to the website of the opinion polling organization Market and Opinion Research International at www.mori.com

Find out how MORI go about asking questions.

2 Search the world wide web for other examples of questionnaires. Assess the strengths and weaknesses of the question design.

YOUNG MASCULINITIES

Stephen Frosh, Ann Phoenix and Rob Pattman (2002)

This research arises out of a large-scale project on 11-14 year old boys in London schools that started in 1997. It explores the experiences of the boys, focusing on how they create a sense of identity.

The boys were taken from 12 secondary schools in London, four of the schools were male only and eight were co-educational. The initial sample consisted of 245 11-14 year old boys.

The boys were studied in focus groups and a second interview took place with 71 of the sample. Twenty-four girls were also interviewed, with the focus on their thoughts about boys.

Interviews took place on school premises. The rooms used were arranged to encourage openness. Group interviews were unstructured but the interviewer had a list of topics and hints in case certain issues did not arise naturally. The interviewer took the role of a facilitator, encouraging the respondent to develop and reflect on issues raised in the conversation. The second interview was used to explore contradictions, gaps and repetitions from the first group interview and offered the respondent the chance to comment on the process of the interview itself.

The interview process was important. The interviewer felt his role was to encourage the boys to talk about themselves and so aimed to create a non-judgmental and positive atmosphere in the room. After each interview he made notes recording his impressions of the interviews, including his emotional response. He began to like the boys even when they were open about their racism, homophobia, bullying and violence.

The study found that boys had to be seen to be different and separate from girls and things that were feminine by association. Popular masculinity also required the male to be 'hard'. This was illustrated through success at sport, 'coolness' and casual attitudes towards school work and the ability to use swear words - 'cussing'.

Adapted from Blundell, J. and Griffiths, J. (2008) *Sociology since 2000*. Lewes: Connect Publications

Frosh, S., Phoenix, A. and Pattman, R. (2002) *Young Masculinities*. Basingstoke: Palgrave

Using the extract above and your own sociological knowledge, explain and evaluate the use of interviewing to investigate the masculine identities of 11-14 year old boys.

 (52 marks)

Grade booster Getting top marks in this question

Your answer will need to make clear the differences between the various methods of asking questions and to explain the reasoning behind the qualitative approaches to questioning used in this study. For example, does the study of identities and experiences require flexible, qualitative methods? Why? The use of individual and group interviews will need to be explained and evaluated in terms of validity, reliability, representativeness and generalisability. In this case, did the researchers focus on validity at the expense of reliability?

TOPIC 6

Secondary sources of data

Getting you thinking

You are a sociologist in the future – 100 years from now. You have access to Facebook profiles in 2008 and want to use them to find out about people's lives in the early years of the 21st century.

1   What insights into life in 2008 could be gained from looking at Facebook profiles?

2   Suggest some ways in which these profiles could be analysed. Think of both qualitative and quantitative approaches.

3   Evaluate the validity and representativeness of Facebook profiles as sources of secondary data.

4   Discuss the usefulness of the worldwide web as a source of secondary data. Use examples to support your points.

Not all research uses primary sources – that is, observing people in real life, sending out questionnaires or carrying out interviews. Many sociologists prefer to use material collected and published by other people. This material is known as **secondary data**.

Secondary data consist of a very wide range of material collected by organizations and individuals for their own purposes, and include sources as complex as official government statistics at one extreme and as personal as diaries at the other. These data include

written material, sound and visual images. Such material can be from the present day or historical data. Finally, and most commonly, secondary sources include the work of sociologists, which is read, analysed and commented on by other sociologists.

Secondary sources are invaluable to sociologists, both on their own and in combination with primary sources. It is unheard of for a researcher not to refer to some secondary sources.

Why sociologists use secondary sources

Some of the main reasons for using secondary sources include the following:

- The information required already exists as secondary data.
- Historical information is needed, but the main participants are dead or too old to be interviewed.
- The researcher is unable for financial or other reasons to visit places to collect data at first hand.
- The subject of the research concerns illegal activities and it is unsafe for the researcher to collect primary data.
- Data need to be collected about groups who are unwilling to provide accounts of their activities – for instance, extreme religious sects who do not want their activities to be open to study.

Errors and biases

Whenever sociologists use a secondary source, they must be aware that the person who first created the source did so for a specific reason, and this could well create **bias**. A diary, for example, gives a very one-sided view of what happened and one that is most likely to be sympathetic. Official statistics may have been constructed to shed a good light on the activities of the government – for example, so that they can claim they are 'winning the war against crime'. Even the work of previous sociologists may contain errors and biases.

Types of secondary data

Sociologists commonly use all these types of secondary data:

- previous sociological research
- official publications, including statistics and reports
- diaries and letters
- novels and other works of fiction
- oral history and family histories
- the media.

Previous sociological research

Previous studies as a starting point

Whenever sociologists undertake a study, the first thing they do is to carry out a **literature search** – that is, go to the library or the internet and look up every available piece of sociological research on the topic of interest. The sociologist can then see the ways in which the topic has been researched before, the conclusions reached and the theoretical issues thrown up. Armed with this information, the researcher can then construct the new research study to explore a different 'angle' on the problem or simply avoid the mistakes made earlier.

However, there are sometimes methodological errors in published research, as well as possible bias in the research findings. There have been many examples of research that

Methods in action

George Davey Smith *et al.* (2003) The health of ethnic minorities: a meta-study

George Davey Smith and his colleagues were concerned that there was relatively little information on the health of ethnic minorities in Great Britain. They therefore conducted a **meta-study** to try to provide an overall picture of health care. They looked at data from a range of surveys including official publications, small-scale surveys and earlier sociological studies. Putting all of this together, they provided a picture of standards of health for different ethnic groups in Britain, taking into account the impact of social class. In order to do this, they also had to review a wide range of theoretical and methodological books and articles. The study therefore includes secondary research based upon both theoretical and statistical studies, from government as well as academic sources.

They found that, overall, the health standards of ethnic minorities in Britain were worse than those of the general population, and that these differences were most apparent in childhood and old age. They found that most previous studies tended to explain any differences in health between ethnic minorities and the majority population in terms of cultural, dietary or genetic differences. However, they concluded that ethnicity by itself does not explain these differences. They suggest instead that differences in health are closely linked to social class and income.

Davey Smith, G., Chaturverdi, N., Harding, S., Nazroo, J. and Williams, R. (2003) *Health Inequalities: Lifecourse approaches*, Bristol: Policy Press

1 Why did the researchers use a meta-study?

2 How did the use of secondary sources allow them to reach different conclusions from earlier research?

has formed the basis for succeeding work and that only many years later has been found to be faulty. A famous piece of anthropological research that was used for 40 years before it was found to be centrally flawed was Mead's *Coming of Age in Samoa* (1928). Mead made a number of mistakes in her interpretation of the behaviour of the people she was studying, but as no one knew this, many later studies used her (incorrect) findings in their work.

Reinterpreting previous studies

Often sociologists do not want to carry out a new research project, but prefer instead to examine previous research in great detail in order to find a new interpretation of the original research results. Secondary data then provides all the information that is needed.

Official publications

Statistics

Statistics compiled by governments and reputable research organizations are particularly heavily used by sociologists. These statistics often provide far greater scale and detail than a sociologist could manage. It is also much cheaper to work on statistics already collected than repeating the work.

The government will usually produce these statistics over a number of years (for example, the government statistical publication *Social Trends* has been published for 30 years), so comparisons can be made over a long period of time.

However, while these official statistics have many advantages, there are also some pitfalls that researchers have to be aware of. The statistics are collected for administrative reasons and the classifications used may omit crucial information for sociologists. For example, sociologists may be interested in exploring issues of 'race'

or gender, but this information might be missing from the official statistics.

Official statistics may be affected by political considerations, such as when they are used to assist the image of the government of the day. They may also reflect a complex process of interaction and negotiation – as is the case with crime statistics – and may well need to be the focus of investigation themselves!

Reports and government inquiries

The civil service and other linked organizations will often produce official reports which investigate important problems or social issues. However, although they draw together much information on these issues, they are constrained by their 'remit', which states the limits of their investigations. The government and other powerful bodies are therefore able to exclude discussion of issues that they do not want to become the centre of public attention. Government discussions on issues related to drugs, for example, are usually carefully controlled so that legalization of drugs is simply not discussed.

Diaries and letters

It is difficult to understand a historical period or important social events if the researcher has no way of interviewing the people involved. Usually, only the official information or media accounts are available. Using such things as letters and diaries helps to provide an insight into how participants in the events felt at the time.

Methods in action

Gina Oliver (2004)
Alone in the mainstream

Gina Oliver's book combines a detailed autobiography of the experience of being deaf throughout the education system in the USA, from primary school to university, and the obstacles which are placed on deaf schoolchildren who seek to be integrated into mainstream schooling.

In order to go beyond her personal experience, Gina Oliver posted a notice on a US website for people who have hearing problems, asking them to contact her with their experiences in the education system. Oliver also wrote to a range of educational institutions and to her own university, asking them to provide publicity for her research. Oliver then asked the respondents to write an essay about their experiences:

≪ *Please write a short (or long, if you like) essay describing the reasons why you would like to be included in this research project. Feel free to share anything you would like about your experience as the only deaf or hard of hearing child in your mainstream school. Feel free to include your suggestions for children who are currently mainstreamed.* ≫

More than 100 respondents chose to respond to this essay question; many wrote quite profusely. Their essays illustrated their eagerness to share their stories and pervasive concern for today's young deaf people.

Having analysed these essays, Oliver then asked a number of people to write about four key themes which she identified, and 60 deaf adults then wrote about their experiences.

Source: Oliver, G. (2004) *Alone in the Mainstream: A Deaf Woman Remembers Public School*, Washington, DC: Gallaudet University Press

1   Why would reading Oliver's work provide us with an unusual insight into the educational experience of deaf children?

2   Why might this be better than asking her and other deaf people about their experiences directly?

3   What weaknesses can you see in Oliver asking other deaf people to write 'essays' about their childhood experiences?

4   Is this work 'value free'? Justify your answer. What issues are raised by your answer?

5   What other ways could this research be done:

   (a) from a quantitative approach?

   (b) from a qualitative approach?

However, problems can occur, as the writers may have distorted views of what happened, or they may well be justifying or glorifying themselves in their accounts. Almost any politician's memoirs prove this.

Novels

Novels can give an insight into the attitudes and behaviour of particular groups, especially if the author is drawn from one of those groups. However, they are fiction and will exaggerate actions and values for the sake of the story. Also, writing books is typically a middle- or upper-class activity, which may limit the insight that can be gained about the particular group featured.

Oral history and family histories

The events to be studied may have taken place some considerable time ago, but there may be older people alive who can recall the events or who themselves were told about them. There may be recordings available of people (now dead) talking of their lives. People often have old cine-film or family photos of events of interest. All of these can be collected and used by the researcher to help understand past events. Of course, the best of all these methods is the interview, with the older person recalling events of long ago (although quite where the line can be drawn between this as secondary research and as a simple interview is rather unclear).

These approaches do all share the usual problems, for instance that events may be reinterpreted by older people or by families to throw a positive light on their actions and, of course, to hide any harm they did to others. Also, memories may be faulty or influenced by intervening knowledge.

The media and content analysis

A huge amount of material is available from newspapers, the internet, magazines and television. In fact, so much material is available that one of the major problems of using the mass media as secondary data lies with the selection of material: on exactly what grounds are items included or excluded? Researchers have to be very careful to include all relevant material and not to be biased in their selection in order to 'prove' their point. Two of the best-known studies using **content analysis** have been strongly criticized for just this. The Glasgow University Media Group's publications have explored a range of topics including television news, representations of mental illness in the media and the portrayal of the 1991 Iraq war; critics claim that they were selective in their choice of material and that they applied their own interpretations to the selections.

However, trying to understand accurately the printed and broadcast media is not just a matter of watching out for bias; there is also the issue of how we interpret the material. When looking at pictures or reading a story in a magazine, different people find different meanings in the material. There are many factors influencing this, but one crucial factor is our own beliefs and attitudes towards the subject that we are reading about. The importance of this for research using secondary data is that we must not assume that what we read or see is the same as it was for the original readers or viewers.

Key terms

Bias where the material reflects a particular viewpoint to the exclusion of others. This may give a false impression of what happened. This is a particularly important problem for secondary sources.

Content analysis exploring the contents of the various media in order to find out how a particular issue is presented.

Literature search the process whereby a researcher finds as much published material as possible on the subject of interest. Usually done through library catalogues or the internet.

Meta-study a secondary analysis using all or most of the published information on a particular topic.

Secondary data data already collected by someone else for their own purposes.

Check your understanding

1 What are secondary data?

2 Why do sociologists use secondary sources?

3 What are the disadvantages of using secondary sources?

4 What are the advantages and disadvantages of using official statistics and other government documents?

5 What are the advantages and disadvantages of using qualitative secondary data such as diaries?

Activities

Research idea

Collect the prospectuses of various universities, colleges or schools. Look at the photographs in each. How do they portray their students? From your own experience of education, do you think this is an accurate portrayal? What motives might there be for the particular images presented? Are there any negative photographs or comments in the text about the educational institution?

Web.tasks

Find the website 'Corporate Watch' at www.corporatewatch.org.uk

Look up information about any two huge corporations (for example, Microsoft or Disney). Then go to the website belonging to that corporation. What are the differences between the information given?
Which do you think is more accurate? Why?

Secondary sources of data

UK CHRISTIAN HANDBOOK: RELIGIOUS TRENDS 6 2006/07

Edited by Peter Brierley (2007)

Christian Research is an organisation that exists to provide helpful information to church leaders. The purpose of the census carried out here is to track the extent of the decline and to determine which forms of Christianity and in which areas are in decline and which are holding their own or even growing.

The census was carried out on 8th May 2005. All 37,501 churches in England were contacted in writing and responses, either mailed or online, were received from just over half (50.02%). The response rate was higher for the larger denominations such as the Church of England and the Roman Catholic Church but much lower for Pentecostal and other churches, which are less likely to have paid leaders. Estimates were made for churches that did not respond, based partly on the assumption that their returns would be like those of similar churches, and partly on responses to earlier surveys.

The two page census form is reproduced in the handbook. It contains questions on attendance at services, the age, gender and ethnic group of those attending, attendance at worship at other times of the week, Alpha courses, support for charities and involvement in local communities.

For the purpose of the census, 'church' was defined as, 'a body of people meeting on a Sunday in the same premises primarily for public worship at regular intervals'. This definition allows for the inclusion of, for example, chapels in hospitals and in the armed forces. In addition, groups meeting on Saturdays such as Seventh Day Adventists were also included, as were groups meeting at least monthly. The day of the census was the 60th anniversary of VE Day, which may have increased attendance when churches held special services. Some churches included all who attended, others left out of the census return those who were not regular attendees whilst others took the census on a different Sunday which would be more 'normal'.

The percentage of the population attending church on the census Sunday was 6.3%. While churchgoing overall was in decline, about a third of churches had grown since 1998. These churches tended to have higher than average proportions of young worshippers.

Adapted from Blundell, J. and Griffiths, J. (2008) *Sociology since 2000.* Lewes: Connect Publications

Brierley, P. (ed.) (2007) *UK Christian Handbook: Religious Trends 6 2006–7.* Swindon: Christian Research

Using the extract above and your own sociological knowledge, explain and evaluate the use of church statistics to investigate changes in religious participation in Britain.

(52 marks)

Grade booster **Getting top marks in this question**

Start by identifying the use of statistics as a form of secondary data. Then move on to explain the advantages of using these church statistics. Sample size and geographical coverage are worth mentioning. But there are many problems that will need to be discussed. Some of these centre around the problems of operationalizing the idea of 'religious participation'. Others concern issues such as the possible lack of objectivity of the organization that collected the figures, variations in the way different churches collected the data and the day chosen to collect the data.

Exam Practice

MIGRANTS' LIVES BEYOND THE WORKPLACE: THE EXPERIENCES OF CENTRAL AND EAST EUROPEANS IN THE UK

Sarah Spencer, Martin Ruhs, Bridget Anderson and Ben Rogaly (2007)

The aim of this study was to investigate the experiences of Central and Eastern European workers in Britain. In-depth interviews and diaries produced qualitative data and a survey was conducted to provide quantitative material. Material was collected from employers, host families of au pairs and from migrants themselves. The people who were analysed in the study cannot be said to be representative of all migrants because there was no database from which names could be randomly selected. Instead, certain types of people were selected to ensure that a wide range of migrants were contacted.

Structured interviews were conducted in the spring of 2004 to provide data for the survey and then re-interviews took place using an in-depth semi-structured format in the winter of that year. The interviews focused on Czechs, Slovaks, Lithuanians and Poles because they constituted a major immigrant group. In addition, Ukrainians and Bulgarians were interviewed because they would not have been affected by the expansion of the EU.

Both the structured survey and in-depth interviews were conducted in the home language of the migrants to ensure that there was clear understanding of the questions. The initial survey interviews took one hour, and the in-depth interviews were designed to be tape recorded. Samples were generally large, with 333 people interviewed in the first wave, 54% of whom were male, though more of the Czechs and Slovaks were female. In addition, 12 respondents from the sample were asked to complete diaries and finally to write an essay. These respondents were spread through the nationalities.

Most migrants intended to return to their home countries. Many had dependents to whom they were sending money. Others had children in the UK and wished to stay for their sake. The longer they stayed in Britain, the more likely they were to want to stay. However, the main reason for people staying in Britain related to the economic situation at home. Most would have preferred to return to their home countries if acceptable and higher-paid work was available.

Adapted from Blundell, J. and Griffiths, J. (2008) *Sociology since 2000*. Lewes: Connect Publications

Spencer, S., Ruhs, M., Anderson, B. and Rogaly, B. (2007) *Migrants' Lives Beyond the Workplace: The Experiences of Central and East Europeans in the UK*. York: Joseph Rowntree Foundation

Explain and evaluate the use of mixed methods to investigate the lives of Eastern European migrants to Britain. *(52 marks)*

Mixed methods are when the researcher combines quantitative and qualitative methods in order to get a balanced and broader picture of society. This is also known as methodological pluralism. Triangulation is when different methods are used to check each other, as Eileen Barker did in her book about the Moonies. Mixing methods should let the sociologist achieve reliability, validity and representativeness.

It is important to study Eastern European migrants as there are so many of them and they might experience racism and discrimination. However, not every nationality is covered in the research.

It is not clear how the sample was collected although it may have been from employers and host families. There was no database available so a random sample could not be selected. However, the researchers did use a large sample of 333 and they did select 'certain types of people to ensure that a wide range of migrants were contacted'. So the sample should have been quite representative and the findings generalisable.

It's always a good idea to define key terms near the start of an answer but they need to be linked to the issue in the question. The last sentence introduces important concepts but their importance is not explained

Good evaluative points although not developed and not linked to the study of migrants.

The question asks about mixed methods rather than sampling so this issue is not explicitly relevant unless linked to the idea of mixed methods by, for example, explaining why a larger sample is possible when using quantitative methods.

Structured interviews were used. These are a quantitative method which are good at producing facts and figures. They would probably have been used to collect background information from the migrants – how long they had lived in Britain, the work they did, their families and so on. Each respondent would have answered the same questions in the same order so there should be good levels of reliability in the data collected.

> A bit of speculation here about the purposes of the structured interviews whish is placed in the context of studying migrants. The point about reliability needs developing.

The interviews were conducted in the language used by the respondents so that would have helped the data be valid and would have helped establish a rapport with the interviewer. We don't know where the interviews took place but if they were in the home of the migrants this would have put them at ease even more and helped validity.

> This paragraph explains the use of structured interviews in terms of their validity and uses information from the extract. A new concept – rapport – is introduced and explained in the context of the research.

However, the structured interviews lasted an hour so the interviewer may have moved away from the set questions, thus affecting reliability. As the questions were probably closed, the interviewer could not have let the respondent express themselves in their own words so they may not have been able to say everything they wanted to so validity could be a problem.

> The word 'however' signals that the answer is now going to look at disadvantages and points are introduced about problems of reliability and validity. However, they could do with further development.

The in depth interviews were qualitative and allowed the migrants to talk at length in their own words and so they could really explain their experiences, which was the aim of the research. These interviews were semi-structured so the interviewer will have guided the respondent, allowing some reliability as well as validity. Also, they were recorded so there will be an accurate record of the data and it can be checked – again helping reliability.

> This paragraph explains the use of semi-structured interviews but needs to be linked to the research context and to develop points rather more – for example, how reliability and validity might have been achieved.

However, the migrants may have been suspicious of the motives of the interviewers so not told them the whole truth, especially if they were working illegally.

> This is a good evaluative point which is not raised in the extract.

The diaries are a method which would allow the researchers to see how the migrants spent their time and the essay would let the migrants express themselves in their own words without any influence from the researchers. These are both qualitative methods. However, if the migrants cannot read or write very well then these methods will not produce valid data.

> Good to notice these two other qualitative methods and they are explained and evaluated in the context of the group being studies, although again, they are not fully developed.

Combining the qualitative and quantitative methods should let the researchers achieve both reliability and validity and mean that the research provides a balanced picture including both facts (from the structured interviews) and feelings, motives and experiences (from the qualitative methods). The best aspects of positivist and interpretive approaches are combined.

> This conclusion focuses on the use of mixed methods but this should have been a more consistent theme of the answer. Similarly, the last line is a bit late to bring in these two theoretical positions – they deserve more discussion.

$\frac{31}{52}$

An examiner comments

There is evidence of understanding in this answer, for example of key methodological concepts and of the study itself. But at times the question about mixed methods gets lost as the answer focuses more on the individual methods rather than their combination. It is only at the beginning and end that paragraphs are devoted to the central issue. Some points are sensitively tied to the research context but at other times general points are made without a specific link to the study of Eastern European migrants. Many of the points raised – although accurate – are in need of development. More explanation is required to get into the higher mark bands. Finally, it is never a good idea to raise significant issues right at the end of an answer and this is exactly what happens here when positivism and interpretive sociology are introduced.

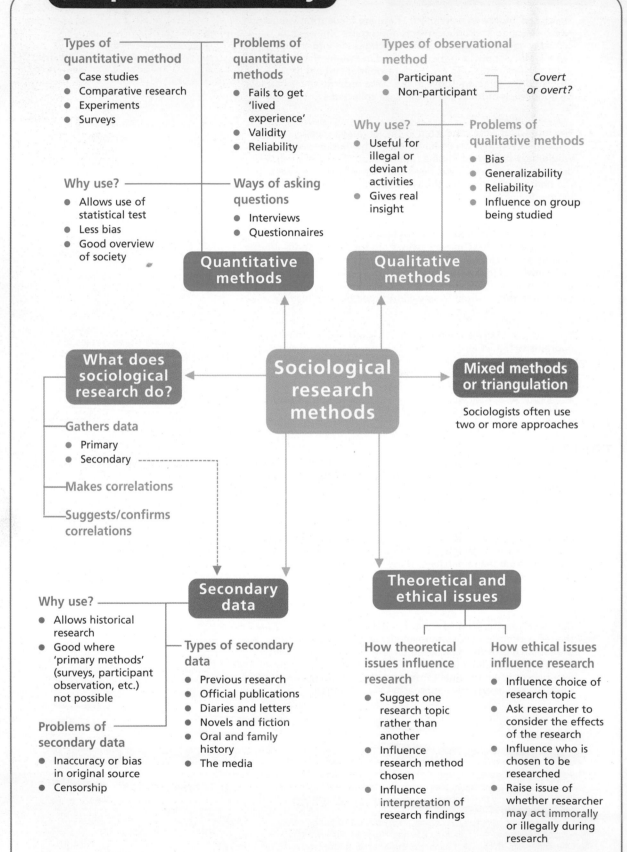

Chapter 3 Summary

Types of quantitative method
- Case studies
- Comparative research
- Experiments
- Surveys

Problems of quantitative methods
- Fails to get 'lived experience'
- Validity
- Reliability

Why use?
- Allows use of statistical test
- Less bias
- Good overview of society

Ways of asking questions
- Interviews
- Questionnaires

Types of observational method
- Participant
- Non-participant

Covert or overt?

Why use?
- Useful for illegal or deviant activities
- Gives real insight

Problems of qualitative methods
- Bias
- Generalizability
- Reliability
- Influence on group being studied

Quantitative methods

Qualitative methods

What does sociological research do?

Sociological research methods

Mixed methods or triangulation

Sociologists often use two or more approaches

Gathers data
- Primary
- Secondary

Makes correlations

Suggests/confirms correlations

Secondary data

Theoretical and ethical issues

Why use?
- Allows historical research
- Good where 'primary methods' (surveys, participant observation, etc.) not possible

Types of secondary data
- Previous research
- Official publications
- Diaries and letters
- Novels and fiction
- Oral and family history
- The media

How theoretical issues influence research
- Suggest one research topic rather than another
- Influence research method chosen
- Influence interpretation of research findings

How ethical issues influence research
- Influence choice of research topic
- Ask researcher to consider the effects of the research
- Influence who is chosen to be researched
- Raise issue of whether researcher may act immorally or illegally during research

Problems of secondary data
- Inaccuracy or bias in original source
- Censorship

Sociology of the Family

OCR specification		Coverage
Key concepts and key trends within the family		
Key concepts and structural trends	• relating to nuclear families, extended families and households, and key structural trends	Covered in Topic 1
Trends in families and households	• over the last 30 years including family size, marriage, divorce, cohabitation, single-parent families and single-person households.	Covered in Topics 3 and 4.
The role of the family in society		
Functionalist views of the role of the family.		Covered in Topics 1 and 2.
Marxist views of the family.		Covered in Topics 1 and 2.
Family diversity		
Different types of contemporary family diversity	• including single-parent families, beanpole families, reconstituted families, cultural diversity, class diversity and sexual diversity.	Covered in Topics 3 and 4.
Contemporary views of family diversity	• including post-modernism, New Right and New Labour views.	Covered in Topics 3 and 4.
Roles, responsibilities and relationships within the family		
Roles, responsibilities and relationships in family life between men and women, and between children and parents		Covered in Topic 5.
Sociological explanations of family relationships	• functionalism, Marxism and varieties of feminism	Covered in Topic 5.
The dark side of family life		Covered in Topic 5.
Demographic changes	• including the ageing of the population and changes in birth and fertility rates and their impact on family life, especially on family size and extended kinship ties.	Covered in Topic 5.

TOPIC 1

The family, social structure and social change

Getting you thinking

Above an Ik village clings to the hillside
Right: an Ik child called Lokiira

1   How do the Ik define the family?

2   Given your own experience of family life, think of three features of the family that you would expect to find in all families, wherever they are. How do these three features differ from the Ik?

3   In what ways might some British families share some of the characteristics of the Ik?

The family does not feature heavily in the culture of the Ik of Northern Uganda. In fact, as far as the Ik are concerned, the family means very little. This is because the Ik face a daily struggle to survive in the face of drought, famine and starvation. Anyone who cannot take care of him- or herself is regarded as a useless burden by the Ik and a hazard to the survival of the others. Families mean dependants such as children who need to be fed and protected. So close to the verge of starvation, family, sentiment and love are regarded as luxuries that can mean death. Children are regarded as useless appendages, like old people, because they use up precious resources. So the old are abandoned to die. Sick and disabled children too are abandoned. The Ik attitude is that, as long as you keep the breeding group alive, you can always get more children.

Ik mothers throw their children out of the village compound when they are 3-years-old, to fend for themselves. I imagine children must be rather relieved to be thrown out, for in the process of being cared for he or she is grudgingly carried about in a hide sling wherever the mother goes. Whenever the mother is in her field, she loosens the sling and lets the baby to the ground none too slowly, and laughs if it is hurt. Then she goes about her business, leaving the child there, almost hoping that some predator will come along and carry it off. This sometimes happens. Such behaviour does not endear children to their parents or parents to their children.

Adapted from Turnbull, C. (1994) *The Mountain People*, London: Pimlico

You probably reacted to the description of the Ik with horror. It is tempting to conclude that these people are primitive, savage and inhuman, and that their concept of the 'family' is deeply wrong. However, sociologists argue that it is wrong simply to judge such societies and their family arrangements as unnatural and deviant. We need to understand that such arrangements may have positive functions. In the case of the Ik, with the exceptional circumstances they find themselves in – drought and famine – their family arrangements help ensure the survival of the tribe. Moreover, you may have concluded that family life in the UK and for the Ik have some things in common. British family life is not universally experienced as positive for all family members. For some members – young and

old alike – family life may be characterized by violence, abuse and isolation.

The problem with studying the family is that we all think we are experts – not surprisingly, given that most of us are born into families and socialized into family roles and responsibilities. For many of us, the family is the cornerstone of our social world, a place to which we can retreat and where we can take refuge from the stresses of the outside world. It is the place in which we are loved for who we are, rather than what we are. Family living and family events are probably the most important aspects of our lives. It is no wonder then that we tend to hold very fierce, emotional, and perhaps irrational, views about family life and how it ought to be organized. Such 'taken-for-granted' views make it very difficult for us to examine objectively family arrangements that deviate from our own experience – such as those of the Ik – without making critical judgements.

Defining the nuclear family

The experiences of the Ik suggest that family life across the world is characterized by tremendous variation and diversity. However, the concepts of variation and diversity have created problems for those sociologists concerned with defining what counts as a family. The functionalist sociologist, George Peter Murdock (1949), for example, defined the family as: 'a social group characterized by common residence, economic co-operation and reproduction. It includes adults of both sexes, at least two of whom maintain a socially approved sexual relationship, and one or more children, own or adopted, of the sexually cohabiting adults'.

Murdock's definition, therefore, is focused on the **'nuclear family'** – a stereotypical two-generation family made up of a heterosexual couple with dependent offspring. This definition of the family has proved very popular with politicians and **right-wing** sociologists who suggest that this is the ideal type of family to which people should aspire. It was generally accepted that this family, which was the statistical norm until the 1980s should have the following characteristics:

- It should be small and compact in structure, composed of a mother, father and usually two or three children who are biologically related (see Figure 3.1).
- They should live together, i.e. share a common residence. Nuclear families are a type of **household**.
- The relationship between the adults should be **heterosexual** and based on romantic love. Children are seen as the outcome of that love and as symbolic of the couple's commitment to each other.
- The relationship between the adults should be reinforced by marriage, which, it is assumed, encourages **fidelity** (faithfulness) and therefore family stability.
- Marriage should be companionate, i.e. based on husband and wives being partners. There is an overlap between male and female responsibilities as men get more involved in childcare and housework. However, some 'natural' differences persist in the form of a gendered or **sexual division of labour** with regard to **domestic labour**. It is taken for granted that women want to have

children and that they should be primarily responsible for **nurturing** and childcare. The male role is usually defined as the main economic breadwinner and head of the household.

- The immediate family comes first and all other obligations and relationships come second. **Kinship**, therefore, is all important.
- It is assumed, almost without question, that the family is a positive and beneficial institution in which family members receive nurturing, unconditional love and care.

New Right views of the family

Traditional beliefs about family life have been dominated by a powerful conservative ideology encouraged by New Right politicians, sociologists and pressure groups like Family and Youth Concern about what families should look like and how family members should behave. For example, the beliefs that the main responsibility for parenting lies with mothers, that lone parents are not as effective as two parents, and that homosexuals should not have the same fertility or parenting rights as heterosexuals, are very influential today in the UK. We can even see such conservative views reflected in our everyday behaviour and attitudes, as Jon Bernardes observes (1997, p.31):

>> *It is not just that many people think of women as the most appropriate carers of children but rather that we all act on this belief in our daily lives. Men may hesitate or not know how to engage in certain tasks or, in public, men may be discouraged from comforting a lost child whilst a woman may 'naturally' take up this role. Examples of family ideology can be found in a wide range of everyday practices, from images on supermarket products to who picks up dirty laundry (or who drops it in the first place).>>

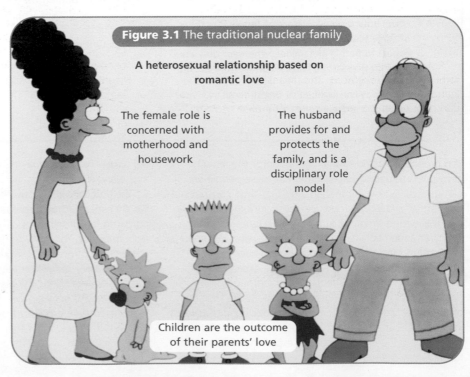

Figure 3.1 The traditional nuclear family

A heterosexual relationship based on romantic love

The female role is concerned with motherhood and housework

The husband provides for and protects the family, and is a disciplinary role model

Children are the outcome of their parents' love

Functionalism, the social structure and the family

Many of our traditional beliefs about the nuclear family are influenced by the theory of functionalism, which dominated thinking in the sociology of the family for many years. Functionalism is a structural theory in that it believes that the social structure of society (which is made up of social institutions such as the economy, education, media, law, religion and family) is responsible for shaping us as individuals and determining our experiences and life chances. Consequently, functionalists are interested in how the family functions for the greater good of society and, in particular, how it contributes to the maintenance of social order. They are also interested in how the family as an institution operates in conjunction with other institutions, particularly the economy, and how these interrelationships also contribute to **social solidarity**. Moreover, functionalists are interested in how the family, as part of the social structure, shapes and benefits its individual members.

The pre-industrial extended family

Functionalist sociologists, such as Talcott Parsons (1965), have attempted to trace the historical development of the family in order to explain why the nuclear family form has been so dominant. Parsons' theory of the family focused on examining the influence of industrialization and the economy on family structures and relationships.

Parsons argued that the economic systems of **pre-industrial** societies were largely based on **extended kinship networks**. Land and other resources were commonly owned or rented by a range of relatives extending well beyond the nuclear family unit. For example, it was not uncommon to live with and work alongside cousins. This extended family was responsible for the production of food, shelter and clothing, and would trade with other family groups for those things they couldn't produce themselves. Very few people left home to go to work. Home and workplace were one and the same thing.

Roles in these families were the product of **ascription** rather than **achievement**. This means that both family status and job were the product of being born into a particular extended family known for a particular trade or skill. For example, if the family were pig farmers, then there was a strong likelihood that all members of the family – men and women, old and young alike – would be involved in some aspect of pig farming. Moreover, these roles would be passed down from generation to generation. Few family members would reject the roles, because duty and obligation to the family and community were key values of pre-industrial society.

In return for this commitment, the extended family network generally performed other functions for its members:

● The family equipped its members with the skills and education they needed to take their place in the family division of labour, although this socialization rarely extended to literacy and numeracy.
● The family functioned to maintain the health of its members, in the absence of a system of universal health care. However, the high infant mortality rates and low life expectancy of the pre-industrial period tell us that this was probably a constant struggle.
● The family also provided welfare for its members. For example, those family members who did make it into old age would be cared for, in exchange for services such as looking after very young children.
● The extended family was expected to pursue justice on behalf of any wronged family member.

The evolution of the nuclear family

Parsons argued that the industrial revolution brought about four fundamental changes to the family (see Fig 3.2):

1   **Industrialization** meant that the economy demanded a more **geographically mobile** workforce. At the same time, achievement became more important than ascription as mass education was introduced. People were, therefore, less likely to defer to their elders or feel a strong sense of obligation to remain near to kin. Parsons argued that nuclear families were formed as people moved away from their extended kin in the countryside in order to take advantage of the job opportunities brought about by industrialization in the towns.

Figure 3.2
Functionalist view of the evolving family

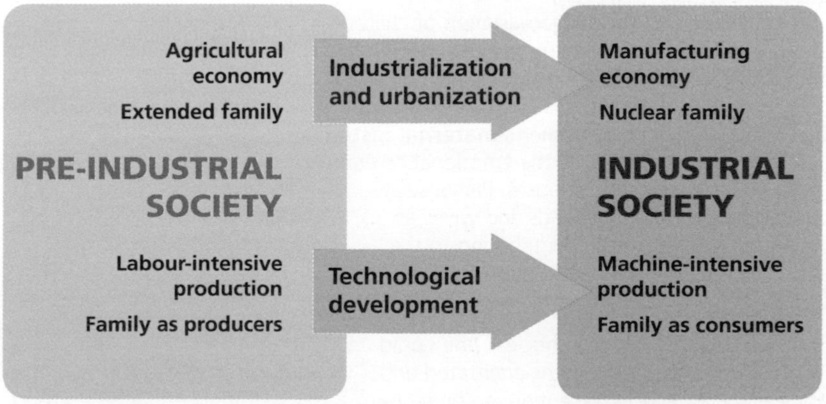

Source: Jorgensen, N. (1995) *Investigating Families and Households*, London: Collins Educational, pp. 14–15

PRE-INDUSTRIAL SOCIETY		INDUSTRIAL SOCIETY
Agricultural economy / Extended family	Industrialization and urbanization →	Manufacturing economy / Nuclear family
Labour-intensive production / Family as producers	Technological development →	Machine-intensive production / Family as consumers

Figure 3.3 Structural differentiation

Multifunctional pre-industrial family

↓

Structural differentiation

Nuclear family with specialized functions

2 Geographical mobility led to people becoming 'isolated' from their relatives and less reliant on kin for economic and social supports. Parsons claims that nuclear family members became more dependent and focused on each other, more home-centred and less prone to pressures from their extended kin and community.

3 Specialized agencies developed which gradually took over many of the functions of the family. Parsons referred to this economic process as **structural differentiation** (see Fig. 3.3 above). For example, after the industrial revolution, families could buy food and clothing mass produced in factories. Companies developed that specialized in the mass production of homes. The result of these processes was that the family became less important as an agency of production. The home and the workplace became separated as people become wage earners in the factory system.

   The state also eventually took over the functions of education, health and welfare. This left the nuclear family to specialize in two essential functions – the primary socialization of children and the stabilization of adult personalities. Parsons claimed that structural differentiation resulted in the family becoming a more streamlined and effective unit in terms of its contribution to the economy.

4 Parsons claimed that the new nuclear unit provided the husband and wife with very clear social roles. The male is the '**instrumental leader**', responsible for the economic welfare of the family group and protection of family members; he goes out to work and earns money. The female is the '**expressive leader**', primarily responsible for the socialization of children and the emotional care and support of family members. It is clearly implied that this sexual division of labour is 'natural' because it is based on biological differences. For example, women's **maternal instincts** made them best suited to be the emotional caretakers of both children and their spouses. Parsons saw relationships between husbands and wives as complementary, with each contributing to the maintenance of the family in a qualitatively different way.

Parsons concluded that only the nuclear unit could effectively provide the achievement-orientated and geographically mobile workforce required by modern industrial economies.

Focus on research

Elizabeth Roberts (1996)
Oral history of working-class women

Elizabeth Roberts interviewed 160 mothers and grandmothers in Lancashire and detailed the everyday lives of ordinary working-class women between 1890 and 1940. She resists the feminist analysis that working-class families were patriarchal institutions that benefited men. Instead, she notes that women blamed poverty, not men, for their plight, and women had power – of a sort – in household and family. The mother/daughter bond was the foundation stone of the family, and women gained much satisfaction from their family achievements such as the management of the family budget, the education and socialization of large families, and the upholding of the family and neighbourhood traditions.

Roberts, E. (1996) *A Woman's Place – an Oral History of Working Class Women, 1890–1940*, Oxford: Blackwell

1 What are the strengths and weaknesses of oral histories?

2 How does Roberts' work challenge critical views of the family?

Historical criticisms of Parsons' view

Historians suggest that Parsons was far too simplistic in his interpretation of the history of the family. They point out that the evidence suggests that industrialization may follow different patterns in different industrial societies. The Japanese experience of industrialization, for example, stressed the importance of a job for life with the same company. Employees were encouraged to view their workmates as part of a larger extended family and consequently duty and obligation were encouraged as important cultural values. The result of this was that extended kinship networks continued to exert a profound influence on their members and the isolated nuclear family failed to gain a significant toehold in Japanese culture.

Laslett's (1972) study of English parish records suggests that only 10 per cent of households in the pre-industrial period contained extended kin. In other words, most pre-industrial families may have been nuclear, and not extended as Parsons claimed. Such small families were probably due to late marriage, early death and the practice of sending children away to become servants or apprentices. It may also be the case that industrialization took off so quickly because nuclear families already existed – and so people could move quickly to those parts of the country where their skills were in demand. However, Laslett's data has been criticized as unreliable because statistics do not give us any real insight into the quality of family life, i.e. how people actually experienced the family or the meaning they attached to family life. For example, people may have lived in nuclear units but may have seen and spent quality time with other relatives on a daily basis.

Michael Anderson's historical study (1971) of the industrial town of Preston, using census records from 1851, also contradicts Parsons' view that, after industrialization, the extended unit was replaced by the nuclear family. Anderson found a large number of households shared by extended kin. These probably functioned as a **mutual economic support system** in a town in which unemployment and poverty were common. In other words, people probably pooled their low wages in order to share the cost of high rents and to help out those who were sick, disabled and elderly.

The evolution of British extended and nuclear families

The British sociologists Young and Willmott (1957) take issue with Parsons over the speed of change. They suggest that the movement towards the nuclear unit was not as sudden as Parsons suggests, but rather that it was more gradual in nature. Their empirical research, conducted in the 1950s in the East End of London (Bethnal Green), showed that extended families existed in large numbers even at this advanced stage of industrialization. This extended kinship network was based upon emotional attachment and obligation. It was also a mutual support network, offering its members assistance with money, jobs, childcare and advice.

Young and Willmott (1973) argue that the extended family unit went into decline in the 1960s, when working-class communities were rehoused in new towns and on council estates after extensive slum clearance. Moreover, the welfare state and full employment in the 1950s undermined the need for a mutual economic support system. Bright working-class young men made the most of the opportunities and qualifications made available by the 1944 Education Act and were less likely to follow their fathers into manual work. Their social mobility into white-collar and professional jobs often meant geographical mobility, i.e. moving away from traditional working-class areas, and less frequent contact with kin. Young and Willmott therefore concluded that the nuclear or **symmetrical family** only became the universal norm in Britain in the late 20th century.

Marxist views

Marxists are critical of the functionalist view that the modern nuclear family has evolved in order to benefit wider society. Instead, Marxists generally see the nuclear family as serving the interests of the ruling class because it mainly promotes capitalist values and so discourages dissent and criticism of inequality and the way capitalism is organized.

In particular, the nuclear family unit is seen as an **ideological apparatus** that promotes values and ways of thinking essential to the reproduction and maintenance of capitalism. It helps to ensure that the working class remain ignorant of the fact that they are being exploited by the capitalist system. For example, nuclear families encourage their members to pursue the capitalist-friendly goals of materialism, consumerism and 'keeping up with the Joneses'. Marcuse (1964) claimed that working-class families are encouraged to pursue 'false needs' in the form of the latest consumer goods and to judge themselves and others on the basis of their acquisitions. He noted that this served the interests of capitalism rather than consumers, because it both stimulated the economy and distracted workers from the need to seek equality and justice.

Marxists argue that the working-class extended family has been deliberately discouraged by the capitalist ruling class, because its emphasis on a mutual support system and collective shared action encourages its members to be aware of their social-class position and hence inequality. Such class consciousness is regarded as threatening, because it may eventually challenge the wealth and power of the capitalist class.

Marxist-feminist views

Marxist-feminists are sceptical about Parsons' claim that the nuclear family meets the needs of industrial society. They, too, suggest that the nuclear family benefits capitalist society and therefore the bourgeoisie at the expense of the working class. Marxist-feminists have focused on the contribution of domestic labour, i.e. housework and childcare, to capitalist economies. They point out that such work is unpaid but has great value for capitalist economies. In other words, capitalism exploits women. Moreover, men benefit from this exploitation.

Margaret Benston (1972) suggested that the nuclear family is important to capitalism because it rears the future workforce at little cost to the capitalist state. Women's domestic labour and sexual services also help to maintain the present workforce's physical and emotional fitness. Mothers and housewives are also a useful reserve army of labour that can be hired cheaply as part-time workers in times of economic expansion and let go first in times of recession. Finally, it can be argued that the capitalist class directly exploit women's domestic labour by hiring women as cleaners, nannies and cooks. This enables the wealthy of both sexes to pursue careers outside the home.

Some feminists suggest that the nuclear family may also be useful to capitalism and men because it provides an emotionally supportive retreat for male workers who may be frustrated at their treatment in the workplace. The focus on a comfortable home and attaining a good standard of living may distract workers from their workplace problems and reduce the possibility of industrial unrest. However, some men may attempt to make up for their lack of power and control in the workplace by exerting control within the family. This may have negative consequences for some females, in the form of domestic violence.

Radical feminist views

Radical feminists argue that the main effect of industrialization was that women were generally excluded from paid work (and therefore, an independent income); they were redefined as mothers and housewives dependent upon the family wage earned by the male breadwinner. Men came to dominate paid work and, consequently, political and cultural power, whereas women were confined to the family in which they were generally exploited and oppressed by men. Radical feminists, therefore, argue that the emergence of the modern nuclear family meets the needs of men rather than the needs of all members of society.

Check your understanding

1   Identify four features of the traditional family.

2   What has been the impact of the traditional model of the family on popular thinking?

3   In Parsons' view:

   (a)   What functions did the pre-industrial family perform?

   (b)   What happened to the functions of the family after industrialization?

4   In what ways do historians challenge Parsons' ideas about family change?

5   From a Marxist perspective, whom does the nuclear family benefit? How?

6   Whom does the nuclear family benefit according to feminist thinkers? How?

Activities

Research idea

Visit your local reference library and ask to see a copy of the 1851 census for your area. Randomly choose a couple of streets and work out how households were organized. Does this evidence support Parsons or Anderson?

Web.tasks

Use an internet search engine such as www.google.co.uk and sites such as www.en.wikipedia.org to find out more about the work of G.P. Murdock, Talcott Parsons, Ronald Fletcher, and particularly Peter Wilmott and Michael Young's research on Bethnal Green in London. However, be cautious in your use of material from the net. Always attempt to check any information against textbook-based data.

Key terms

Achievement the allocation of roles and status on the basis of individual merit, e.g. through the acquisition of qualifications.

Ascription the allocation of roles and status on the basis of fixed characteristics, e.g. on the basis of gender or what family you are born into.

Conservative a belief in traditional ideas and institutions; suspicious of radical change.

Domestic labour housework and childcare.

Expressive leader Parsons' term for the female function of mother/housewife.

Extended kinship networks relationships between family members beyond the nuclear family, e.g. grandparents, cousins.

Fidelity being faithful to one's partner.

Geographical mobility the ability to move quickly around the country.

Heterosexual attracted to the opposite sex.

Household a social group sharing common residence.

Ideological apparatus according to Marxists, any institution that is involved in the transmitting of ruling-class ideas, e.g. education, mass media.

Ideology set of powerful ideas.

Industrialization the process (occurring during the 18th and 19th centuries in Britain) whereby societies moved from agricultural production to industrial manufacturing. It had a huge impact, creating cities (urbanization), changing the sort of work people did, and fundamentally altering their social experiences and relationships.

Instrumental leader Parsons' term for the male breadwinner.

Kinship related to each other by blood, marriage, etc.

Maternal instinct a 'natural' instinct to desire motherhood and want to care for children.

Mutual economic support system a system in which family members work to support each other.

Nuclear family family group consisting of two generations, i.e. parents and children, living in the same household.

Nurturing caring for and looking after others.

Pre-industrial before the industrial revolution.

Right-wing political ideas that are supportive of tradition.

Sexual division of labour the division of both paid work and domestic labour into men's jobs and women's jobs.

Social solidarity the feeling of belonging.

Structural differentiation the process by which the family lost many of its pre-industrial functions to outside agencies such as manufacturing industry and the welfare state.

Symmetrical family a nuclear family in which both spouses perform equally important roles.

The family, social structure and social change

the opening sentence of each paragraph should clearly highlight the reason

whatever it is that you have identified must be discussed in some depth using sociological studies and examples

each reason needs to be developed into a very detailed paragraph which must be clearly distinguishable from the other

(a) Identify and explain two reasons why extended families are still important in contemporary Britain.

(17 marks)

contemporary means studies of extended families conducted in the last 10–20 years

begin your answer with a clear definition of what is meant by this concept

you should attempt to write two very detailed paragraphs in about 15 minutes

a detailed description of the view is required using sociological concepts, theories and studies

it is important to assess the merits of the functionalist theory of the family in some detail, either by raising specific strengths or criticisms of the theory or by presenting alternative theoretical perspectives

this view is a functionalist perspective

you should attempt to write at least 2 sides of the answer book in about 30 minutes

(b) Outline and evaluate the view that the nuclear family evolved to meet the needs of modern industrial society.

(33 marks)

Grade booster Getting top marks in this question

You need to describe the functionalist theory of the evolution of the family in detail. Begin by describing how Parsons views the pre-industrial family in terms of its structure and functions. Describe the effect industrialisation had on the evolution of the family in terms of size and contemporary functions. You should make some points of evaluation –these might be historical or be taken from other sociological perspectives, e.g. Marxism and feminism, or even functionalism itself, e.g. Wilmott & Young or Fletcher.

TOPIC 2

The role of the family in society

Getting you thinking

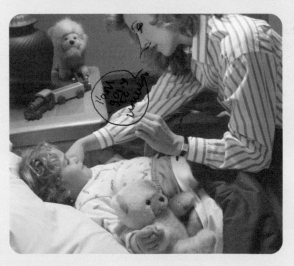

1   Examine the photographs carefully. What functions are family members performing?

2   How do you think your family functions to benefit you?

3   In your opinion, can family functions be performed just as effectively by other agencies?

It is likely that you have identified several family functions after examining the photographs and discussing your own families. You have probably concluded too that very few social institutions can perform these functions as well as the family. You will no doubt be pleased to see that your conclusions parallel those of many sociologists. However, it is important to understand that the experience of family functions is not the same for all of us. There may be very different experiences shaped by social class, ethnicity, age, gender and religion. Furthermore, some of these experiences may be damaging rather than beneficial.

The functionalist theory of the family

For many years, the sociology of the family was dominated by the theory of functionalism. Functionalists assume that society has certain basic needs or **functional prerequisites** that need to be met if it is to continue successfully into the future. For example, a successful society is underpinned by social order and economic stability, so the role of the social institutions that make up society is to make sure this continues by:

- transmitting values, norms, etc., to the next generation in order to reproduce **consensus** and therefore the culture of a society
- teaching particular skills in order that the economy – the engine of society – operates effectively
- allocating people to family and occupational roles which make best use of their talents and abilities.

Functionalists see the family as playing a major role in achieving these social goals. They view the family as the cornerstone of society because it plays the dominant role amongst all social institutions in making individuals feel part of wider society. Furthermore, the family is seen as meeting the needs of individuals for emotional satisfaction, social support, identity and security. Overall, then, functionalists see the family as extremely **functional**, i.e. its existence is both beneficial and necessary for the smooth running of society and the personal development of individuals.

The work of G.P. Murdock

Murdock (1949) compared over 250 societies and claimed that the nuclear family was universal, i.e. that some form of it existed in every known society, and that it always performed four functions essential to the continued existence of those societies:

- *Reproductive* – Society requires new members to ensure its survival – **procreation** generally occurs within a marital and family context.
- *Sexual* – This function serves both society and the individual. Unregulated sexual behaviour has the potential to be socially disruptive. However, marital sex creates a powerful emotional bond between a couple, encourages fidelity and therefore commits the individual to family life. Sex within marriage contributes to social order and stability because marital fidelity sets the moral rules for general sexual behaviour.
- *Educational* – Culture needs to be transmitted to the next generation, so children need to be effectively socialized into the dominant values, norms, customs, rituals, etc., of a society.
- *Economic* – Adult family members show their commitment to the care, protection and maintenance of their dependents by becoming productive workers and bringing home an income. This underpins the family standard of living with regard to shelter or housing, food, quality of care, etc. It also benefits society because it is assumed without question that family members should take their place in the economy and the **division of labour** as specialized wage-earners, thereby contributing to the smooth running of the economy and society.

Evaluation of Murdock

Interpretivist sociologists argue that Murdock fails to acknowledge that families are the product of culture rather than biology, and that, consequently, family relationships and roles will take different forms even within the same society. For example, a range of different attitudes towards bringing up children can be seen in the UK which have their roots in different religious beliefs, access to economic opportunity, belief in particular child psychology approaches, etc. Think about how the educational function may differ in an upper-class White family compared with a Muslim family or a White family living on a deprived inner-city estate.

Murdock's definition of the family and its functions is also quite conservative in that it deprives certain members of society of family status; it implies that certain types of parenting – single, foster, homosexual and surrogate – are not quite as beneficial as the classic two heterosexual parents' model. In this sense, Murdock's model is political because it is clearly saying there are 'right' and 'wrong' ways to organize family life.

Family functions

Despite these doubts about the universality of the nuclear unit, functionalist sociologists have focused their attention on the functions of the family in order to assess its benefits for both the social structure and its members. Several functions have been identified that allegedly contribute to the wellbeing of society as well as parents and children.

Primary socialization of children

As we saw in Topic 1, Parsons (1955) saw the pre-industrial extended family as evolving into the modern nuclear family which specialized in the primary socialization of children. Parsons believed that personalities are 'made not born' – for Parsons, a child could only become a social adult by internalizing the shared norms and values of the society to which they belonged. He therefore saw nuclear families as 'personality factories', churning out young citizens committed to the rules, patterns of behaviour and belief systems which make involvement in social life possible. In this sense, the family acts as a bridge between children and their involvement in wider society.

As Cheal (2002) puts it, more simply: 'Parents today are encouraged to believe they have a special responsibility to ensure every child grows up happy, strong, confident, articulate, literate and skilled in every possible respect.'

Other sociologists point out that the family is important in terms of both political and religious socialization. Many of our beliefs, prejudices and anxieties may be rooted in the strong emotional bonds we forge with our parents during childhood.

Parsons saw mothers as playing the major role in the process of nurturing and socialization in families. Mothers, he claimed, were the 'expressive leaders' of the family who were biologically suited to looking after the emotional and cultural development of children. Such ideas reflect the dominant domestic arrangements in the UK where women have long held primary responsibility for looking after children and housework. These arrangements will be further explored in Topic 5.

Although the family is viewed as the main agent of socialization, it is important to remember that socialization is a life-long process. It does not end with the onset of adulthood or when a child leaves home. We acquire experience and knowledge throughout our lives from a range of different sources. It is therefore important to acknowledge the existence of secondary agents of socialization, such as the educational system, religion, the mass media and the workplace. Such agencies also strongly support what goes on in families. Fletcher (1988), for example, argued that childrearing in families is made more effective by the support offered by state institutions in the form of antenatal and postnatal care, health clinics, doctors, health visitors, social workers, teachers and housing officers.

Stabilization of adult personality

Parsons argued that the second major specialized function of the family is to relieve the stresses of modern-day living for its adult members. This theory, often called the 'warm bath' theory, claims that family life 'stabilizes' adult personalities. Steel and Kidd note the family does this by providing 'in the home a warm, loving, stable environment where the individual adults can be themselves and even "let themselves go" in a childish and undignified way. At the same time, the supervision and socialization of children gives parents a sense of stability and responsibility' (Steel and Kidd 2001, p.42). This emotional support and security, and the opportunity to engage in play with children, acts as a safety valve in that it prevents stress from overwhelming adult family members and, as a result, it strengthens social stability. In this sense, Parsons viewed the family as a positive and beneficial place for all its members – a 'home sweet home', a 'haven in a heartless world' and a place in which people can be their natural selves (see Fig. 3.4).

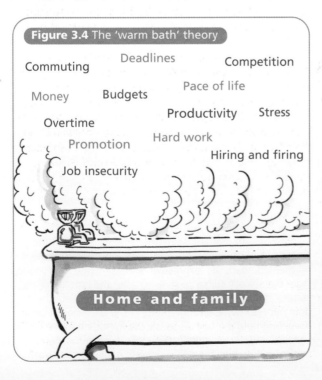

Figure 3.4 The 'warm bath' theory

Commuting
Deadlines
Competition
Money
Budgets
Pace of life
Productivity
Stress
Overtime
Promotion
Hard work
Hiring and firing
Job insecurity

Home and family

Gender-role socialization

A further important aspect of socialization is that children learn the cultural patterns of behaviour expected of their gender, i.e. what is regarded as appropriate masculine or feminine behaviour. From an early age, people are trained by their parents' childrearing practices to conform to social expectations of how males and females should behave.

Chapman (2004, p.200) notes that traditionally:

<< *girls, through play, through the chores they did and through formal schooling would learn the right kind of attitudes and skills to perform their adult role of homemaker and mother. Boys, by the same token, were aimed squarely at the role of breadwinner by toning down their emotionality so that they would have what were presumed to be the right kinds of skill for work.* >>

In this sense, then, gender differences are not biological or natural but are socially constructed by society. These differences too are further reinforced by secondary agents of socialization, such as education and the mass media.

Social control

The family serves as an important agent of **social control** and, alongside secondary agencies such as religion, the criminal justice system and the mass media, polices the behaviour of society's members in order to maintain value consensus and social order. As Murdock pointed out, the family is generally regarded as the moral centre of society and sets the rules with regard to how people should behave, particularly with regard to sex and sexuality, e.g. it is generally regarded as deviant to engage in adulterous behaviour.

Setting the boundaries of deviant behaviour is an important consequence of primary socialization. Effective childrearing involves the development of a moral conscience that trains children to know the difference between 'right' and 'wrong'. This is backed up through parental use of positive sanctions (e.g. rewards) and negative sanctions (e.g. punishments). In this sense, the family contributes to the maintenance of other social institutions by ensuring the moral education of children who usually grow up to become decent, law-abiding citizens and workers.

Social status

Being born into a family results in the acquisition of a number of **ascribed statuses** – i.e. status allocated by age, gender, birth order, ethnicity, religion and social class. There is some evidence that the socio-economic status of our family provides us with a sense of family identity. It also has a profound influence over the quality of opportunities that we experience as we grow up. For example, the social and cultural supports we receive from parents with regard to education, e.g. nursery education, private tuition, attendance at private schools, access to computers and so on, are often dependent upon the economic supports our parents can offer us. Some families are able to offer their children considerable economic support, not only during their early years of dependence, but often well after they have flown the family nest, e.g. to go on to university or to set up homes of their own. Bernardes argues that such inequalities in economic maintenance result in helpless newborn infants being channelled into becoming a wide range of very unequal mature adults.

Economic consumption

In Topic 1, we saw that the pre-industrial family was responsible for the production of goods. Industrialization, however, led to factories taking over this function. Family companies, farms and shops continue to exist in the 21st century, but it can be argued that the family's economic function today is as a unit of **consumption** – goods and services provided by the economy are mainly consumed by the family unit. As Day Sclater notes:

<< *from ready-made meals, through washing machines and cars, to telecommunication services, the advertisers on our TV sets and in magazines clearly regard families as providing the main market for the goods and services they promote. Family income is expended largely on things for the family.*>> (Sclater 2000, p.24)

Recreation and leisure

During the 20th century, the family became an important centre for recreation and leisure. This was especially true for children in the 1990s, when parents started to interpret the world as a much riskier place for children and children began to spend more time in the home. Evans and Chandler (2006) note how homes, and specifically children's bedrooms, are often now furnished with media and technological entertainment, such as televisions, DVD players and computer games.

Protective and welfare function

Unlike many newly-born animals, the human baby is generally helpless and requires adult physical support and protection for a prolonged period of time. However, the welfare support that a child receives from its parents, e.g. shelter, diet and education, very much depends on the family's socio-economic status. This, in turn, is dependent on the occupation and income of the major wage-earners.

The welfare function also takes the form of family members being cared for and supported by other family members if they are ill, disabled, elderly or in poverty. The family, therefore, makes an important contribution to the health and welfare of the more vulnerable members of society, and works alongside social institutions such as the National Health Service.

Functionalists, therefore, see the family as a crucial social institution functioning positively to bring about healthy societies and individuals.

Criticisms of functionalist views of the family

Functionalists tend to view the family as very harmonious but as we shall see in Topic 5, this view has been challenged by accounts of child abuse, domestic violence and the fall-out from divorce. As Cheal notes, functional relationships can easily slip into **dysfunctional** relationships, and love can often turn into hate in moments

of intense emotion. He notes that 'we have to face the paradox that families are contexts of love and nurturance, but they are also contexts of violence and murder' (Cheal 2002, p.8).

Functionalist analyses of the nuclear family tend to be based on middle-class and American versions of family life, and they consequently neglect other influences, such as ethnicity, social class or religion. For example, Parsons does not consider the fact that wealth or poverty may determine whether women stay at home to look after children or not. Since Parsons wrote in the 1950s, many Western societies, including the UK, have become **multicultural**. Religious and ethnic **subcultural** differences may mean that Parsons' version of the family is no longer relevant in contemporary society.

Social and cultural changes may mean that some of the functions of the family have been modified or even abandoned altogether as demonstrated in Table 3.1.

The Marxist critique

Marxists are very critical of the process of primary socialization in the nuclear family because they argue that it reproduces and maintains class inequality. They argue that the main function of the nuclear family is to distract the working class from the fact they are exploited by capitalism. This is done in two ways:

● The hierarchical way in which nuclear families are traditionally organized (e.g. the male as the head of the household) discourages workers from questioning the hierarchical nature of capitalism and the inequalities in wealth and power that result from it.
● Parents are encouraged to teach their children that the main route to happiness and status lies in consumerism and the acquisition of material possessions. Consequently, the organization of capitalism (and its inequalities) often goes unchallenged by a generation fixated on the acquisition of the latest designer labels and trendy gadgets.

From a Marxist perspective, then, the functions of the nuclear family benefit those who run the capitalist system rather than the whole of society, as functionalists suggest.

The Marxist-feminist critique

Marxist feminists argue that the nuclear family functions to benefit capitalism and, therefore, the wealthy rather than the whole of society. Men too benefit from family life at the expense of women. Marxist-feminists argue that the focus on women as mothers puts considerable cultural pressure on women to have children and to take time out of the labour market to bring them up. These children become the workforce of the future at little or no expense to the capitalist class. This also benefits men, because it means that women cannot compete on a level playing field for jobs or promotion opportunities if their first priority is looking after children.

Furthermore, it is argued that socialization of children ensures that the pattern of male dominance and female subordination (symbolized by men's traditional role as main economic earner and head of household, and the idea that women should primarily be responsible for children) is reproduced generation after generation.

The radical-feminist critique

Radical feminists argue that the nuclear family mainly functions to benefit men because gender-role socialization results in males and females subscribing to a set of ideas that largely confirm male power and superiority. They argue that the nuclear family is the main arena in which **patriarchal ideology** is transmitted to children. This ideology encourages the notion that the **sexual division of labour** is 'natural' and unchangeable. It also results in the exploitation of women because patriarchal ideology mainly views women as sexual objects when single, and mothers/housewives when married.

Evaluating Marxism and feminist theories of the family

Feminist theories of the family have dated fairly badly, because they fail to account for recent economic and social changes, such as the **feminization of the economy**, the educational success of young females, women's use of divorce, and many women's rejection of domestic labour as their unique responsibility.

Feminist theories portray women as passively accepting their lot – the reality, however, is that women can adopt a range of active social identities today, many of which do

Table 3.1 Changes in the functions of the family

Family function	Recent social trends – have these undermined or supported family functions?
Procreation	The size of families has declined as people choose lifestyle over the expense of having children. Many women prefer to pursue careers and are making the decision not to have children. The UK birth rate has consequently fallen.
Regulating sex	Sex outside marriage is now the norm. Alternative sexualities, e.g. homosexuality, are becoming more socially acceptable.
Stabilizing personalities	A high percentage of marriages end in divorce. However, some argue that divorce and remarriage rates are high because people continue to search for emotional security.
Economic	Although welfare benefits are seen by some as undermining family economic responsibilities, the family is still a crucial agency of economic support, especially as the housing market becomes more expensive for first-time buyers, and young people spend longer periods in education with the prospect of debt through student loans.
Welfare	A decline in state funding of welfare in the 1980s led to the encouragement of 'community care', in which the family – and especially women – became responsible for the care of the elderly, the long-term sick and the disabled.
Socialization	This is still rooted in the family, although there are concerns that the mass media and the peer group have become more influential, with the result that children are growing up faster.
Social control	Power has shifted between parents and children as children acquire more rights. This trend, alongside attempts to ban smacking in England and Wales, is thought by some sociologists to undermine parental discipline. Some sociologists argue that families need fathers and see the absence of fathers in one-parent families as a major cause of **delinquency**.

not involve playing a secondary role to men. In other words, many young women are resisting traditional male definitions of what their role should be.

There is an implicit assumption in feminist theories that all male–female relationships involve male exploitation of women. However, the bulk of male–female relationships are probably based on mutual love and respect rather than exploitation, domination and subordination.

Both Marxism and feminism have a good deal in common with functionalism despite their ideological differences. All three theories see the functions of the family as determined by the needs of society and the economy. All three theories are guilty of overemphasizing the nuclear family and neglecting the rich diversity of family types in modern society. (This diversity will be explored further in Topics 3 and 4.)

From an interpretivist point of view, functionalism, feminism and Marxism tend to neglect the meanings families have for individuals and how family members interpret family relationships. Both feminism and Marxism, for example, can be accused of deliberately ignoring those accounts of family life in which some females suggest motherhood is a fulfilling and rewarding experience.

Marxism and feminism are also very critical of the nuclear family but fail to offer any practical alternatives to it.

Key terms

Ascribed status inherited status.

Consensus common agreement on shared values.

Consumption the ways in which individuals use goods and services.

Delinquency youth crime.

Dysfunctional having negative consequences.

Feminization of the economy an economic trend that began in the 1990s whereby the majority of newly available jobs were aimed at women.

Functional beneficial, fulfilling a purpose.

Functional prerequisites the basic needs of society, such as the need for social order.

Multicultural having more than one culture.

Patriarchal ideology male-dominated ideas.

Procreation having children.

Sexual division of labour the distribution of childcare and housework tasks according to gender.

Social control process of persuading, encouraging and enforcing conformity.

Subcultural subscribing to cultural values and norms that may be different from the mainstream.

Check your understanding

1 What are the four universal functions of the family according to Murdock?

2 What did Parsons mean when he described the nuclear family as a personality factory?

3 What is the 'warm bath' theory?

4 In what ways might recent social trends challenge the idea that the nuclear family functions to relieve the stresses of modern living for adults?

5 How are functionalist, feminist and Marxists alike in their analyses of the functions of the nuclear family?

Activities

Research idea

Using this chapter, make a list of the functions that the family performs. Find five people of different ages and ask them to rate on a scale of 1 to 5 how important these functions are to them (where 1 is 'very important' and 5 'not important'). Also ask two open questions 'what is a family?' and 'what are families for?'

Web.tasks

Visit websites dedicated to the family, such as:
www.familyeducation.com
www.familiesonline.co.uk
www.mumsnet.com

Look at the content of these sites in terms of advice, news and letters from parents. What functions should families be performing according to these sites? Do such functions support the functionalist theory of the family?

The role of the family in society

the opening sentence of each paragraph should clearly highlight the way

whatever it is that you have identified must be discussed in some depth using sociological studies and examples

you should attempt to write two very detailed paragraphs in about 15 minutes

each way needs to be developed into a very detailed paragraph which must be clearly distinguishable from the other

(a) Identify and explain two ways in which the nuclear family benefits men at the expense of women.

(17 marks)

begin your answer with a clear definition of what is meant by this concept

think about how women might be exploited by men in the family according to feminist theory

a detailed description of the view is required using sociological concepts, theories and studies

it is important to assess the merits of the functionalist theory of the functions of the family in some detail, either by raising specific strengths or criticisms of the theory or by presenting alternative theoretical perspectives

this view is a functionalist perspective

you should attempt to write at least 2 sides of the answer book in about 30 minutes

(b) Outline and evaluate the view that the major function of the family is to make individuals feel part of wider society.

(33 marks)

Grade booster Getting top marks in this question

You need to describe the functionalist theory of the functions of the family in detail and how it fits with their consensus view of society. You need to describe the kinds of functions they see the family as performing and explain how these benefit society as well as individuals. You must evaluate this functionalist view by using different feminist views and/or Marxist views of the role of the family in benefiting men or the ruling class. Use concepts such as stabilisation of primary socialisation, stabilisation of adult personality, patriarchy, capitalism and reproduction of labour.

TOPIC 3

Marriage, divorce and family diversity

Getting you thinking

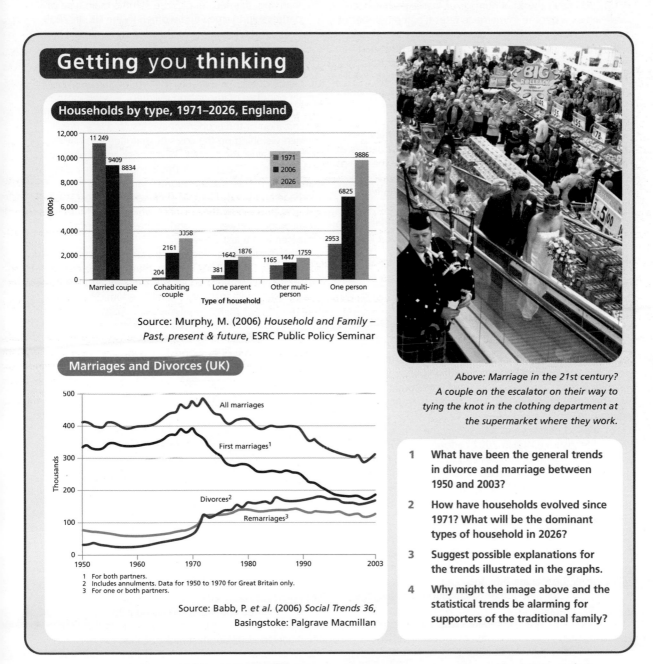

Households by type, 1971–2026, England

(000s)

Married couple: 11 249 (1971), 9409 (2006), 8834 (2026)
Cohabiting couple: 204 (1971), 2161 (2006), 3358 (2026)
Lone parent: 381 (1971), 1642 (2006), 1876 (2026)
Other multi-person: 1165 (1971), 1447 (2006), 1759 (2026)
One person: 2953 (1971), 6825 (2006), 9886 (2026)

Legend: 1971, 2006, 2026

Type of household

Source: Murphy, M. (2006) *Household and Family –
Past, present & future*, ESRC Public Policy Seminar

Marriages and Divorces (UK)

Thousands

All marriages
First marriages[1]
Divorces[2]
Remarriages[3]

1950   1960   1970   1980   1990   2003

1 For both partners.
2 Includes annulments. Data for 1950 to 1970 for Great Britain only.
3 For one or both partners.

Source: Babb, P. *et al.* (2006) *Social Trends 36*,
Basingstoke: Palgrave Macmillan

*Above: Marriage in the 21st century?
A couple on the escalator on their way to
tying the knot in the clothing department at
the supermarket where they work.*

1   **What have been the general trends in divorce and marriage between 1950 and 2003?**

2   **How have households evolved since 1971? What will be the dominant types of household in 2026?**

3   **Suggest possible explanations for the trends illustrated in the graphs.**

4   **Why might the image above and the statistical trends be alarming for supporters of the traditional family?**

It is not difficult to see why supporters of the traditional family, such as the New Right, are so alarmed by figures and images such as those above. They believe these indicate a crisis in the family, which will inevitably result in increasing antisocial behaviour and moral breakdown.

Many postmodernists and feminists look at the figures and images in a very different way – they see them as indicators of greater personal choice in our private lives,

and as evidence of a rejection of patriarchal family arrangements. So who is right?

Marriage

In 1972, the highest ever number of couples (480 000) since the Second World War got married. According to the

Office for National Statistics (ONS), this was due to the baby boom generation of the 1950s reaching marriageable age and these people choosing to marry at a younger age compared with previous generations. However, the annual number of marriages in England and Wales then went into decline and, despite a slight revival in marriage in 2004 when 273 000 couples got married, reached an all-time low in 2005 when only 244 710 couples tied the knot.

This decline in the total number of marriages has been paralleled by a decline in marriage rates (i.e. the number of people marrying per 1000 of the population aged 16 and over). In 1994, the marriage rate was 11.4 but this had declined to 10.3 by 2004. The male rate declined from 36.3 in 1994 to 27.8 in 2004 whilst the female rate declined from 30.6 to 24.6. Furthermore, only 32 per cent of marriages in 2004 involved a religious ceremony, compared with 51 per cent in 1991.

We can also see some ethnic variations in marriage. Research by Berthoud (2000) suggests that three quarters of Pakistani and Bangladeshi women are married by the age of 25, compared with just over half of White women. Moreover, British African-Caribbeans are the group least likely to get married – only 39 per cent of Caribbean adults under the age of 60 are in a formal marriage, compared with 60 per cent of White adults.

The future of marriage?

These figures have recently provoked a keen debate between New Right commentators and feminists. New Right commentators express concerns about the decline in marriage. Patricia Morgan (2000) argues that marriage involves unique 'attachments and obligations' that regulate people's behaviour. For example, she claims that married men are more likely to be employed than unmarried or cohabiting men, and earn more (i.e. 10 to 20 per cent more in 2001) because they work harder than any other male group.

An analysis of marriage statistics by the Office for National Statistics (ONS) in 2007 concludes that marriage is good for the health of couples and that married people live longer than single or **divorced** people, although Murphy (2007) suggests that it could be bad relationships rather than divorce that makes people unhappy and hence ill.

However, fears about what marriage statistics reveal are probably exaggerated for four reasons:

1   People are delaying marriage rather than rejecting it. Most people will marry at some point in their lives. However, people are now marrying later in life, probably after a period of cohabitation. The average age for first-time brides in 2003 was 29 years and for all grooms 31 years, compared with 22 for women and 24 for men in 1971. Women may delay marriage because they want to develop their careers and enjoy a period of independence.
2   British Social Attitude Surveys indicate that most people, whether single, divorced or cohabiting, still see marriage as a desirable life-goal. People also generally believe that having children is best done in the context of marriage. Few people believe that the freedom associated with living alone is better than being married to someone.
3   Two fifths of all marriages are remarriages (in which one or both partners have been divorced). These

people are obviously committed to the institution of marriage despite their previous negative experience of it. (An interesting new trend is the number of young men – aged under 25 – who are marrying women significantly older than them, i.e. 'toy-boy' marriages. One in three of first-time grooms in 2004 was younger than his bride, more than double the number in 1963.)
4   Despite the decrease in the overall number of people marrying, married couples are still the main type of partnership for men and women in the UK. In 2005, seven in ten families were headed by a married couple.

Wilkinson (1994) notes that female attitudes towards marriage and family life have undergone a radical change or 'genderquake'. She argues that young females no longer prioritize marriage and children, as their mothers and grandmothers did. Educational opportunities and the feminization of the economy have resulted in young women weighing up the costs of marriage and having children against the benefits of a career and economic independence. The result of this is that many females, particularly middle-class graduates, are postponing marriage and family life until their careers are established. This is supported by the statistics which show that births to women aged between 35 and 39 have dramatically increased in the last 20 years.

Other feminist sociologists are sceptical about the value of marriage. Smith (2001) argues that marriage creates unrealistic expectations about **monogamy** and faithfulness in a world characterized by sexual freedom. She argues that at different points in people's life cycles, people need different things that often can only be gained from a new partner. Campbell (2000) suggests that marriage benefits men more than it does women.

Cohabitation

A constant source of concern to the New Right has been the significant rise in the number of couples cohabiting during the last decade. The proportion of non-married people cohabiting has risen sharply in the last 20 years from 11 per cent of men and 13 per cent of women in 1986 to 24 per cent and 25 per cent respectively. In 2007, the ONS suggested that cohabiting couples are the fastest growing family type in the UK. Around 2.2 million families are cohabiting couples with or without children. This family type has grown by 65 per cent since 1997. In fact, the numbers are likely to be higher than this because the ONS data did not include same-sex couples living together. The ONS predict that by 2014, as a consequence of this growth, married couples could account for less than half of British families. The ONS data also suggests that a third of teenagers in 2007 are destined to cohabit rather than marry, compared with one in ten of their grandparents.

New Right commentators claim that cohabitation is less stable than marriage. A report by the Institute for the Study of Civil Society (Morgan 2000) claimed that cohabiting couples were less happy and less fulfilled than married couples, and more likely to be abusive, unfaithful, stressed and depressed. In 2007, ONS data analysed by Murphy suggested that children whose parents live together but are not married get worse results at school, leave education earlier and have a higher risk of developing a serious illness.

Is cohabitation replacing marriage?

However, surveys indicate that few people see cohabitation as an alternative to marriage. The fact that cohabiting couples are much younger than married couples suggests cohabitation is seen by many participants as a test of compatibility and a prelude to marriage. Kiernan (2007) notes that it is difficult to generalize about cohabiting couples. These may include people who are about to marry, those who oppose marriage and those who are just testing the strength of their relationship in a situation that has become more socially acceptable in the last ten years. Kiernan also points out that the educational and health disadvantages that the ONS study purports to identify might come about because people in cohabiting relationships are more likely to be socially disadvantaged and poor in the first place.

Other research suggests that cohabitation is a temporary phase lasting on average about five years. Approximately 60 per cent of cohabiting couples eventually marry – usually some time after the first child is born. Although cohabitation marks a dramatic change in adult living arrangements – as recently as the 1960s, it was regarded as immoral – cohabiting couples with and without children only accounted for 10 per cent of households in 2006. There is also some evidence that a significant number of people live together simply because they are waiting for a divorce. For example, in 2005, 23 per cent of cohabiting men were separated from a previous partner whilst 36 per cent were divorced. Finally, as we saw earlier, marriage rather than cohabitation is still the main cultural goal for most people in the UK.

Marital breakdown

Types of marital breakdown

Marital breakdown can take three different forms: divorce, separation and **empty-shell marriages**:

● *Divorce* refers to the legal ending of a marriage. Since the Divorce Reform Act of 1969, divorce has been granted on the basis of '**irretrievable** breakdown' and, since 1984, couples have been able to petition for divorce after the first anniversary of their marriage. 'Quickie' divorces are also available, in which one partner has to prove the 'fault' or 'quilt' of the other, for matrimonial 'crimes' such as adultery, although these tend to be costly.
● *Separation* is where couples agree to live apart after the breakdown of a marriage. In the past, when divorce was difficult to obtain or too expensive, separation was often the only solution.
● *Empty-shell marriages* are those in which husband and wife stay together in name only. There may no longer be any love or intimacy between them. Today, such marriages are likely to end in separation or divorce, although this type of relationship may persist for the sake of children or for religious reasons.

The divorce rate

Britain's divorce rate is high compared with other European societies. In 1938, 6000 divorces were granted in the UK. This figure had increased tenfold by 1970, and in 1993, numbers peaked at 180 000. By 2000, this figure had fallen to 154 600 although the years 2001–04 have seen a gradual rise to 167 100. People who had been divorced before constitute about 20 per cent of this total. There are now nearly half as many divorces as marriages and, if present trends continue, about 40 per cent of current marriages will end in divorce.

New Right sociologists argue that such divorce statistics are one of the symptoms of a serious crisis in the family. They suggest that divorce is too easily available, with the result that people are not as committed to marriage and the family as they were in the past. Many New Right sociologists see a direct relationship between divorce, one-parent families and antisocial behaviour among the young, and argue for a return to traditional family values as well as a toughening up of the divorce laws.

New Right sociologists argue that children who experience the divorce of their parents suffer a range of problems as they get older, such as being more prone to crime and unemployment. It is claimed that such children are themselves likely to experience divorce when they marry. Research by Rodgers and Pryor (1998) found that children from separated families are more likely than children from two-parent families to suffer behavioural problems, to underachieve at school, to become sexually active and, if female, become pregnant at an early age, and to smoke, drink and use drugs during adolescence. When they become adults, they are more likely to experience poverty.

Flouri and Buchanan's (2002) study of 17 000 children from families that had experienced separation and divorce found that in families where fathers were still involved with their children, the children were more successful in gaining educational qualifications and continued to seek out educational opportunities in adult life. They are less likely to get into trouble with the police and less likely to become homeless. Such children also grow up to enjoy more stable and satisfying relationships with their adult partners. However, Buchanan found that if conflict continued after divorce between parents, children could become vulnerable to mental health problems.

Why is the divorce rate increasing?

Changes in divorce law have generally made it easier and cheaper to end marriages, but this is not necessarily the cause of the rising divorce rate. Legal changes reflect other changes in society, especially changes in attitudes. In particular, sociologists argue that social expectations about marriage have changed. Functionalist sociologists even argue that high divorce rates are evidence that marriage is increasingly valued and that people are demanding higher standards from their partners. Couples are no longer prepared to put up with unhappy, 'empty-shell' marriages. People want emotional and sexual compatibility and

equality, as well as companionship. Some are willing to go through a number of partners to achieve these goals.

Feminists note that women's expectations of marriage have radically changed, compared with previous generations. In the 1990s, most **divorce petitions** were initiated by women. This may support Thornes and Collard's (1979) view that women expect far more from marriage than men and, in particular, that they value friendship and emotional gratification more than men do. If husbands fail to live up to these expectations, women may feel the need to look elsewhere.

Women's expectations have probably changed as a result of the improved educational and career opportunities they have experienced since the 1980s. Women no longer have to be unhappily married because they are financially dependent upon their husbands. Moreover, Hart (1976) notes that divorce may be a reaction to the frustration that many working wives may feel if they are responsible for the bulk of housework and childcare. Similarly, it may also be the outcome of tensions produced by women taking over the traditional male role of breadwinner in some households, especially if the male is unemployed.

Divorce is no longer associated with stigma and shame. This may be partly due to a general decline in religious practices. The social controls, such as extended families and **close-knit communities**, that exerted pressure on couples to stay together and that labelled divorce as 'wicked' and 'shameful', are also in decline. Consequently, in a society dominated by **privatized nuclear families**, the view that divorce can lead to greater happiness for the individual is more acceptable. It is even more so if divorce involves escaping from an abusive relationship or if an unhappy marriage is causing emotional damage to children. However, it is important to recognize that such attitudes are not necessarily a sign of a casual attitude towards divorce. Most people experience divorce as an emotional and traumatic experience, equivalent to bereavement. They are usually also aware of the severe impact it may have on children.

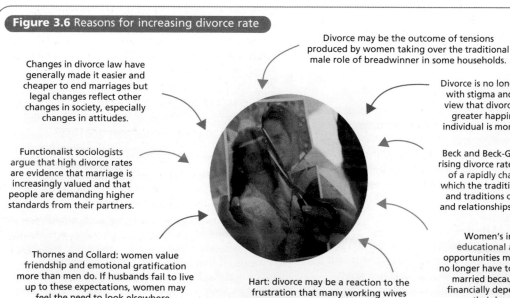

Figure 3.6 Reasons for increasing divorce rate

Changes in divorce law have generally made it easier and cheaper to end marriages but legal changes reflect other changes in society, especially changes in attitudes.

Functionalist sociologists argue that high divorce rates are evidence that marriage is increasingly valued and that people are demanding higher standards from their partners.

Thornes and Collard: women value friendship and emotional gratification more than men do. If husbands fail to live up to these expectations, women may feel the need to look elsewhere.

Divorce may be the outcome of tensions produced by women taking over the traditional male role of breadwinner in some households.

Divorce is no longer associated with stigma and shame. The view that divorce can lead to greater happiness for the individual is more acceptable.

Beck and Beck-Gernsheim (1995): rising divorce rates are the product of a rapidly changing world in which the traditional rules, rituals and traditions of love, romance and relationships no longer apply.

Women's improved educational and career opportunities mean that they no longer have to be unhappily married because they are financially dependent upon their husbands.

Hart: divorce may be a reaction to the frustration that many working wives may feel if they are responsible for the bulk of housework and childcare.

Postmodern approaches to divorce

Beck and Beck-Gernsheim (1995) argue that rising divorce rates are the product of a rapidly changing world in which the traditional rules, rituals and traditions of love, romance and relationships no longer apply. In particular, they point out that the modern world is characterized by individualization, choice and conflict.

- *Individualization* – We are under less pressure to conform to traditional collective goals set by our extended family, religion or culture. We now have the freedom to pursue individual goals.
- *Choice* – Cultural and economic changes mean that we have a greater range of choices available to us in terms of lifestyle and living arrangements.
- *Conflict* – There is now more potential for antagonism between men and women because there is a natural clash of interest between the selfishness encouraged by individualization and the selflessness required by relationships, marriage and family life.

Beck and Beck-Gernsheim argue that these characteristics of the modern world have led to personal relationships between men and women becoming a battleground (they call it the 'chaos of love') as evidenced by rising divorce rates. However, Beck and Beck-Gernsheim are positive about the future because they note that people still generally want to find love with another in order to help them cope with a risky, rapidly changing world. In particular, love helps compensate for the stress and, particularly, the impersonal and uncertain nature of the modern world. Love is the one thing people feel is real and that they can be sure of. Divorce and remarriage may simply be signs that people still have faith that they will one day find the true love they need to help them cope with the complexity of modern life.

Divorce trends suggest that monogamy (one partner for life) will eventually be replaced by **serial monogamy** (a series of long-term relationships resulting in cohabitation and/or marriage). However, the New Right panic about divorce is probably exaggerated. It is important to remember that although four out of ten marriages may end in divorce, six out of ten succeed; over 75 per cent of children are living with both natural parents who are legally married. These figures suggest that society still places a high value on marriage and the family.

Single-parent families

The number of one-parent families with dependent children tripled from 2 per cent of UK households in 1961 to 7 per cent in 2005. There are now approximately 1.75 million lone-parent families in Britain, making up about 23 per cent of all families. About 26 per cent of people under the age of 19 live in a one-parent family. Ninety per cent of single-parent families are headed by women. Most of these are ex-married (divorced, separated or widowed) or ex-cohabitees. The fastest growing group of single parents is made up of those who have never married or cohabited. Haskey estimated this group to be 26 per cent of all single mothers in 2002. Contrary to popular opinion, most single mothers are not teenagers – teenage mothers make up just 3 per cent of lone parents. The average age of a lone parent is actually 34.

Ford and Millar (1998) note that lone parenthood is seen by some as an inherently second-rate and imperfect family type, reflecting the selfish choices of adults against the interests of children. For example, New Right thinkers see a connection between one-parent families, educational underachievement and delinquency. They believe that children from one-parent families lack self-discipline and can be emotionally disturbed because of the lack of a firm father figure in their lives. In addition, New Right thinkers are concerned about the cost of one-parent families to the state. Public expenditure on such families increased fourfold in the 1990s. It is suggested that the state offers

Focus on research

Burghes and Brown (1995)
Teenage single mothers

A qualitative study using unstructured interviews with 31 mothers who were teenagers at conception and who have never been married was carried out by Burghes and Brown in 1995. They found that most of the pregnancies were unintended. However, nearly all the respondents expressed strong anti-abortion views and adoption was rarely considered. Most of the mothers reported that their experience of lone motherhood was a mixture of hard work and enormous joy. For the most part, the mothers interviewed preferred to be at home caring for their children. All the mothers intended to resume training or employment once their children were in school. Marriage was also a long-term goal.

Burghes, L. and Brown, M. (1995) *Single Lone Mothers: Problems, prospects and policies*, York: Family Policy Studies Centre

How does this research challenge stereotypes about teenage mothers?

'perverse incentives', such as council housing and benefits, to young females to get pregnant.

Ford and Millar note that the 'perverse incentives' argument is flawed when the quality of life of lone parents is examined. Many experience poverty, debt and material hardship, and try to protect their children from poverty by spending less on themselves. Ford and Millar also suggest that poverty may be partly responsible for lone parenthood. Single women from poor socio-economic backgrounds living on council estates with higher than average rates of unemployment are more likely than others to become solo mothers. Motherhood is regarded as a desired and valued goal by these women and may be a rational response to their poor economic prospects. Surveys of such women suggest that children are a great source of love and pride, and most lone parents put family life at the top of things they see as important.

Feminist sociologists maintain that familial ideology causes problems for the one-parent family because it emphasizes the nuclear family ideal. This ideal leads to the **negative labelling** of one-parent families by teachers, social workers, housing departments, police and the courts. Single parents may be **scapegoated** for inner-city crime and educational underachievement, when these problems are actually the result of factors such as unemployment and poverty. The New Right also rarely consider that single parenthood may be preferable to the domestic violence that is inflicted by some husbands on their wives and children – or that the majority of one-parent families bring up their children successfully.

Reconstituted families

The **reconstituted** or stepfamily is made up of divorced or widowed people who have remarried, and their children from the previous marriage (or cohabitation). Such families are on the increase because of the rise in divorce. In 2003, it was estimated that 726 000 children were living in this type of family.

Reconstituted families are unique because children are also likely to have close ties with their other natural parent. An increasing number of children experience co-parenting, where they spend half their week with their mother and stepfather and spend the other half with their father. Some family experts see co-parenting as a characteristic of binuclear families – two separate post-divorce or separation households are really one family system as far as children are concerned.

De'Ath and Slater's (1992) study of step-parenting identified a number of challenges facing reconstituted families. Children may find themselves pulled in two directions, especially if the relationship between their natural parents continues to be strained. They may have tense relationships with their step-parents, and conflict may arise around the extent to which the step-parent and stepchild accept each other, especially with regard to whether the child accepts the newcomer as a 'mother' or 'father'. Strained relations between step-parents and children may test the loyalty of the natural parent and strain the new marriage. These families may be further complicated if the new couple decide to have children of their own, which may create the potential for envy and conflict among existing children.

Single-person households

One of the most dramatic post-war changes in Britain has been the increase in single-person households. More than 6.5m people now live on their own – three times as many as 40 years ago – and 29 per cent of all households comprised just one person in 2005. The increase in elderly single-person households is mainly due to longer life expectancy. However, we have also seen a corresponding increase in young, single-person households. For example, in 1971, only 6 per cent of households were made up of single people under state pension age. This had increased to 15 per cent by 2005. There are a number of explanations for this increase:

● *The increase in female employment/career opportunities* – More women are gaining financial independence and choosing singlehood as a creative option for themselves before they elect eventually to settle down, although some are opting for voluntary childlessness.

● *The expansion of higher education* – More people are now going to university. This obviously delays the start of their careers and thus is likely to delay 'settling down' tendencies.

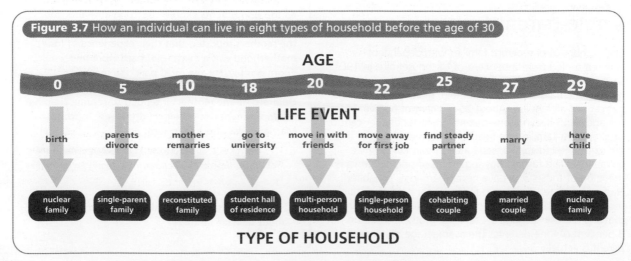

Figure 3.7 How an individual can live in eight types of household before the age of 30

AGE

| 0 | 5 | 10 | 18 | 20 | 22 | 25 | 27 | 29 |

LIFE EVENT

| birth | parents divorce | mother remarries | go to university | move in with friends | move away for first job | find steady partner | marry | have child |

TYPE OF HOUSEHOLD

| nuclear family | single-parent family | reconstituted family | student hall of residence | multi-person household | single-person household | cohabiting couple | married couple | nuclear family |

- *Changes in attitude/priorities* – Trends in marriage suggest that people are marrying later and have other priorities, such as education and careers. For example, Sharpe (1994) found girls in the 1970s were concerned with love, marriage, husbands, children, jobs and careers, in that order. In the 1990s, when she repeated the research, she found that girls' priorities had changed and that they were more focused on jobs and careers. The pressure to 'settle down and have children' is not as great as it used to be.
- *The increase in divorce* – Divorce creates both single-parent families and single-person households.

However, it is also important to note that for some young people, singlehood might only be a temporary phase before they establish a couple relationship and a nuclear family.

Check your understanding

1   Why have marriage rates declined in recent years?

2   Why is cohabitation not a threat to marriage?

3   Why are women more likely to initiate divorce proceedings than men?

4   What social problems are caused by divorce according to New Right sociologists?

5   What reasons, apart from legislation making divorce easier, might be responsible for the rise in divorce since the 1970s?

6   How might reconstituted family life differ from that experienced in nuclear families?

7   Why do feminist sociologists think that one-parent families are seen as a 'problem'?

Key terms

Close-knit community a community in which there are close relationships between people (everyone knows everyone else).

Divorce the legal ending of a marriage.

Divorce petition a legal request for a divorce.

Empty-shell marriage a marriage in which the partners no longer love each other but stay together, usually for the sake of the children.

Irretrievable unable to be recovered. Broken down for ever.

Monogamy the practice of having only one partner.

Negative labelling treating something as being 'bad' or 'undesirable'.

Privatized nuclear family a home-centred family that has little contact with extended kin or neighbours.

Reconstituted families stepfamilies.

Scapegoated unfairly blamed.

Serial monogamy a series of long-term relationships.

Activities

Research idea

1   Carry out a mini-survey across three different age groups (e.g. 15 to 20, 25 to 30, and 35 to 40), investigating attitudes towards marriage, cohabitation, one-parent families, step-families, co-parenting, teenage pregnancy, etc.

2   Interview two males and two females to find out what characteristics they are looking for in a future partner. Do your findings support the view that females set higher standards in relationships?

Web.tasks

1   Use the archives of either the *Guardian* or the *Daily Telegraph* websites to research the debate about divorce. The latter is excellent for links to relevant sites such as www.divorce-online.co.uk, the family law consortium and the Lord Chancellor's Department.

2   Visit the websites of the following organizations and work out whether they support familial ideology:
- www.themothersunion.org
- www.civitas.org.uk – this site has a collection of interesting fact sheets on the family, plus excellent links to traditionalist family sites
- www.oneplusone.org.uk

3   Use the web to research one-parent families. The following websites contain a range of useful data and information:
- www.gingerbread.org.uk
- www.opfs.org.uk
- www.oneparentfamily.co.uk
- www.careforthefamily.org.uk

the opening sentence of each paragraph should clearly highlight the reason

whatever it is that you have identified must be discussed in some depth using sociological studies and examples

you should attempt to write two very detailed paragraphs in about 15 minutes

each reason needs to be developed into a very detailed paragraph which must be clearly distinguishable from the other

(a) Identify and explain two reasons why the number of single-person households has increased in the last thirty years. **(17 marks)**

begin your answer with a clear definition of what is meant by this concept

a detailed description of the view is required using sociological concepts, theories and studies

it is important to assess the merits of the New Right view of trends in marriage, cohabitation and divorce in some detail, either by raising specific strengths or criticisms of the view or by presenting alternative theoretical perspectives

this view is a New Right perspective

you should attempt to write at least 2 sides of the answer book in about 30 minutes

(b) Outline and evaluate the view that recent trends in marriage, cohabitation and divorce indicate a decline in family life. **(33 marks)**

treat each of these social phenomena as equally as possible

Grade booster Getting top marks in this question

Begin by identifying some of the patterns of marriage, cohabitation and divorce. Take each in turn and explain why the New Right see these trends as indicating a decline in the quality of family life. Contrast these arguments with those feminist and postmodernist sociologists who claim that these changes indicate positive change for the family. For example, examine those arguments which suggest that marriage is still popular, that cohabitation is not an alternative to marriage and that divorce is an indicator of a healthy marriage system and a cause of very positive family diversity.

TOPIC 4

The impact of demographic changes on family life and diversity

Getting you thinking

Births[1,2] and deaths[1,2] (UK)

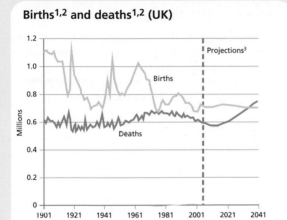

1 Data for 1901 to 1921 exclude Ireland which was constitutionally
  a part of the United Kingdom during this period.
2 Data from 1981 exclude the non-residents of Northern Ireland.
3 2004-based projections for 2005 to 2041.

International migration into and out of the United Kingdom: by gender

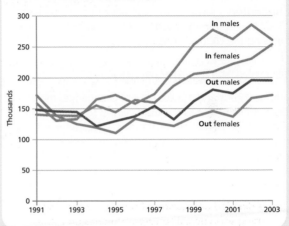

Source (both graphs): Babb, P. *et al.* (2006) *Social Trends 36*,
Basingstoke: Palgrave Macmillan

© Posy Simmonds (from *The Observer*, 25 October 1998)

1   Examine the graphs above – what trends can be observed?

2   How do you think that the trends relating to births, deaths and migration will influence the nature of family life in the UK?

3   How do the family setups portrayed in the cartoon challenge the traditional view of the family?

The study of **demography** is focused on how the number of births and deaths, and the number of people entering and leaving the country (migration) all affect the size, sex and age structure of the population. As we shall see, demographic changes over the past 100 years have had a major influence on British family life. The nuclear family is no longer the main way in which living arrangements are organized in the UK. Consequently, some sociologists, notably Rapoport *et al.* (1982), have been very critical of the functionalist and New Right view that the typical family is nuclear. They point out that even back in 1978, only 20 per cent of families fitted the traditionalist idea of a married couple household, i.e. a father who went out to work and a mother who stayed at home to look after the two children. Rapoport and colleagues argue that family life in Britain today is actually characterized by **diversity**. A range of family types exists with diverse internal setups reflecting the changing demography of British society.

The population of the UK

The population of the United Kingdom grew steadily between 1971 and 2003 to reach 59.8 million people in 2004. Population projections suggest that it will reach 65 million in 2023 and 67 million by 2031. The rate of population change over time depends upon four demographic factors:

- the **birth rate** – refers to the number of live births per 1000 of the population over a year
- the **fertility rate** – refers to the number of live births per 1000 women aged 15 to 44 over one year
- the **death rate** – refers to the number of deaths per 1000 of the population over the course of a year
- **migration** – refers to the number of people entering the UK (i.e. **immigration**) and the number of people leaving the UK (i.e. **emigration**).

Reasons for population growth

Up to the 1950s and 1960s, natural change (i.e. more births than deaths) was the main reason for population growth in the UK, although from the 1980s onwards, net migration (i.e. immigration exceeding emigration) has been the main factor. For example, in the 1950s, natural change accounted for 98 per cent of population change and net migration for only 2 per cent. Between 2001 and 2004, net migration accounted for two thirds of the increase in the UK population.

Changes in the birth rate

Only 716 000 children were born in 2004. This is 34 per cent fewer births than in 1901 and 21 per cent fewer than 1971. However, if we examine the birth rate over the course of the century, it has not been a straightforward history of decline. It is actually a history of fluctuations. There was a fall in births during the First World War, followed by a postwar 'baby boom', with births peaking at 1.1 million in 1920. The number of births then fell and remained low during the interwar period. Births increased again after the Second World War with another 'baby-boom'. There was also an increase in births in the late 1980s and early 1990s. This was the result of the larger cohort of women born in the 1960s entering their childbearing years. Since 2001, the birth rate has steadily risen. In 2007, the ONS announced that the 2006 birth rate was the highest for 26 years.

There are a number of reasons why the number of births in the 21st century is lower than the number of births in 1901:

- A major decline in the infant mortality rate, (i.e. the number of children dying at birth or in their first year of life per 1000 births) occurred. This began in the 19th century because of improvements in sanitation, water supplies and nutrition, and continued into the 20th century. Contrary to popular belief, medicine was not mainly responsible for children surviving into adulthood. Mass vaccination was not introduced until after the Second World War, although it obviously contributed to the better health enjoyed by children. The decline in child mortality rates meant that parents

did not need to have lots of children to ensure that a few survived.
- As standards of living increased, having children became an expensive business. It is estimated that an average child costs about £140,000 to bring up. Parents have therefore chosen to limit the size of their families
- Attitudes towards women's roles dramatically changed during the course of the 20th century and this had a profound effect upon women's attitudes towards family life, having children, education and careers. In particular, it resulted in a decline in fertility as women chose to have fewer children and some chose not to have children at all.

Changes in the fertility rate

The fertility rate generally refers to the number of children that women of childbearing age have in any one year. Fertility rates have generally declined over the past 100 years. For example, in 1900 there were 115 live births per 1000 women aged 15 to 44, compared with only 57 in 1999 and 54.5 in 2001.

Another way of looking at fertility is to examine the Total Fertility Rate (TFR) – the number of children that are born to an average woman during her childbearing life. In 2004, the UK had a TFR of 1.77 children per woman but recent ONS data suggests that the first baby boom of the 21st century may be on its way because the fertility rate rose to 1.8 babies per woman in 2005 and again to 1.87 in 2006. This was the fifth annual rise in a row and resulted in the most babies being born in a single year since 1993.

Fertility and age

There is evidence that women are delaying having families. Changes in fertility rates suggest that women are having children at an older age than they were 30 years ago. In general, fertility rates for women aged 30 and above have increased, while those for women aged below 30 have declined. The average age of married women giving birth has increased by six years since 1971 to 30 in 2003. The highest rate of fertility is found in the age group 30 to 34 whilst 2005 ONS figures showed a seven per cent increase in births among women aged between 35 and 39. Moreover, the number of children born to women aged 40 and over has doubled in the last 20 years.

Explanations for changes in fertility rate

There are three main reasons why fertility rates fell towards the end of the 20th century:

- Reliable birth control, particularly the contraceptive pill, gave women far greater power over reproduction.
- Educational opportunities expanded for females, particularly entry into university. This coincided with an increase in job opportunities for females as the service sector of the economy expanded. There is some evidence that the recent rise in the fertility rate of women aged 35 and above is due to high earners who took up their university places in the 1980s.
- Attitudes towards family life underwent a profound cultural change as a result of economic change. Women could see that there were other lifestyle

choices in addition to getting married and having children.

The recent rise in fertility has been credited to the increase in the number of immigrants to the UK who tend to have larger families. For example, in 2005, 146 944 children were born to mothers who did not come from Britain. In 1998 the total was 86 345. Babies born to mothers from overseas accounted for 21.9 per cent of all births in 2005, up from 20.8 per cent in 2004.

Dual-earner families

There is some evidence that declining fertility rates have encouraged the decline of the full-time mother and encouraged the growth of dual-career families in which couples combine paid work with family life and childcare. Over 60% of couples with children now combine jobs and family life. There are generally two types of dual-earner families. Some professional couples are extremely committed to their careers but make the decision to have a child once these careers are established. These couples are probably partly responsible for the doubling in the number of women aged 40 or over having babies in the last 20 years. These couples can probably also afford professional childcare services such as nannies, au-pairs and private nurseries.

The other more common type of dual-earner family is composed of the husband who earns the major share of the family income and the female who works part time. In this situation, it is likely that it is she who takes the major responsibility for childcare and the upkeep of the home.

Births outside marriage

New Right commentators have been especially disturbed by the fact that one in three babies is now born outside marriage. In particular, media **moral panics** have focused on the fact that the UK has the highest rate of teenage pregnancy in Europe. For example, in England and Wales in 2003, there were 34 138 pregnancies in the 16 to 17 age group, 7690 pregnancies in the 15 to 16 age group and 334 pregnancies in the 14 and under age group. Only 54 per cent of these conceptions resulted in a birth.

However, according to the National Council for One Parent Families, the under-16 conception rate has fallen considerably, compared with the 1960s, and it has fallen slightly over the last ten years to approximately 8 per 1000 girls. Only 3 per cent of unmarried mothers are teenagers, and most of them live at home with their parents. Experts are generally sceptical that such teenagers are deliberately getting pregnant in order to claim state housing and benefits. Moreover, four out of five births outside marriage are registered to both parents, and three-quarters of these are living at the same address. Most births outside marriage, therefore, are to cohabiting couples. It should also be pointed out that a significant number of marriages break up in the first year after having a child, which suggests that marriage is not always the stable institution for procreation that the New Right claim it is.

Childlessness

Some sociologists argue that we should be more concerned about the trend towards childlessness that has appeared in recent years. The Family Policy Studies Centre estimates that one woman in five will choose to remain childless, and this figure is expected to double in the next 20 years (McAllister 1998). In 2000, one in five women aged 40 had not had children compared with one in ten in 1980, and this figure is expected to rise to one in four by 2018.

The death rate

The annual number of deaths has remained relatively steady since 1901. There were peaks in the number of deaths during both the First and Second World Wars. The peak of 690 000 in 1918 represented the highest annual number of deaths ever recorded; these were due both to losses during the First World War and the influenza epidemic which followed it. However, as the population has increased, life expectancy has increased and death rates have fallen; between 1971 and 2004 the death rate for all males fell by 21 per cent, while the death rate for all females fell by 9 per cent.

Life expectancy

In 1851, life expectancy at birth in England and Wales was 40 years for males and 44 years for females. Just 150 years later, in modern-day industrialized UK, life expectancy has nearly doubled from Victorian levels: children born in 2004 will, on average, live for 78 years. This increase in life expectancy is the result of improved public health (sanitation and hygiene), medical technology and practice (drugs such as vaccines and antibiotics), rising living standards (which have improved nutritional intake and housing quality) and better care and welfare facilities (which have been mainly provided by the State).

However, life expectancy is not uniform across the country. There is some evidence that life expectancy differs according to region, e.g. male life expectancy in 2002 was 76.2 years in England, but 73.5 in Scotland. There is also evidence that life expectancy also depends on social class and ethnicity – those in middle-class jobs tend to live longer than those in manual jobs and the unemployed, whilst some ethnic minorities have lower life expectancy than White people.

The ageing population

The decline in the death rate, especially the infant mortality rate, and the increase in life expectancy has led to an ageing of the UK population. There are increasing numbers of people aged 65 and over and decreasing numbers of children under 16. In 1821, there were very large numbers of young people but very few of them were surviving into old age. Today, there are fewer young people – only 12 per cent of the population is aged under 10 years compared with 27 per cent in 1821, whilst the numbers of those aged over 80 years have increased from 1 per cent in 1821 to 4 per cent in 2004. However, the UK also saw an acceleration in this process in the late 20th century – the number of people aged under 16 declined by 18 per cent between 1971 and 2004 whilst the number of people aged over 65 increased by 29 per cent in the same period. It is predicted that people aged over 65 years will outnumber people aged under 16 for the first time in 2014 and that the gap will widen thereafter.

Elderly one-person households

The ageing of the population has led to an increase in the number of one-person households over state pension age as a proportion of all households. In 2005, 14 per cent of all households were of this type. Women aged 65 and over were more likely to live alone than men because of their superior life expectancy and because they tend to marry men older than themselves. In 2005, 59 per cent of women aged 75 and over were living alone.

Extended kinship ties

Although older people are increasingly living alone, this does not mean that they are isolated. Evidence suggests that many of them have regular contact with extended kin. There is evidence that working-class families, in particular, still see great virtue in maintaining **extended families**. The study *Villains* by Janet Foster (1990) – of an East End London community – found that adults chose to live only a few streets away from their parents and other close relatives such as grandparents, aunts, uncles and cousins, and visited them regularly. Ties between mothers and children were particularly strong. Emotional and material support was frequently offered to family members.

Other research by Phillipson and Downs (1999), and O'Brien and Jones (1996) found that children and grandchildren saw their elderly relatives on a frequent basis, whereas ONS survey data collected in 2003 found that 61 per cent of grandparents saw their grandchildren once a week. Many elderly relatives were using new technology such as e-mail to keep in contact with their extended kin.

Ross *et al.* (2006) found in their study that grandparents spoke positively about becoming and being a grandparent (see Focus on research below). When grandchildren were younger, time was spent together on outings and playing together, or with the grandparents teaching skills and providing childcare. As grandchildren grew older, the relationships were more likely to revolve around talking, giving advice and support.

Beanpole families

Brannen (2003) notes that the ageing of the population, the increasing tendency of women to pursue both higher education and a career, the consequent decline in fertility and the availability of divorce has led to the recent emergence of four-generation families – families that include great-grandparents and great-grandchildren. She notes that families today are less likely to experience horizontal intragenerational ties, i.e. we have fewer aunts, uncles and cousins. Brannen argues that we are now more likely to experience vertical intergenerational ties, i.e. closer ties with grandparents and great-grandparents (see Focus on research on p. 95). Brannen calls such family setups 'beanpole families'. She argues that the 'pivot generation', i.e. that sandwiched between older and younger family generations is increasingly in demand to provide for the needs of both

Focus on research

Ross et al. (2006)
Exploring intergenerational relationships

Interviews and group discussions were held with 73 grandparents aged between 55 and 88 and 75 grandchildren aged between 10 and 19 to explore in depth the meaning and significance of grandparent–grandchild relations.

Grandparents generally spoke positively about becoming and being a grandparent. When grandchildren were younger, time was spent together on outings and playing together, or with the grandparents teaching skills and providing childcare. Grandparents often referred to providing financial support to assist their grandchildren, ranging from pocket money to school fees. As grandchildren grew older, the relationships were more likely to revolve around talking, giving advice and support. Both generations described how grandparents usually played a key role in 'listening' to grandchildren. Many young

people said they could share problems and concerns with their grandparents and referred to the way grandparents would sometimes act as go-betweens in the family, particularly when there were disagreements between themselves and their parents.

Grandparents also provided a bridge to the past by acting as sources of family history, heritage and traditions: storytellers who kept grandchildren aware of their own family experiences and their culture. They were also active in keeping wider sets of relatives connected.

Ross, N., Hill, M., Sweeting, H. and Cunningham-Burley, S. (2006) *Grandparents and Teen Grandchildren: Exploring Intergenerational Relationships*, Edinburgh: Centre for Research on Families and Relationships

1 Why might the research methods used by the researchers have increased the validity of the findings?

2 How did grandparents and grandchildren interpret each other's family role?

elderly parents and grandchildren. For example, 20 per cent of people in their fifties and sixties currently care for an elderly person, while 10 per cent care for both an elderly person and a grandchild. Such services are based on the assumption of 'reciprocity', i.e. the provision of babysitting services is repaid by the assumption that daughters will assist mothers in their old age.

Migration

Historically, the population of Great Britain was made up of people from a White British ethnic background. The pattern of migration since the 1950s has produced a number of distinct, minority ethnic groups within the general population. In 2001, the majority of the population in Great Britain were White British (88 per cent). The remaining 6.7 million people (11.8 per cent of the population) belonged to other ethnic groups – White Other was the largest group (2.5 per cent), followed by Indians (1.8 per cent), Pakistanis (1.3 per cent), White Irish (1.2 per cent), those of mixed ethnic backgrounds (1.2 per cent), Black Caribbeans (1.0 per cent), Black Africans (0.8 per cent) and Bangladeshis (0.5 per cent).

Migration during the latter part of the 20th century also led to religious diversity in Great Britain. Christianity was the main religion in Great Britain; 41 million people identified themselves as Christians in 2001, making up 72 per cent of the population. Muslims formed the largest non-Christian religious group, comprising 3 per cent of the total population. Hindus were the next largest group (1 per cent), followed by Sikhs (0.6 per cent), Jews (0.5 per cent) and Buddhists (0.3 per cent).

Cultural diversity

Immigration has led to cultural and religious diversity in family life. Research carried out at Essex University in 2000 indicates that only 39 per cent of British-born African-Caribbean adults under the age of 60 are in a formal marriage, compared with 60 per cent of White adults (Berthoud 2000). Moreover, this group is more likely than any other group to intermarry. The number of mixed-race partnerships means that very few African-Caribbean men and women are married to fellow African-Caribbeans and only one-quarter of African-Caribbean children live with

two Black parents. Ali (2002) notes that such marriages result in interethnic families and mixed-race (sometimes called 'dual heritage') children. Some sociologists have suggested that these types of families have their own unique problems, such as facing prejudice and discrimination from both White and Black communities.

African-Caribbean families

There is evidence that African-Caribbean families have a different structure to White families. African-Caribbean communities have a higher proportion of one-parent families compared with White communities – over 50 per cent of African-Caribbean families with children are one-parent families. Rates of divorce are higher but there is also an increasing tradition in the African-Caribbean community of mothers choosing to live independently from their children's father. Berthoud notes two important and increasing trends:

- 66 per cent of 20-year-old African-Caribbean mothers remain single compared with 11 per cent of their White peers, while at 25 years, these figures are 48 per cent and 7 per cent respectively.
- At the age of 30, 60 per cent of African-Caribbean men are unattached, compared with 45 per cent of their White peers.

These trends indicate that African-Caribbean women are avoiding settling down with the African-Caribbean fathers of their children. Berthoud (2003) suggests that the attitudes of young African-Caribbean women are characterized by 'modern individualism' – they are choosing to bring up children alone for two reasons:

- African-Caribbean women are more likely to be employed than African-Caribbean men. Such women rationally weigh up the costs and benefits of living with the fathers of their children and conclude that African-Caribbean men are unreliable as a source of family income and are potentially a financial burden. Surveys indicate that such women prefer to be economically independent.
- Chamberlain and Goulborne (1999) note that African-Caribbean single mothers are more likely to be supported by an extended kinship network in their upbringing of children – interestingly, African-Caribbean definitions of kinship often extends to including family friends and neighbours as 'aunts' and 'uncles'.

Asian family life

The Essex study also found that the Pakistani and Bangladeshi communities are most likely to live in old-fashioned nuclear families, although about 33 per cent of Asian families – mainly Sikhs and East African Asians – live in extended families. East African Asian extended families are likely to contain more than one generation, while Sikh extended units are organized around brothers and their wives and children.

Berthoud argues that South Asians tend to be more traditional in their family values than Whites. Marriage is highly valued and there is little divorce (although this may indicate empty-shell marriages). Marriage in Asian families – whether Muslim, Hindu or Sikh – is mainly arranged and

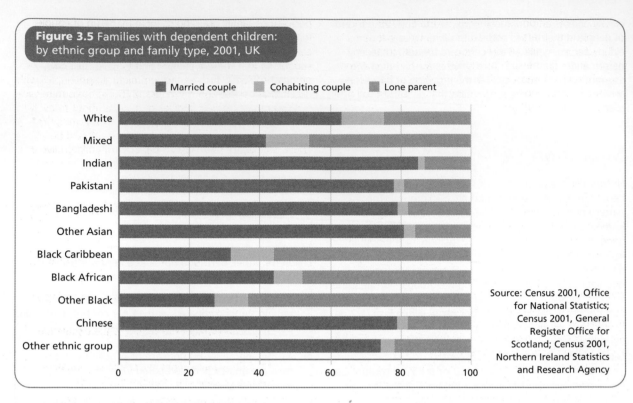

Figure 3.5 Families with dependent children: by ethnic group and family type, 2001, UK

■ Married couple ■ Cohabiting couple ■ Lone parent

White
Mixed
Indian
Pakistani
Bangladeshi
Other Asian
Black Caribbean
Black African
Other Black
Chinese
Other ethnic group

0   20   40   60   80   100

Source: Census 2001, Office for National Statistics; Census 2001, General Register Office for Scotland; Census 2001, Northern Ireland Statistics and Research Agency

there is little intermarriage with other religions or cultures. There is also evidence that Bangladeshi and Pakistani women have more children than Indian and White women, and at younger ages. Relationships between Asian parents and their children are also very different from those that characterize White families. Children tend to respect religious and cultural traditions, and they feel a strong sense of duty to their families, and especially to their elders. South Asian families, particularly, feel a strong sense of duty and obligation to assist extended kin in economic and social ways. This is important because Bangladeshi and Pakistani families in the UK are more likely to be in poverty compared with Indian and White families. Such obligations often extend to sending money to relatives abroad on a regular basis and travelling half way around the world to nurse sick or dying relatives.

Class diversity

Rapoport *et al.* (1982) suggest that there may be differences between middle-class and working-class families in terms of the relationship between husband and wife and the way in which children are socialized and disciplined. Some sociologists argue that middle-class parents are more child-centred than working-class parents. They supposedly take a greater interest in their children's education, and consequently pass on cultural advantages in terms of attitudes, values and practices (i.e. cultural capital) which assist their children through the educational system. However, critical sociologists argue that working-class parents are just as child-centred, but that material deprivation limits how much help they can give their children. Therefore, the working-class child's experience is likely to be less satisfactory because of family poverty, poor schools, lack of material support, greater risks of accidents both in the home and in the street, and so on.

There is also evidence that extended kinship ties are important to the upper class, in their attempt to maintain wealth and privilege. The economic and political **elite** may use marriage and family connections to ensure 'social closure' – that is, to keep those who do not share their culture from becoming part of the elite.

Sexual diversity

The New Right have expressed concern at the increasing number of same-sex couples who are cohabiting – and particularly the trend of such couples to have families through adoption, artificial insemination and surrogacy. In 1999, the law lords ruled that a homosexual couple can be legally defined as a family, and the Government is now looking to introduce legislation which will mean that long-term same-sex partners will have similar rights to heterosexual married couples with regard to inheritance (of property and pensions, for example) and next-of-kin status. New Right commentators have suggested that such family setups are 'unnatural' and that children will either be under pressure to experiment with the lifestyles of their parents or will be bullied at school because of the sexuality of their parents. In the courts, such fears have meant that in the past mothers who have come out as lesbians have lost custody of their children.

There have been a number of sociological studies of homosexual couples and children. Studies of couples suggest that relationships between partners are qualitatively different from heterosexual partners in terms of both domestic and emotional labour because they are not subject to gendered assumptions about which sex should be responsible for these tasks. There may, therefore, be more equality between partners.

Studies of children brought up in single-sex families show no significant effects in terms of gender identification or sexual orientation. For example, Gottman (1990) found that adult daughters of lesbian mothers were just as likely to be of a heterosexual inclination as the daughters of heterosexual mothers. Dunne (1997) argues that children brought up by homosexuals are more likely to be tolerant and see sharing and equality as important features of their relationships with others.

Postmodernism and family diversity

Postmodernists argue that postmodern family life is characterized by diversity, variation and instability. For example, women no longer aspire exclusively to romantic love, marriage and children. Premarital sex, serial monogamy, cohabitation, economic independence, single-sex relationships and childlessness are now acceptable alternative lifestyles. Men's roles too are no longer clear cut in postmodern society, and the resulting 'crisis of masculinity' has led to men redefining both their sexuality and family commitments. Beck and Beck-Gernsheim (1995) argue that such choice and diversity have led to the renegotiation of family relationships as people attempt to find a middle ground between individualization and commitment to another person and/or children.

Demography and diversity – some conclusions

As we can see, demographic changes in the number of births and deaths, the fertility rate and migration have had a fairly profound effect on the structure and internal organization of families in the modern UK. In particular, these demographic changes have undermined the traditionalist New Right view that the nuclear family is the most common type of family in the UK. In 2005, only 37

per cent of family households were made up of couples with dependent children. However, demographic changes also tell us that family life is not static – rather it is constantly in a state of change and flux. For example, 25 per cent of family households are made up of couples with no children. These and single-person households may have evolved out of nuclear families or may be about to evolve into them. It is important, therefore, not to dismiss the nuclear family as redundant, although we should be constantly aware that over 40 per cent of children live in a non-traditional family today.

Check your understanding

1 How have changes in the fertility rate affected the relationship between women and family life?

2 What have been the main causes of the ageing of the UK population?

3 What effects might the ageing of the population have on family life in the UK?

4 What differences might exist between working-class and middle-class families in the UK?

5 Identify three main differences in family life in multicultural Britain?

Activities

Research idea

1 If you know people from ethnic or religious backgrounds different from your own, ask if you can interview them about their experience of family life. Make sure your questionnaire is sensitive to their background and avoids offending them.

2 Design a research tool that allows you to gather quantitative and qualitative information about your classmates' relationships with their elderly relatives. Does this confirm or challenge previous sociological research?

Web.tasks

Visit the following sites which focus on recent research into family life. What changes have they documented in family life since the turn of the century?

● The Institute for Social and Economic Research: www.iser.essex.ac.uk

● Centre for Family Research: www.ppsis.cam.ac.uk/CFR/

● Joseph Rowntree Foundation: www.jrf.org.uk

● Families, Life Course and Generations Research Centre: www.leeds.ac.uk/family

Key terms

Birth rate number of live births per 1000 of the population.

Death rate number of deaths per 1000 population.

Demography the study of population change.

Diversity difference, variation.

Elite the most powerful, rich or gifted members of a group.

Emigration people moving abroad.

Extended family a family in which sons and daughters live in the same neighbourhood as their parents, see each other

on a regular basis and offer each other various kinds of support.

Fertility rate number of children born per 1000 women aged 15 to 44.

Immigration people settling in the country to live or work.

Migration the number of people entering and leaving the country.

Moral panic public concern over some aspect of behaviour, created and reinforced in large part by sensational media coverage.

The impact of demographic changes on family life and diversity

the opening sentence of each paragraph should clearly highlight the feature

whatever it is that you have identified must be discussed in some depth using sociological studies and examples

you should attempt to write two very detailed paragraphs in about 15 minutes

each feature needs to be developed into a very detailed paragraph which must be clearly distinguishable from the other

(a) Identify and explain two features of the cultural diversity of family life in the UK.   (17 marks)

begin your answer with a clear definition of what is meant by this concept

a detailed description of the view is required using sociological concepts, theories and studies

it is important to assess the merits of the view in some detail, either by raising specific strengths and criticisms of the view or by presenting alternative theoretical perspectives

this view is shared by a number of perspectives

you should attempt to write at least 2 sides of the answer book in about 30 minutes

(b) Outline and evaluate the view that recent demographic changes have resulted in changes in the nature of family life in the UK.   (33 marks)

clearly define what specific changes are demographic

Grade booster   Getting top marks in this question

You need to describe what is meant by demographic changes and to outline the trends and patterns in the birth rate, fertility rate, death rate and migration rate in the past 30 years. Take each of these demographic trends in turn and show how they impact on the family. For example, the decline in the birth rate has contributed to smaller family size and the emergence of new family units such as the beanpole family. Note too how the decline in the death rate and increasing life expectancy has led to the ageing of the population which has great implications for the way family life is organised. Finally, make reference to immigration and emigration and how this is shaping the cultural diversity of modern family life.

TOPIC 5

Roles, responsibilities and relationships within the family

Getting you thinking

1. Consider the list of tasks above. Which adult in your home was mainly responsible for each task when you were aged 5 to 7?

2. What other aspects of power and control in the home are neglected if we only focus on household tasks?

3. Who exercises power in your home and what forms does this take?

(a) Making sure that you had sandwiches for lunch or the money to pay for a school dinner.

(b) Making sure that your favourite food was in the fridge.

(c) Arranging with other parents for you to go to a party or around to somebody's house for tea.

(d) Making sure that you had a clean swimming costume and towel on the days of school swims.

(e) Changing the sheets on your bed.

(f) Supervising your bathtime.

(g) Picking you up from school.

(h) Buying a present for you to take to another child's birthday party.

(i) Reassuring you if you had a bad dream in the night.

(j) Anticipating that you needed a new pair of shoes because you were about to grow out of your old pair.

In 1973, Young and Willmott claimed that the traditional **segregated division of labour in the home** – men as breadwinners and women as housewives/mothers – was breaking down. The relationship between husband and wife (the **conjugal relationship**) was becoming – at least in middle-class families – more joint or **symmetrical**. This trend towards **egalitarian** marriage, they argued, was caused by the decline in the extended family, and its replacement in the late 20th century by the privatized nuclear family, as well as by the increasing opportunities in paid employment for women. Some media commentators were so convinced by these arguments that in the 1980s, it was claimed that a 'new man' had appeared, i.e. males who were in touch with their feminine side and who were happy to meet women's emotional and domestic needs.

However, the exercise above should have shown you that much of women's labour in the home is neglected by studies that focus only on obvious and highly visible tasks. A good deal of what women do in the home is mental and emotional as well as physical, involving anticipating and fulfilling the needs of family members. These more subtle responsibilities tend to be missed by researchers, some of

whom have concluded that men and women are becoming more equal in the home on the basis of their sharing some of the more glamorous domestic tasks, such as cooking. These sorts of surveys can also miss other influences that ensure that power and control in the home remain firmly in male hands – violence, the lack of status associated with the full-time mother/housewife role, the belief that working mothers damage children, the fact that being a mother limits job opportunities, and so on.

Do men and women share roles equally within the family?

The idea that equality is a central characteristic of marriage is strongly opposed by feminist sociologists. Studies of professional couples indicate that only a minority genuinely share housework and childcare. For example, Dryden's (1999) qualitative study of 17 married couples found that women still had major responsibility for housework and childcare.

Surveys investigating the distribution of housework and childcare tasks suggest that men today are more involved in domestic tasks than their fathers and grandfathers. However, the Time Use Survey of 2005 carried out by Lader *et al.* (2006) found that women in paid work spent 21 hours a week on average on housework, compared with only 12 hours spent by men on the same. Overall, this survey found that 92 per cent of women do some housework per day, compared with only 77 per cent of men. Surprisingly, there was little sign that the traditional sexual division of labour in the home was changing. In 2005, women still spent more time than men cooking, washing up, cleaning, tidying, washing clothes and shopping. DIY and gardening tasks were still male dominated.

Furthermore, data from the British Household Panel Survey (2001) suggests that whatever the work–domestic set-up, women do more in the home than men. For example, when both spouses work full time, and even when the man is unemployed and his wife works, women put more hours into domestic labour than men. Some sociologists have suggested that unemployed men actually resist increased involvement in housework because they interpret it as unmasculine and as further threatening their role as breadwinner. McKee and Bell (1986) found that unemployed men in their study found it degrading to do housework and to be 'kept' by their employed wives.

The quantifiable evidence, therefore, indicates that women are still likely to experience a **dual burden or double shift** – in that they are expected to be mainly responsible for the bulk of domestic tasks, despite holding down full-time jobs. Sclater (2000) points out that household technologies, such as washing machines and vacuum cleaners, advertised as making life easier for women have actually increased this burden because they have raised household standards of cleanliness and increased time spent on housework.

Sociological studies have also noted that the distinction between work and leisure or free time is less clear cut for married women. For example, Green (1996) found that wives usually interpret leisure time as time free from both paid work and family commitments, whereas husbands saw all time outside paid work as their leisure time.

It has been suggested by Kilkey (2005) that working parents are now experiencing a 'time famine' with regard to childcare, which is resulting in the delegation of some childcare to external carers, especially kin such as grandparents. Brannen's observations about beanpole families outlined in Topic 3 seem to support this. However, Dryden found that gender inequality in the distribution of childcare and housework tasks was still a major source of dissatisfaction in marriage for women. Indeed, studies, such as the one by Bittman and Pixley (1997), suggest this inequality is a major cause of divorce today

Emotion work

Women are also responsible for the emotional wellbeing of their partners and children. Studies such as that carried out by Duncombe and Marsden (1995) have found that women felt that their male partners were lacking in terms of 'emotional participation', i.e. men found it difficult to express their feelings, to tell their partners how they felt

about them and to relate emotionally to their children. Duncombe and Marsden argue that this increases the burden on women because they feel they should attempt to compensate and please all parties in the home. Consequently, women spend a great deal of time soothing the emotions of partners and children. This leads to the neglect of their own psychological wellbeing, and can have negative consequences for their mental and physical health. For example, Bernard's study of marriage (1982) confirms this – she found that the men in her study were more satisfied with their marriage than their wives, many of whom expressed emotional loneliness. Moreover, these men had no inkling that their wives were unhappy.

Decision-making

Surveys of young married couples with children conclude that the decision to have children, although jointly reached, dramatically changes the life of the mother rather than the father. As Bernardes (1997) notes, in the UK, most female careers are interrupted by childbirth, but only a small minority of mothers return to their pre-baby jobs and most experience downward mobility into precarious, low-paid, part-time jobs with few rights.

Some sociologists have focused on the distribution of power within marriages. Hardill *et al.* (1997) discovered that middle-class wives generally deferred to their husbands in major decisions involving where to live, the size of the mortgage, buying cars etc. They concluded that the men in their sample were able to demand that the interests of their wives and families should be subordinated to the man's career because he was the major breadwinner. However, Gillian Leighton (1992) discovered that the power to influence and make family decisions changed when males became unemployed. In her study of professional couples, working wives often took over responsibility for bills and initiated cutbacks in spending.

Fatherhood

An important part of the New Right critique of one-parent families is the view that most of them lack fathers. Dennis and Erdos (2000), for example, suggest that fatherless children are less likely to be successfully socialized into the culture of discipline and compromise found in nuclear families, and so are less likely to be successful parents themselves. It is suggested that such children lack an authority figure to turn to in times of crisis and, as a result, the peer group and mass media have an increased influence. It is argued that such influence is likely to lead to an increase in social problems, such as delinquency, sexual promiscuity, teenage pregnancy and drug use.

De-partnering and de-parenting

There is no doubt that de-partnering, whether from marriage or cohabitation, leads to some degree of de-parenting, i.e. one or other parent, usually the father in the UK, becomes less involved in the parenting of a child. Furthermore, the law in the UK tends to uphold traditional ideas about gender roles, and custody of children is mainly awarded to the mother. Bernardes notes that the Children

Act clearly states that the mother should have parental responsibility for a child if the parents are not married. It is estimated that 40 per cent of fathers lose touch completely with their children after two years; others will experience irregular contact or conflict with their ex-partners about access arrangements.

The quality of fathering

Other commentators have suggested that we should focus on the quality of fathering. In the early 1990s, many sociologists concluded that the role of fathers was changing. For example, men in the 1990s were more likely to attend the birth of their babies than men in the 1960s, and they were more likely to play a greater role in childcare than their own fathers. Burghes (1997) found that fathers were taking an increasingly active role in the emotional development of their children. Beck (1992) notes that, in the postmodern age, fathers can no longer rely on jobs to provide a sense of identity and fulfilment. Increasingly, they look to their children to give them a sense of identity and purpose.

However, Warin et al. (1999), in their study of 95 families in Rochdale, found that fathers, mothers and teenage children overwhelmingly subscribed to the view that the male should be the breadwinner, despite changes in employment and family life, and that mothers were the experts in parenting. The researchers do note that children increasingly expected their fathers to support them emotionally as well as provide for their material comforts. Research by Gray (2006) supports this view. Her research showed that fathers emphasized the need to spend quality time with their children. They wanted more time to get to know their children, to take them out, to help them with homework and to talk to them. Fathers viewed time spent with children in outings, sport, play and conversation as an expression of fatherhood rather than as a form of domestic work.

However, it is important not to exaggerate men's role in childcare. Looking after children is still overwhelmingly the responsibility of mothers, rather than jointly shared with fathers. Recent research has focused on the pressures of work in the 21st century. A survey by Dex in 2003 found that 30 per cent of fathers (and 6 per cent of mothers) worked more than 48 hours a week on a regular basis. Gray found that many fathers would like to spend more time with their children but are prevented by long work hours from bonding effectively with their children.

The social capital approach

Lately, researchers have taken a 'social capital' approach to childcare. This has resulted in parenting being re-defined as investing time in children which will benefit them educationally, economically and emotionally. Social capital research therefore focuses on how parents interpret time spent with children. Gray's research found that both male and female parents in her study saw spending time with children as an important aspect of family relationships. Fathers, in particular, saw spending time alone with a child as quality time because they were more likely than women to be doing it out of choice rather than obligation.

Focus on research

Reynolds et al. (2003)
Caring and counting

The researchers interviewed 37 mothers and 30 fathers in couples who had at least one pre-school child (Reynolds et al. 2003). The mothers were working in a hospital or in an accountancy firm. All the mothers in the study had strong, traditional views about what being a 'good mother' and a 'good partner' was about. Employment did not necessarily lead to more egalitarian relationships with their partners.

In fact, most of the mothers and fathers interviewed subscribed to highly traditional and stereotypical views about the gendered division of labour within the home. The mothers had primary responsibility for the home and the conduct of family life. Mothers who worked full time were just as concerned as those working part time to 'be there' for their children and to meet the needs of their children and their family.

The researchers found no evidence of mothers becoming more 'work centred' at the expense of family life.

Apart from increasing the family income, mothers also felt their employment was helping them to meet their children's emotional and social development. Separate interviews with the women's partners revealed widespread agreement that the mother's work was having a positive impact on family relationships. Most fathers felt their children had benefited from their mothers' work, which provided a positive role model for their children.

Some mothers, nevertheless, expressed concern that their job had a negative impact on the family, particularly when they were overstretched at work, felt tired or had trouble 'switching off' from a bad day at work. A number of fathers also felt uneasy about the demands placed on their partners at work and the effect that work-related stress could have on their children and their relationship with each other.

Reynolds, T., Callender, C. and Edwards, R. (2003) Caring and Counting: The impact of mothers' employment on family relationships, York: Joseph Rowntree Foundation (www.jrf.org.uk)

1 Comment on the sample used in the study.

2 How did parents feel that mothers' employment was having a positive effect on their families?

3 What concerns were expressed about mothers' employment?

Patriarchal ideology

Feminists have highlighted the influence of patriarchal ideology on the perceptions of both husbands and wives. Surveys indicate that many women accept primary responsibility for housework and childcare without question, and believe that their career should be secondary to that of their husband. Such ideas are also reflected in state policy, which encourages female economic dependence upon men. Moreover, patriarchal ideology expects women to take on jobs that are compatible with family commitments. Surveys suggest that a large number of mothers feel guilty about working. Some actually give up work altogether because they believe that their absence somehow damages their children.

The mother/housewife role and work

Some feminist sociologists have concluded that women's participation in the labour market is clearly limited by their domestic responsibilities. Because of these responsibilities, very few women have continuous full-time careers. Mothers, then, tend to have 'jobs', while their husbands have 'careers'. As a result, women don't have the same access to promotion and training opportunities as men. Some employers may believe that women are unreliable because of family commitments and, consequently, discriminate against them.

Modern marriages, therefore, do not appear as equal as functionalists suggest. On all the criteria examined so far – the distribution of housework and childcare tasks, decision-making, and the impact of being a mother/housewife on employment – we see women at a disadvantage compared with men.

Violence in families

Another important aspect of power within marriage is domestic violence – the power of men to control women by physical force. This type of violence is estimated to be the most common type of violence in the UK although, because it takes place behind closed doors, often without witnesses, it is notoriously difficult to measure and document. It is also difficult to define – as Sclater (2000) notes, some behaviour, such as kicking and punching, is easily recognizable as violent, but behaviours such as threats, verbal abuse, psychological manipulation and sexual intimidation are less easy to categorize and may not be recognized by some men and women as domestic violence.

The official statistics tell us that violence by men against their female partners accounts for a third of all reported violence. Stanko's (2000) survey found that one incident of domestic violence is reported by women to the police every minute in the UK. Mirrlees-Black (1999), using data from the British Crime Survey, found that women were more likely to suffer domestic violence than men – 70 per cent of reported domestic violence is violence by men against their female partners. These figures are thought to be an

underestimate because many women are reluctant to come forward for various reasons:

- They love their partners and think they can change them.
- They blame themselves in some way for the violence.
- They feel they may not be taken seriously.
- They are afraid of the repercussions.

Some sociologists have reported increases in female violence on men, but it is estimated that this constitutes, at most, only 5 per cent of all domestic violence. Moreover, as Nazroo's (1999) research indicates, wives often live in fear of men's potential domestic violence or threats, while husbands rarely feel frightened or intimidated by their wives' potential for violence.

Focus on research

British Crime Survey
Computer-assisted interviewing

Questions on domestic violence are now part of British Crime Surveys, which aim to gain an insight into the true amount of crime in society by talking to victims. The designers of this survey realized that face-to-face interviewing was an unreliable method because victims are often too embarrassed to talk about their experiences of violence. The 1996 survey was the first to use the alternative method of computer-assisted interviewing, in which a laptop is passed over to the respondent, who reads the questions on screen and enters their answers directly onto the computer without the interviewer being involved. It is thought that the confidentiality factor associated with this type of interviewing on such a sensitive issue has improved both the reliability of the method (and produced on average a 97 per cent response rate) and the validity of the data collected, i.e. people are more willing to open up.

1 What is computer-assisted interviewing?

2 Identify the advantages and disadvantages of computer-assisted interviewing.

3 To what extent is computer-assisted interviewing likely to achieve valid and reliable data about domestic violence?

Feminists suggest that domestic violence is a problem of patriarchy. In particular, research indicates that men's view that women have failed to be 'good' partners or mothers is often used to justify attacks or threats. These gendered expectations may be particularly reinforced if a woman goes out to work and earns more than her partner. Many boys and men are still brought up in traditional ways to believe that they should have economic and social power as breadwinners and heads of household. However, the feminization of the economy and male unemployment has led to some sociologists suggesting that men are undergoing a 'crisis of masculinity'. Violence may be an aspect of the anxiety men are feeling about their economic and domestic role, an attempt to re-exert and maintain power and control in a rapidly changing world. Feminists also point out that society has, until fairly recently, condoned male violence in the home. Both the state and the criminal justice system have failed to take the problem seriously, although there are positive signs that the Labour government and police forces are now willing to condemn and punish such violence. Whatever the explanation, some feminists would argue that as long as men have the capacity to commit such violence, there can never be equality within marriage.

Theoretical explanations of inequalities in power and control in families

There are four major theoretical perspectives on the distribution of power and control in the family:

1 *Functionalists* see the sexual division of labour in the home as biologically inevitable. Women are seen as naturally suited to the caring and emotional role, which Parsons terms the 'expressive role'. (see Topic 2, p.?)
2 *Liberal feminists* believe that women have made real progress in terms of equality within the family and particularly in education and the economy. They generally believe that men are adapting to change and, although they culturally lag behind women in terms of attitudes and behaviour, the future is likely to bring further movement towards domestic and economic equality (see Topic 2, p.?).
3 *Marxist–feminists* argue that the housewife role serves the needs of capitalism in that it maintains the present workforce and reproduces future labour-power (see Topic 2, p. 83).
4 *Radical feminists* such as Delphy (1984) believe that 'the first oppression is the oppression of women by men – women are an exploited class'. The housewife role is, therefore, a role created by patriarchy and geared to the service of men and their interests (see Topic 2, p. 83).

Criticisms of these theories

- These theories fail to explain why women's roles vary across different cultures. For example, the mother/housewife role does not exist in all societies.
- Feminism may be guilty of devaluing the mother/housewife role as a 'second-class' role. For

many women, housework and childcare, like paid work, have real and positive meaning. Such work may be invested with meaning for women because it is 'work done for love' and it demonstrates their commitment to their families. Thus, boring, routine work may be transformed into satisfying, caring work.

- Feminists may underestimate the degree of power that women actually enjoy. Women are concerned about the amount of housework men do, but they are probably more concerned about whether men show enough gratitude or whether men listen to them, etc. The fact that many women divorce their husbands indicates that they have the power to leave a relationship if they are unhappy with it. Catherine Hakim (1996) suggests that feminists underestimate women's ability to make rational choices. It is not patriarchy or men that are responsible for the position of women in families. She argues that women choose to give more commitment to family and children, and so have less commitment to work than men have.

Relationships between children and parents

Cunningham (1976) notes that modern parenting of children is based on three inter-related principles:

- Children are vulnerable and are therefore in need of protection from certain aspects of adult society.
- The world of the adult and the world of the child should be separate worlds.
- Children have the right to happiness.

Children and the state

The parenting of children is assisted by the state which over the years has become more involved in supervising childhood and family life. The state supervises the socialization of children through compulsory education, which lasts 11 years. The role of social services and social workers is to police those families in which children are thought to be at risk. The government also takes some economic responsibility by paying child benefit and children's tax credits to parents. The 2004 Children Act has produced the influential policy 'Every Child Matters' which focuses on the wellbeing of children and young people from birth to age 19. This stresses 'better outcomes' for children, such as 'being healthy, staying safe', and 'achieving economic wellbeing' at the centre of all government policies. In 2007, the government set up the Department for Children, Schools and Families to ensure that all children and young people:

- stay healthy and safe
- secure an excellent education and the highest possible standards of achievement
- enjoy their childhood
- make a positive contribution to society and the economy
- have lives full of opportunity, free from the effects of poverty.

Increasingly, children have come to be seen as individuals with rights. The Child Support Act (1991) deals with the care, bringing up and protection of children. It protects children's welfare in the event of parental separation and divorce, emphasizing that the prime concern of the state should be the child, and what children themselves say about their experiences and needs. Some children have recently used the act to 'divorce' their parents, while others have used it to 'force' their separated/divorced parents to see them more regularly.

Lewis argues that Labour have particularly taken the idea of 'social investment in children' seriously and have increasingly recognized that family forms are changing. Lone mothers have ceased to be condemned as a moral problem and threat. Rather, Labour has introduced policies such as the New Deal of 1998, aimed at helping lone mothers back into paid work.

Labour has also recognized that there are few families in the 21st century which have exclusively a male breadwinner. Most families rely on two incomes and most women work (albeit often part time). Lewis notes that Labour has:

- invested in subsidies for nursery childcare
- lengthened maternity care from 14 weeks to nine months
- almost doubled maternity pay
- introduced the right for parents of young children to ask for flexible working patterns from their employers.

However, this explicit family policy has attracted criticism that it is undermining family privacy and that Labour has constructed a 'nanny state' which over-interferes in personal living arrangements. Furthermore, despite these innovations, the government is still accused of conforming to conservative family ideology in that the policy emphasis is still overwhelmingly on motherhood rather than on parenting in general or fatherhood, as seen in the limited rights of fathers to take paid paternity leave. Moreover, some cabinet ministers have regularly stated that married parents create the best environment for bringing up children. Critics suggest that, on the whole, state policy continues to reinforce traditional ideas about the family.

Is childhood under threat?

Some sociologists suggest that parenting is decline and consequently it is argued that childhood is under threat from and in need of protection from adult society.

This approach suggests that successful childrearing requires two parents of the opposite sex, and that there is a 'right' way to bring up a child. Such views often 'blame' working mothers or single mothers, and/or inadequate parents, for social problems such as delinquency. They also see children as in need of protection from 'threats' such as homosexuality and media violence. Postman (1982), for example, sees childhood as under threat because television exposes them too soon to the adult world (see Focus on research below).

In Toxic Childhood (2007), Sue Palmer argues that adults are benefiting enormously from living in a wealthier

Focus on research

Neil Postman (1982)
Is childhood disappearing?

Postman argues that childhood is disappearing. His view is based on two related ideas.

1 The growth of television means that there are no more secrets from children. Television gives them unlimited access to the adult world. They are exposed to the 'real world' of sex, disaster, death and suffering.

2 'Social blurring' has occurred so there is little distinction between adults and children. Children's games are disappearing and children seem less childlike today. They speak, dress and behave in more adult ways, while adults have enjoyed looking more like their kids and youth generally. Over time, nearly all the traditional features that mark the transition to adulthood – getting a job, religious confirmation, leaving home, getting married – no longer apply in any clear way.

Postman's analysis has been heavily criticized. His arguments do not appear to be based on solid evidence, while recent studies indicate that adults are actually taking more and more control of their children's lives. For example, David Brooks (2001) diagnoses parents today as obsessed with safety, and ever more concerned with defining boundaries for their kids and widening their control and safety net around them.

Perhaps it is children that are disappearing rather than childhood. Children are a smaller percentage of our overall population today and are diminishing in relative proportion to other age groups.

Adapted from Allen, D. (2001) 'Is childhood disappearing?', *Studies in Social and Political Thought,* 6(1), 2001

1 What methods could be used to collect data about the impact of television on children?

2 To what extent do you believe that childhood is disappearing? What evidence can you use to support your view?

society in which electronic technologies have enriched their lives. However, the same technologies are harming children because all too often parents are using them as an alternative to traditional parenting practices. Instead of spending quality time with their children and reading them stories, Palmer claims parents are too happy to use television, electronic games and junk food to keep them quiet. Children are therefore deprived of traditional childhood and family life, and she claims that 'every year children become more distractible, impulsive and self-obsessed – less able to learn, to enjoy life, to thrive socially' because of these trends.

Furthermore, some children's experiences of childhood may be damaging. Different types of child abuse have been rediscovered in recent years, such as neglect and physical, sexual and emotional abuse. The NSPCC points out that each week at least one child will die as a result of an adult's cruelty, usually a parent or step-parent, while 30,000 children are on child protection registers because they are at risk from family members. For some children, then, the experience of parenting and family life can be exploitative, dangerous and traumatic.

The interpretivist view of family life

Interpretivist sociologists have focused on researching how children see and interpret the world around them. They suggest that functionalist and New Right arguments assume that children are simply empty vessels. Family life is presented as a one-way process in which parenting and socialization aim to transform children into good citizens. However, this view ignores the fact that children have their own unique interpretation of family life, which they actively employ in interaction with their parents. In other words, the relationship between parents and children is a two-way process in which the latter can and do influence the nature and quality of family life. For example, research by Morrow (1998) found that children can be constructive and reflective contributors to family life. Most of the children in Morrow's study had a pragmatic view of their family role – they did not want to make decisions for themselves but they did want a say in what happened to them (see Topic 2, p.113)

Focus on research

Jonathan Gershuny (2000)
Standards of parenting

A major theme of those who believe that the family is in decline is working parents and particularly working mothers. However, research illustrates the complexity of the debate about whether standards of parenting have fallen. In 2000, Jonathan Gershuny, using data from the diaries of 3000 parents, suggested that the quality of parenting had significantly improved compared with the past. He noted that the time British parents spent playing with and reading to their children had increased fourfold and this was the case for both working and non-working parents.

1   How could the use of diaries in Gershuny's research be criticized?

Check your understanding

1   What did Young and Willmott claim about conjugal roles in the 1970s?

2   What have recent surveys concluded about the distribution of domestic tasks between husbands and wives?

3   In what circumstances might wives acquire more power over decision-making in the home?

4   What do sociological studies tell us about fatherhood?

5   What effect does the mother/housewife role have on women's job opportunities?

Key terms

Conjugal relationship the relationship between married or cohabiting partners.

Double shift or dual burden refers to wives taking responsibility for the bulk of domestic tasks as well as holding down full-time jobs.

Egalitarian based on equality.

Segregated division of labour in the home a traditional sexual division of labour in which women take responsibility for housework and mothering, and men take responsibility for being the breadwinner and head of the household.

Symmetrical similar or corresponding.

Activities

Research idea

1   Conduct a survey of parents using the lists of tasks in the 'Getting you thinking' exercise on p. 108. An interesting variation is to ask parents separately whether they think they and their partner are doing enough around the home. Ask a set of parents to keep a time-use diary documenting time spent on housework and childcare.

2   Interview a selection of mothers in different social situations – e.g. full-time mothers, those who have full-time or part-time jobs, those who have children who have left home. Try to construct an interview schedule that measures how they feel about the mother/housewife role.

Web.tasks

Use the web to research domestic violence. The following websites contain a range of useful data and information:

- www.homeoffice.gov.uk/crime-victims/reducing-crime/domestic-violence/
- www.womensaid.org.uk
- www.met.police.uk/dv/
- www.womenandequalityunit.gov.uk/domestic_violence

1   Visit the websites www.child-abuse.com/childhouse and www.unicef-irc.org/research/

    These contain links to a number of excellent sites that look at childhood and children's rights across the world.

2   Visit the NSPCC website www.nspcc.co.uk to get an idea of the degree of child abuse in UK society.

3   Visit the government websites www.dfes.gov.uk and www.everychildmatters.gov.uk to see how social policy is now shaped by official concerns for the welfare of children.

Roles, responsibilities and relationships within the family

the opening sentence of each paragraph should clearly highlight the way

whatever it is that you have identified must be discussed in some depth using sociological studies and examples

you should attempt to write two very detailed paragraphs in about 15 minutes

each way needs to be developed into a very detailed paragraph which must be clearly distinguishable from the other

(a) Identify and explain two ways in which government social policy protects the interests of children.

(17 marks)

begin your answer with a clear definition of what is meant by this concept

a detailed description of the view is required using sociological concepts, theories and studies

it is important to assess the merits of the view in some detail, either by raising specific strengths and criticisms of the view or by presenting alternative theoretical perspectives

this view is mainly argued by functionalist sociologists

you should attempt to write at least 2 sides of the answer book in about 30 minutes

(b) Outline and evaluate the view that the domestic division of labour in most marriages is characterised by equality.

(33 marks)

clearly define what these concepts mean in your introduction

Grade booster Getting top marks in this question

This view is generally a functionalist one and is associated with sociologists such as Parsons and Wilmott and Young whose ideas on equality within marriage with regard to housework and childcare should be clearly outlined. Examine the evidence for these ideas by describing contemporary studies of the distribution of housework and childcare. Sociological studies of who controls decision-making in families, emotion work, fathering and domestic violence should also be referenced. Use concepts such as segregated and joint conjugal roles, egalitarian, symmetrical, patriarchy, dual burden, triple shift etc whenever possible.

(a) Identify and explain two ways in which social policy may affect the extent of family diversity. *(17 marks)*

One of the most influential pieces of government policy relates to divorce. Before the 1970s divorce was a complex and expensive business in which people had to prove that their husband or wife was guilty of a matrimonial crime in a court of law. As a result, many people who were unhappy with their marriages decided either to stay together in an empty shell marriage or they separated. Many poorer people, especially women, could not afford to divorce.

The Divorce Reform Act of 1969 changed all this. People can still get a quickie divorce under the old rules but the 1969 Act said that all people now need to do is to separate for two years. If both husband and wife agree that the marriage has irretrievably broken down they can have a divorce after two years. Divorce increased ten times in the 1970s because of this social policy and had the effect of increasing the number of single parent families as women tended to get custody of children after divorce. Single-parent families last on average five years because single-parents tend to meet someone else and get re-married forming reconstituted families or step-families. The social policy on divorce has therefore led to family diversity in the form of an increase in the number of one-parent families and reconstituted families.

This section demonstrates a very perceptive and detailed level of knowledge and understanding. Sociological concepts such as divorce, matrimonial crime, single parent families and reconstituted families are clearly understood and applied to the ways in which social policy affects family diversity.

Secondly, social policy relating to homosexuality has also affected family diversity. Before the 21st century, homosexual people had few rights with regard to marriage and family life. Since the election of the Labour government in 1997, homosexuals have been given the right to have civil partnerships (a form of marriage) and to adopt children. In 1999 the law lords ruled that homosexuals could be legally defined as a family and the government is going to introduce social policy which will result in homosexual couples having the same legal rights as heterosexual couples in relation to being regarded as next-of-kin and property inheritance. As a result of these changes, modern family life is now characterised by sexual diversity because of the growing number of homosexual and lesbian families with children.

Although this section is not as detailed as the previous section, it contains some very relevant and focused knowledge of sexual diversity in family life. It is difficult to see how this might have been improved and therefore the candidate was awarded the full 17 marks.

17/17

(b) Outline and explain the view that the ageing of the population will have significant effects on both family structure and relationships. *(33 marks)*

Britain today has an ageing population because the death rate is lower than the birth rate in the UK. In fact the birth rate has decreased by a third compared with 1900 and 21% compared with 1971. This has led to more of the population being aged over 65 because family size has fallen in each generation. Families were likely to have five children back in the 1950s but this has fallen to less than 2 children in 2010.

This is a rather confused introduction which raises more questions than it answers. The relationship between an ageing population and both the death rate and birth rate needs to be better organised.

The birth rate fell during the early part of the 20thcentury because the infant mortality rate had fallen dramatically at the end of the 19th century because children began to survive childhood because of better diet, housing and living standards. As living standards increased, so too did the expense of having children so people chose to have less.

The relevance of this section to the question is not clear.

The birth rate was therefore influenced by the fertility rate – the numbers of children that women of child-bearing age have in any one year. Fertility rates like birth rates have generally declined as women choose to have less children because of the contraceptive pill which was introduced in the 1960s. The feminisation of the

Although there are some interesting concepts used in this section, and the fertility rate is relevant to an ageing population, this paragraph fails to make the connection in a convincing way.

economy – especially the expansion of the service sector – meant there was more opportunity for women to have careers. This led to what Wilkinson calls a 'genderquake' – women became less interested in having children and more interested in getting their career started before they thought about having children.

There are a number of effects of an ageing population for family life. There may be a change in family structure as nuclear families include older family members such as grandparents and great-grandparents who can't afford to live alone or in a residential home. Families which contain these two extra-generations have been described as 'beanpole families' by Brannen who uses this term to describe the vertically extended families that have children, parents, grandparents and great-grandparents living in the same house or in the same general neighbourhood.

> This is better –the candidate is back on track and is now focused on addressing the question using a very relevant study in an accurate fashion.

Brannen notes that because the generation in their late 50-60s are generally still able to look after themselves and are themselves likely to have parents in their 80s, they often become the carers of them. They also become carers of their grandchildren while their children are at work. Brannen calls this generation the 'pivot generation'. These services are usually offered with the assumption of 'reciprocity' – when they are older they expect their children to return the favour by looking after them when they are older.

> Good knowledge and understanding is demonstrated here.

Ross carried out interviews with grandparents and their grandchildren and argued that the quality of family relationships had improved because of the ageing of the population. Grandparents were very positive about being grandparents and spent quality time with their grandchildren on outings and teaching them skills. They also often helped out financially. Young people said they often shared problems and concerns with their grandparents that they could not share with their parents. Grandparents were happy to give advice and support.

> Excellent knowledge and understanding of a very relevant study is demonstrated in this section.

However, the idea that families should look after aged grandparents has always existed within ethnic minority communities. Many Asian families, regardless of religion, feel a strong sense of duty and obligation towards their parents and grandparents. In fact, it is seen as dishonourable if children neglect their parent's needs or put them in a residential home. This leads to an increase in vertically extended Muslim families in the UK.

> This section makes a good evaluative point but it needed to be more focused on addressing the central issue of the question, i.e. the ageing of the population.

However caring for the elderly can have some negative effects upon some family members. Firstly, it may increase the domestic burden on women who take most responsibility for caring in families. They may have to give up any ambition they might have in terms of a career to look after their aged parents. Secondly, it may result in financial hardship for the family because one partner may have to give up work in order to care full-time for elderly relatives. Thirdly, caring for others can increase stress and consequently result in ill-health for carers.

> Some good evaluative points are made in this section about the effects of an ageing population on other family members.

23/33

An examiner comments

After a rather confused and unfocused beginning, this response settles down to display a reasonably good level of knowledge and understanding of such key concepts as the beanpole family and relevant sociological studies such as Brannen and Ross. However, the candidate does not really get to grips with the reasons why an ageing population has come about. There was also potential for other effects of an ageing population to be explored. For example, the candidate failed to consider elderly single-person households, sheltered housing and residential homes. The candidate was therefore awarded 8 marks for knowledge and understanding. With regard to interpretation and application, the candidate needed to construct a context in which the reasons for an ageing population were explained. Moreover, the response was sometimes not focused on addressing the question. The candidate was therefore awarded 9 marks for interpretation and application. Evaluation was not well developed. There were some attempts at analysis but apart from the final paragraph, assessment was superficial and unfocused. 6 marks are awarded for analysis and evaluation.

Chapter 3 Summary

Functionalism
- Nuclear family norm
- Industrialization
- Structural differentiation

Historical perspectives
- Gradual evolution
- Symmetrical family

Marxism
- Ideological capitalist apparatus
- Promotes ruling-class ideology

Feminism
- Marxist-feminist: family benefits capitalism & men
- Radical feminist: family benefits men – patriarchal

G.P. Murdock
- Family as universal institution
- Performs reproductive, sexual, educational and economic functions

Marxism
- Family functions to distract working class from inequality

Parsons
- Primary socialization of children
- Stabilization of adult personalities

Feminism
- Family is patriarchal and promotes male dominance

Family, social structure & change

Family functions

State policy

Labour family policy
- Department for Children, Schools and Families
- Child Support Acts

Families and households

Demographic changes & family life

Birth rates & fertility rates
- Effect on family size
- Effect of birth control, educational opportunity and genderquake

Death rate
- Life expectancy
- Ageing population
- Beanpole families

Migration
- Cultural diversity in family life
- Extended kinship ties

Marriage, divorce & family diversity

Marriage
- In decline or merely postponed?
- Effect of genderquake
- Threat of cohabitation

Marital breakdown
- Divorce rate
- Effects of divorce on children
- Influence of postmodern world

Single-parent families
- Stereotypes vs facts
- Reconstituted families

Types of diversity
- Sexual diversity
- Class diversity

Roles, responsibilities and relationships between men and women

Housework and childcare
- Equality vs dual burden
- Decision-making
- Fatherhood

Violence
- Definitions
- Role of patriarchy

Roles, responsibilities and relationships between parents and children

Is childhood under threat
- Toxic childhood
- Interpretivist accounts

Sociology of health

OCR specification

	Coverage
Key concepts and the social construction of health and illness	
Key concepts, particularly, health, illness, sickness, morbidity and mortality as well as different approaches for understanding health and illness, specifically the bio-medical and social models of health	Covered in Topic 1
The social construction of health and illness using cultural relativity/differences, lay definitions and approaches which stress the social process of becoming ill	Covered in Topic 1
Patterns and explanations of ill health in society	
Patterns of ill health in society by social class, gender and ethnicity	Covered in Topic 2.
Sociological explanations for differences in mortality and morbidity, particularly artefact, social selection, cultural and structural explanations.	
The social construction of mental illness and disability	
Definitions, diagnosis and trends of mental illness by ethnicity, class and gender	Covered in Topic 3.
Sociological explanations of mental illness, particularly structural and interactionist explanations.	Covered in Topic 3.
The social construction of disability – changing definitions over time and the medical and social models	Covered in Topic 3.
The role of health professionals in society	
Sociological explanations of the role of health professionals in society, particularly functionalist, Marxist, Weberian and feminist theories	Covered in Topic 4.
The rise of complementary/alternative medicines and their relationship to health professionals	Covered in Topics 1 and 4.

The social construction of health and illness

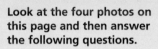

Look at the four photos on this page and then answer the following questions.

1   Which of these people are, in your opinion, 'abnormal' and which are 'normal'?

2   What suggestions can you make for helping 'abnormal' people make themselves 'normal'?

3   Next, indicate which of these people, if any, are 'ill'.

4   In small groups, compare your answers and explain how you made your decisions.

5   Do you think that health and illness and normal bodies have anything to do with society, or are they just natural, biological states?

This topic investigates the ways in which **health**, **illness** and **disability** are defined in our society and the implications for people who are defined as ill or disabled. The majority of the population pass most their lives taking for granted the normal, routine state of their bodies, until this 'normality' is disrupted in some way. At this point, people often say they are 'ill'. However, it is very unclear just what illness is. Surely, such an important concept does not vary simply according to how each individual feels? Anyway, how does anyone know what is 'normal'?

A second, linked area is the notion of 'abnormality'. If there is such a thing as 'normality', then there must be something which is 'abnormal'. This category might include those suffering from chronic (long-term) illness, such as multiple sclerosis, those with a 'mental illness' or those with a physical 'disability'.

Sociologists also want to understand how terms such as 'abnormality' and 'disability' are constructed and what implications there are for the people so labelled.

We begin by looking at how health and illness are defined and the implications of these definitions for society.

Definitions of health and illness

At some time, most of us will have woken up in the morning not really feeling very well. Despite telling our parents this, it may have been difficult to persuade them that we really were too ill to go to school or college (particularly if there was an exam that day or a particular lesson they knew we loathed). Only when we produced some real evidence, such as vomiting or a rash, were we believed. Our parents may also be rather less than supportive when it turns out that we have been drinking pretty heavily the night before. Ill or just hung over? And anyway, why is being hung over not being ill – after all, we feel awful? The answer from disapproving parents might well be that being hung over is the price we pay for a night's drinking and that it therefore does not count as a 'real' illness.

This situation illustrates a number of issues. First, it is not clear exactly what we mean by being 'healthy' and being 'unwell'. It seems that these concepts may well have different meanings depending upon who is defining them. In this case, us and our parents. Furthermore, there is a 'moral' element involved. If feeling ill is a result of having drunk too much, then this may be classified as just a 'hangover' and hence our own fault.

Definitions of illness and their consequences (get the day off college or have to endure a miserable day attending) form the starting point for the sociology of medicine.

To unravel this complex issue, we will look first at how ordinary, or **lay**, people construct their definitions of health and illness. We will then move on to look at the competing models amongst health practitioners themselves.

Lay definitions of health and illness

If definitions of health and illness vary, then we need to know just what factors appear to influence the way in which individuals define their sense of being healthy or ill. Sociologists have suggested that culture, age, gender and social class are particularly important.

Cultural differences

Different social groups have differing ideas of what constitutes illness. For example, Krause (1989) studied Hindu and Sikh Punjabis living in Bedford, and in particular focused on their illness called 'sinking heart' (*dil ghirda hai*) which is characterized by physical chest pain. According to Krause, this illness is caused by a variety of emotional experiences – most importantly, public shame of some sort. No such illness exists in other mainstream cultures in Britain.

Age differences

Older people tend to accept as 'normal' a range of pains and physical limitations which younger people would define as symptoms of some illness or disability. As we age, we gradually redefine health and accept greater levels of physical discomfort. In Blaxter's (1990) national survey of health definitions, she found that young people tend to define health in terms of physical fitness, but gradually, as people age, health comes to be defined more in terms of being able to cope with everyday tasks. She found examples of older people with really serious arthritis, who nevertheless defined themselves as healthy, as they were still able to carry out a limited range of routine activities.

Gender differences

According to Hilary Graham (2002), men have fewer consultations with doctors than women and appear to have lower levels of illness. This is partly due to the greater number of complications associated with childbirth and menopause that women face, but it is also partly due to the fact that men are less likely to define themselves as ill or as needing medical attention. The idea of 'masculinity' includes the belief that a man should be tough and put off going to the doctor.

Focus on research

Talcott Parsons
The sick role: sickness as deviance

According to Talcott Parsons (1975), being sick is a deviant act which can prevent a person undertaking their normal social functions. Society therefore controls this deviance through a device known as 'the sick role'. This is illustrated in Figure 7.1 below.

Figure 7.1 The sick role

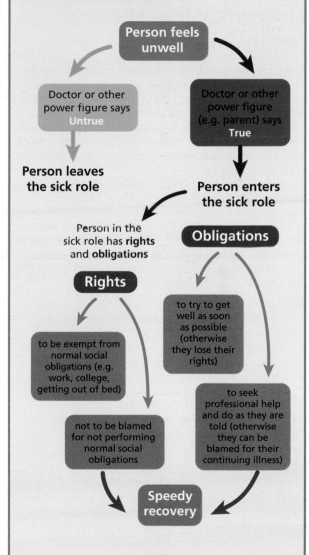

1 Think of examples of people you know who have 'unfairly' claimed the sick role. What do you think about them and their behaviour?

2 Are there some illnesses which, in your opinion, do not deserve the 'rights' of the sick

Despite the greater readiness of men to define themselves as healthy and to visit **GPs** less often, men have considerably higher mortality (death) rates than women.

Social class differences

Blaxter's research also showed that working-class people were far more likely to accept higher levels of 'illness' than middle-class people. Blaxter describes working-class people as 'fatalistic' – that is, they accepted poor health as 'one of those things'. As a result, people from lower social classes are less likely to consult a GP than middle-class people. This may be because they will accept a higher level of pain and discomfort before considering themselves ill enough to visit a doctor.

Bio-medical definitions of health and illness

There is a distinction in most people's minds between those who think they are ill and those who really are ill. In contemporary society, the role of deciding whether the person is truly ill lies with doctors. If they decide that a person is ill, then a series of benefits flow, both formal (in the provision of medical help, or time off work or college) and informal (such as sympathy, release from household tasks and so on).

However, if they decide that you are not really ill, then you receive no benefits and may, in fact, be open to accusations of **malingering**.

Doctors use a particular 'scientific' measure of health and illness in order to decide whether someone really is ill or not. This model is known as the **biomedical model**, and it is the basis of all Western medicine. The elements of this model include the following:

- Illness is always caused by an identifiable (physical or mental) reason and cannot be the result of magic, religion or witchcraft.
- Illnesses and their causes can be identified, classified and measured using scientific methods.
- If there is a cure, then it will almost always be through the use of drugs or surgery, rather than in changing social relationships or people's spiritual lives.
- This is because the cause almost always lies in the actual physical body of the individual patient.

At its simplest, this model presents the human body as a type of machine and, just as with a machine, parts can go wrong and need repairing. Over time, the body 'wears out' just as a machine does and will eventually stop working completely. This is why the contemporary medical model is sometimes referred to as the 'bio-*mechanical*' model.

Illness and disease

What emerges from the discussion of health and illness is that individuals, using lay concepts of health, may define themselves as 'ill' or not, depending upon a range of social factors. On the other hand, doctors claim that they can scientifically determine, via medical tests, whether or not a person is ill. Eisenberg (1977) has therefore suggested that we should make a distinction between illness and disease.

Illness is an individual's subjective experience of symptoms of ill health, whereas diseases are clinical conditions defined by medical professionals. It is therefore perfectly possible, as Blaxter has pointed out, to have an illness without a disease and a disease without an illness!

Traditional and non-Western cultural definitions of health and illness

The biomedical model contrasts markedly with concepts of illness in traditional and non-Western cultures, where illness is seen as the result of a wider range of factors than just the body itself.

In traditional societies, for example, these factors could include witchcraft – where the blame for the illness lies in the bad wishes of others, or possibly the 'will of God'. A more complex model of health exists in non-Western societies, where the body and the mind are seen as completely linked. Any understanding of the body must be linked with the person's mental state, and the two need to be treated together.

However, over the last two hundred years, the biomedical model of health has come to dominate healthcare and has excluded other approaches. This supremacy is linked to the wider development of science and scientific methods as the predominant form of knowledge in modern societies.

Social model of health and illness

In contrast to the bio-medical model of health, the social model of health and illness has developed as a sociological critique of the bio-medical model. This model suggests that definitions of health and illness are socially constructed. This means they are the product of the social interactions and relationships that make up society. The social model is therefore focused on how people actually experience health and illness.

The social process of becoming ill

The social model notes that the very process of becoming ill is socially constructed. In other words, there are a number of social factors which influence whether a person is regarded as ill. Firstly, people have to recognize that they are unwell. However, this may depend on factors such as gender or age. For example, evidence suggests that elderly people are more willing to put up with symptoms of illness that may not be tolerated by younger people whereas males may feel that their masculinity is undermined if they complain about being ill.

Secondly, people need to define their symptoms as serious enough to visit a doctor. Most people self-medicate or are looked after by their immediate family when ill. Official morbidity statistics derived from doctors' records suggest that there may a **clinical iceberg** of illness that never comes to the attention of doctors. The bio-medical model's view of illness and disease may therefore be undermined by the fact that it is based on only a small amount of total illness coming to the attention of the medical profession.

Thirdly, the decision to go to the doctor is also a social process which might be influenced by a variety of social factors such as the longevity of the illness (i.e. do you need official permission to take time off work or school?), the nature of the illness (is the illness embarrassing?), previous interactions with the doctor (is he or she approachable?) etc. Factors such as social class, gender, religion and ethnicity may influence decision-making at this stage.

The sick role

The functionalist sociologist, Talcott Parsons, suggested that illness and sickness were deviant in that they could potentially disrupt the smooth running of society. For example, if crucial workers suffered long-term sickness this could disrupt the specialized division of labour and undermine economic efficiency. Parsons argued that as part of our socialization into culture, we learn to play a **sick role**. We learn that to be officially recognized as sick by doctors and other people in authority such as employers, we must conform to recognized modes of behaviour, e.g. after a period of self-medication, we must visit a doctor and always follow their orders. In return, society and doctors have obligations to fulfill on behalf of the sick, e.g. the patient is put first and all possible medical expertise is used to restore his or her health. Figure 7.1 on page 147 illustrates these ideas in more detail.

Public health

There is no doubt that the biomedical model has made a major contribution to getting rid of the major killer infections of the 19th and early 20th century in Britain, e.g. smallpox, polio, tuberculosis etc. However, the bio-medical is not totally responsible for these improvements. McKeown (1979) suggests public health factors such as better diet and housing, and the introduction of clean water supplies and sanitation are more important in explaining the radical improvement in health experienced by the British people during the course of the 20th century. He points out that infant mortality rates improved dramatically towards the end of the 19th century. The NHS was only set up in 1948 and the mass immunization of children were not introduced until 1970.

Preventative medicine

Sociologists such as Trowler (1989) argue that biomedicine directs medical resources into the wrong areas. It is argued that the biomedical model's focus on the body as a machine means that money and resources are mainly focused on cure and treatment, i.e. drugs and surgery. Trowler argues that the NHS is a national sickness service because it reacts after illness has been diagnosed rather than preventing the illness from occurring in the first place. He suggests that resources would be better spent on health promotion to prevent people getting ill in the first place.

Iatrogenesis

Illich (1975) was a major critic of the biomedical model of medicine because he believed that medical intervention did

Focus on research

Writing about health and sickness: an analysis of contemporary autobiographical writing from the british mass-observation archive

Helen Busby (2000)

In 1981, 1,400 volunteers were invited to write about their experiences or the experiences of others around them on various themes. The writing took various forms including letters, questionnaires, diaries, autobiography and accounts of interviews. The sample of writers was weighted towards older people and women and tends to have a middle class bias. There were 249 responses in 1998 to a directive which asked the sample to write about what people felt they needed to stay well and what they thought undermined people's health experiences.

Most of the respondents wrote in terms of 'keeping going' rather than responding to symptoms and, because the directive was issued in winter, the symptoms were often related to colds and flu. Most people viewed health as something which must be worked at and symptoms as things to be ignored or worked through.

However, older people tended to view good health as a matter of luck. Women tried harder than men to avoid being sick whereas men worked through sickness at busy times and took sick leave when work was less busy. When sick leave was taken, it was often in response to a boring or disliked job although many people worried about the cost of time off and those who worked freelance would not allow themselves to be sick if they then lost pay.

Many people felt they could stay well through the exercise of self control. People were more likely to seek medical help if their symptoms interfered with their ability to work. They would disguise symptoms if they were not able to take time off. In addition, some illness was interpreted as 'shadow illness' in the sense that people felt unwell but also felt that they did not have clearly identifiable and understood symptoms that could enable them to take time off work or convince a doctor. The findings also suggested that on the whole people felt a strong moral duty not to be ill.

Source: adapted from Blundell. J. and Griffiths, J. (2008) *Sociology since 2000*. Lewes: Connect Publications

1   How do the findings of this research support the view that illness is a social process?

2   Is there support in these findings for Parsons' concept of a sick role?

more harm than good. Illich suggested that doctors are responsible for a great deal of illness. He refers to these negative consequences of biomedicine as 'iatrogenesis'.

Direct harm to the patient caused by medical intervention is known as clinical iatrogenesis. These harms include deaths and injuries caused by errors during surgery, the side-effects of drugs such as pain-killers, anti-depressants and the contraceptive pill and deaths in hospitals from hospital super-bugs such as MRSA.

Illich also argues that the bio-medical model is increasingly expanding its influence over aspects of social life which were previously not regarded as the province of health professionals. For example, Gomm notes that this **medicalisation of social life** has resulted in alcoholism, obesity, learning difficulties, children's misbehaviour, sexual problems, shyness etc being defined as medical problems in recent years. This is reflected in the dramatic increase in the number of psychiatric counsellors in the UK in the last ten years. Illich refers to this increasing medicalisation of social life as social iatrogenesis. He also argues that our increasing dependency as a society on all things medical – a cure for all ills – suggests modern societies are increasingly experiencing cultural iatrogenesis.

Postmodernist views of the body and health

So far in this chapter, we have questioned common-sense ideas held about what is sickness and health and have raised some challenging questions about these ideas. However, we can go further and question a closely related concept upon which notions of illness are ultimately based: the concept of 'the body'.

All of us exist in 'bodies' that, *objectively*, are different shapes, heights, colours and physical abilities; they are also *subjectively valued* as attractive or ugly, young or old, short or tall, weak or strong.

Let us look first at the objective differences. The two most common explanations for objective differences between bodies are, first, that people's bodies vary according to genetic differences (height, weight, etc.) and, second, that bodies change as people age. However, sociologists point out that the shapes of people's bodies are often actually linked to diets, type of employment and general quality of life. A huge range of research indicates that poorer people are more likely to:

- eat 'unhealthy' foods and to smoke cigarettes
- be employed in repetitive, physically demanding work or the other extreme of boring, sedentary employment
- have worse housing conditions
- live in more deprived neighbourhoods.

All of these factors impact upon the condition of a person's body and health. We can see then that the physical shapes of bodies are strongly influenced by social factors.

If we look next at the differences in how bodies are subjectively valued, we can see that the culture – and media – of different societies promote very different valuations of body shapes. What is considered as attractive or ugly, normal or abnormal has varied over time and society. Currently, for example, in affluent societies the idea of slimness is highly valued, yet historically in most societies the ideal body shape for a woman was a 'full figure' with a noticeable belly, while in middle-aged men, a large stomach indicated that they were financially successful in life – poor people looked thin and ill nourished.

Body shapes and appearance have never been neutral; they have always sent out social messages which others evaluate. However, in late modernity, the body has become an especially important 'site' for making statements about oneself. Giddens (1991) argues that in contemporary society our individual identity has come to be something which people 'work at', with everyone consciously constructing the image (personality, clothing, style of speech, ethnic affiliation) which they want to present to others as their real 'selves'. Giddens calls this **reflexive mobilization**. One very important part of this is how we wish our body to be viewed by others and what message we wish it to give. Chris Shilling (2003), for example, has pointed out that bodies are coming to be seen more and more as **unfinished products**, by which he means that bodies are no longer seen as something which people just 'have', to be accepted as they are. Increasingly, he argues, people wish to alter their bodies in order to express their individuality or to achieve some desired state. Shilling points to the growth of cosmetic surgery, tattooing, dieting and body building, all of which are undertaken by individuals to achieve a desired image of themselves.

Sociologists, then, are suggesting that we should not just view the body in biological terms, but also in social terms. The physical body and what we seek to do with it change over time and society. This has significant

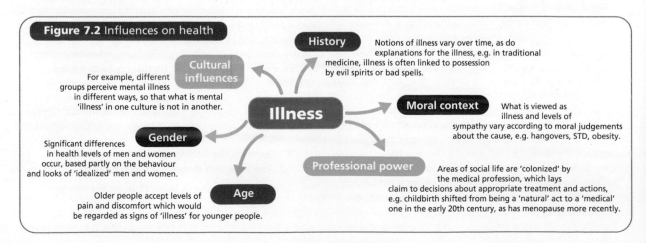

Figure 7.2 Influences on health

Cultural influences
For example, different groups perceive mental illness in different ways, so that what is mental 'illness' in one culture is not in another.

History
Notions of illness vary over time, as do explanations for the illness, e.g. in traditional medicine, illness is often linked to possession by evil spirits or bad spells.

Illness

Moral context
What is viewed as illness and levels of sympathy vary according to moral judgements about the cause, e.g. hangovers, STD, obesity.

Gender
Significant differences in health levels of men and women occur, based partly on the behaviour and looks of 'idealized' men and women.

Professional power
Areas of social life are 'colonized' by the medical profession, which lays claim to decisions about appropriate treatment and actions, e.g. childbirth shifted from being a 'natural' act to a 'medical' one in the early 20th century, as has menopause more recently.

Age
Older people accept levels of pain and discomfort which would be regarded as signs of 'illness' for younger people.

implications for medicine and ideas of health. Thus, the idea of people being 'obese' is *physically* related to excessive amounts of processed food, coupled with lack of exercise. However, *socially* it has become a medical problem as a result of people coming to define this particular body shape as 'wrong' and unhealthy. In many traditional African and Pacific island cultures, however, a large or (as we now call it) **obese** body shape was a sign of success and a shape to be aimed at.

The social patterns of health and illness

Finally, Coward (1989) argues that the biomedical model tends to stress that health problems are individual, both in terms of the causes and the cures. Coward argues that this ignores the wider social factors that cause ill health, such as poverty, poor housing, job-related stress and pollution, amongst others. These social patterns in mortality and morbidity are examined in Topic 2.

Complementary medicine

In recent years, there has been a major growth in alternative or **complementary** forms of health provision. These include therapies such as homeopathy, herbal medicines and acupuncture. Following the ideas of Giddens (1991) about the development of new ways of thinking and acting in contemporary society, which he characterizes as **late modernity**, Hardey (1998) has argued that in late modernity, there has been a decline in the uncritical acceptance of the authority of professionals, such as doctors. A second relevant feature of late modernity has been the growth in self-expression and individual choice. The idea that some people should give themselves completely into the power of doctors, and

subject themselves to treatments which they may not even understand has therefore become increasingly questioned.

Hunt and Lightly (1999) document five reasons for the increased popularity of alternative medicines and therapies. Firstly, the popularity of alternative approaches has arisen out of frustration with the rate of scientific advance in conventional medicine. Secondly, people have become critical of the iatrogenic effects of medicine especially the side effects of drugs. Thirdly, people are increasingly dissatisfied with the organisation and administration of health services especially long waiting lists, the failure to effectively treat chronic disease and the lack of power they perceive patients to have. One of the attractions of alternative medicine is that they encourage more input from patients and empower the sick. Fourthly, people may be attracted to the psychological and spiritual dimensions of alternative medicine which is seen to be lacking in conventional medicine. Finally, Hunt and Lightly suggest there is a growing section of the population that wants to experiment with their potential. In this sense, alternative medicine is part of a new age cultural movement which embraces ideas and practices such as vegetarianism, yoga, meditation etc.

The evidence suggests that one in seven people are receiving treatment from practitioners of alternative medicine and that 96 per cent of the British population have tried an alternative therapy at least once. However Crawford (1977) argues that these alternative therapies are not that radical or alternative. This is because like the biomedical approach, they still focus on the individual as the main site of the disease and ignore the social context in which people live which may be the main cause of illness and disease. Crawford suggests alternative medicines should not be seen as signs that the general public is rejecting the biomedical approach. Instead he argues that alternative medicines, despite the criticisms they have received from medical experts, are an extension of conventional medicine because of their failure to address the primary social and economic sources of many illnesses.

Key terms

Biomedical model of health the conventional Western model. It sees the body as very much like a biological machine, with each part of the body performing a function. The doctor's job is to restore the functions by solving the problem of what is wrong. Ideas about the environment or the spiritual health of the person are not relevant.

Clinical iceberg illness which does not come to the attention of doctors because it is self-medicated

Complementary medicine alternative forms of health intervention, such as homeopathy.

General practitioner (GP) a local doctor who deals with general health issues.

Health a person's perception of the state of their body's wellbeing.

Illness perception of feeling unacceptably worse than normal body state.

Iatrogenesis the idea that medicine and doctors can actually harm people

Lay definitions of health 'lay' refers to the majority of the public who are not medical practitioners and who therefore use common-sense ideas about health and illness.

Malingering pretending to be ill in order to avoid work or other responsibilities.

Medicalisation of social life the increasing tendency of doctors and psychiatrists to suggest that some aspects of social behaviour are actually illnesses, e.g. shyness

Obesity a medical term for being overweight.

Sick role the social norms that both ill people and doctors are expected to conform to

Activities

Research idea

Select a small sample of people, ideally from different generations, and ask them to rate their degree of sympathy on a scale of 1 to 5 for people with the following 'illnesses': hangover, headache (not caused by a hangover!), impotence, cirrhosis of the liver (caused by drinking too much alcohol), anorexia, heart disease, breast cancer, lung cancer caused by smoking, sexually transmitted disease.

Do your results show any different attitudes to illness and disease amongst people? What explanations can you suggest for your findings?

Web.tasks

Search online for information and advice on health – for example, Men's Health Magazine at www.menshealth.co.uk

Does the advice make assumptions about what is normal and abnormal in terms of body shape and styles of life?

Visit www.iatrogenesis.org in order to document the latest examples of clinical iatrogenesis.

Check your understanding

1 How does the public define health?

2 Identify and explain any three factors that affect the definition of health and illness.

3 What is the clinical iceberg and how does its existence challenge the biomedical model?

4 Why is the 'sick role' functional to the smooth running of industrial societies?

5 How do McKeown's observations about public health challenge the biomedical approach?

6 What is iatrogenesis?

7 What is the difference between clinical and cultural iatrogenesis?

8 What does Gomm mean by the 'medicalisation of social life'?

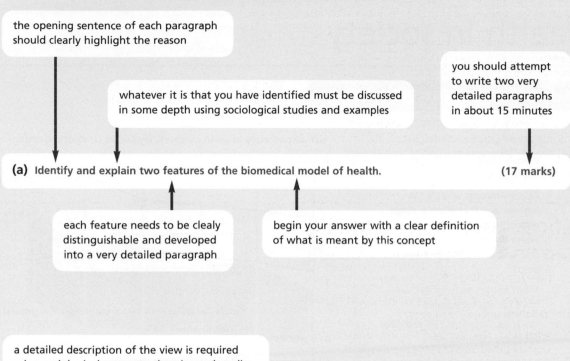

the opening sentence of each paragraph should clearly highlight the reason

whatever it is that you have identified must be discussed in some depth using sociological studies and examples

you should attempt to write two very detailed paragraphs in about 15 minutes

(a) Identify and explain two features of the biomedical model of health. **(17 marks)**

each feature needs to be clealy distinguishable and developed into a very detailed paragraph

begin your answer with a clear definition of what is meant by this concept

a detailed description of the view is required using sociological concepts, theories and studies

it is important to assess the merits of the social construction view, either by raising specific strengths or criticisms of the theory or by contrasting it with the biomedical model

(b) Outline and evaluate the view that health and illness are socially constructed. **(33 marks)**

this view means that health and illness are a product of the relationships and interactions that make up society

you should attempt to write at least 2 sides of the answer book in about 30 minutes

Grade booster Getting top marks in this question

You need to begin by describing the dominant view of how health and illness come about, i.e. the biomedical model, in detail. Contrast this with the view that health and illness are socially constructed by examining the social process of becoming ill especially the clinical iceberg. Parsons' theory of the sick role should be discussed next because this suggests that society has social expectations about how patients and doctors should behave. Go on to examine the relationship between health and illness, public health, preventative medicine and alternative approaches. Finally, explore Illich's idea of iatrogenesis and the medicalisation of social life.

TOPIC 2

Patterns and explanations of ill health in society

Look at the graph on the right.

1 Who is likely to live longer on average, men or women?

2 Approximately, what is the highest age that women could expect to live to in 2001 (the latest figures currently available) and what is the highest age for men?

3 What impact does social class have on age expectancy?

4 What explanations can you offer for these differences?

Life expectancy at birth in years, by social class and gender

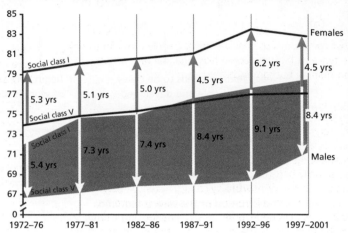

Source: Department of Health (2005) *Tackling Health Inequalities*, London: DoH

Life expectancy, healthy life expectancy and disability-free life expectancy at birth: by gender (Great Britain)

	Males		Females	
Years				
	1981	2002	1981	2002
Life expectancy	70.9	76.0	76.8	80.5
Healthy life expectancy	64.4	67.2	66.7	69.9
Years spent in poor health	6.4	8.8	10.1	10.6
Disability-free life expectancy	58.1	60.9	60.8	63.0
Years spent with disability	12.8	15.0	16.0	17.5

Source: *Social Trends 37*, 2007

Look at the table on the left.

5 Although people live longer nowadays, what does the table tell us about the health of older people? What implications might this have for women in particular?

6 In your opinion, is it a curse or a blessing to live longer (on the basis of these statistics)?

If ever anyone sought proof that social factors have a significant impact upon people's lives, then they only have to look at the relationship between a person's life experiences and their chances of illness and early death. The chances of an early death, of a serious long-term illness and of a disability are closely related to social class, income, gender, area of residence and ethnic group.

But why should this be? Health, illness and disability are generally thought of as linked to the luck of our genes – that is, they are biologically caused. Yet sociologists argue that the evidence from research indicates that it is the interaction of our social experiences with our biological make-up that determines our health. If pressed, they might well argue that the more important of the two sets of factors is actually the social rather than the biological. In this chapter, we will explore the major social determinants of our health: social class, gender and ethnicity. We will look at each area in turn.

Social class

Mortality

Over the last 25 years, **life expectancy** has risen for both men and women, in all social classes. But overall they have risen more for those in the higher social classes, so that the difference between those in the higher and those in the lower social classes has actually grown. For example, in the 1970s, the **death** or **mortality rate** among men of working age was almost twice as high for those in class V (unskilled) as for those in class I (professional). By 2003, it was almost two and a half times as high. Men in social class I can expect to live for almost eight and a half years longer than men from social class V, while women in social class I can expect to live four and a half years longer than their social class V counterparts.

Deaths from heart disease and lung cancer (the two most common causes of death for people aged 35 to 64) are twice as high in people from manual backgrounds as non-manual backgrounds.

Morbidity

Although death rates have fallen and life expectancy has increased, there is little evidence that the population is experiencing better health than 20 years ago. In fact, there has actually been a small increase in **self-reported** long-standing illness or **morbidity**, and differences between the social classes are still quite clear. However, as we saw in Topic 1, what is defined as 'health' changes over time. So it may be that people are actually in better health but don't believe it. Bearing this in mind, among the 45 to 64 age group, 18 per cent of people from 'managerial or professional backgrounds' reported a limiting long-standing illness, compared to over 32 per cent of people from 'routine or manual backgrounds' (ONS 2007).

In adulthood, being overweight is a measure of possible ill health, with obesity a risk factor for many chronic diseases. There is a noticeable social-class gradient in obesity, which is greater for women than men. According to the Department of Health (2007), about 32 per cent of women in the poorest fifth of the population are obese, compared to 16 per cent of women in the richest fifth of the population.

Explanations for differences in health between social classes

Different ways of explaining class differences in **mortality** and **morbidity** have been suggested.

The artefact approach

An **artefact** is something observed in a scientific investigation that is not naturally present, but occurs as a result of the investigative procedure. Perhaps the link between class and health is not real but a statistical illusion. Illsley (1986) argues that the statistical connection between social class and illness exaggerates the situation. For example, he points out that the number of people in social class V has declined so much over the last 30 years that the membership is just too small to be used as the basis for comparisons with other social classes.

Focus on research

Socio-economic circumstances at different life stages and smoking

by Christine Power, Hilary Graham and Orly Manor (2005)

This study was based on secondary data collected from the National Child Development Study which is a longitudinal study that has been following about 17,000 people born during a single week of March 1958 using postal questionnaires and interviews. Members of the sample were last interviewed aged 41. 11,373 subjects reported information about smoking at this stage. The aims were to find the link between social class and smoking behaviour from the age of 16 to 41, and to establish whether there is a link between early and lone parenthood and smoking.

The study found a strong link between smoking and social class. Manual workers were more likely to start smoking than other social groups and they started to smoke at an earlier age. Two-thirds of these still smoked at the age of 41. In contrast, two-thirds of smokers from the higher social classes had given up smoking by the age of 41.

There was also a link between childhood poverty and smoking patterns. Working-class women were much less likely to give up smoking than any other social group. Other risk factors for heavy adult smoking included lack of educational qualifications and, for women, motherhood before the age of 23 and lone motherhood before the age of 33. Those who remained in the lower social classes were likely to remain smokers.

Source: adapted from Blundell. J. and Griffiths, J. (2008) *Sociology since 2000*. Lewes: Connect Publications

1   **How does this evidence support the culturalist position on the poor health of the working-class?**

2   **How might this evidence be used support the materialist and structuralist positions on working-class health?**

However, the 'Independent Inquiry into Inequalities in Health' (Acheson 1998) showed that, even when the classes were regrouped to include classes IV and V together, significant differences remained. For example, in the late 1970s, death rates were 53 per cent higher among men in classes IV and V, compared with those in classes I and II.

Social selection

This approach claims that social class does not cause ill health, but that ill health may be a significant cause of social class. For example, if a person is chronically ill (i.e. has a long-term illness) or disabled in some way, it is usually difficult for them to obtain a secure, well-paid job.

The fit and healthy are more likely to be successful in life and upwardly mobile in terms of social class.

The problem with this approach is that studies of health differences indicate that poor health is a result of poverty rather than a cause of it.

Cultural explanations

The **cultural explanations** approach stresses that differences in health are best understood as the result of cultural choices made by individuals or groups in the population.

- *Diet* – Manual workers consume twice as much white bread as professionals, and have higher sugar and salt consumption and eat less fresh fruit and vegetables.
- *Cigarette smoking* – Over 40 per cent of males and 35 per cent of females in social classes IV and V regularly smoke, whereas only about 12 per cent of males and females in social class I smoke.
- *Leisure and lifestyle* – Middle-class people are more likely to take exercise and engage in a wider range of physical and sporting activities than the working classes. These reduce levels of stress and help maintain a higher standard of health and fitness.
- *Alcohol* – Alcohol consumption is directly related to social class, with much higher consumption amongst the 'lower' social classes.

The cultural approach, however, fails to ask why these groups have poor diets and high alcohol and cigarette consumption. Critics point out that there may be reasons why people are 'forced' into an unhealthy lifestyle. These critics have put forward an alternative **material explanation**.

Social class and health inequalities

Materialist explanations

Materialist sociologists point out that the choice of an unhealthy lifestyle may be rational. A study of food purchasing by Dobson (1994) found that working-class attitudes towards shopping for food were shaped by poverty. Working-class mothers were reluctant to experiment with healthy foods because they were critical of the expense of such foods and they did not want to risk wasting money on food their children might not eat. They therefore bought 'unhealthy' foods such as biscuits and white bread because they knew their children would eat them. Many of the mothers interviewed by Dobson were critical of the costs of putting healthy eating into practice. The decision, therefore, to buy unhealthy food was rational in terms of their difficult economic circumstances.

Blackburn (1991) notes that poverty results in a greater proportion of working-class people's incomes being taken up by the cost of food. This results in decisions being made to purchase cheaper less healthy food. The poor are also more likely to live in 'food deserts' – inner city areas which lack large supermarkets with a choice of healthy nutritious foods. Instead they have to rely on corner-shops or smaller supermarkets which generally have less choice and are more expensive.

The role of poverty

Materialists stress that poverty is the key factor in understanding and explaining health inequalities. The poor have unique experiences and characteristics that lead to poor health and low life expectancy. For example, when in work, they are likely to be earning below average income. Many of the poor –particularly single mothers, the elderly and disabled people – are claiming benefits such as income support or disability benefit.

A good example of the impact of poverty on health is Shettleston, an inner city area of Glasgow, which has a mortality rate of 234 which is more than twice the national average. Shaw (1999) estimates that 71 per cent of deaths in Shettleston are premature and could have been avoided if the population was lifted out of poverty. Mitchell estimates that 11,508 lives would be saved every year in the UK if child poverty was eradicated and governments did more to reduce inequalities in income and wealth.

Materialists point out that poverty leads to the quality of life of the poor being affected in a variety of ways which impact negatively on morbidity and mortality levels. The poor are more likely to experience low quality rented accommodation with problems such as dampness, vermin and overcrowding being common. Poorer areas are also poorer environments in terms of pollution, litter, vandalism, graffiti and anti-social behaviour. There is often a lack of facilities, especially for the young and limited access to transport, health care (e.g. medical surgeries in poorer areas generally have more patients than surgeries in more affluent areas) and to shops with a wide selection of cheap and healthy foodstuffs.

Structuralist explanations

Many of the above problems associated with poverty are blamed by structuralist sociologists, particularly Marxist sociologists, on the way British society is organised. In other words, the British economy is structured or organised along capitalist lines and this has produced great inequalities in the distribution of wealth and income. From this perspective, poverty exists because wealth is concentrated in so few hands. Structuralists also see poverty as being caused by the free market economic policies of successive British governments which have resulted in unemployment as industries have gone into decline or re-located their businesses to other parts of the world.

Inequality and cohesion

Wilkinson and Pickett (2009) argue that the greater the inequality in a society like the UK, the less social cohesion (i.e. sense of belonging) it has. Insecurity and isolation is more likely to be experienced by the poorest social groups. For example, if crime rates in particular areas are high, this increases people's feelings of mutual suspicion, fear, anxiety etc. He argues that the poor are less likely to feel a sense of belonging to society if they feel that they have no control over their everyday circumstances.

Wilkinson (1999) notes too that the physical experience of living in poor communities can lead to increased anxiety and stress. For example, low income can lead to worry about how bills are going to be paid and debt. Some residents may realistically fear being a victim of crime or anti-social behaviour. Unemployment could lead to feelings of shame, depression and hopelessness. Wilkinson argues that all these experiences lead to stress which can undermine our immune systems and our ability to fight off infection and disease, as well as mental illness.

Wilkinson compares the UK with Sweden because these countries have a great deal in common in terms of their standards of living. However, he notes that Sweden enjoys better levels of health and lower death rates than the UK. He argues that this is because the UK exhibits greater levels of inequalities in wealth, income and educational success between the different social classes whereas in Sweden there are fewer economic differences between social groups. Wilkinson concludes that greater income equality in the UK would greatly reduce health differences in illness and death rates.

Work and ill-health

Other structuralist sociologists have looked at how the organization of the British workforce might contribute to ill-health. Davey Smith (1990) argues that mortality rates can be linked to position at work. He found that workers with little power or control over their work are likely to experience worse health than those given more responsibility. His research on civil servants has shown that routine clerical workers are much more likely to die young than workers in higher grades. If the lowest and highest grades are compared, those in the lowest grades are actually three times more likely to die before reaching the age of 65.

Marxists have also drawn attention to the numbers of deaths of workers in factories, on building sites etc because of employer breaches of health and safety laws. On average, about 500 workers die at work every year. Furthermore, thousands are injured. Industrial diseases too contribute to the poor health of working-class people. Industries vary in how dangerous they are to their employees. For example, respiratory diseases are common amongst those working in road and building construction, as a result of the dust inhaled, while various forms of cancer are associated with chemical industries.

The inverse care law

The inverse care law, associated with Julian Tudor Hart (1971), suggests that health care resources tend to be distributed in inverse proportion to need. This means that those regions or social groups whose need is least get the most resources, while those regions or social groups whose need is greatest get the least. For example, Easington in County Durham, a very deprived area, should be receiving an additional £26.5 million a year in funding, while Kensington and Chelsea, one of the richest places in Britain, is receiving £30.3 million a year, more than the official government funding formula requires. In general, in practice this means that working-class areas have fewer GPs, dentists, hospitals, specialist units such as cancer screening etc than more affluent middle-class areas. It has been suggested that one reason for this may be because the medical professionals are middle-class themselves.

There is some evidence that the inverse care law is also underpinned by a north-south divide. Some experts have even described this unequal access to health services as a 'postcode lottery'. For example, an examination of NHS facilities reveals that the industrial areas of northern England and Wales have:

● Fewer and older hospitals.
● Fewer high status hospitals, i.e. foundation trust hospitals which are given higher levels of funding than other hospitals.
● Fewer and less adequate specialised facilities, such as for cancer and kidney treatments.
● Fewer hospital beds per head of population.
● Fewer GP practices and therefore higher patient-doctor ratios – so there are fewer doctors for those most likely to get ill.
● Slower access to diagnostic tests, anti-cancer drugs and chemotherapy.

Gordon et al. (1999) argue that there is a large body of evidence to support what they describe as the 'inverse prevention law' in front-line healthcare. By this, they mean that those social groups who are in greatest need of preventative care – that is, the poor – are least likely to have routine regular access to preventative services such as health promotion, dental check-ups, immunisation and cancer screening. These inequalities have real consequences. For example, people in the cities of northern England are almost twice as likely to die of cancer compared with those who live in the affluent areas of the south. The death rate from cancer is 60 per cent higher in Liverpool than in east Dorset.

Conclusions

It is a fact that working-class people are more susceptible to illness and consequently that they are more likely to die younger than their middle-class or upper-class counterparts. The evidence strongly suggests that material, structural and psycho-social forces that are beyond the control of working-class people are responsible rather than irresponsible lifestyle choices.

Gender and health

Women live longer than men, e.g. in the UK, a female born in 2004 can expect to live until she is 81.1 years old, while a male born in the same year can expect to reach the age of 76.7 years. Men's death rates are almost double those of women in every single class. They also have higher levels of chronic illness, mental illness and disability. This has led some sociologists to conclude that men die and women suffer. However, this apparently contradictory pattern – higher morbidity combined with a longer life span – has led some observers to argue that it is not that women are more likely to be ill than men, but that they are more willing to visit the doctor.

Explanations for the link between gender and health

Biology

The idea that women experience more morbidity or illness, and consequently visit the doctor more often may be exaggerated by the biological function of their bodies.

Focus on research

Health survey for England 2005: the health of older people

Edited by Rachel Craig and Jennifer Mindell (2007)

The Health survey is an annual survey focused on the health of British people which in 2005 carried out 2673 structured interviews with people aged over 65 years about their general health, alcohol use, smoking, consumption of fruit and vegetables, as well as their general experience of health and use of health care facilities. Trained nurses also visited these households to measure height and weight and take various medical samples.

The survey found that older women were more likely than men to have a chronic illness or condition that affected their lives in some way. A quarter of all women aged over 65 but only 14% of men had walking problems. Women were more likely to be morbidly obese than men. Obesity can result in chronic conditions such as diabetes, arthritis and raised blood pressure. This then predisposes people to strokes and heart attacks. High blood pressure is also associated with high intake of salt and is more common among poorer income groups.

The study found that poor health is linked to poor social capital- those who experienced bad health were those who saw fewest people and who went out the least often. Men were more likely than women to have poor social capital in the sense that they were less likely to have a social network of friends and family that they regularly saw. On the other hand, women were more likely to belong to clubs and social associations, and see family members on a regular basis.

Men were less likely than women to go to a doctor but were more likely to have attended a hospital outpatient appointment. Those who were in good health were far more likely to visit a dentist than those who were ill.

Women were more likely to experience symptoms of depression than men although among men, those most likely to experience depression were in the lower income groups.

Source: adapted from Blundell. J. and Griffiths, J. (2008) *Sociology since 2000.* Lewes: Connect Publications

1. **How do the research findings support the idea that there are differences in morbidity between men and women?**

2. **How do the findings on social capital support the ideas of Wilkinson?**

Nettleton (2006) notes that these so-called high rates of illness have more to do with the maintenance of the female body with regard to menstruation, contraception, infertility and pregnancy. In other words, women do not visit doctors because they suffer higher rates of illness than men but because the nature of their body mean that such visits cannot be avoided. For example, the act of giving birth puts great strain on the female body. Women may also suffer more ill health than men because they live longer.

Cultural/behavioural explanations

The process of gender role socialization means women and men are socialized into completely different sets of values, norms and social roles which may impact on their health and life expectancy. This can be illustrated in a number of ways:

O'Brien et al (2005) conducted interviews with fourteen focus groups composed of men from a variety of social backgrounds. They found that the majority of men preferred to tolerate symptoms of illness and to put off visiting a doctor. Most men interpreted masculinity as being able to cope with pain. Admitting pain or the need for medical help was regarded as a sign of weakness. In particular, men admitted that they regarded feelings of anxiety or depression as a type of vulnerability that needed to be avoided because they interpreted it as directly challenging their masculinity.

Socialization into femininity in the UK encourages women to express their emotions and to talk about their problems more than men. This may mean that women are more comfortable than men in taking their physical and emotional problems to doctors.

Boys and men are socialized into 'high risk' behavior which may have a negative effect upon health and life expectancy. For example, men are more likely to drink and smoke, e.g. they may drink in order to cope with anxiety, stress and depression rather than visit the doctor for prescription drugs. They are also socialized into being more aggressive and this may mean that they are much more willing to take risks which result in more harm and death from violence and road accidents. For example, about 40% of death of boys aged 1-14 are due to accidents and violence compared with 26% of girls.

The materialist/structural explanation

There is some evidence that the organization of work in capitalist society may negatively impact on men's health and life expectancy. For example, work is a central part of masculinity and unemployment therefore can have a severe effect on men's physical and mental health. Furthermore, working- class men are at risk from the nature of their jobs. For example, hundreds at men a year are killed in the workplace and thousands are injured. They are more likely than women to be exposed to toxic materials and to develop industrial diseases. Retirement has traditionally come later for men compared with women. There is some evidence that retirement results in a loss of identity, self-esteem and purpose. It may also result in social isolation as retirement cuts off a major source of social contact. All these factors may have a negative effect on health, especially mental health and life expectancy.

The experience of work may affect women's health too. Annandale (1998) argues that women who have careers and enjoy economic independence enjoy better health than women who do not. However, one drawback of this is that evidence from the USA suggests that the life expectancy of career women is dropping to the level of men's life expectancy.

Despite the improvement in women's job opportunities, the evidence suggests that many women are in low-paid, low-skilled insecure part-time work. Consequently they are more likely to be in poverty which means that they are likely to experience an inadequate diet, poor quality housing, debt and a threatening urban environment. Wilkinson notes that these experiences of deprivation may trigger stress-related diseases and result in these women being less able to fight off illness or infection.

Feminist explanations

Bernard (1972) takes the view that women may suffer more ill-health because of marriage. In her study, she found that married women were less healthy than single women and full-time housewives were less healthy than women who worked full-time. Furthermore, married men were healthier than single men.

Bernard notes that many women suffer a 'triple burden' of being low-paid workers, who are mainly responsible for childcare and housework, as well as managing their family's emotions. Moreover, women's stress is increased by having less leisure time than males. Bernard therefore concludes that giving up work and becoming a full-time mother-housewife can lead to depression, social isolation and nervous anxiety. However, Bernard's measurement of women's health was measured by visits to the doctor which we have already seen may be problematical.

Feminists argue that women' health is more at risk from clinical iatrogenesis, especially the increased risk of cancer or heart conditions associated with the contraceptive pill. Women's use of mental health services may mean that iatrogenesis is also caused by addiction to anti-depressants and sleeping pills.

Busfield (1988) claims women's health is not taken seriously by the medical profession. She notes that female illnesses such as pre-menstrual tension and post-natal depression have only recently been recognized by the medical profession as legitimate illnesses. Busfield also notes that the same symptoms in men and women are diagnosed, labelled and treated quite differently. For example, anxiety and stress in a man may be diagnosed as symptoms of over-work and rest might be advised. Similar symptoms in a woman maybe viewed as a 'natural' aspect of women's 'weaker' character that can only be treated with drugs. Women are therefore more likely to be diagnosed as depressed or suffering from anxiety than men. They are also more likely to be treated in mental hospitals. Both these trends may have more to do with how male doctors interpret female symptoms rather than objective scientific analysis.

Feminists argue that women often experience health problems such as depression because of the patriarchal nature of the family, e.g. women may be disproportionately responsible for housework and childcare even when they work full-time. However, feminists claim that male doctors tend to see women's ill-health as a function of their emotional weaknesses which undermines their ability to be good wives and mothers rather than because of women's lack of power and control in a patriarchal society.

Oakley notes that male doctors have extended their power and control over areas such as gynaecology and childbirth which have traditionally been dominated by female medical professionals such as midwives. She found that over two-thirds of first-time mothers in her study of maternity felt that they had little control over their childbirth. The mothers in her study also complained that doctors showed little interest in listening to their concerns and anxieties.

However, in criticism of these feminist views, there is evidence that health services benefit women more than men. Women still live longer than men and the NHS's funding of screening for breast and cervical cancer is significantly higher than that for prostate cancer which kills about 10,000 males a year (approximately 2000 women die a year from cervical cancer) and testicular cancer.

Ethnicity and health

Ethnicity refers to a person's culture (or way of life) and sense of cultural identity. We normally use the term to refer to the values, norms and customs shared by the major ethnic minority groups in the UK – Asian people from a Pakistani, Bangladeshi and Indian background, African-Caribbeans, Chinese and Africans. White people constitute the majority ethnic population in the UK. Most ethnic minority groups have higher mortality rates than the white population and consequently ethnic minority life expectancy is generally lower than the White majority population. In particular, infant mortality rates tend to be significantly higher than the white population.

People from African-Caribbean, Indian, Pakistani and Bangladeshi backgrounds are more likely to die from tuberculosis, liver cancer and diabetes compared with the White population. However, apart from liver cancer, all ethnic minority groups have lower levels of death from cancer than the White population. Indians and Pakistanis are the ethnic groups most likely in the UK to die from heart disease whereas African-Caribbeans have the lowest level of death from such disease. However Africans and African-Caribbeans are more likely to suffer from strokes and high blood pressure than other ethnic groups whilst African-Caribbeans are more likely to suffer from the genetic blood disorder sickle cell anaemia.

Indians and African-Caribbeans are more likely to experience mental illness, especially schizophrenia compared with other ethnic groups. Furthermore African-Caribbeans are five times more likely than other ethnic groups to be hospitalised for mental illness.

Explanations for the link between ethnicity and health

The biomedical explanation

This theory sees biology as the main source of illness. For example, African-Caribbean people are more likely to experience sickle cell disease because of a mutated gene. However biological explanations are only relevant in a minority of illnesses. They are unable to account for consistent differences in mortality and morbidity between different ethnic groups that experience no significant genetic or physical differences.

The culturalist explanation

Culturalist explanations suggest that the culture of ethnic minorities is responsible for their mortality and morbidity rates. It is suggested that ethnic minorities choose to pursue particular courses of action that result in ill-health.

- In particular, diet is blamed for the high rates of heart disease amongst Asians –especially ghee, a supposedly less healthy form of cooking fat. The high rate of diabetes among Asians is blamed on high carbohydrate foods which encourage obesity. It is argued that Asian foods also tend to lack vitamin D and that this may account for the higher level of rickets found among Asian children.
- Levels of smoking are high among Asian and Black groups compared with whites.
- Asian people are less likely to engage in physical exercise and sport compared with other ethnic groups.

However, critics of the culturalist approach suggest it is not Asian culture that is responsible for their poor health but the NHS response to ethnic minority cultures. For example, despite big improvements, there is still a lack of information available in minority ethnic group languages as well as a lack of translation services.

Moreover Asian women prefer to see female doctors but there is a shortage of female GPs in those areas with the largest numbers of Asian households. Also, health professionals may fail to meet the health needs of ethnic minorities because they are not familiar enough with the religious, cultural and dietary practices of ethnic minority cultures.

The materialist explanation

Materialists are very critical of culturalists for failing to acknowledge that cultural practices are not voluntarily chosen – rather they are shaped by the economic and social circumstances of the individual over which the individual has little or no control.

Sociologists such as Shaw (2006) suggest that poverty is more likely to be experienced by ethnic minorities. 40% of ethnic minority communities live in poverty compared with 20% of the White community. This figure increases to 69% for people of Pakistani and Bangladeshi origin. Kempson (1996) argues that poverty leads to debt, poor diet and nutrition and stress which impacts negatively on communities by increasing both the chances of illness and early death.

Poverty caused by unemployment and low pay

Ethnic minorities experience high unemployment rates compared with white people – in 2004, 5% of Whites were unemployed compared with 14% of African-Caribbeans, 13% of Bangladeshis and 11% of Pakistanis.

Ethnic minorities, even when working, experience lower rates of pay than White people because:

- They are more likely to be over-concentrated in lower paid semi-skilled and unskilled work which often involves working night-shifts in hazardous and toxic work environments.
- White people are twice as likely as ethnic minority men to be in a well-paid skilled trade.

- In 2007 ethnic minorities in management and professional jobs earned up to 25% less than their white colleagues.

Poverty and low quality housing

Poverty also leads to housing inequalities. 70% of ethnic minority people in the UK live in council housing in the 88 most economically and socially deprived local authority districts. Only 2% of Whites live in poor, damp and overcrowded housing compared with 30% of Bangladeshis and 22% of Pakistanis. Alcock found that poor damp housing often leads to poor health in ethnic minority children, as well as time off school and few qualifications leading to low-paid low-skilled jobs or unemployment.

Poverty, racism and poor health

Much of the poverty and exclusion experienced by ethnic minorities is actually caused by racism. Racist name-calling, racial attacks, racial harassment, employer racism and institutional racism also contributes to poor levels of physical and mental health. All these experiences of abuse may increase fear, stress and isolation.

The Inverse Care Law

Tudor Hart suggests that areas that need health care the most actually have less NHS funding and fewer specialist hospitals, consultants and general practitioners (GPs). This is especially true of those areas in which there are concentrations of ethnic minorities in the North of England or inner city areas of London.

Furthermore it is argued that what NHS services exist do not cater sufficiently for ethnic minority cultural and religious needs. The NHS has been criticised for being an 'ethnocentric' or institutionally racist institution – it is mainly focused on the needs of the majority white population rather than all social groups. Surveys indicate that Asians report higher levels of dissatisfaction about health care than White people.

It has been suggested that ethnic minority people may be put off seeking medical help because:

- Some ethnic groups, e.g. Muslims prefer women to be treated by female doctors but there may not be enough of these in areas with large Muslim communities to guarantee this.
- Ethnic minorities, especially Muslims, Hindus and Sikhs, may have unique religious and dietary needs. However, NHS hospitals may fail to cater for these needs. For example, after death Muslims must follow specific religious and funeral practices with regard to the dead body. It has been suggested that NHS personnel are often ignorant and disrespectful of these needs.

Social constructionist or interactionist theories

Interactionist accounts of health focus on the treatment of African-Caribbeans with regards to mental health. Nazroo (2001) argues that African-Caribbeans, especially Rastafarians are more likely than any other group to be diagnosed as 'mentally ill'. However, Nazroo argues this may not reflect real illness. Rather he accuses White psychiatric doctors of wrongly interpreting and negatively labelling behaviour which is culturally or religious 'different' as mental illness' or 'schizophrenia'.

For example, many Rastafarians refuse to co-operate, usually by refusing to communicate, with the White authorities because they subscribe to the religious view that White society is 'evil' (Babylon) for enslaving Africans during the slave trade. Nazroo argues that the price they pay for this non-cooperation is being remanded to psychiatric units for reports. He argues that this is not scientific diagnosis – rather it is a form of white social control.

Once a person has been admitted to a psychiatric institution it can be quite difficult to get out because all behaviour is interpreted in the context of the 'mentally ill' label. There is some evidence too that continuing non-cooperation leads to greater controls over African-Caribbeans inside the system through the use of drugs and electric shock treatment.

Marxism

Marxists are not surprised that ethnic minorities experience high rates of morbidity and mortality. They note that the organisation of capitalism results in great inequalities in wealth and income, and therefore poverty which is more likely to be experienced by members of ethnic minority groups.

Psycho-social explanations

Wilkinson (1996) suggests that those who are low in the socio-economic hierarchy such as ethnic minorities have less social control over their working and living conditions and consequently they experience greater stress and greater feelings of low self-esteem.

Wilkinson also argues that income inequality affects health because it undermines social cohesion – the sense that we are all valued equally by society. Our general sense of happiness and contentment is dependent on how strongly we feel a sense of belonging to society. Wilkinson argues that extreme inequalities weakens our sense of social cohesion because inequality generates feelings of desperation, hopelessness, helplessness, depression, bitterness, fear, insecurity, envy, hostility and inferiority, which lead to stress. Wilkinson notes that social cohesion is at its weakest in deprived inner city areas in which ethnic minorities are more likely to live.

Wilkinson claims these negative experiences trigger off psycho-social behaviour such as smoking and drinking, poor eating habits and inactivity. As a result, this in turn increases depression, high blood pressure and weakens resistance to disease and infection, all of which contribute to the high mortality and morbidity rates experienced within ethnic minority communities.

161

Key terms

Artefact approach an approach that believes that the statistics about class and health exaggerate the real situation.

Caribbean commonwealth parts of the West Indies that are in the Commonwealth, such as Barbados.

Cultural explanations explanations that emphasize lifestyle and behaviour.

Death rate the number dying per 1000 of a population per year.

Indian subcontinent the section of south Asia consisting of India, Pakistan and Bangladesh.

Life expectancy the number of years that a person can expect to live on average in a given population.

Material explanations explanations that focus on the make-up of society: for example, on inequalities of income and wealth.

Morbidity refers to statistics about illness.

Mortality refers to statistics of death.

Self-reported the result of asking people themselves.

Activities

Research idea

Ask a sample of 20 people how much fresh fruit they eat each day. You might wish to divide the sample by gender or by age or even by parental occupation. Do any differences emerge?

Web.tasks

Go to the Department of Health's Community Health Profiles website at:

www.communityhealthprofiles.info/index.php

Here you can look up your own area and obtain a full health profile.

Check your understanding

1   Identify four factors that are closely linked to health.

2   Why might some areas of Britain have worse health than others?

3   Give one example of health differences between the social classes.

4   What explanations have been suggested for health differences between the social classes?

5   Explain, in your own words, the meaning of the 'artefact approach'.

6   Do biological factors alone explain the differences in health between men and women?

7   What three explanations have been given for the differences in health between the various ethnic minorities and the majority of the population?

An eye on the exam
Patterns and explanations of ill health in society

the opening sentence of each paragraph should clearly highlight the reason

whatever it is that you have identified must be discussed in some depth using sociological studies and examples

begin your answer with a clear definition of what is meant by this concept

(a) Identify and explain two aspects of marriage that might account for higher morbidity levels for females.

(17 marks)

each aspect needs to be clealy distinguishable and developed into a very detailed paragraph

you should attempt to write two very detailed paragraphs in about 15 minutes

a detailed description of the view is required using sociological concepts, theories and studies

it is important to assess the merits of the culturalist theory of health in some detail, either by raising specific strengths or criticisms of the theory or by presenting alternative theoretical perspectives such as materialist or structuralist perspectives

this view is a culturalist perspective

(b) Outline and evaluate the view that working-class people experience worse health because they make the wrong cultural choices.

(33 marks)

you should attempt to write at least 2 sides of the answer book in about 30 minutes

Grade booster Getting top marks in this question

You need to describe working-class experience of mortality and morbidity showing very clearly that in contrast with other social classes that they experience inequality. Outline in detail using illustrative examples, how culturalist sociologists suggest that working-class people engage in unhealthy behaviour relating to diet, exercise, smoking and alcohol. Criticise this perspective with references to materialist studies of diet and smoking which show such behaviour to be rational in the context of poverty. Outline in detail how poverty impacts on both mortality and morbidity. Link these ideas to the structuralist emphasis on inequalities in wealth and income, and the psycho-social consequences for health and illness.

TOPIC 3

The social construction of mental illness and disability

Getting you thinking

'Normal children given drugs'

By **David Derbyshire** and **Roger Highfield** at the British Association science festival The Daily Telegraph (filed: 09 September 2004)

THE RISE OF attention deficit hyperactivity disorder has led to concerns that doctors and drugs companies are turning unpleasant, but essentially normal, human behaviour into medical conditions. Its most serious form, known as hyperkinetic disorder, affects 1.4 per cent of children. Sufferers are unable to concentrate, forgetful, disorganized and easily distracted. At school they are disruptive, find it almost impossible to learn ...

While the most serious cases are generally recognized as psychiatric disorders, diagnosis of milder forms of ADHD, is more controversial. One person's ADHD victim is another's naughty child. Some researchers are concerned that drugs such as Ritalin, the 'chemical cosh', are used to suppress essentially normal but disruptive behaviour. In the UK, only 0.3 per cent of all children receive medication for ADHD, compared with six per cent in America.

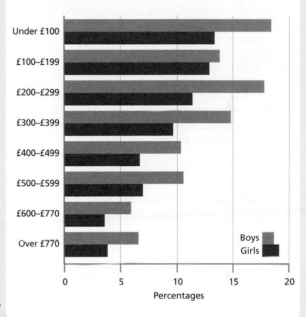

Prevalence of mental disorders among children: by gender and gross weekly household income, Great Britain, 2004

1   Provide a short summary of what the chart above tells you about the relationship between mental illness and (a) gender (b) family income.

2   Can you suggest any explanations for these links?

3   There is considerable debate concerning the very existence of ADHD. Some people argue that it is simply a way of labelling bad behaviour as mental illness and therefore taking the blame away from parents and the children. What is your view?

4   Do you think that it is right to use drugs to alter the behaviour of children?

5   Look at the photo of the anorexic/very thin young women. Is anorexia a mental illness in your opinion?

6   What conclusions can you draw about how we define mental illness and who decides whether it exists or not?

Mental illness has been the forgotten twin to physical illness, in terms of the attention paid to it and the funding provided by the NHS. The issue only comes to the fore when a particularly spectacular event hits the headlines. However, mental health is a major problem in society, with about one in seven of the population claiming to have mental health problems at some point in their lives. But mental health is dogged with debates over definitions and over the differences in the extent of mental health problems across different groups in society.

According to the government publication *Social Trends 2007* (Self and Zealey 2007), about one in six British people aged 16 to 74 reported experiencing a neurotic disorder (self-diagnosed), such as depression, anxiety or a phobia, in the seven days before a national survey on mental health.

Overall, when looking at which group is most likely to suffer from high rates of mental illness, the poorest and most excluded are massively overrepresented.

Members of ethnic minorities have significantly different chances of mental illness compared to the majority White population. According to Nazroo (2001) people of 'South Asian origin' have very low rates of mental illness, while those of African-Caribbean origins have particularly high levels of schizophrenia, with levels between three and five times higher than the population as a whole.

Women are more likely than men to exhibit behaviour defined as mental illness. Overall, women have rates about one third higher than men, but in some specific forms of mental illness the figures are much higher. For example, women are at least three times more likely to suffer from depression.

Defining mental illness

Sociology is split between two different approaches regarding how to define mental illness. The two approaches are **social realism** and **social constructionism**.

Social realism

Social realism is a general term used to describe the approaches of sociologists who, broadly speaking, accept that there are distinctive sets of abnormal behaviour that cause distress to individuals and to those around them. These forms of abnormal behaviour are classified as mental illness. Social realists such as Pilgrim and Rogers (1999) accept that, at different times and in different cultures, there are variations in what is considered as mental illness. Nevertheless, they argue that, although mental illness may have different names and may or may not be recognized in different cultures, it does actually exist as a real condition.

This view is very similar to the bio-medical approach discussed in Topic 1. This approach sees the causes of mental health as situated in the physical body, e.g. as a result of brain damage, genetic factors, chemical and hormonal influences etc or as the result of external factors that damage mental development, e.g. poor diet, pollution etc.

The bio-medical approach believes that symptoms can be scientifically diagnosed and categorised. Mental health practitioners, e.g. psychiatrists have therefore diagnosed problematic human behaviour into over 350 psychiatric categories or conditions, e.g. neuroses, phobias, anxieties, depression, psychotic episodes etc. Consequently, they see treatment as allopathic, i.e. cure-orientated through the use of drugs, electric shock treatment, surgery etc. The biomedical model has recommended that sufferers from extreme mental health problems be isolated from wider society in secure mental health institutions, i.e. asylums.

Social constructionism

Social constructionist perspectives have been very influential in sociological approaches to mental illness and start from the argument that what is considered normal varies over time and from society to society. For example, over the last two hundred years in Britain, alcohol consumption has been seen variously as normal, as morally wrong or even illegal, as a sign of being mentally ill and as a central part of a religious ritual. In fact, most of these different attitudes to alcohol can still be found in Britain today!

Even greater extremes of behaviour have been seen as normal in some societies and as evidence of madness in others. For example, saying that you are possessed by the spirit of your ancestor would suggest madness in contemporary Britain, but for native Americans, or in some West African religions, it would be a perfectly reasonable statement which most people would believe was true.

Mental illness: the labelling perspective

The degree of flexibility about what constitutes normal and abnormal behaviour has been taken furthest by labelling theorists. Labelling theory examines how the labelling of mental illness occurs in the first place and what effects it has on those who are labelled. Thomas Szasz (1973), for example, argues that the label 'mental illness' is simply a convenient way to deal with behaviour that people find disruptive. Szasz is particularly critical of psychiatrists for diagnosing children with Attention Deficit Hyperactivity Disorder (ADHD) and calling ADHD a disease. He argues that diseases are biological problems that can physically be observed or measured within the body. For example, cancer is a disease that can be spotted using blood tests and biopsies. It can be cut out of the body with surgery or physically attacked with radiotherapy or chemotherapy. In an autopsy, it can be seen as a physical presence that caused death.

Szasz argues that none of these criteria can be applied with regard to ADHD and other so-called mental diseases. Instead ADHD involves people with power - parents, teachers and psychiatrists -making judgements about children's behaviour. If that behaviour is judged too 'naughty' or disruptive then the child may be diagnosed as suffering from ADHD and prescribed a drug -ritalin- that subdues the child and controls that behaviour. However Szasz argues that other parents, teachers and psychiatrists could quite easily judge the same behaviour as normal for a child that age or as merely a product of childish tantrums. Furthermore Szasz argues that giving a child ritalin is a form of physical child abuse because the child has no say in the matter. Labelling theory therefore rests firmly upon a social constructionist definition of mental illness.

The effects of labelling

According to Scheff (1966), whether someone becomes labelled or not is determined by the benefits that others might gain by labelling the person 'mentally ill'. So, those people who become a nuisance, or who prevent others from doing something they want to do, are far more likely to be defined as being mentally ill than those who pose no threat or inconvenience, and may be ignored. A good example of this is the way political dissidents were treated in the Soviet Union in the 1970s. People who were critical of life under communism were often labelled mentally ill and packed off to asylums for 'treatment' rather than arrested and put on trial. The diagnosis of mental illness sent out the ideological message that life was so good in the Soviet Union only a mad person would complain about it!

Once labelled, there are a number of negative consequences for the person, because it is then assumed that all their behaviour is evidence of their mental state. A famous study by Rosenhan (1973) illustrates this. In the early 1970s in the USA, Rosenhan asked eight perfectly 'normal' researchers to enter a number of psychiatric institutions after phoning up and complaining that they were 'hearing voices'. Once the researchers had been admitted into the institutions, doctors and staff regarded them as truly mentally ill and reinterpreted all their behaviour as proof of this. However, the researchers were under strict instructions to behave completely normally at all times. For example, Rosenhan asked one of his pseudo-patient to take notes of everything he saw and did. When Rosenhan eventually accessed the hospital records of this particular 'patient' he found that both nurses and doctors had expressed concern about the 'writing behaviour'. In other words, this normal behaviour was seen and interpreted as abnormal behaviour within the context of a psychiatric hospital ward.

In a later study, new staff in a psychiatric hospital were told that this experiment was to be repeated in their institution, and they were asked to uncover these researchers who were just pretending to be ill. In this study, staff routinely judged people who were 'genuinely ill' as merely pretending. It would seem, therefore, that there is some confusion as to how even experts can decide who is actually mentally ill.

Erving Goffman (1961) followed the **careers** of people who were genuinely defined as being mentally ill. He suggested that, once in an institution, people are stripped of their **presenting culture** – by which he means the image that we all choose to present to the world as 'us'. This may include a style of haircut, make-up, or the requirement that people address us as 'Mr' or 'Mrs' rather than 'Michael' or 'Sarah'. The 'patient' may also lose their right to make decisions about their life and may be required to take medication, which can disorientate them.

Quickly, the self-image that a patient has – perhaps of being a respectable, witty, middle-aged person – is stripped away, leaving them bewildered, vulnerable and ready to accept a new role. In this powerless situation, any attempts to reject the label of mental illness can actually be interpreted as further signs of illness, and perhaps as indicating a need for increased medication or counselling. In fact, accepting the role of being mentally ill is seen as the first sign of recovery.

Criticisms of the labelling perspective

The labelling perspective on mental illness has not gone unchallenged. Gove (1982) suggests that the vast majority of people who receive treatment for mental illness actually have serious problems before they are treated and so the argument that the label causes the problem is wrong. Furthermore, he argues that labelling theory provides no adequate explanation for why some people start to show symptoms in the first place.

According to Gove, labelling may help explain some of the responses of others to the mentally ill, but it cannot explain the causes of the illness.

Foucault's perspective on mental illness

A second, very distinctive version of social constructionist theory emerges in the work of the French sociologist, Foucault (1965). He explains the growth in the concept of mental illness by placing it in the context of the changing ways of thinking and acting which developed in the early 18th century. According to Foucault, during the **Enlightenment**, more traditional ways of thinking, based on religious beliefs and on emotions, were gradually replaced by more rational, intellectually disciplined ways of thinking and acting. These eventually led to the significant scientific and engineering developments that formed the basis of the 'industrial revolution'. Foucault argues that as rationality developed into the normal way of thinking, irrationality began to be perceived as deviant.

This shift away from the irrational and towards the rational was illustrated, according to Foucault, by the growth in asylums for those considered mad. Foucault suggests that having mad people in asylums, both symbolically and literally, isolated mad people away from the majority of the population. The asylums symbolized the fact that madness or irrationality was marked out as behaviour that was no longer acceptable.

Although Foucault's writing is very dense and complicated, the essential message is that madness, as we understand it, is a relatively modern invention which emerged from the development of modern 'rational' ways of thinking and acting.

Structuralist perspectives on mental health

Structuralist perspectives on mental health are closely tied to the social realist definition of mental illness. These approaches accept the reality of mental illness and set out to discover what factors in society might cause the illness. As a result of research by sociologists working within this tradition, evidence of clear mental health differences between social groups has emerged.

Mental illness and ethnicity

Writers within the structuralist perspective, such as Virdee (1997), explain the fact that some ethnic minorities are more likely to develop mental health problems by arguing that the sorts of pressures and stresses that can cause people to develop mental illness are more likely to be experienced by members of ethnic minorities because they encounter racism and disadvantage throughout their lives.

However, labelling theorists have argued that some of the behaviour of Afro-Caribbean adults, in particular, has been seen as inappropriate in British society, and has therefore been labelled as a symptom of mental illness. For example, cultural differences between White society and African-Caribbean culture can sometimes lead to African-Caribbean behaviour, especially within the criminal justice system, being seen and interpreted as aggressive and problematic. Consequently, African-Caribbeans are more likely than any other ethnic minority group to be remanded for psychiatric reports by the courts. Once in the mental health care system, they are much more likely than other social groups to experience more harsh and invasive forms of treatment such as electroconvulsive or shock therapy.

However, Nazroo is critical of the structuralist approach. He points out that people of Bangladeshi origin, who are amongst the most deprived groups in the British population and are also victims of racism, actually have lower levels of mental illness than the general population. Nazroo therefore concludes that mental illness cannot just be caused by racism and deprivation.

Mental illness and gender

Structuralists, such as Brown *et al.* (1995), argue that women are more likely to lead stressful lives because they often combine the dual burden of careers and responsibility for the bulk of housework and childcare. Women are also more likely to experience poverty, poor housing conditions, debt and the stress of living on the margins of society.

However, labelling theorists and feminist sociologists, such as Chesler (1972), go further and argue that the behaviour of women is more likely to be defined as evidence of mental illness because the defining is done by a male-dominated profession. Rather than looking for the real reasons – which are most likely to be related to the stress that might result from being responsible for the bulk of childcare and housework, or women's low status in society – GPs and psychiatrists are more interested in defining the problem in terms of an individual woman's mental state without any reference to her social experiences.

Busfield (1988) has suggested that the structuralist position and the labelling approach have a great deal in common because women are more likely to experience patriarchal exploitation, inequality and hardship, which leads to higher levels of mental illness, but they are also more likely to have their problems defined as mental illness by psychiatrists.

Inequality, social class and mental illness

Link and Phelan (1995) reviewed all the evidence collected over a period of 40 years which focused on the link between social class and mental illness, and concluded that all the research clearly pointed to a close relationship between deprivation and low levels of mental health. A government study (Office for National Statistics Study 2004) found that children from the poorest backgrounds were three times more likely to have behaviour disorders than those whose parents were in professional occupations. Structuralist writers, such as Myers (1975), have suggested a '**life-course**' model, which suggests that poor people experience mental illness because as they get older, they experience more severe social problems. However they lack the educational, social and economic resources to overcome these problems which get progressively worse. This stress of trying to cope year in, year out , leads to mental illness.

A second type of structuralist explanation focuses on the concept of **social capital**. Putnam (2000) argues that people who have extensive and strong social networks of friends and relatives are more likely to be happy, to have lower levels of stress and to feel they 'belong' to their local community. The result of this is that they are less likely to suffer from mental illness.

In a similar analysis, Wilkinson argues that the poor are more likely to be living in severely deprived areas with high crime rates and little sense of community. He suggests that the more vulnerable living in these communities often experience fear of crime. They are less likely to know or trust their neighbours because of the high turnover of people in these areas. They are more likely to be socially isolated and lonely. They are more likely to be struggling to make ends meet and to pay their bills. Wilkinson argues that all these experiences are stress triggers and that they are likely to set off mental health problems such as depression.

Mental illness: conclusion

Mental illness is a highly contested issue in sociology. There are arguments over the very definition of the term and how to explain the differences in mental illness rates in the population. However, the different approaches actually have a great deal in common and Busfield's approach is one that has received much support. She argues that it is probably true that some groups are much more likely to find their behaviour defined as mental illness, compared to the behaviour of other groups. However, it is also true that these very same groups – ethnic minorities, women and the socially excluded – all suffer high levels of stress and so one would expect them to have higher levels of mental illness. Both these processes therefore reinforce each other.

The social construction of disability

It is assumed that disabled people have some physical or mental impediment that prevents them from operating 'normally'. This perception starts from the assumption that there is a 'normal' body, and a 'normal' range of activities associated with it which are disrupted in some way.

The biomedical model of disability

This definition originates with the medical model of **disability** which mainly focuses on the physical and mental impairments that result in disability. This model assumes that:

● The disabled are sick and abnormal.

- The disabled are dependent on the able-bodied and are unable to function effectively without their constant help.
- Normalization can only occur through either medical cure or through round-the-clock care.
- Disability is a **personal tragedy** and consequently the disabled deserve our pity. The disabled person has to be 'helped' to come to terms with the physical and psychological problems that they face.

The social model of disability

However, it has been pointed out by critics such as Oliver (1996) that the obstacles imposed by society are just as great as those imposed by the physical impairment. He notes that it is society which disables physically impaired people because the disabled are deliberately excluded from full participation in society by the stereotypical attitudes held by able-bodied people. In other words, physically impaired people are actually disabled by society.

Disabled by society

Disability activists and sociologists have suggested that most of the UK population are impaired in some way but they are rarely classified as 'disabled'. They argue that there are degrees of difference in disability or impairment; for example, the author of this chapter is impaired in that his eyesight is extremely poor without glasses or contact lenses. However, he is not socially labelled as 'disabled' because society does not define shortsightedness as a problem and so society does not produce a social environment in which people who wear glasses or contact lenses are handicapped. However, people who have to use wheelchairs are handicapped by society's failure to provide a social environment in which they can be as mobile as able-bodied people.

Furthermore, the social model of disability notes that not everyone is able to do everything as well as others – for example, run, catch or throw a ball – yet we do not describe those who are less able as being 'disabled'. We just accept these differences as part of the normal range of human abilities. This range of normality could be extended to include those defined as 'disabled' especially if physical facilities and social attitudes were adjusted to include those with disabilities – for example, by altering the way we construct buildings, and by regarding sport played by disabled people as equal to 'traditional' types of sport.

It is with this in mind that the World Health Organization has distinguished between impairment, disability and handicap:

- *Impairment* refers to the abnormality of, or loss of function of, a part of the body.
- *Handicap* refers to the physical limits imposed by the loss of function.

Focus on research

Meershoek et al. (2007)
Doctors' power of judgement

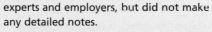

The Netherlands and the UK operate a similar system whereby people applying for long-term state benefits on the grounds of disability will be assessed by a specialist doctor. Because of the difficulty in deciding precisely what 'disabled' means, a great deal of discretion is given to the doctors. Meershoek and colleagues set out to uncover the grounds on which the doctors made their judgements about whether a person was truly disabled or not and hence about their entitlement to state benefits.

Meershoek and colleagues undertook an ethnographic study of the specialist doctors employed to do this work in The Netherlands. This involved observing over 500 consultations between clients and 20 different doctors, in different phases of the sick leave, including final judgments for long-term disability pension. They made field notes of the consultations and of the doctors' comments beforehand and afterwards. They also interviewed the 20 physicians about their decision-making processes. In order to have a background understanding, they also followed the doctors in their contacts and meetings with other experts and employers, but did not make any detailed notes.

They made notes of all the consultations and then agreed between them on certain themes and patterns which emerged on the basis of 'grounded theory' (that is, not making any assumptions before gathering data and then building up a theory as the information becomes available). They then re-analysed their notes to look at the specific responses of doctors to the replies of people claiming disability benefit whom the doctors considered 'problematic'.

Meershoek, A., Krumeich, A. and Vos, R. (2007) 'Judging without criteria? Sickness certification in Dutch disability schemes', *Sociology of Health and Illness* 29(4), pp.497–514

1   What is meant by an ethnographic approach?

2   The researchers made notes of the meetings, but did not make any (electronic) recordings. Do you think this might present some problems?

3   The researchers did not make detailed notes of their interviews with the experts and employers. Do you think making detailed notes would have been useful?

4   Grounded theory is commonly used in ethnographic research – how does this compare with more positivistic approaches?

- *Disability* refers to the socially imposed restriction on people's abilities to perform tasks as a result of the behaviour of people in society.

According to this approach, disability has to be understood as much in social terms as physical ones; so, a person can have an impairment without being disabled.

The origins of disability

Marxists such as Finkelstein (1980) have suggested that our negative cultural attitudes towards the disabled may be the product of capitalism's emphasis on work as a source of identity, status and power. He suggests that in pre-industrial societies, the idea that disabled people should be segregated and treated differently simply did not exist. However, industrialization was responsible for a dramatic shift in cultural attitudes because capitalist society required a healthy and fit workforce to generate profits for the capitalist class; in this context, the disabled become an economic burden for society and are defined as abnormal and as a social problem.

Focus on research

Anderson and Kitchin (2000)
Stereotyping, sexuality and disability

Anderson and Kitchin studied the attitudes of health professionals working in family planning clinics in Northern Ireland and found that many of them subscribed to cultural myths about the sexual behaviour of disabled people. For example, professionals tended to believe that:

- disabled people were unable to take part in sexual activities
- disabled people were sexually irresponsible and therefore needed to have their sexual appetite and behaviour controlled by professionals
- some disabled people were unable to sustain long-term relationships
- some disabled people lacked a sex drive.

Source: Best, S. (2005) *Understanding Social Divisions*, London: Sage, p. 112

1   **Do the beliefs held by health professionals in Northern Ireland support the medical or social model of disability?**

2   **How might these beliefs undermine integration and encourage learned helplessness among the disabled?**

Stigma and disability

The social action sociologist Goffman suggests that certain groups of people are defined as having 'discredited identities' because their characteristics are seen as 'negative', e.g. criminals, paedophiles etc.

Disability is a discredited status because able-bodied people assume that being blind or being in a wheelchair means that the disabled person is dependent on the able-bodied and incapable of having normal social relations. However, the problem really lies with the able-bodied who negatively stigmatise or label the disabled. They are the ones who find it awkward to have normal social relations with those who are 'discredited'. They may be embarrassed, avoid eye contact or ignore the 'obvious' disability.

The concept of 'master status'

When the discrediting status becomes the main way in which people are seen by others, then Goffman calls this a 'master status'. The stigma then completely dominates the way the person is treated, and any other attributes are seen as less important. The person who is unable to walk unaided is seen simply as 'wheelchair-bound' (not as an intelligent, articulate woman, for example).

Learned helplessness

Goffman points out that the individuals themselves may accept this master status and come to see themselves solely in terms of their stigmatized status. In other words, disabled people may respond to the constant assumption that they are helpless and dependent by developing low social esteem and worth. A **self-fulfilling prophecy** therefore results – the disabled person behaves as society expects.

A classic study which illustrates this self-fulfilling prophecy very well is Scott's (1969) study of blind people. After observing the interaction between medical professionals and blind people in the USA, Scott argued that the blind developed a 'blind personality' because they internalized the experts' view that they should be experiencing psychological problems in adjusting to their loss of sight. Part of this process also involved '**learned helplessness**', i.e. that they should rely on sighted people for help. In other words, they became dependent because this is what the experts expected them to do.

Mass media representations of the disabled

A number of studies indicate that negative stereotypes about disability may be reinforced and encouraged by mass media representations. Longmore (1987) suggests that disabled people tend to be represented on television as evil, as monsters, as inhuman, as dependent on others, as maladjusted, as the objects of pity or charity, and as dangerous and deviant. If the disabled are portrayed as courageous, this is often contrasted with the tragedy of their situation. These stereotypes may reinforce prejudice and discrimination. As Cumberbatch and Negrine (1992) argue, media representations of the disabled rarely present them as 'a person, an individual who also happens to have a disability'.

Prejudice and discrimination

Stereotypes and prejudices about the disabled affect their quality of life in several ways:

- The disabled may find themselves segregated from able-bodied society, e.g. in special schools, which consequently makes it more difficult for them to be 'normal' and for them to integrate into society.
- Prejudice may be translated into discrimination in the field of employment as employers may be reluctant to take them on. The disabled therefore may be more likely to be on welfare benefits and to experience poverty.
- Kallianes and Rubenfeld (1997) argue that women with disabilities are often discriminated against compared with other women. It is assumed by professionals that such women should not be having sex and that they are likely to make unsuitable mothers. There have been a number of cases in which disabled women have been forcibly sterilized or have had their children forcibly taken into care.

The disabled identity and resistance

The social model of disability argues that more positive disabled identities should be promoted stressing independence, choice and autonomy for disabled people. They believe that the state should invest in a disabled-friendly social environment and should address prejudice and discrimination against the disabled.

Recent sociological studies suggest that disabled people are more likely to resist those definitions of disability that stress dependence and helplessness. Antle (2000) found that children with disabilities do not qualitatively differ in how they see themselves compared with children without disabilities. Olney and Kim (2001) argue that the disabled people in their study felt positive about their disability despite their awareness that people without disabilities negatively evaluated them. They rejected the medical labels and had a very positive self-image.

Critiques of the social model of disability

Critiques of the social model of disability have recently appeared. These acknowledge that prejudice and discrimination need to be addressed and that the social environment in which we live is not always conducive to the disabled. However, they argue that we cannot ignore the fact that physical and biological factors such as pain, mental impairment, and so on, do negatively impact on how disabled people experience social life and can make it unpleasant and difficult. The disabled identity is therefore probably made up of coping both with the limitations caused by the physical impairment of the body and mind, and the limitations of the social environment shaped by negative and stereotypical attitudes towards disability.

Key terms

Career refers, in this context, to the gradual changes in people as a response to a label (for example, 'mental patient').

Disability the socially imposed restriction on people's abilities to perform tasks as a result of the behaviour of people in society.

Enlightenment a period of intellectual change in the late 17th to the late 18th centuries.

Learned helplessness learning how to be dependent.

Life-course model suggests that the accumulation of social events experienced over a whole lifetime, not just individual important events, influence people and their mental state.

Personal tragedy a term used by Oliver to describe the way disability is seen as a personal as opposed to a social problem.

Presenting culture a term used by Goffman to refer to how people like to portray themselves to others.

Schizophrenia a form of mental illness where people are unable to distinguish their own feelings and perceptions from reality.

Self-fulfilling prophecy predictions about the behaviour of social groups that come true as

a result of positive or negative labelling.

Social capital refers to a network of social contacts.

Social constructionism the approach which suggests that mental illness (and all other social phenomena) exists because people believe it does.

Social realism a sociological approach which suggests that mental illness does really exist.

Activities

Research idea

1   Conduct a small-scale survey. Ask 20 people: what the first words are that pop into their minds when you say the words 'mental illness' to suggest the two main reasons for people being mentally ill.

Collate your answers – what do they suggest about people's views of mental illness. Do the sociological ideas contained in this topic ring true?

2   Conduct a survey into how many disabled people are portrayed on contemporary television and in films and whether they are positively or negatively represented.

Web.tasks

1   Find the website of the mental health charity MIND at **www.mind.org.uk**. Use the 'links' section to explore the work of some of the organizations connected with mental health issues. Make a list of all the mental health issues covered. How important an issue is mental health in the UK today?

2   Visit the websites below which are run by disabled people. How do the images and statements made on these sites challenge the biomedical model of disability?
   www.disabilityalliance.org
   www.radar.org.uk
   www.ilanet.co.uk

Check your understanding

1 Identify the two sociological approaches to defining mental illness.

2 Explain the key differences between the two approaches you have identified.

3 How does the idea of 'labelling' help us to understand mental illness?

4 What is meant by a structural explanation for mental illness?

5 How does Busfield suggest that the structuralist and labelling approaches can be combined?

6 Why are people from certain ethnic minorities more likely to be defined as suffering from mental illness?

7 What argument do feminist writers use to explain why women are more likely to be defined as suffering from mental illness?

8 How does the biomedical model view disability?

9 Identify five ways in which people with impairments are disabled by society.

10 What is the relationship between learned helplessness and the self fulfilling prophecy?

An eye on the exam — The social construction of mental illness and disability

the opening sentence of each paragraph should clearly highlight the reason

whatever it is that you have identified must be discussed in some depth using sociological studies and examples

begin your answer with a clear definition of what is meant by this concept

(a) Identify and explain two ways in which disabled people are disabled by society. **(17 marks)**

each way needs to be clealy distinguishable and developed into a very detailed paragraph

you should attempt to write two very detailed paragraphs in about 15 minutes

a detailed description of the view is required using sociological concepts, theories and studies

it is important to assess the merits of the labelling theory of mental illness in some detail, either by raising specific strengths or criticisms of the theory or by presenting alternative theoretical perspectives such as the biomedical approach

this view is a labelling or interactionist perspective

you should attempt to write at least 2 sides of the answer book in about 30 minutes

(b) Outline and evaluate the view that mental illness is simply a label applied by others. **(33 marks)**

Grade booster — Getting top marks in this question

Begin by defining what is meant by mental illness and by briefly outlining the facts about mental illness in terms of its extent and which groups in society are likely to suffer from it. Briefly describe the conventional or biomedical explanation of it. This view should be evaluated by outlining the labelling ideas of Szasz and Scheff which can be supported by descriptions of experiments conducted by Rosenhan and Katz. Examine sociological ideas about the relationship between labelling, gender and ethnicity. Studies of the consequences of being labelled mentally ill especially the work of Goffman should be explored in detail. Finish by examining both structuralist and psycho-social perspectives.

TOPIC 4

The role of health professionals in society

Getting you thinking

Trust me, doctors are paid too much

By Nick Britten

A JUNIOR DOCTOR yesterday called for doctors' pay to be reduced into line with that of nurses and other public sector workers, saying that his senior colleagues enjoyed an 'opulent' way of life while other hospital staff had to get by on a 'piffling' amount.

Mark Jopling, a first-year pre-registration house officer, said doctors allowed themselves to be placed on a 'golden pedestal' and were happy to be regarded as 'awesome life savers', earning large amounts of money, driving luxury cars and living in grand houses.

The British Medical Association said Dr Jopling's views were 'not widely held' among doctors, but he won support from the Royal College of Nursing for 'helping expose nurses' poor pay'.

Dr Jopling, 24, yesterday accepted that his comments might well upset his senior colleagues. He said: 'If I became a consultant, the taxpayer would be sending me home with about £90,000. Were I to prefer a nine-to-five job as a GP, I would be raking in a fat £100,000 – even more, if I played the system well.'

Doctors, Dr Jopling said, were 'quick to justify' their salaries 'with a series of compelling arguments: we work hard, we have big responsibilities, we are also well qualified and have to endure a protracted training'. But he added: 'Teachers, social workers and other professionals in the public sector work long hours too, however, some of these at home and unrecognised.

It is unfair that our salaries dwarf theirs. In medicine there has been a long-standing acknowledgment that nurses work hard and are underpaid. A nurse starts on a relatively modest £16,000 and regularly works nights and weekends. It is usually nurses who give patients most support during their stay in hospital.'

A spokesman for the BMA said: 'This is one doctor's point of view. Unsurprisingly, it isn't widely held in the medical profession. The facts support the case for paying doctors more, not less. The new GP contract pays doctors for raising the quality of patient care they provide.'

Source: nbritten@telegraph.co.uk

Nurses fear for futures as morale plummets

By Nicole Martin

MORALE AMONG NURSES has reached an all-time low, according to a survey that paints a picture of a profession in crisis.

A poll of 9,000 nurses found that despite the Government pouring billions of pounds into the health service, many still feel overworked, under-valued and fear for their futures.

More than half – 55 per cent – said they were too busy to deliver the level of care they would like, and 30 per cent said they would quit the profession if they could.

Source: www.telegraph.co.uk/news/main.jhtml?xml=/news/2007/07/16/nnurse116.xml

1 Why are doctors paid higher salaries than nurses or teachers?

2 Do you think that only outstanding people can become doctors?

3 Break into small groups and decide whether, as a group, you agree with Dr Jopling's arguments or those of the BMA.

4 Which occupational group, if any, do you trust more than doctors?

Members of the medical profession are among the most prestigious and well-paid groups in society. But how did they get this superior status? Was it really through their greater abilities, as they would have us believe? Sociologists are always suspicious of the claims groups make about themselves and, as you might expect, their views are not always totally supportive of the caring, dedicated image the medical professions like to present. In this topic, we are going to explore the reasons for the power, prestige and affluence of the medical professions.

There are five main sociological approaches to understanding the position and role of the medical professions. These are:

- *the functionalist argument* – this perspective argues that the medical profession benefits society and that doctors are primarily motivated by the desire to heal the sick.
- *the Weberian approach* – this theory suggests that the professionalisation of medicine is just an occupational strategy to achieve higher income and status
- *the Marxist view* – this theory argues that the medical profession works on behalf of the capitalist class control workers and is rewarded for this by the ruling class
- *the postmodernist view* – this theory argues that the power of the medical profession has emerged as a result of their ability to define what counts as prestigious knowledge
- *the feminist approach* – these theories argue that the medical profession is a patriarchal agency that can best be understood by seeing how it has controlled and marginalized women.

The functionalist approach: professions as a benefit to society

The first approach to understanding the role of the professions developed from the functionalist school of sociology, associated with the writing of Talcott Parsons, which seeks to show what functions the various parts of society play in helping society to exist.

Barber (1963) argued that professions, especially the medical professions, are very important for society because they deal with people when they are in particularly vulnerable positions. It is, therefore, in the interests of society to have the very best people, who maintain the highest standards, to provide medical care. These people must not only be competent but they must also be totally trustworthy. According to functionalists, true professions can be recognized by the fact that they share a number of 'traits'. These are as follows:

- They have a *theoretical basis* to their knowledge – Doctors have a full understanding of medical theories about the body. This allows them to make independent decisions about the cause of illness and the best cure.
- They are *fully trained* to the highest possible standards – Only the most intelligent can enter the medical profession and succeed.

- Competence is *tested by examination* – There is no favouritism and doctors are in their position as a result of their ability alone.
- The profession has a *strict code of* **ethics** – Doctors deal with people at their most vulnerable and the code of ethics ensures that no patient is exploited.
- They are *regulated and controlled* through an organization (the General Medical Council) which decides who can enter the profession. This professional body has the power to punish and strike doctors off the practicing register if they are found guilty of unprofessional behaviour.

Critics of the functionalist approach

Waitzkin (1979) argues that for many years these professional characteristics and standards were mainly used as a barrier to prevent groups, other than upper-middle-class white males, from entering the profession. It is only in the last 20 years that there has been a significant recruitment of women and ethnic minorities into the medical profession.

Functionalists claim that people become doctors because they are public spirited –they are putting the community before self-interest. However, the existence of private medicine and the high financial rewards paid to particular types of doctors, (i.e. many plastic surgeons are highly rewarded for non-critical work such as enhancing the female form) suggests that financial reward may the main driving force for many doctors.

Illich suggests some doctors do more harm than good and that clinical iatrogenesis (i.e. mistakes made by doctors in surgery and diagnosis as well as the tendency to prescribe drugs with side-effects or addictive qualities) is responsible for a high number of patient deaths, harms etc.

Some sociologists are critical of the role of the General Medical Council which is supposed to supervise the profession. It is argued that they often fail to investigate accusations of incompetence against doctors. Final sanctions such as striking a doctor off the medical register, are used very rarely and are usually due to doctors being found guilty of sexual misconduct rather than gross incompetence or negligence.

The Weberian approach: professionalization as a strategy

The second approach to understanding the power of the medical professions is that, rather than being constructed for the good of the community, they are, in fact, constructed for the good of the medical professions themselves. This argument has developed from the original writings of Max Weber, an early 20th-century sociologist who argued that all occupational groups compete with each other for status and high rewards. He noticed that one way in which they did this was to organize themselves along professional lines, i.e. to form professional associations in order to bargain with employers and protect their financial interests.

Parry and Parry (1976) suggest that professionalisation is an occupational strategy aimed at controlling the labour

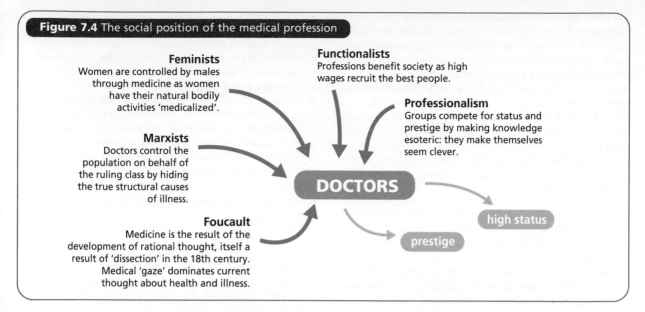

Figure 7.4 The social position of the medical profession

Feminists
Women are controlled by males through medicine as women have their natural bodily activities 'medicalized'.

Functionalists
Professions benefit society as high wages recruit the best people.

Professionalism
Groups compete for status and prestige by making knowledge esoteric: they make themselves seem clever.

Marxists
Doctors control the population on behalf of the ruling class by hiding the true structural causes of illness.

Foucault
Medicine is the result of the development of rational thought, itself a result of 'dissection' in the 18th century. Medical 'gaze' dominates current thought about health and illness.

DOCTORS

prestige

high status

market so that it economically benefits doctors. With this objective in mind, the process of professionalisation has a number of important dimensions:

1 *The production of a body of* **esoteric** *knowledge* – This means creating an apparently complex body of knowledge that can only be understood and practised by medical experts, i.e. doctors.

2 *Educational barriers* – The medical profession has managed to gain control over the training, qualifications and entry requirements necessary to become a doctor. The number of new doctors is deliberately kept quite low in order to ensure scarcity and consequently this means they can demand or charge more for their services.

3 *Exclusion of competition* – Doctors have managed to convince the government that only their members are qualified to carry out medical diagnosis and treatment. This monopoly is backed by law – it is a criminal offence to impersonate a doctor and to carry out medical diagnosis.

The medical profession has used its legal monopoly to discredit and exclude any competition to its expertise and knowledge. Alternative medical approaches such as faith healing, homeopathy, aromatherapy etc are often dismissed as inferior forms of treatment by doctors who claim that only scientific medicine and surgery are effective.

A good example of this exclusion in practice has been provided by Cant and Sharma (2002), who studied the relationship between the medical profession and the practitioners of chiropractic medicine. (This is the manipulation of the spine, joints and muscles in order to realign them.) For over 60 years, chiropractors campaigned to gain legal recognition, which was finally granted in an act of parliament in 1994. But Cant and Sharma point out that in order to get this recognition, chiropractors effectively had to subordinate themselves to doctors. In other words, they do not have the same status as doctors – they are effectively para-medical practitioners who have patients referred to them by doctors.

4 *Maintenance of privilege* – Medical professionals are concerned with maintaining their privileges and status. Doctors have fought all attempts to impose any controls over them –they demand clinical freedom - the right to do what they think best – and they fight any attempts to hand over part of their work to others, such as allowing nurses to prescribe medicines.

5 *Maintenance of standards* – All doctors have to belong to the British Medical Association. This means that doctors can claim they are maintaining the highest public standards because they also claim the right to investigate any wrongdoings by their members as well as the right to punish them. This makes it difficult for other interested parties such as those who manage the NHS, the police and politicians to examine the activities of doctors.

Parry and Parry argue that doctors' claims to be altruistic distracts from the fact that they adopt market strategies that maximize their earning power. In particular, controlling access to the profession and limiting the number of doctors being trained have been a very effective strategy in ensuring that doctors enjoy high pay, job security and privilege. From a Weberian perspective, then, the medical profession looks after its own interests as well as those of its patients.

Marxist approaches

Marxists, such as Navarro (1977), argue that in capitalist societies such as Britain, a small ruling class exploits society for its own benefit. He argues that doctors are agents of this capitalist class and their high status and salaries are the rewards they receive from the capitalist ruling class for playing their part in maintaining economic inequality and exploitation.

Marxists argue that doctors are agents of the state who work on behalf of the capitalist class in a number of ways:

● Doyal (1979) argues that doctors and the health service, alongside other ideological apparatuses such as education and the mass media, legitimate the organisation of capitalism (with all its inequalities) by persuading the workforce that capitalism 'cares' for them. The NHS as part of the welfare state promises workers and their families that it will look after them from the cradle to the grave. This functions to reduce the potential for class conflict and political unrest.

- Doctors mislead the workforce as to the real causes of any illness they might suffer. This is because the medical profession explains health and illness in terms of the actions and genetics of individuals rather than focusing on poor working conditions, poverty, poor housing and inequalities in wealth and income which Marxists claim are the true, underlying causes of ill health.

- Doctors guarantee the good health and fitness of the manual workforce so that capitalist production, exploitation and profit-making can continue undisturbed. Marxists argue that the NHS exists to benefit the capitalist class rather than the working-class because its true ideological function is to make sure that workers continue to be healthy in order to make profits for their employers.

- Marxists point out that health and illness in a capitalist society are carefully linked to being able or not being able to work. Doctors play a key role in deciding who is fit to work and who is sick enough to be eligible for state disability and sickness benefits. In this sense, doctors socially control the workforce on behalf of the capitalist class.

However, critics point out that Marxism ignores the genuinely beneficial work that doctors do, and that to characterize their work as mainly focused on misleading and controlling the population is inaccurate. Doctors do mainly work in the context of individual problems but they also recognize and acknowledge stress in the workplace and the role of poverty. Some Marxists, notably McKinley suggest that Navarro and Doyal exaggerate the power of doctors. He argues that their professional freedom has been weakened by the state to the extent that doctors too are exploited by the capitalist bourgeoisie. McKinley argues that their role has been reduced to 'drug pushers' in that they prescribe drugs for all ills and so generate greater profits for the bourgeoisie who own and control the drug companies.

Postmodernist approaches

There is an old saying, 'knowledge is power' and in Foucault's analysis of medicine, this is literally true. According to Foucault (1976), in every society, groups are 'battling' to look after their own interests. The best way of doing this is to get control of what is regarded as 'truth' or 'knowledge'. If other people believe that what you say is 'true' and what others say is 'false', then you have a high chance of getting them to do what you want. So you seek to create an overall framework of thought and ideas,

Focus on research

Lorelei Jones and Judith Green (2006)
The attitudes of younger GPs

Lorelei Jones and Judith Green wanted to find out whether newly qualified GPs had different views from older GPs about the nature of professionalism. Traditionally, GPs have perceived their jobs as a vocation, in which they had a duty to their patients and society. Their motivation was as much moral as financial. Jones and Green wished to know if, in late modernity, this vocational attitude to being a GP was still dominant. They discovered that the traditional vocational approach had been replaced by one in which younger GPs seek nice work, by which they meant good pay, pleasant surroundings, interesting and varied work and decent patients.

A purposive sampling strategy was used to select interviewees who were working in general practice from across England, Wales and Scotland in a range of rural and urban locations. In total, 20 GPs, aged 32–37 (14 women, 6 men) were included in the study, reflecting the gender composition of new GPs.

Interviews, lasting about an hour, were audio-taped and transcribed. In all interviews, participants were prompted for reasons for choosing general practice, career histories, descriptions of their work, satisfactions and dissatisfactions with the job and plans for the future. Participants were encouraged to elaborate when

they raised other topics. The results were transcribed and formed the basis of a second interview.

Follow-up interviews took place some months later and participants were asked to reflect on questions arising from analysis of the earlier replies. These second replies were also transcribed.

The research was based on 'grounded theory', in which the theoretical ideas emerge during the research in the process of discussion and analysis. The researchers used computer software which can be used to generate 'themes'. The analysis of the transcripts showed the key theme of 'nice work'.

Before the research, the interviewees were assured that they would remain anonymous and all the interviewees were given pseudonyms in the published academic article.

Jones, L. and Green, J. (2006) 'Shifting discourses of professionalism: a case study of general practitioners in the United Kingdom', *Sociology of Health and Illness*, 28(7), pp. 927–50

1 What sort of sampling technique was used?

2 The researchers interviewed a total of 20 GPs. Do you think that it is possible to make generalizations for all younger GPs based upon this number?

3 What do we mean by 'grounded theory'? How does this differ from traditional positivistic research methods?

4 Why was it important to the accuracy of the research that the GPs remained anonymous?

within which all the more specific debates (what Foucault calls 'discourses') are conducted.

Foucault argues that, over time, doctors have led the way in helping to construct an idea of 'science', through their activities in dissecting bodies and demonstrating to people the ways in which bodies are constructed in the form of a 'biological machine'. This has resulted in a society where rational scientific thought is prized above all else, where other forms of thought are regarded as inferior, and where doctors have significant prestige and power. So, medicine has played a major part in constructing the way we think and act in contemporary society. In the process, the medical professions have gained considerable benefits in terms of status and financial rewards.

However, postmodernists argue that the dominance of scientific and medical 'meta-narratives' has been challenged in recent years. Doctors are no longer seen as infallible and the concept of iatrogenesis has undermined the concept of medical professionalism. However, the biggest external challenge to the power of doctors has come from complementary or alternative medicines, which include homeopathy, herbal remedies, acupuncture and a range of other techniques.

Giddens (1991) has argued that this challenge is the result of two characteristics of late modernity:

● There has been a decline in conformity. There is now a greater stress on individual desire and choice. People are therefore looking beyond conventional medicine to alternative therapies to improve the quality of their lives.
● People are now more likely to be disillusioned with the claim that medical professionals and experts should have the monopoly over medical knowledge. There has been a decline in the idea that 'doctor knows best' because the general public is increasingly aware that doctors can and do make frequent mistakes.

Feminist approaches

Feminist sociologists, such as Oakley (1986) and Witz (1992), suggest that the activities of doctors contribute to the social control of women, both as patients and as medical practitioners. They point out that medicine has traditionally been a male occupation, with women excluded or marginalized into junior roles. This simply reinforces the subordinate position of women in society. Feminists point out that historically, women have always held a key role in healing and traditional healthcare. For example, women dominated health care in medieval Britain as herbal healers. However, feminists claim that women's power as healers threatened patriarchal power in this period and women who practiced herbal medicine were consequently labelled 'witches' and punished accordingly. Similarly, women in Victorian Britain were not legally prevented from entering the medical profession but the patriarchal values of this period meant that women were generally excluded from higher education which meant that they were effectively barred from becoming doctors. In recent years, feminist sociologists such as Oakley have complained that doctors have attempted to take control of areas of health such as childbirth that were previously dominated by female health workers such as midwives. Graham points out that men still dominate the top jobs in the NHS, i.e. consultants and surgeons. Women consultants are disproportionately represented in stereotypically feminine areas such as paediatrics.

Feminists argue that women's illnesses result from patriarchal factors such as women's subordinate position in society and in the family. However these causes are turned into a medical problem by a male-dominated medical profession. This shifts the issue away from the position of women in general, to the particular medical condition of a single woman. Furthermore, feminist sociologists claim that symptoms reported to doctors by females are often dismissed as 'women's problems' which are deemed less serious than other medical problems. There is evidence too that women are more likely than men to be victims of clinical iatrogenesis because of the side effects of contraceptives, anti-depressants and tranquillisers which are disproportionately prescribed to women.

Key terms

Clinical freedom the right of doctors to do what they think is best without other people having a say.

Discourse a way of thinking about issues.

Esoteric obscure and accessible only to a few.

Ethics a code of behaviour.

Professionalization tactic used by occupational groups to gain prestige and financial rewards.

Check your understanding

1   Give two examples of the 'traits' of a profession, according to functionalists.

2   According to the Weberian approach, how do professions exclude other competing occupational groups?

3   How do the actions of doctors, in explaining why we are ill and then prescribing medicines, help capitalism?

4   Give one example of how doctors have 'medicalized' a normal activity of women?

5   According to Foucault, what is the relationship between knowledge and power over people?

Activities

Research idea

1   Ask a small sample of people to identify five characteristics they associate with doctors. Do your results support the points made in the topic?

2   Identify a small sample of people who have actually used some form of 'alternative' healing. Conduct unstructured interviews to uncover their motives in seeking the treatment and the meaning they gave to their experiences.

Web.tasks

1   Visit the Royal College of Nursing website at **www.rcn.org.uk**

    What aspects of the discussion in this topic are illustrated here? You will find useful to look at the section on the RCN's 'mission'.

2   Visit the General Medical Council website at **www.gmc-uk.org**

    What points in this topic does this website illustrate (and also perhaps challenge!)?

3   Visit the Institute for Complementary Medicine website at **www.icmedicine.co.uk**

    What ideas about 'the body' and healing lie behind these therapies and treatments? To what extent are they similar to, or different from, the conventional Western 'biomedical model'?

whatever it is that you have identified must be discussed in some depth using sociological studies and examples

begin your answer with a clear definition of what is meant by this concept

(a) Identify and explain two examples of iatrogenesis. **(17 marks)**

the opening sentence of each paragraph should clearly highlight the reason

each aspect needs to be clealy distinguishable and developed into a very detailed paragraph

you should attempt to write two very detailed paragraphs in about 15 minutes

it is important to assess the merits of the functionalist theory of the medical profession in some detail, either by raising specific strengths or criticisms of the theory or by presenting alternative theoretical perspectives

this view is a functionalist perspective

(b) Outline and evaluate the view that the medical profession works for the good of society. **(33 marks)**

a detailed description of the view is required using sociological concepts, theories and studies

you should attempt to write at least 2 sides of the answer book in about 30 minutes

Grade booster   Getting top marks in this question

You need to describe the functionalist theory of the medical profession in detail. Begin by describing using illustrative exemplars the features which functionalists like Barber suggest members of the medical profession share and how these allegedly function for the greater good of society. Be willing to evaluate this view with specific criticisms such as Illich's ideas on iatrogenesis. Functionalist ideas need to be contrasted with a detailed outline of Weberian theories such as Parry and Parry who argue that the medical profession has developed characteristics primarily aimed at improving their status and wealth, and Marxist theories such as Doyal or Navarro who see the medical profession as agents of the capitalist class. Finish with some feminist observations about how a patriarchal medical profession might be used to socially control women.

177

Chapter 5 Sociology of health

(a) Identify and explain two reasons for gender differences in mortality. *(52 marks)*

One reason for the difference in mortality or death between men and women may be gender role socialization. Feminist sociologists note that In Britain our culture socialises boys into a particular type of masculine behaviour and outlook. For example, boys are expected to keep their emotions in check and not to express any outward signs of distress. They are not expected to cry. Generally, boys do not talk with others about their problems. On the other hand, Browne argues that females are expected to be emotional and when they are upset, it is expected that they cry or confide in others. This may mean that when they are older that they are better at dealing with stress, anxiety etc because they can let it out whereas men lack this ability. Keeping stress in may raise blood pressure and increase the possibility of death from heart attack or stroke.

> This first reason is focused accurately on gender role socialization and is quite wide-ranging in its discussion. However, despite the reference to feminism and Browne, it is a little generalised.

Another reason might be related to the types of jobs men and women do. Men tend to be employed full-time in jobs with long hours. Some men are in dangerous jobs which involve risks and the possibility of accidents and exposure to toxic substances. About 500 men are killed each year at work, e.g. delivering goods, on construction sites and in factories. Thousands more are injured or disabled because of accidents at work. Work gives men identity, status, purpose and social contacts. Losing a job because of redundancy or retirement might lead to some men experiencing stress and depression.

> There is some good knowledge and understanding displayed in this paragraph but apart from statistics relating to deaths in the workplace, there is little contemporary evidence cited. Moreover not all the examples cited relate to mortality. Overall, there is good rather than excellent knowledge and understanding of reasons demonstrated in this response. There needed to be more use of sociological concepts and sociological studies to access the top of the marking scheme.

15/17

(b) Outline and evaluate the view that cultural factors are the main reason working-class people die younger and suffer more illness and disability than middle-class people. *(52 marks)*

On average working-class people die younger and experience more chronic illness and disability than middle-class people. Men in social class I on average live almost eight and a half years longer than men from social class 5. Also, babies born to professional fathers have levels of infant mortality half that of babies born to unskilled manual fathers.

> This is a good introduction which contextualises the debate. Accurate and fairly wide-ranging knowledge is cited of patterns and trends in health and illness.

Culturalist theories argue health inequalities are caused by the working class making the wrong lifestyle choices. Culturalist explanations very firmly blame the cultural behaviour of the poor for their ill health and reduced life expectancy. They argue that the poor make poor decisions about diet – they consume too much junk food, fried food, white bread, sugar and salt, and not enough fresh fruit and vegetables. They also note that the working class are three times more likely to smoke than the middle class and also consume more alcohol. Furthermore, they point out that that the working class engage in less exercise than the middle-class who are much more likely to take part in sports and exercise such as walking and jogging , and are more likely to visit gym and health clubs.

> This is a very focused paragraph which demonstrates an excellent level of knowledge and understanding of the culturalist perspective on health.

However, materialist critics suggest that culturalists fail to see that so-called lifestyle choices are the product of the economic and social environment of the working-class and poor, e.g. smoking may be a way of compensating for the stress of poverty or it may be the sole pleasure in life generally denied pleasure.

> This paragraph contains explicit and relevant evaluation of the culturalist perspective although other points could have been raised, e.g. culturalist theories tend to over-generalise about working-class culture.

Materialists argue that these inequalities are the result of the fact that working-class people are more likely to experience poverty as a consequence of being either unemployed or because they are low paid. It is argued by Shaw that this poverty limits healthy lifestyle choices in terms of diet and exercise. For example, people on benefits and low wages may not be able to afford a car or expensive public transport to get to supermarkets which have a wider choice of healthy foods. They may not be able to afford to join gyms or health clubs. Kempson notes that poverty involves a great deal of stress-related illnesses because of debt and worrying about how bills are to be paid or children are to be fed.

> On the whole, some excellent knowledge and understanding is demonstrated in this section. The candidate displays a wide-ranging knowledge of concepts and studies. There is a good level of depth and detail and the material is interpreted in an accurate fashion.

Materialists also argue that working-class people are more likely to live in poor quality rented accommodation in polluted inner city environments. Alcock found that poor damp housing often leads to poor health in working-class children, time off school and few qualifications leading to low-paid low-skilled jobs or unemployment. Wilkinson notes that poor areas suffer from low social cohesion – people feel that there is little sense of community support. They feel threatened by high crime rates, vandalism, graffiti etc. They feel isolated, lonely, anxious and depressed. Consequently, stress levels are high which contributes to both poor physical and mental health.

> The candidate displays a perceptive understanding of a range of concepts and sociological theories in this section.

Finally, Tudor Hart's inverse care law theory argues that those working-class areas in greatest need get less funding than middle-class areas which generally enjoy good health. Tudor Hart argues that this results in inequalities in resources such as the number of hospitals, hospital beds, GPs and nurses.

> Good knowledge of the inverse care law is demonstrated in this section although the candidate misses the opportunity to explain why such inequalities come about.

An examiner comments

Altogether this response is awarded 9 marks for knowledge and understanding because it impresses with regard to culturalist and materialist theories but falls a little short in terms of explaining why the inverse care law exists. There was also a need to explore other theories of poor working-class health – the candidate could have also examined Marxist and psycho-social theories. Knowledge of counter arguments, e.g. the materialist position was clearly presented. In terms of interpretation and application, the candidate showed a very good ability to select and interpret sociological material. Lots of very relevant illustrative examples were used. The candidate therefore was awarded 11 marks out of a possible 13 for this skill. Finally, although there was brief specific evaluation of the culturalist argument, evaluation was the weakest skill demonstrated by this candidate. There needed to be more specific and balanced evaluation of all the theories summarised. Evaluation was largely by juxtaposition. The candidate was awarded 7 marks out of the 10 marks available for this skill.

Chapter 5 Summary

Patterns of health
Vary according to social group:
- Ethnicity
- Social class
- Gender

Explanations for variations
- Artefact/statistical
- Cultural
- Structural
- Materialist
- Psycho-social

The biomedical approach
- The body as a machine
- Allopathic - cure based

Health inequalities

Physical illness

Illness and health socially constructed

Lay definitions
- Based on common sense
- Vary by culture, age, gender, etc.

The social model of health
- The social process of becoming ill
- The sick role
- Public health
- Preventative medicine
- Iatrogenesis
- Postmodernism and the body
- Alternative medicine

Health, illness and medicine

Biomedical approaches
- Ethnic minorities
- Women
- Poor

Social construction of mental illness
- The myth of mental illness
- Labelling theory
- The effects of institutionalisation
- Foucault – shift to radical thinking
- Structual factors
- Psycho-social factors

Mental illness

Social constructionism
- Foucault – shift to rational thinking
- Labelling theory

The medical professions

To whose benefit do they operate?
- Men – the feminist approach
- Themselves – Weberian approach
- The ruling class – Marxist approach
- Society as a whole – the functionalist approach

Disability

Disability
- The biomedical approach
- Disabled by society
- Learned helplessness
- Media representations

The Sociology of Religion

OCR specification			Coverage
Key concepts and the changing nature of religious movements in society			
Key concepts	• Religious belief • Religious membership	• Religious commitment • Religiosity	These terms are explained in Topic 1
Different types of religious institutions and movements	• Churches • New religious movements • Religious fundamentalism	• Denominations • New Age movements	Religious organizations are explained in Topic 1
The role of religion in society			
Sociological explanations	• Functionalism • Weberianism	• Marxism	Covered in Topic 2
Postmodern views			Postmodern views are covered in Topic 2 but also referred to in other Topics
Religion and social position			
Religiosity according to:	• Ethnicity • Social class	• Gender • Age	Covered in Topic 3
New religious movements/ New Age movements			
The strength of religion in society			
Evidence indicating the secularization of society			Covered in Topic 4. Important background material regarding defining and measuring religion in Topic 1.
Evidence against the secularization of society			

Religion and religious organizations

Getting you thinking

Buddhism

Buddhism is a spiritual tradition that focuses on personal spiritual development and the attainment of a deep insight into the true nature of life. Buddhism teaches that all life is interconnected, so compassion is natural and important.

- Buddhism is 2500 years old.
- There are currently 376 million followers worldwide.
- According to the 2001 census, there are around 151 816 Buddhists in Britain.
- Buddhism arose as a result of Siddhartha Gautama's quest for Enlightenment in the 6th century **BCE**.
- There is no belief in a personal God. It is not centred on the relationship between humanity and God.
- Buddhists believe that nothing is fixed or permanent – change is always possible.
- Buddhists can worship both at home or at a temple.
- The path to Enlightenment is through the practice and development of morality, meditation and wisdom.

Adapted from www.bbc.co.uk/religion/religions/ buddhism/ataglance/glance.shtml

1 What beliefs are shared by Paganists, Buddhists and the Amba?

2 How might these beliefs help believers deal with the 'big' questions in life – for example, about suffering and death?

3 Do you consider each of these to be religions? Explain your answers.

4 What is your definition of religion?

Beliefs of the Amba

People like the Amba and their kinsmen believe profoundly that the world is ruled by supernatural forces. ... For this reason, nothing happens by chance. ... Let us consider this example: Sebuya is driving his car, has an accident and dies. ... That very day, all over the world, millions of cars reached their destination safely – but Sebuya had an accident and died. White people will search for various causes. For instance, his brakes malfunctioned. ... But this kind of thinking leads nowhere, explains nothing. ... Sebuya died because someone cast a spell on him. ... Speaking in the most general terms, a wizard did it.

Adapted from Kapuscinski, R. (1998) *The Shadow of the Sun: My African Life*, London: Penguin

Paganism

Paganism describes a group of contemporary religions based on a reverence for nature. These faiths draw on traditional religions throughout the world.

- Paganism encompasses a diverse community, including Wiccans, druids, shamans, sacred ecologists, Odinists and heathens.
- Some groups concentrate on specific traditions or practices, such as ecology, witchcraft, Celtic traditions or certain gods.
- Most Pagans share an ecological vision that comes from the Pagan belief in the organic vitality and spirituality of the natural world.
- Because of persecution and misrepresentation, it is necessary to define what Pagans are not, as well as what they are. Pagans are not sexual deviants, do not worship the devil, are not evil, do not practise 'black magic', and their practices do not involve harming people or animals.
- The Pagan Federation of Great Britain estimate that the number of Pagans in the British Isles is between 50 000 and 200 000 (2002).

Adapted from www.bbc.co.uk/religion/religions/ paganism/ataglance/glance.shtml

At some point in their lives everyone asks some 'big' questions about those things that are beyond our everyday experiences. These might include '… sleep and dreams, death, catastrophes, war, social upheaval, the taking of life, suffering and evil' (Hamilton 2001).

Berger (1971) points out that every culture across the world and throughout history has developed ways of dealing with these issues in order to prevent anxiety and social disruption. These consist of sets of beliefs that give some meaning to the world for individuals. He refers to these beliefs as a '**sacred canopy**' that gives significance to everyday life as it becomes seen as something that is part of a larger purpose. For Berger, it is religion that provides this sacred canopy.

What is religion?

Working out an acceptable definition of religion is a problem that has troubled sociologists since the earliest days of the subject. Across the world and throughout history, the nature of beliefs has varied so widely that it is very difficult to identify the kinds of common factors that allow for simple definitions. For example, should the witchcraft and **magic** of the Amba (see 'Getting you thinking' opposite) be seen as religious belief? Similarly, Buddhism, which does not include the idea of a personal God or a relationship between humans and God (see opposite)? And what about fanatically following a football team or a political view – can these be seen as religious?

Sociological approaches to defining religion can be divided into three broad categories:

1   **Substantive definitions** – These attempt to explain what religion actually is.
2   **Functional definitions** – These define religion in terms of its uses and purposes for individuals and societies.

Substantive definitions

One of the simplest definitions of religion dates from over 100 years ago. Tylor (1903) defined religion as 'belief in spiritual beings'. This definition was criticized for ignoring religious practices – the things people do to show their belief, for example forms of worship and ceremonies. Durkheim (1915) introduced the idea of practices into his definition. Religion, he said, is:

>> *a unified system of beliefs and practices relative to* **sacred** *things, that is to say, things set apart and forbidden – beliefs and practices which unite into one single moral community called a Church all those who adhere to them.* >> (Durkheim 1915)

Durkheim focuses on religion as a group activity and the way that certain symbols are imbued with a sacred power: they are regarded with awe and are often associated with rituals – an example might be the cross as a symbol in Christianity.

Substantive definitions of religion are dogged by the problem of which beliefs should and should not be included as 'religious'. For example, should the Amba's belief in magic be seen as religious, or should magic be a separate category as it may not include belief in god or gods or practices such as worship? And what about New Age ideas such as belief in the power of crystals, or cults such as scientology?

Functional definitions

These kinds of definitions state what religion actually does – its functions. There is an element of functionality about Durkheim's definition above, as it talks about uniting followers into 'one single moral community'. The assumption behind these definitions is that, as religion is a product of society, it needs to be defined in terms of its contributions to society. Because of this, these definitions are sometimes associated with the functionalist perspective.

An example of a functional definition is Yinger's:

<< *Religion is a system of beliefs and practices by means of which a group of people struggles with the ultimate problems of human life.* >> (Yinger 1970)

There are, however, problems with functional definitions of religion:

1   They are too broad – for example, belief systems that are specifically anti-religious could be included, such as Marxism. As Scharf (1970) puts it, functional definitions are cast in such wide terms that they 'allow any kind of enthusiastic purpose or strong loyalty, provided it is shared by a group, to count as religion'. To get around this problem, the term 'civil religion' is sometimes used to describe these types of belief systems (see Topic 2, pp. 193–194).
2   Functional definitions simply assume that religion plays a useful role in society. Anything that contributes to social stability can be considered as a religion without any need for evidence.

Measuring religiosity

Sociologists sometimes use the term religiosity to refer to the extent to which people are religious, in other words, their 'religiousness'. Judging religiosity is by no means a simple matter. When a functional definition of religion is used for example, all sorts of behaviour and belief can be categorised as religious, for example, fanatical support for a football team or political movement.

Table 1.1 Population of Great Britain: by religion, April 2001

	Total population (Numbers)	Total population (Percentages)	Non-Christian religious population (Percentages)
Christian	41,014,811	71.8	
Muslim	1,588,890	2.8	51.9
Hindu	558,342	1.0	18.3
Sikh	336,179	0.6	11.0
Jewish	267,373	0.5	8.7
Buddhist	149,157	0.3	4.9
Any other religion	159,167	0.3	5.2
All non-Christian religious population	3,0593108	5.4	100.0
No religion	8,596,488	15.1	
Religion not stated	4,433,520	7.8	
All population	57,103,927	100.0	

Religious belief

Problems in defining religion mean there is no clear idea of the boundaries of religious belief. Is a belief in fate, luck or superstition a religious belief? What about belief in ghosts and guardian angels?

The 2001 Census asked questions about religious belief. As Table 1.1 shows, just over 77 per cent of people claimed to have a religious belief, with 71.8 per cent identifying themselves as Christian. The second largest group was people with 'no religion'. The largest of the non-Christian religions was Islam with 2.8 per cent of respondents identifying themselves as Muslim.

But what do these figures actually tell us? Just because someone identifies themselves as religious when prompted in a survey does not necessarily mean that their behaviour is affected by that belief. They may not be a member of any religious organization or attend any religious services. In fact, we know that church attendance on Sundays halved between 1967 and 2006 yet there was no great decline in those identifying themselves as Christian. It seems that most people are still identifying with religion in terms of their own *private* beliefs but are less willing to express that belief *publicly* by attending religious events. Grace Davie (1994) describes this trend as 'believing without belonging'.

An alternative way of interpreting the data about religious belief is provided by Day (2007). She argues that the high levels of religious affiliation found in surveys may reflect a desire to belong to a community rather than real religious belief. In her sample, a little over half were what she termed 'adherent Christians' who believed in God and in heaven, and attended church. However, of the remainder, there were a significant number who neither 'belonged' nor 'believed'. They fell into one of three categories.

1 *Natal Christians* saw themselves as Christians because they were born into a Christian family or baptized.
2 *Ethnic Christians* saw Christianity in terms of Englishness and, therefore, as a way of identifying with an ethnic group.
3 *Aspirational Christians* saw Christianity as a sign of goodness and respectability.

These groups were attracted to the idea of religion as a way of feeling part of a wider community rather than as a reflection of their personal belief.

Religious commitment

How do people express their commitment to religion and how can sociologists measure that commitment?

Attendance at religious services

Counting up the number of people attending religious events seems an obvious and simple method but there are many problems.

1 There are many types of religious organization and a decision needs to be made about which are to be included. For example, are 'New Age' movements to be included?
2 How is attendance to be measured? What about people who only attend a few times a year, for example at Christmas, or those who go to church simply for 'rites of passage' such as christenings, marriages and funerals?
3 Different organizations collect attendance data in more or less reliable ways. Sociologists have to rely on the secondary data provided by the organizations themselves. It has been suggested that the Catholic Church may underestimate attendance figures to reduce the fees they have to pay to church authorities while the Church of England may be motivated to exaggerate figures where a small church is in danger of closure.

4 Attendance at religious services may not be a valid indicator of religious commitment. Martin (1969) points out that religious attendance was a sign of respectability in Victorian England rather than an expression of religious commitment. Today people might only participate in religion for friendship and support.

Membership of religious organizations

An alternative way of measuring commitment to religious organizations is to count the numbers of people who have actually become members. Membership of the large churches such as the Church of England is declining but this is partly offset by increases in membership of smaller Christian groups such as Jehovah's Witnesses and Mormons, and of activity in non-Christian religions such as Islam. However, this is not necessarily a reliable indicator of religious commitment because membership may be counted in different ways. For example, anyone baptized a Roman Catholic is a member of that church although they may not have attended church since. Similarly, every Jewish head of household is considered to be a member of the Jewish religion. Membership figures for smaller religious groups are not likely to be reliable.

Religious clothing and symbols

Religious commitment can be expressed through clothing. This is most obviously the case with some religions associated with minority ethnic groups such as Islamic dress codes such as the hijab (see Topic 3 for a more detailed discussion). Symbols and clothing make a public statement about and an individual's religious commitment and values.

Private and personal religious activity

This is probably an impossible form of religious commitment to measure. People may pray, send messages to their personal gods or involve themselves in a range of superstitious and spiritual activities, from avoiding walking under ladders to attending séances.

These debates about operationalizing the concept of religion affect the argument about the strength of religion in society today, which is the subject of Topic 4.

Religious organizations

Religious organizations can be broadly grouped into four main types:

- churches
- sects
- denominations
- cults.

Churches and sects

Weber (1920) and Troeltsch (1931) were the first to distinguish between churches and sects. A church is a large, well-established religious body, such as the mainstream organizations that represent the major world religions – Christian churches (such as the Roman Catholic, Anglican and Eastern Orthodox churches), Judaism, Islam, Hinduism, and so on. However, the term 'church' is particularly associated with the Christian religion and today many prefer to call religions such as Islam and Hinduism 'faiths'. A sect is a smaller, less highly organized grouping of committed believers, usually setting itself up in protest at what a church has become – as Calvinists and Methodists did in preceding centuries (they are now considered to be denominations within the Christian Church – see below). In terms of membership, churches are far more important than sects. The former tend to have hundreds of thousands or even millions of members, whereas sect members usually number no more than a few hundred. Hence, the often widespread media attention given to sects is somewhat disproportionate.

Denominations

According to Becker (1950) a denomination is a sect that has 'cooled down' to become an institutionalized body rather than an active protest group. Niebuhr (1929) argues that sects that survive over a period of time become denominations because a **bureaucratic**, non-hierarchical structure becomes necessary once the charismatic leader dies. Hence, they rarely survive as sects for more than a generation. While they initially appear deviant, sects gradually evolve into denominations and are accepted as a mere offshoot of an established church. They no longer claim a **monopoly of truth**, and tend to be tolerant and open, requiring a fairly low level of commitment. However, Bryan Wilson (1966) rejects Niebuhr's view and suggests that some sects do survive for a long time without becoming denominations and continue to require a high level of commitment.

Cults

There is some disagreement among sociologists over how to classify a cult, but most agree that it is the least coherent form of religious organization. The focus of cults tends to be on individual experience, bringing like-minded individuals together. People do not formally join cults, rather they subscribe to particular theories or forms of behaviour. Scientology, for example, is claimed to have eight million members worldwide.

Table 1.2 The differences between churches, denominations, sects and cults

This table illustrates key differences between types of religious organization. It is inevitably an oversimplification, as religious organizations do not always fit neatly into these categories.

Feature	Churches	Denominations	Sects	Cults
Scope	National (or international); very large membership; inclusive	National (or international); large membership; inclusive	Local or national. Tend to start small but can become extremely large.	Local, national or international; inclusive; vary in size
Internal organization	Hierarchical; bureaucratic	Formal bureaucratic	Voluntary; tight-knit; informal	Voluntary; loose structure
Nature of leadership	Professional clergy with paid officials	Professional clergy; less bureaucratic; use lay preachers	No professional clergy or bureaucratic structure; often charismatic leader	Individualistic; may be based on a common interest or provision of a service; inspirational leader
Life span	Over centuries	Often more than 100 years	Sometimes more than a generation; may evolve into a denomination	Often short-lived and die with the leadership
Attitude to wider society	Recognize the state and accept society's norms and values. Often seen as the establishment view	Generally accepted but not part of formal structure; seen as a basis of non-conformist views	Critical of mainstream society; often reclusive with own norms and values	May be critical or accepting of society, but have a unique approach that offers more
Claims to truth	Monopoly view of truth; strong use of ritual with little arousal of strong emotional response	No monopoly on truth; less ritual but clear emphasis on emotional fervour	Monopoly view of truth; aim to re-establish fundamental truths	No monopoly; borrow from a range of sources
Type of membership	Little formal commitment required; often by birth	Stronger commitment and rules, e.g. teetotalism or nongambling	Exceptional commitment	Membership flexible
Examples	Anglicanism, Roman Catholicism, Islam, Judaism, Hinduism, Sikhism	Baptists, Methodists, Pentecostalists	Mormons, Jehovah's Witnesses, Moonies, Branch Davidian, Salvation Army	Scientology, spiritualism, transcendental meditation, New Age ideas

The terms 'sect' and 'cult' are often used interchangeably by the media to describe new forms of religious organization and there can be considerable **moral panic** about them, as we shall see in the next topic. Recently, sociologists such as Wallis (1984) have developed the terms 'new religious movement (NRM)' and 'New Age movement (NAM)' to describe these new forms of religion.

Table 1.2 below summarizes the differences between churches, denominations, sects and cults.

Postmodernity and organized religion

For some sociologists, the advent of postmodern society has resulted in:

- previously powerful religious organizations becoming less significant
- an increase in fundamentalist factions within all major world religions
- new types of religious movements and networks, and the development of the **'spiritual shopper'**.

According to Lyotard (1984), postmodern society is characterized by a loss of confidence in **meta-narratives** – the 'grand' explanations provided by religion, politics, science and even sociology. The 'truths' that these subjects and belief systems claim to be able to reveal have not been forthcoming. This has led to what Bauman (1992) calls a 'crisis of meaning'. Traditional religions, in particular, seem unable to deal with this crisis. Take, for example, the social conflicts caused in the name of religion and religion's inability to reconcile this with the claim to preach love rather than hate. Consequently, newer expressions of religiosity have become more individualistic and less socially divisive. This has enabled individuals to restore meaning to their lives without having to rely on religious institutions imposing their monopoly of truth. This can be seen in the decline of religious monopolies and the rise of NRMs and NAMs. Some established religions have attempted to respond to these changes by watering down their content – according to Herberg (1960), they have undergone a process of internal secularization. Examples of this include the increased acceptance of divorce, homosexuality and the ordination of women in the Christian church, and the increasing popularity of Reform Judaism and Progressive Judaism.

Fundamentalism

Other established religions have encouraged a counterresponse to internal secularization and perceived moral decline by returning to the fundamentals, or basics, of their religious roots. Hence, there has been a rise in religious fundamentalism. Examples include Zionist groups in Israel, Islamic fundamentalists in Iran, Afghanistan and elsewhere, and the Christian Right in the USA. In the past 30 years, both Islamic and Christian fundamentalism have grown in strength, largely in response to the policies of modernizing governments and the shaping of national and international politics by globalization. The increasing influence of Western consumerism, for example, on less developed societies may be perceived as a threat to their faith and identity, thus provoking a defensive fundamentalist response. As Bauman puts it (1992), 'fundamentalist tendencies may articulate the experience of people on the receiving end of globalization'.

According to Holden (2002), fundamentalist movements, such as Jehovah's Witnesses, offer hope, direction and certainty in a world that seems increasingly insecure, confusing and morally lost.

Fundamentalism can sometimes lead to violence, especially where fundamentalists value their beliefs above tolerance of those who do not share them. In some cases, these beliefs can be so strong as to overcome any respect or compassion for others. They can sometimes even overcome the basic human values of preserving one's own life and the lives of others. The bombing of abortion clinics in the USA, the attacks on the Pentagon and World Trade Center Towers on 11 September 2001, and the suicide bomb attacks in Madrid (March 2004) and London (July 2005) are specific examples.

Features of fundamentalist groups

Sociologists such as Caplan (1987), Hunter (1987), and Davie (1995) provide a useful summary of some of the key features of fundamentalist groups (see Table 1.3 below).

Individual choice and the postmodern world

Postmodernists argue that the tendency for individuals to assert their identity through individual consumption rather than group membership has led to the growth of NRMs. The information explosion created by new technologies has provided an opportunity for people to pick and choose from a vast array of alternatives in a virtual 'spiritual supermarket'. Those in developed countries where this choice is greatest, act as 'spiritual shoppers', picking those beliefs and practices that suit their current tastes and identity, but dropping them or substituting them for other products if those identities change.

Table 1.3 Key features of fundamentalist groups

What fundamentalists do	Why they do it
They interpret 'infallible' sacred texts literally.	They do this in order to counter what they see as the diluting influence of excessive intellectualism among more **liberal** organizations. They often use texts from scriptures selectively to support their arguments.
They reject **religious pluralism**.	Tolerance of other religious ideas waters down personal faith and consequently fundamentalists have an 'us' and 'them' mentality.
Followers find a personal experience of God's presence.	They define all areas of life as sacred, thus requiring a high level of engagement. For example, fundamentalist Christians are 'born again' to live the rest of their lives in a special relationship with Jesus.
They oppose secularization and modernity and are in favour of tradition.	They believe that accommodation to the changing world undermines religious conviction and leads to moral corruption.
They tend to promote conservative beliefs, including patriarchal ones.	They argue that God intends humans to live in heterosexual societies dominated by men. In particular, they condemn abortion and detest lesbian and gay relationships.
They emerge in response to social inequality or a perceived social crisis.	They attract members by offering solutions to desperate, worried or dejected people.
Paradoxically, they tend to make maximum use of modern technology.	To compete on equal terms with those who threaten their very existence, the Christian Right, for example, use television (in their view the prime cause of moral decay) to preach the 'Word'. Use of the internet is now widespread by all fundamentalist groups.

The emergence of new religious movements (NRMs)

As we saw earlier, membership of established 'mainstream' churches has dropped dramatically. However, affiliation with other religious organizations (including Pentecostal, Seventh-Day Adventists and Christian sects) has risen just as noticeably. It is estimated that there may now be as many as 25 000 new religious groups in Europe alone, over 12 000 of whose members reside in the UK (see the 'Focus on research' on the right).

Difficulties in measuring affiliation to NRMs in the UK

There are a number of difficulties in measuring affiliation to NRMs in the UK:

- Many of the organizations listed in the 'Focus on research', right, have a large number of followers who are not formally registered in any way. It is estimated that about 30 000 people have attended meditation courses run by Brahma Kumaris, for example.
- Some groups have disbanded their organizations but still have 'devotees' – an example is the Divine Light Mission, whose followers, once initiated with 'the Knowledge', continue to practise the techniques of meditation independently.
- Many organizations are based overseas and their supporters in the UK are not traceable.
- The commitment required varies enormously between organizations. While those who devote themselves full time to their movement are generally quite visible, part-time commitment is more difficult to identify.

Affiliation through practice and belief is much higher than formal membership for both traditional and new religions.

Classifying NRMs

Sociologists have attempted to classify such movements in terms of shared features. One way is to identify their affinities with traditional mainstream religions. For example, some may be linked to Hinduism (e.g. Hare Krishnas) and others to Buddhism (various Zen groups). Some NRMs, such as the Unification Church (Moonies), mix up a number of different theologies, while others have links with the Human Potential Movement, which advocates therapies such as transcendental meditation and Scientology to liberate human potential.

Wallis (1984) identifies three main kinds of NRM:

1 world-affirming groups
2 world-rejecting groups
3 world-accommodating groups.

World-affirming groups

These are usually individualistic and life-positive, and aim to release 'human potential'. They tend to accept the world as it is, but involve techniques that enable the

Focus on research

Peter Brierley
Membership of NRMs

Membership of new religious movements, UK 1980 to 2000

	1980	1990	2000
The Aetherius Society	100	500	700
Brahma Kumaris	700	900	1500
Chrisemma	–	5	50
Da free John	35	50	70
Crème	250	375	510
Eckankar	250	350	450
Elan Vital*	1200	1800	2400
Fellowship of Isis	150	250	300
Life training	–	250	350
Mahikari	–	220	280
Barry Long Foundation	–	400	–
Outlook seminar training	–	100	250
Pagan Federation	500	900	5000
The Raelian movement	100	100	100
Shinnyo-en UK	10	30	60
Sahaja Yoga	220	280	365
Solara	–	140	180
3HO	60	60	60
Hare Krishna	300	425	670
Others	50	575	1330
Total	3925	7710	14 625
% of UK population	0.007	0.014	0.028

* previously known as the Divine Light Mission

Compiled from: Brierley, P. (ed.) (2000) *Religious Trends 2000*, London: HarperCollins

1 **Assess the reliability of the figures above.**

2 **Identify key patterns in the figures and suggest explanations for them.**

individual to participate more effectively and gain more from their worldly experience. They do not require a radical break with a conventional lifestyle, nor strongly restrict the behaviour of members. Research suggests that these are more common amongst middle-aged, middle-class groups – often in people who are disillusioned and disenchanted with material values and in search of new, more positive meanings. These groups generally lack a church, ritual worship or strong ethical systems. They are often more like 'therapy groups' than traditional religions. Two good examples of world-affirming groups are:

- *The Church of Scientology* founded by L. Ron Hubbard – Hubbard developed the philosophy of 'dianetics', which stresses the importance of 'unblocking the mind' and leading it to becoming 'clear'. His church spread throughout the world (from a base in California). Its business income is estimated at over £200 million per year through the courses members pay for, as well as through the sale of books.
- *Transcendental Meditation* (or TM) was brought to the West by the Hindu Mahareshi Mahesh Yogi in the early 1950s and was further popularized through the interest shown in it by the Beatles in the 1960s. Adherents build a personal **mantra**, which they then dwell upon for periods each day. Again, the focus is on a good world – not an evil one – and a way of 'finding oneself' through positive thinking.

World-rejecting groups

These organizations are usually sects, in so far as they are always highly critical of the outside world and demand significant commitment from their members. In some ways, they are quite like conventional religions in that they may require prayer and the study of key religious texts, and have strong ethical codes. They are exclusive, often share possessions and seek to relegate members' identities to that of the greater whole. They are often **millenarian** – expecting divine intervention to change the world. Examples include:

- The Unification Church (popularly known as the Moonies), founded in Korea by the Reverend Sun Myung Moon in 1954. The Unification Church rejects the mundane secular world as evil and has strong moral rules, such as no smoking and drinking.
- Members of Hare Krishna (Children of God, or ISKCON International Society for Krishna Consciousness) are distinguished by their shaved heads, pigtails and flowing gowns. Hare Krishna devotees repeat a mantra 16 times a day.

World-rejecting sects are the movements that have come under most public scrutiny in recent years, largely because of the public horror at the indoctrination that has even led to mass suicide. There is a growing list of extreme examples:

- the mass suicide of Jim Jones's People's Temple in Jonestown, Guyana in 1987
- the Aum Supreme Truth detonating poisonous gas canisters on a Tokyo underground train in 1995, leaving 12 dead and 5000 ill

- the suicidal death in 1997 of the 39 members of the Heaven's Gate cult in California.

Signs of cultist behaviour

Robbins (1988) identifies the following signs of cultist behaviour:

- *Authoritarianism* – Control of the organization stems from an absolute leader or a small circle of elite commanders.
- *Infallibility* – The chosen philosophy is the only path to salvation, and all others are worthless. Anyone who questions or challenges what the cult offers is denied access or exiled.
- *Programming* – The belief in the infallibility of the cult's philosophy, experiential panacea and leader are derived from the abandonment of critical and rational thinking.
- *Shunning* – Members are encouraged to sever communications and relationships with friends and family members.
- *Secret doctrines* – Certain teachings are 'secret' and must never be revealed to the outside world.
- *Promised ones* – Members of the cult are encouraged to believe they were chosen, or made their choice to join the cult, because they are special or superior.
- *Fire and brimstone* – Leaving the cult, or failing at one's endeavour to complete the requirements to achieve its panacea, will result in consequences greater than if one had never joined the cult in the first place.

Cult apologists

Cult apologists, such as Haddon and Long (1993), while not members themselves, both defend the right of such groups to exist and argue for more religious tolerance. They claim that:

- most cults are simply misunderstood minority 'religions'
- these movements only seem weird because people don't know enough about them and believe sensational media accounts
- anticult organizations and individuals misrepresent the beliefs and practices of such movements
- anticult organizations are intolerant of religious freedom.

World-accommodating groups

This final category of religious movement is more orthodox. They maintain some connections with mainstream religion, but place a high value on inner religious life. The Holy Spirit 'speaks' through the Neo-Pentecostalists, for example, giving them the gift of '**speaking in tongues**'. Other examples include spiritualists who claim to be able to contact the spirits of the dead; many Spiritualists draw inspiration from faiths with a deep mystical tradition such as Sufism, the Kabbalah, Hinduism and Buddhism. Such religions are usually dismayed at both the state of the world and the state of organized mainstream religions. They seek to establish older certainties and faith, while giving them a new vitality.

New Age movements (NAMs)

The term 'New Age' refers to a large number of religions and therapies that have become increasingly important since the 1970s. Many New Age movements can be classed as 'world affirming' (see above) as they focus on the achievement of individual potential.

Bruce (1996) suggests that these groups tend to take one of two forms:

1   *Audience cults* involve little face-to-face interaction. Members of the 'audience' are unlikely to know each other. Contacts are maintained mostly through the mass media and the internet as well as occasional conferences. Both astrology and belief in UFOs are good examples of these. Audience cults feed a major market of 'self-help therapy' groups and books which regularly appear in best-seller lists.

2   *Client cults* offer particular services to their followers. They have led to a proliferation of new 'therapists' (from astrological to colour therapists), establishing new relationships between a consumer and a seller. Amongst the practices involved are tarot readings, **crystals** and astrology. Many bookshops devote more to these sorts of books than to books on Christianity.

NAMs seem to appeal to all age groups, but more especially to women (see also Topic 3). Bruce (1995) suggests that those affiliated, however, already subscribe to what Heelas calls the '**cultic milieu**' (Heelas 1996) or '**holistic milieu**' (Heelas *et al.* 2004) – a mish-mash of belief in the power of spirituality, ecology and personal growth, and a concern that science does not have all the answers.

Key terms

Bureaucratic centralized form of organization run by official representatives.

Religious pluralism where a variety of religions co-exist, all of which are considered to have equal validity.

Crystals belief in the healing power of semiprecious stones.

Cult apologists non-cult members who are religiously tolerant and challenge the misinterpretation of cult practice common in the wider society.

Cultic or holistic milieu a range of activities involving the mind, body and spirit, such as yoga, tai chi, healing and self-discovery.

Functional definitions of religion definitions that focus on the role religion plays for societies and individuals.

Liberal a concern with individual freedoms.

Magic events not explained by traditional science.

Mantra personal word or phrase given by a religious teacher (guru) which is used to free the mind of non-spiritual secular awareness and provide a focus for meditation.

meta–narrative belief system, such as religion or science, that claims to explain the world.

Millenarian belief in a saviour.

Monopoly of truth a view that only the viewpoint of the holder can be accepted as true.

Moral panic media-induced panic about the behaviour of particular groups.

Religious pluralism where a variety of religions co-exist, all of which are considered to have equal validity.

Religious practices rituals and rites associated with religion.

Sacred regarded with awe and reverence.

Sacred canopy Berger's term for beliefs that give meaning to the world.

Speaking in tongues the power to speak in new (but often incomprehensible) languages believed to be a gift from God.

Spiritual shoppers a postmodern idea that people consume religion in much the same way as any other product.

Subjectivization the increasing relevance of the self and personal experiences as a dominant feature of religion in late-modern society.

Substantive definitions of religion those that attempt to explain what religion actually is.

Check your understanding

1   How has Durkheim's definition of religion been challenged?

2   What problems are associated with functional definitions of religion?

3   Briefly define 'church', 'denomination', 'sect' and 'cult', giving examples of each.

4   In your own words, outline the key features of fundamentalism.

5   Give two possible reasons for the rising number of fundamentalist groups across the globe.

6   What do you understand by the term 'spiritual shopper'?

7   Why are the numbers of those involved with NRMs probably much higher than membership figures suggest?

8   Briefly explain what Wallis means by the term 'world-affirming movements'. Give examples.

9   How does Bruce classify New Age movements?

10 What does Wallis mean by the term 'world rejecting movements'? Give examples.

Activities

Research idea

Ask your friends some 'big questions' about, for example, the meaning of life, and life after death. Make sure you get informed consent from them before the interview, as this sort of questioning might upset some people. What sort of belief systems do their answers reveal? To what extent can their beliefs be described as 'religious'?

Web.tasks

1 Go to the BBC's 'religions' website at **www.bbc.co.uk/religion/religions**. Choose four religions and draw up a table to compare them using the categories: beliefs, customs, rites and values.

2 Go to the website of the Cult Information Centre at **www.cultinformation.org.uk** and explore some of the organizations and incidents mentioned. Then go to the website of Inform at **www.inform.ac/infmain.html** and compare the attitude to NRMs, cults and sects on each site.

An eye on the exam Religion and religious organizations

Make sure you make the two problems clear, identify them at the beginning of paragraphs

The question requires careful consideration of this word. What are the different aspects of religiosity?

(a) Identify and explain two problems in measuring religiosity.　　　(17 marks)

The problems need to be discussed in some depth using sociological concepts and studies

Aim to write for about 15 minutes

A detailed description of the view is required using sociological concepts, theories and studies

Put forward the case that there are similarities as well as differences

You need to explain what these differences are

(b) Outline and evaluate the view that the differences between types of religious organization have been exaggerated.　　　(33 marks)

This means blown out of proportion

Aim to write at least two sides of the answer book in about 30 minutes

Grade booster Getting top marks in this question

Show the examiner that you are aware of the variety of different types of religious organization – these should include churches, denominations, sects, cults and a variety of new religious and New Age movements. These will need to be described and their key characteristics and differences identified. Then you need to discuss similarities between, say, churches and denominations and sects and cults. You might discuss how sects can become denominations and then churches. It is likely that you will stress the diversity of new religious movements and top answers will stress that what is considered a 'religious' organization depends on what kind of definition of religion is used.

The role of religion in society

Getting you thinking

Left: A funeral

Above: Members of a church meet for coffee in the vestry

Right: God can both explain poverty and offer hope of salvation from it

1 **What purpose does religion serve for the individuals in each picture?**

2 **What might happen to these individuals if religion suddenly ceased to exist?**

3 **Suggest some ways in which religion helps people in modern society to cope with disruptive influences in their lives.**

Sociologists who have studied the role of religion in society often tend to fall into one of two broad camps:

1 Those who see religion as a **conservative** force – 'Conservative' means keeping things the way they are. These sociologists see religion as a force for stability and order. They may well favour a functionalist or a Marxist point of view.

2 Those who see religion as a force for social change – Supporters of this position point to the role of religion in encouraging societies to change. They may be influenced by the writings of Max Weber or by some neo-Marxist thinkers.

Inhibiting change

Both functionalists and traditional Marxists adopt the view that religion inhibits change – that is, they identify a similar role for religion. However, functionalists tend to view this as a 'good' thing, while Marxists view it as a 'bad' thing.

Functionalism and religion

The key concern of functionalist writing on religion is the contribution that religion makes to the wellbeing of society – its contribution to social stability and value consensus. In his famous work, *The Elementary Forms of Religious Life*, Durkheim (1912) relates religion to the overall structure of society. He based his work on a study of **totemism** among Australian aborigines. He argued that totemism represents the most elementary form of religion.

The totem is believed to have divine properties that separate it from those animals or plants that may be eaten or harvested. There are a number of ceremonies and rituals involved in worship of the totem which serve to bring the tribe together as a group and consequently to reaffirm their group identity.

Durkheim defined religion in terms of a distinction between the **sacred** (holy or spiritual) and the **profane** (unspiritual, non-religious, ordinary). Sacred people, objects and symbols are set apart from ordinary life, and access to them is usually forbidden or restricted in some way.

Why is the totem so sacred?

Durkheim suggests that the totem is sacred because it is symbolically representative of the group itself. It stands for the values of the community, who, by worshipping the totem, are effectively 'worshipping' their society.

Durkheim's distinction between the sacred and profane, is, in effect, the distinction between society and people. The relationship between god and humans (power and dependence) outlined in most religions is a reflection of the relationship between society and humans. It is not god who makes us behave and punishes our misdemeanours, but society.

Durkheim argues that religion is rarely a matter of individual belief. Most religions involve collective worship, ceremony and rituals, during which group solidarity is affirmed or heightened. An individual is temporarily elevated from their normal profane existence to a higher level, in which they can recognize divine influences or gods. These divine influences are recognized as providing the moral guidance for the particular social group concerned. For Durkheim, however, gods are merely the expression of the influence over the individual of what he calls the '**collective conscience**' – the basic shared beliefs, values, traditions and norms that make the society work. The continual act of group worship and celebration through ritual and ceremony serves to forge group identity, creating cohesion and solidarity. God is actually a recognition that society is more important than the individual.

In maintaining social solidarity, religion acts as a conservative force; when it fails to perform this function, new ideas may emerge that effectively become the new religion. Thus, Durkheim regarded **nationalism** and **communism** as examples of the new religions of industrial society, taking over from Christianity, but performing the same essential functions. Durkheim and other functionalists are not saying that religion does not change – clearly its *form* does – but what remains unchanged is its *function*, and that, essentially, is to offer support for the status quo. Politics and its associated rituals, flag waving, parades and so on, are the new forms by which collective sentiments are symbolically expressed. Consequently, religion, in one form or another, is a necessary feature of any society.

The functions of religion in modern society

The key functions of religion can be summarized as follows.

Socialization

In modern societies, the major function of religion is to socialize society's members into a value consensus by investing values with a sacred quality. These values become 'moral codes' – beliefs that society agrees to hold in the highest regard and socialize children into. Consequently, such codes regulate our social behaviour – for example, the Ten Commandments (from the Old Testament) are a good example of a set of moral codes that have influenced both formal controls, such as the law (e.g. 'Thou shalt not kill/steal'), as well as informal controls, such as moral disapproval (e.g. 'Thou shalt not commit adultery').

Social integration and solidarity

Encouraging collective worship is regarded by functionalists as particularly important for the integration of society, since it enables members to express their shared values and strengthens group unity. By worshipping together, people develop a sense of commitment and belonging; individuals are united into a group with shared values, so that social solidarity is reinforced, deviant behaviour restrained and social change restricted. Also, religion and its associated rituals foster the development of the collective conscience or moral community, which helps people to understand the reality of social relations, communicate with others and establish obligations between people.

Civil religion

In modern societies, ritual and ceremony are common aspects of national loyalties. In the UK, street parades, swearing allegiance to Queen and country, and being part of a flag-waving crowd all remind us of our relationship to the nation.

This idea has been developed by some functionalist thinkers into the theory of '**civil religion**'. This refers to a situation where sacred qualities are attached to aspects of the society itself. Hence, religion in one form or another continues to be an essential feature of society. This is very evident in America where the concept of civil religion was first developed by Bellah (1970), himself American. America is effectively a nation of immigrants with a wide range of co-existing cultural and religious traditions. What does unite them, however, is their faith in 'Americanism'. While traditional religion binds individuals to their various communities, civil religion in America unites the nation. Although civil religion need not involve a connection with supernatural beliefs, according to Bellah, God and Americanism appear to go hand in hand. American coins remind their users 'In God we trust', and the phrase 'God bless America' is a common concluding remark to an important speech. Even the phrase 'President of the United States of America', Bellah argues, imbues the country's leader with an almost divine quality. The God that Americans are talking about, however, is not allied to a particular faith;

he is, in a Durkheimian sense, the God of (or that is) America.

Bellah, however, suggests that even civil religion is in decline, as people now rank personal gratification above obligation to others and there is, in his view, a deepening cynicism about established social institutions. However, the events of 11 September 2001 and their aftermath have undoubtedly led to a reaffirmation of Americanism and its associated symbolism.

Preventing anomie

Durkheim's main fear for modern industrial society was that individuals would become less integrated and their behaviour less regulated. Should this become widespread, **anomie** (a state of confusion and normlessness) could occur whereby society could not function because its members would not know how they should behave relative to one another.

Religious and civil ceremony prevents this happening by encouraging an awareness of common membership of an entity greater than, and supportive of, the individual. Some religious movements seem to have grown in times of social upheaval when anomie may have been occurring. For example, the industrial revolution in Britain was marked by a series of revivalist movements, such as Methodism and Presbyterianism.

Coming to terms with life-changing events

Functionalist thinkers, such as Malinowski (1954) and Parsons (1965), see religion as functioning to relieve the stress and anxieties created by life crises such as birth, puberty, marriage and death. In other words, such events can undermine people's commitment to the wider society and, therefore, social order. Religion gives such events meaning, helping people come to terms with change. Most societies have evolved religious **rites of passage** ceremonies in order to minimize this social disruption. For example, the death of a loved one can cause the bereaved to feel helpless and alone, unable to cope with life. However, the funeral ceremony allows people to adjust to their new situation. The group mourning also reaffirms the fact that the group outlives the passing of particular individuals and is there to support its members.

Criticisms of functionalism

● Church attendance is declining in most Western societies, such as the UK. It is difficult to see how religion can be functioning to socialize the majority of society's members into morality and social integration, if only a minority of people regularly attend church.

● Some have argued that Durkheim's analysis is based on flawed evidence: he misunderstood both totemism and the behaviour of the aboriginal tribes themselves.

● Religion can have a negative effect on societies – it can be dysfunctional. Rather than binding people together, many of the world's conflicts have been caused by religion, for example between Sunni and Shiite Muslims, Hindus and Muslims in India, and Christians and Muslims throughout the world. The latter situation prompted Islamic scholars in October 2007 to write to

Pope Benedict XVI and other Christian leaders suggesting a joint emphasis on mutual understanding and shared aspects of the religions, such as an emphasis on 'loving your neighbour'.
- Much functionalist analysis is based upon the idea that a society has one religion, but many modern societies are multicultural, multifaith societies.
- The idea that religion can be seen as the worship of society depends on an assumption that worship is a collective act – people joining together to celebrate their god or gods. However, religious belief may be expressed individually.

Durkheim did recognize that religion had a strong social control function, as the following quotation illustrates.

<< Religion instructed the humble to be content with their situation, and, at the same time, it taught them that the social order is providential; that it is god himself who has determined each one's share, religion gave man a perception of a world beyond this earth where everything would be rectified; this prospect made inequalities seem less noticeable, it stopped men from feeling aggrieved. >> (Durkheim 1912)

Marxists take this argument much further. They argue that religion, far from being an instrument of social solidarity, is an instrument of social control and exploitation.

Marxism and religion

The following quotations provide a summary of the classic Marxist position on religion.

<< Religion is the sigh of the oppressed creature, the sentiment of a heartless world ... the soul of soulless conditions. It is the opium of the people. >> (Marx 1844)

<< Religion is a kind of spiritual gin in which the slaves of capital drown their human shape and their claims to any decent life. >> (Lenin 1965)

Like Durkheim, Marx also argued that religion was a conservative force in society. However, he did not agree that this force was essentially positive and beneficial to society. Rather, Marx argues that the primary function of religion is to reproduce, maintain and justify class inequality. In other words, religion is an **ideological apparatus**, which serves to reflect ruling-class ideas and interests. Moreover, Marx describes religion as the 'opium of the people', because in his view it prevents the working classes from becoming aware of the true nature of their exploitation by the ruling class and doing anything about it. Instead, they see it all as 'God's will' and passively accept things as they are, remaining in a state of false consciousness. Religion acts as an opiate – a pacifying drug – in that it does not solve any problems people may have, but merely dulls the pain and, therefore, argued Marx, most religious movements originate in the oppressed classes.

However, as Engels pointed out:

<< The history of early Christianity has notable points of resemblance with the modern working-class movement. Like the latter, Christianity was originally a movement of oppressed people: it first appeared as the religion of slaves and emancipated slaves, of poor people deprived of all rights, of peoples subjugated or dispersed by Rome. Both Christianity and the workers' socialism preach forthcoming salvation from bondage and misery; Christianity places this salvation in a life beyond, after death, in heaven; socialism places it in this world, in a transformation of society. >>
(Marx and Engels 1975)

Religion is seen by Marx as being ideological in three ways, as outlined below (Marx and Engels 1957).

1 Legitimating social inequality

Religion serves as a means of controlling the population by promoting the idea that the existing hierarchy is natural, god-given and, therefore, unchangeable. We can particularly see this during the **feudal period**, when it was widely believed that kings had a divine right to rule. During the 18th and 19th centuries, it was generally believed that God had created both rich and poor, as reflected in the hymn 'All Things Bright and Beautiful'. This stated (in what is now a little-used verse):

<< The rich man in his castle,
the poor man at his gate,
God made them, high or lowly,
and order'd their estate. >>

2 Disguising the true nature of exploitation

Religion explains economic and social inequalities in supernatural terms. In other words, the real causes (exploitation by the ruling class) are obscured and distorted by religion's insistence that inequality is the product of sin or a sign that people have been chosen by God.

3 Keeping the working classes passive

Some religions present suffering and poverty as a virtue to be accepted – and even welcomed – as normal. It is suggested that those who do not question their situation will be rewarded by a place in heaven. Such ideas promote the idea that there is no point in changing society now. Instead, people should wait patiently for divine intervention. Religion offers hope and promises happiness in a future world. The appeal to a God is part of the illusion that things will change for the better. This prevents the working class from actually doing anything which challenges the ruling class directly.

Marx was interested in industrial capitalist societies and Christianity was at the centre of his thinking. However, other religions can be seen to have the same effect, whether it is the Buddhist focus on individual meditation, or the Hindu caste system, which fixes status for this life in one caste and only allows for improvement after reincarnation.

Religion thus discourages people from attempting change, so the dominant groups can retain their power. Religion is used by the ruling class to justify their position. Church and ruling class are mutually reinforcing:

<< The parson has ever gone hand in hand with the landlord. >> Communist Manifesto (Marx 1848)

However, evidence for the traditional Marxist position is partial and tends to be of a documentary nature, looking at the nature of faith and the way in which the religion of the poor concentrates on the afterlife. Also, some traditional Marxists adopt the view that religion can bring about social change, a position also adopted by some neo-Marxists and discussed further in the next topic.

Evidence to support Marxist views

- Halevy (1927) argued that the Methodist religion played a key role in preventing working-class revolution in 19th-century Britain. Most European nations, apart from Britain, experienced some type of proletarian attempt to bring about social change in this period. Halevy argued that working-class dissatisfaction with the establishment in Britain was, instead, expressed by deserting the Church of England, which was seen as the party of the **landed classes**. Methodism attracted significant numbers of working-class worshippers, and Halevy claims Methodism distracted the proletariat from their class grievances by encouraging them to see enlightenment in spirituality rather than revolution. In this sense, religion inhibited major social upheaval and, therefore, social change.
- Leach (1988) is critical of the Church of England because it recruits from what is essentially an upper-class base (80 per cent of bishops were educated at public school and Oxbridge). The Church is also extremely wealthy. Leach argues that, as a result, the Church has lost contact with ordinary people. He suggests it should be doing more to tackle inequality, especially that found in the inner cities.
- Religion is used to support dominant groups in America. It has been suggested that modern Protestant **fundamentalist religions** in the USA support right-wing, conservative and anticommunist values. Fundamentalists (the **Christian Right**) often suggest that wealth and prosperity are a sign of God's favour, while poverty, illness and homosexuality are indicators of sin.
- Hook (1990) noted that the (then) Pope, John Paul II, had a very conservative stance on contraception, abortion, women priests and homosexuality (a stance shared by his successor, Benedict XVI). He points out that the Vatican's stance on contraception is causing problems in less developed areas of the world, such as South America. Hook also suggests that the considerable wealth of the church could be doing more to tackle world poverty.

Neo-Marxist views on religion

Not all Marxists have followed the view that religion is purely 'the opium of the people' (see p. 195). Some have emphasized the revolutionary potential of religion. O'Toole (1984) has pointed out that:

>> *Marxists have undoubtedly recognized the active role that may be played by religion in effecting revolutionary social change.* >>

Writers who have tried to update the ideas of Marx to suit new developments in society are known as neo-Marxists. Some neo-Marxists have rejected the classic Marxist idea that all the cultural institutions in society, such as the media, the law and religion, are inevitably under the control of the ruling class. They argue that ruling-class domination is actually more effective if its members are not directly involved in these cultural institutions. This is because it will then appear that the media and so on are independent when, in fact, the economic power of the bourgeoisie means that no matter who fills particular roles in these institutions, they are still under ruling-class control. Neo-Marxists call this apparent independence of cultural institutions **relative autonomy**.

The Italian neo-Marxist Antonio Gramsci (1971) wrote in the 1920s and 30s. Although he was aware at the time that the church was supporting ruling-class interests, he did not believe this to be inevitable. He argued that religious beliefs and practices could develop that would support and guide challenges to the ruling class, because the church, like other cultural institutions, was not directly under their control. Members of the working class could challenge the dominant class through the distribution of more radical ideas.

Otto Maduro (1982), also argued for the relative autonomy of religion, suggesting that in situations where there is no other outlet for grievances, such as in Latin America, the clergy can provide guidance for the oppressed in their struggle with dominant groups.

Criticisms of Marxism

- Like functionalism, the Marxist theory of religion fails to consider **secularization**. Surely the ideological power of religion is undermined by the fact that fewer than 10 per cent of people attend church?
- Marx failed to explain the existence of religion where it does not appear to contribute to the oppression of a particular class. Nor does Marxism explain why religion continues to exist when, in theory at least, oppression has come to an end. In the USSR under communism after the 1917 revolution, the state actively discouraged religion and many places of worship were closed. The communist state placed limits on religious activity and the religious instruction of children was banned. Nevertheless, religion did not die out under communism, as Marx predicted it would.
- There are also some examples of religious movements that have brought about radical social change and helped remove ruling elites. They demonstrate that religion can legitimize radical revolutionary ideas as well as ideologically conservative ones. Marx failed to recognize this. Neo-Marxists have recognized the way in which religion is sometimes used as the only means to oppose the ruling class. Recently in Britain, for example, churches have often provided safe havens for immigrant groups facing deportation by the government, enabling such groups to publicize their case further and to gain time and support.

Both the functionalist and Marxist approaches suggest that religion generally plays a conservative role in society –

preventing change and supporting the existing social order. This topic looks at an alternative position – that it is possible for religion to change societies.

Weber and religion

Max Weber, in his famous work *The Protestant Ethic and the Spirit of Capitalism* (1958, originally 1905), argued that it was possible for religious ideas to cause social change. He focused on the role of one particular religious group in bringing about the change from that may have helped to facilitate dramatic social change.

The Protestant ethic and the spirit of capitalism

Calvinists were a Protestant group who emerged in the 17th century and believed in predestination. According to them, your destiny or fate was fixed in advance – you were either damned or saved, and there was nothing you or any religious figure could do to improve your chances of going to heaven. There was also no way of knowing your fate. However, it was believed that any form of social activity was of religious significance; material success that arose from hard work and an **ascetic** life would demonstrate God's favour and, therefore, your ultimate destiny – a place in heaven.

Weber argued that these ideas helped initiate Western economic development through the industrial revolution and capitalism. Many of the early **entrepreneurs** were Calvinists. Their obsessive work ethic and self-discipline, inspired by a desire to serve God, meant that they reinvested, rather than spent, their profits. Such attitudes were ideal for the development of industrial capitalism.

The influence of religious leadership on social change

According to Weber, religious and other authority takes one of three forms:

1 *Charismatic* – People obey a religious leader because of their personal qualities. Well-known **charismatic** figures might include Jesus Christ and Hitler. Charisma has been a common feature of leadership in some religions, particularly cults and sects, which can, if the charismatic leader attracts enough followers, bring about significant changes to the societies in which they originate.

Focus on religion and violent social change

The attacks on **11 September 2001** in New York and on **7 July 2005** in London – and the American and British response (the so-called 'war on terror') – have often been presented in religious terms, as 'good versus evil', for example. Both sides have used religion to try to change the world.

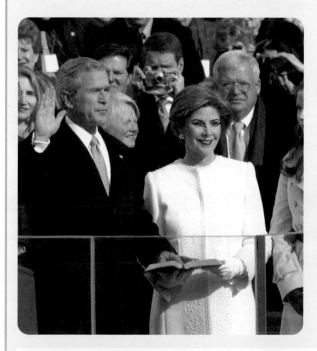

Photo left: George W. Bush, US president at the time of the bombings in 2001 and 2005

Photo right: the bombers making their way to London on 7 July 2005

1 How has religion motivated the individuals in each picture?

2 How might their actions be viewed if religion did not exist?

3 To what extent do you think religion causes or justifies social change?

2 *Traditional* – Those who exercise authority do so because they continue a tradition and support the preservation and continuation of existing values and social ties. Those in authority give orders (and expect to be obeyed) because the office they fill gives them the right to. Though generally conservative, this kind of authority can be responsible for change in the face of modernizing regimes. The authority of the Islamic leaders in Afghanistan and Iran are recent examples.

3 *Legal–Rational* – This type of authority is not based on the personal qualities of the individual but on laws and regulations. Orders are only to be obeyed if they are relevant to the situation in which they are given. Individuals within the legal system, government and state institutions exercise this form of authority.

Social change can be caused by influential religious leaders who have challenged legal–rational authority – the form exercised by the state or government. Charismatic leaders, in particular, have been responsible for the establishment of many alternative social arrangements, often causing conflict with mainstream society or much negative publicity through the harmful influences of their leaders.

Criticisms of Weber

● Some countries with large Calvinist populations, such as Norway and Sweden, did not industrialize. However, as Marshall (1982) points out, Weber did not claim that Calvinism *caused* capitalism; he only suggested that it was a major contributor to a climate of change. Calvinist beliefs had to be supplemented by a certain level of technology, a skilled and mobile workforce, and rational modes of law and bureaucracy.

● Some commentators have suggested that slavery, colonialism and piracy were more important than

Calvinist beliefs in accumulating the capital required for industrialization.

● Marxists are also critical because, as Kautsky (1953) argued, capitalism predates Calvinism. He argued that early capitalists were attracted to Calvinism because it made their interests appear legitimate.

● Aldridge (2000) points out that charismatic leadership can be unstable, in that movements often disintegrate once the charismatic leader dies. Such leadership does not, therefore, contribute significantly to long-lasting social change.

Postmodernism and religion

Topic 1 explained some of the views of postmodern sociologists towards religion. They believe that religion has become just one of many sets of beliefs which compete for attention in postmodern culture. People are 'consumers' of beliefs or 'spiritual shoppers' who decide which belief systems suit their needs at any particular time. The 'spiritual supermarket' now contains a very wide range of 'products' including many NRMs and NAMs. The growth of NRMs and NAMs reflects people's disillusionment with science and rational thinking and their search for meaning in an increasingly unstable and unpredictable world. In this context fundamentalist beliefs are also attractive because they offer absolute certainties and crystal-clear moral guidelines.

Unlike Marxists and functionalists, postmodern sociologists do not believe it is possible to generalise about the role of religion in society. What is required is an analysis of specific religious beliefs and practices in particular social situations.

Key terms

Anomie a state of confusion and normlessness.

Christian Right fundamentalist and right-wing Christian groups, particularly powerful in the southern states of America.

Civil religion events or activities that involve ritualistic patterns and generate the collective sentiments usually associated with established religions.

Collective conscience beliefs, values and moral attitudes shared by members of a society

that are essential to the social order.

Communism political philosophy originated by Karl Marx that advocates common ownership of land and business.

Conservative supporting things staying as they are.

Feudal period medieval period when wealth in society was based on the ownership of land.

Fundamentalist religions belief systems that argue the need to subscribe or return to traditional values and practices, usually involving the literal

translation of, and belief in, a religious text.

Ideological apparatus agencies (such as religion, education and the mass media) that transmit ruling-class ideology to persuade subordinate groups (e.g. the working class) that inequality is natural and normal, thereby ensuring their consent to it.

Landed classes wealthy, land-owning aristocracy.

Nationalism patriotic feelings towards a nation; belief that your nation is superior to others

Profane ordinary, unreligious aspects of life.

Rites of passage a ceremony or event that marks an important change in a person's life

Sacred holy or spiritually significant.

Secularization a process whereby religious beliefs and practices lose their social significance.

Totemism a primitive religion involving the worship of certain objects seen to have a widespread influence over tribal life.

Check your understanding

1 What is the distinction between the sacred and the profane?

2 What is Durkheim's explanation of the true nature of the 'totem' and 'god'?

3 Identify and explain four functions of religion.

4 Explain, using examples, how civil religion performs similar functions to religion as it is usually understood.

5 How have functionalist ideas about religion been criticized?

6 How, according to Marxists, does religion benefit the capitalist class?

7 What evidence is there to support such views?

8 How can Marxist views on religion be criticized?

9 What does Weber mean by the 'Protestant ethic'?

10 How did Weber suggest that the Protestant ethic contributed to the development of capitalism?

11 Give an example that shows in each case how charismatic and traditional leadership have caused social change.

12 What criticisms have been made of Weber's work?

Activities

Research idea

Interview (or conduct a focus group with) a small number of fellow students who attend religious events on a regular basis. Try to cover a range of religions. Ask them about their beliefs and their views about society.

● Do they argue for social change or are they content with the way things are?
● If they want change, what sort of changes are they looking for?
● How do they think these might come about?

Web.tasks

1 Go to the website of the *Guardian* newspaper at www.guardianunlimited.co.uk and, in the archive search section, key in the words 'government' and 'church'. What evidence can you find for the continuing influence of the church on politics in modern society?

2 Go to a search engine and type in the phrase 'Christian Right + USA'. Investigate the extent to which they lend support for the Republican party (an American political party with conservative views).

An eye on the exam   The role of religion in society

The two ways need to be stated clearly, probably at the beginning of paragraphs

Bear in mind the different types of religious belief and organization

Aim to write for about 15 minutes

(a) Identify and explain two ways in which religion may cause social change.   (17 marks)

Each of the two ways need to be discussed in depth, using sociological concepts, studies, examples and theories

The focus must be on change, not keeping societies stable

The functionalist view needs to be described in some detail, including examples of key writers and concepts

This view stresses the role of religion in maintaining social stability and order

(b) Outline and evaluate functionalist views of religion.   (33 marks)

Include criticisms of the functionalist view as well as putting forward alternative perspectives

Although the question focuses on religion, it might help to provide a brief description of the key points of the functionalist perspective

Aim to write at least two sides of the answer book in about 30 minutes

Grade booster   Getting top marks in this question

Key functionalist writers such as Durkheim, Parsons and Malinowski need to de discussed as well as concepts such as 'collective conscience', social order and civil religion. The evaluative section of your answer should include criticisms of functionalism such as the failure of that perspective to deal with societies based on religious pluralism and the privatized expression of belief. Other perspectives such as Weberianism and Marxism can be used as contrasts to functionalism, although bear in mind that Marxism too sees religion as playing a role in social control.

TOPIC 3

Religion and social position

Getting you thinking

Group	1970	1980	1990	2000	
Christian: Trinitarian* of whom:	9272	7529	6624	5917	mainly White ethnic majority
Anglican	2987	2180	1728	1654	
Catholic	2746	2455	2198	1768	
Free Churches	1629	1285	1299	1278	
Presbyterian	1751	1437	1214	989	
Orthodox	159	172	185	235	
Christian: Non-Trinitarian**	276	349	455	533	
Buddhist	10	15	30	50	mainly ethnic minority
Hindu	80	120	140	165	
Jewish	120	111	101	88	
Muslim	130	305	495	675	
Sikh	100	150	250	400	
Others	20	40	55	85	

Membership in the UK (thousands)

Adapted from Brierley, P. (ed.) *Religious Trends 2000*, London: HarperCollins

*Trinitarian churches are those that accept a view of God as the three eternal persons: God the Father, God the Son and God the Holy Spirit. These are the great majority of Christian churches.

**Non-Trinitarian churches accept a range of different views of God. These include sects such as: Christian Scientists, the Church of Scientology, Jehovah's Witnesses, Mormons (Church of Jesus Christ of Latter Day Saints), Spiritualists and the Unification Church (Moonies).

Church attendance and experience in the UK, by gender

(%)	All	Men	Women	Christian	No religion
Regular churchgoer	15	11	19	28	1
Fringe churchgoer	3	3	4	6	1
Occasional churchgoer	7	6	8	11	3
Open de-churched [1]	5	3	6	7	2
Closed de-churched [2]	28	28	27	29	31
Open non-churched [3]	1	1	1	1	1
Closed non-churched [4]	32	38	27	18	57
Other religions	6	7	6	0	0
Unassigned	2	3	2	1	3

Source: Ashworth, J. and Farthing, I. (2007) *Churchgoing in the UK: A research report from Tearfund on church attendance in the UK*, Teddington: Tearfund

1 Open de-churched: former churchgoers who may return.
2 Closed de-churched: former churchgoers unlikely to return.
3 Open non-churched: have never been churchgoers but are likely to be in future.
4 Closed non-churched: never been to church and unlikely to do so.

Look carefully at the two tables.
The first shows membership of different religious organizations over the last 40 years.

1 Which religious organizations have made the most gains in membership since 1970? Suggest reasons for this.

2 Which have lost the most members Suggest reasons for this.

The second divides the UK population up in terms of their participation in religion and links this to gender.

3 What does this table show about the relationship between gender and religious participation? Suggest reasons why there may be a link between gender and religious participation?

Of course religious beliefs are individual. In a multi-cultural, multi-faith society like Britain today we are all free to express our beliefs however we wish and, as we have seen in previous topics, there are a wide variety of spiritual options available. However, as the exercise above demonstrates, it is still the case that religious belief and behaviour are related to social factors such as gender, ethnicity, social class and age. This topic explores these relationships and shows that social characteristics cannot be analysed in isolation from each other.

Gender

Feminism and religion

Simone de Beauvoir in her pioneering feminist book, *The Second Sex* (1953), saw the role of religion in a similar way to Marx. However, she saw it as oppressive to women in particular. Religion is used by the oppressors (men) to control the oppressed group (women). It also serves as a way of compensating women for their second-class status. Like Marx's proletariat, religion gives women the false belief that they will be compensated for their suffering on earth by equality in heaven. She concludes:

<< [Religion] gives her the guide, father, lover, divine guardian she longs for nostalgically; it feeds her daydreams; it fills her empty hours. But, above all, it confirms the social order, it justifies her resignation by giving hope of a better future in a sexless heaven. >>

El Sadaawi (1980), a Muslim feminist, does not blame religion in itself for its oppressive influences on women, but blames the patriarchal domination of religion that came with the development of **monotheistic** religions. Such religions, she argues, 'drew inspiration and guidance from the patriarchal and class societies prevalent at the time'. Men wrote their scriptures, and the interpretation of them was almost exclusively male-orientated. This has, on many occasions, enabled men to use religion as an abuse of power. In the 14th century, for example, the Catholic Church declared that women who treated illnesses without special training could be executed as witches. Clearly, the traditional remedies administered by women were seen as as a threat to the authority of the emerging male-dominated medical profession.

Is religion necessarily patriarchal?

It should not be assumed that all religions are equally oppressive to women and there have been some successful challenges to the patriarchal structure of organized religion. Gender-neutral language has been introduced in many hymns and prayers, and the requirement in the Christian marriage ceremony for the bride to promise to obey her husband is now also optional.

Leila Badawi (1994) has noted aspects of Islam that are positive for women, such as being able to keep their own family name when they marry. In fact, most converts to Islam are female. Numerous writers have highlighted how veiling (the covering of the entire face and hair in the company of men outside the family), rather than being a submission to patriarchy, is in fact a means of ethnic and gender assertiveness. Leila Ahmed (1992) suggests that the veil is a means by which Muslim women can become involved in modern society while maintaining a sense of modesty and correctness. As she puts it: '[Islamic dress] is a uniform of both transition and arrival, signalling entrance into and determination to move forward in modern society.'

Focus on research

Helen Watson (1994)
The meaning of veiling

According to the Qu'ran, women should exercise religious modesty or *hijab* because their seductiveness might lead men astray. Many writers, including some Islamic feminists, have argued that this has been misinterpreted by men to mean that women must cover their bodies and faces in the presence of men who are not relatives, with the patriarchal motive of controlling women. Western commentators also are critical of the practice, seeing it as evidence of repression. As Julie Burchill (2001) writing in *The Guardian* commented, 'such women carry round with them a mobile prison'.

Watson (1994), however, demonstrated that the veil also has the potential to liberate. She interviewed three Muslim women who had alternative perspectives on the practice of veiling. Nadia, a second-generation British Asian woman studying medicine at university, chose to start wearing a veil at 16. She commented, 'It is liberating to have the freedom of movement to be able to communicate without being on show'. She found that far from being invisible it made her stand out as a Muslim and also helped her to avoid 'lecherous stares or worse' from men. The second woman, Maryam, was a middle-aged Algerian living in France. Upon moving to France she felt it more appropriate to wear a veil. She commented that 'it is difficult enough to live in a big foreign city without having the extra burden of being molested in the street because you are a woman'. The third respondent, Fatima, was an older woman. She was less positive about veiling, seeing it as 'just a trend', but recognized that to turn against some of the less desirable Western values, e.g. the over-emphasis on women as sex objects, was a good thing. In her opinion veiling should be a matter of choice.

Adapted from Watson (1994) 'Women and the veil: personal responses to global process', in A. Ahmed and H. Donnan (eds) *Islam, Globalisation and Postmodernity*, London: Routledge

1 **What criticisms could be made of Watson's research?**

2 **How does Watson's work serve as a caution to sociologists who interpret the practices of unfamiliar religions in simplistic terms?**

Why are women more religious than men?

Whatever women's influence and status may have been in religious organizations, and despite a recent drift away from mainstream Christianity, studies have consistently shown that women are more religious than men. Miller and Hoffmann (1995) report that women:

- are more likely to express a greater interest in religion
- have a stronger personal religious commitment
- attend church more often.

Until relatively recently, these patterns appeared to hold true throughout life, irrespective of the kind of religious organization (cult, sect or church) or religious belief (astrology, magic, spirits, and so on). It is only during the last 20 years or so that women have begun to leave the church at a faster rate than men. According to Brierley (2006), between 1989 and 1998, more than 65 000 women were lost from churches each year, 57 per cent of all those leaving churches. From 1998 to 2005, the figure was slightly lower (51 000 per year) but throughout this time, women were leaving churches at about twice the rate of men.

Aune *et al.* (2008) cite a number reasons for the decline in church attendance and why certain women in particular are not going to church as much as they once did:

- *Fertility levels* – Women have fewer children and so the older generation lost from the church is not being replaced.
- *Feminist values* – Feminist values began influencing women in the 1960s and 1970s, challenging traditional Christian views about women's roles and raising women's aspirations.
- *Paid employment* – At the beginning of the 20th century, a third of women were in paid work; now, a century later, two-thirds are in the labour market. Juggling employment with childcare and housework causes time pressures and attending church is one activity to suffer.
- *Family diversity* – Compared to wider society, churches include fewer non-traditional families. Family forms which are growing, such as singleness, lone-parent families and cohabitation, are underprovided for and even discouraged by churches.
- *Sexuality* – The church's ambivalence towards sexuality is driving women to leave, feeling that the church requires them to deny or be silent about sexual desire and activity.

However, an explanation for the persistence of a greater degree of religious orientation among women overall is offered by Greeley (1992). He argues that before women acquire a partner and have children, their religiosity is not dissimilar to men's (although slightly more committed). But, 'once you start "taking care" of people, perhaps, you begin implicitly to assume greater responsibility for their "ultimate" welfare'. Greeley contends that women are more involved in caring than in practical responsibilities. Caring, it seems, tends to be associated with a more religious outlook.

Miller and Hoffmann (1995) identify two main explanations for such gender differences:

1 *Differential socialization* – Females are taught to be more submissive, passive, obedient and nurturing than males. These traits are compatible with religiosity, as such characteristics are highly esteemed by most religions. By the same token, men who internalize these norms tend to be more religious than men who do not.
2 *Differential roles* – Females have lower rates of participation in paid work and this, it is argued, gives women not only more time for church-related activities, but also a greater need for religion as a source of personal identity and commitment. They also have higher rates of participation in child-rearing, which in turn increases religiosity because it coincides with a concern for family wellbeing.

However, changes in women's roles are having an impact on their religious orientation. Linda Woodhead (2005), in attempting to explain the diversity of responses that modern women have begun to demonstrate towards religion, divides contemporary women into three groups:

1 *Home-centred women,* whose priority is their home and families, even if they engage in part-time work. They tend to be traditionally Christian because Christianity affirms their priorities.
2 *Jugglers,* who combine home and work. These women are more likely to be found in alternative spirituality because alternative spiritualities do most to help women who are negotiating private/public boundaries, affirming their commitments to their families while also endorsing female **empowerment** and the search for fulfilment outside the home.
3 *Work-centred women,* who are more likely to follow male patterns of religiosity, abandoning church because it doesn't fit with their demanding work schedules and taking on a more secular outlook.

Women and NRMs

Sects

Women tend to participate more in sects than men. Although it is difficult to estimate, Bruce (1995) has suggested that the ratio of female-to-male involvement is similar to that in established religion at about 2:1.

Women are more likely than men to experience poverty, and those who experience economic deprivation are more likely to join sects. As Thompson (1996) notes: 'They may not have the economic and social standing of others in society, but sect members have the promise of salvation and the knowledge that they are enlightened.'

Glock and Stark (1969) identify a number of different types of deprivation in addition to the economic, all of which are more likely to apply to women. They suggest that people who form or join sects may have experienced one or even a number of these.

- *Social deprivation* – This may stem from a lack of power, prestige and status. For example, if people experience a lack of satisfaction or status in employment, they may seek these goals via a religious sect. Those in unsatisfying lower-middle-class jobs (mainly occupied by women) may find satisfaction in the **evangelical goals** set by **conversionist** sects, such as Jehovah's Witnesses or Mormons.

- *Organismic deprivation* – This is experienced by those who suffer physical and mental problems (again more likely among women than men). For example, people may turn to sects in the hope of being healed or as an alternative to drugs or alcohol.
- *Ethical deprivation* – People may perceive the world to be in moral decline and so retreat into an **introversionist sect** that separates itself from the world, such as Jim Jones' People's Temple. Again, women tend to be more morally conservative than men.

In the 19th century, many sects were initiated by women: Ellen White set up the Seventh Day Adventists, Mary Baker Eddy founded Christian Science, Ann Lee founded the Shakers, and the Fox sisters began the Spiritualist movement.

Cults

Cults involve a highly individual, privatized version of religious activity. This is mainly involved with promoting a notion of personal 'improvement'. Even where wider issues are addressed (such as social problems of crime, unemployment or the destruction of the environment), the solutions offered tend to be couched in personal terms (meditation, greater consciousness, etc.). This 'private sphere' of cult activity relates to traditional gender roles for women, which are based in the 'private' arena of the home. Women are also more inclined to see in themselves a need for self-improvement.

Women and NAMs

Historically, wherever nature is conceptualized, the role of women has been seen in terms of their 'essential femininity', that is, as being naturally different creatures to males – more attuned to the supposed natural rhythms of life. Thus, within the philosophies of New Age cults, women tend to be afforded a much higher status than men. This is one reason that may explain higher female involvement in NAMs, as many of them emphasize the 'natural', such as herbal and homeopathic remedies, aromatherapy and massage. Research by Glendinning and Bruce (2006) confirms that middle-class women more often than men subscribe to alternative therapies associated with NAMs, such as yoga and meditation, whereas younger working-class women more often believe in astrology and fortune-telling.

Women and fundamentalism

The resurgence of religious fundamentalism over the past decade has played a major role in attempting to reverse the trend of women's increasing autonomy and their pursuit of fulfilment beyond motherhood.

- In the USA, opposition to women controlling their fertility through abortion has sometimes ended in violence, with right-wing, religious pro-life groups adopting near terrorist tactics to close clinics down.
- Despite India's long history of reform and modernization, the rise of Hindu fundamentalism has made it difficult for governments there to intervene in

family life or encourage greater freedom for women, despite their commitment to preventing the oppression of members of lower castes.

- Fundamentalist groups in Iran, Israel, Afghanistan and elsewhere similarly insist on ruthlessly conserving or reinstating women's traditional positions.

Cohen and Kennedy (2000) suggest that 'the desire to restore fundamentalist religious values and social practices is associated with the fear that any real increase in women's freedom of choice and action will undermine the foundations of tradition, religion, morality and, it could be argued, male control'.

Women's traditional roles centre around childrearing and the home. They are thus responsible for transmitting religious values from one generation to the next and upholding all that is most sacred in the lives of family members. Fundamentalism, both in the West (such as the Christian Right or the **Nation of Islam** in the USA) and elsewhere, has often emphasized the significance of protecting and defending women. The spin-off is that this re-empowers men by removing some of the **ambiguities** that have been associated with the modern world. But, as feminists assert, the apparent position of importance such women experience in upholding the faith, brings with it powerlessness and sometimes abuse at the hands of husbands and kinsmen.

However, not all women are unwilling victims of the return to traditional roles – as the work on Muslim women and veiling demonstrates. Research by Woodhead and Heelas (2000) shows how women converting to orthodox Judaism in the US are actually attracted by the status in the home that it provides them with. Such women can also be seen as seeking to remove the ambiguities of modernity, as they perceive them.

Ethnicity

Clear evidence of greater religiosity among ethnic minorities comes from the first detailed Home Office survey of the nation's belief (O'Beirne 2004). When asked what they considered important to their identity, religion was cited tenth by White Christians behind family, work, age, interests, education, nationality, gender, income and social class. For Black people, 70 per cent of whom say they are Christian, religion was third, while Asians placed it second, only behind family. People of mixed race ranked their religion seventh.

There are various possible reasons why immigrants to Britain have placed a greater emphasis on religion than the long-established population:

- People had high levels of belief before migration and, as Weber (1920) has suggested, being members of deprived groups, they tended to be more religious. Religion provides an explanation for disadvantage and possibly offers hope of salvation, if not elsewhere on earth then in the afterlife.
- Religion helps bond new communities – particularly when under threat. As Durkheim (1912/1961) has argued, it provides members with a sense of shared

norms and values, symbolized through rituals that unite them as a distinctive social group.

However, religion has also become a basis for conflicts between cultures. The dominant culture often sees minority cultures in a negative light, as there is the feeling that newcomers to British society should **assimilate**. Ethnic-minority issues, such as arranged marriages, and the growth in the number of religious temples and mosques (while many Christian churches have closed) suggest an unwillingness to assimilate and have created resentment from the host community. However, many second- and third-generation ethnic-minority Britons were born in the UK and their refusal to assimilate fully has led to a re-evaluation of what being British actually means.

In studying religion and ethnicity, it is clear that religions offer much more than just spiritual fulfilment. They have the power to reaffirm the ethnic identity of their adherents, albeit in uniquely different ways – as is clear from Table 1.4 below.

Religion and ethnic identity

While there are significant differences in religiosity within the Asian and African-Caribbean communities, it is possible to make some initial generalizations about them. African-Caribbeans were mainly Christian on arrival in the UK, but when they tried to join existing religious institutions, they often had to come to terms with the racism displayed by the church and its congregations, a racism pervasive in British society at the time. On the other hand, Hindus, Sikhs and Muslims (for whom religion was part of their 'difference') had virtually no existing religious organizations and places of worship in Britain to join. They had to make a collective effort to establish and practise their faith in a radically new social setting. As Modood *et al.* (1994) point out, for Asians their religion was intricately connected with their status as an ethnic group, but this was not the case for African-Caribbeans (see Table 1.5).

Below: Worshippers at a Pentecostal service. How do you account for the growth of Pentecostal churches in the UK?

Even for those who saw their Christianity as part of family tradition and culture, their religion was not significantly part of their sense of ethnic difference.

Nonetheless, distinctively African-Caribbean forms of Christian spirituality in both the mainstream churches and in the Black-led churches have mushroomed in the past 20 years, as some African-Caribbeans have sought to establish their own churches. Many have adopted an evangelical affiliation to Christianity, which stresses belief in personal conversion and the factual accuracy of the Bible alongside a commitment to seek new converts. Such Christianity, practised by the **charismatic** and **Pentecostal** movements has grown dramatically over the last decade.

An average of three new churches a week have been started since 1998 (Christian Research 2006) – half this growth is from ethnic-minority churches, especially Black churches. Quite apart from African-Caribbean Pentecostalism in the UK, evangelical movements have drawn millions of Africans to Christian churches across the continent of Africa and, since 2001, a third of all immigrants to Britain have come from Africa. There has also been a growth of Chinese, Croatian, Portuguese and Tamil churches, especially in London. However, at the same time,

Table 1.4 Differences in the significance of religion for first-generation Asian and African-Caribbean migrants to Britain		
	African-Caribbean	**Asian**
Role of religion	Religion is used as a means of coping with the worries and the pressures of life through the joyful nature of prayer, as much through its immediacy and mood-affecting quality as its long-term contribution to personal development.	Asian groups tend to speak of control over selfish desires and of fulfilling one's responsibilities to others, especially family members. Prayer is seen in terms of duty, routine and the patterning of their lives.
Religion and family life	Used to develop trust, love, mutual responsibilities and the learning of right and wrong within the context of the family. African-Caribbeans express an individualistic or voluntaristic view of religion. Children should decide for themselves whether they maintain religious commitment into adulthood.	Used in a similar way, but Asians tend to adopt a collective or conformist approach. The expectation of parents is that their children will follow in adulthood the religion they have been brought up in; not to do so is to betray one's upbringing or to let one's family down.
Religion and social life	Little importance beyond fostering and maintaining a spiritual, moral and ethical outlook. The church offers opportunities to socialize and to organize social events in an otherwise privatized community of member families.	Muslims tend to see conformity to Islamic law and Islam as a comprehensive way of life, affecting attitudes to alcohol, food, dress and choice of marriage partner. The influence of religion is less extreme for most Sikhs and Hindus, but its importance for the first generation is still great.

Adapted from Modood, T., Beishon, S. and Virdee, S. (1994) *Changing Ethnic Identities*, London: Policy Studies Institute

slightly more than three churches a week have closed. Changes in the composition of practising Christians is, therefore, coming mainly from an increase in ethnic-minority and Pentecostal churches. In 2005, 17 per cent of churchgoers were from non-White ethnic groups, an increase from 12 per cent in 1998. Pentecostal churches have replaced Methodist churches as the third largest Christian denomination and were the only denomination that grew in the period 1998 to 2005 (Brierley 2006). Half of Pentecostal churches are predominantly Black (ESRC Society Today 2006). While the Roman Catholic Church lost the greatest number and proportion of members of any denomination from 1998 to 2005, there has also been a growth in the membership of particular Catholic churches – for example, there appears to be revitalization of some inner-city Catholic communities as a result of migration from Eastern Europe, especially Poland (reported in Bates 2006).

Differences in styles of worship

While worship in Anglican churches is dominated by older people and women, and demands limited formal involvement of the congregation, Pentecostal church congregations comprise every age group and an equal balance of the sexes. There is a greater emphasis on religious experience than **religious dogma**, and worship is concerned with demonstrating publicly the joyous nature of religious conversion and the power of religion to heal people, both physically and mentally. Considerable involvement is required from worshippers in the form of dancing and 'call and response' between congregation and clergy.

Bird (1999) suggests that Pentecostalism has played a dual role for African-Caribbean people:

1   For some, it has enabled them to cope with and adjust to a racist and unjust society. It serves as an 'opium' for the people, as Marx has suggested. Beckford (2000) also suggests that evangelical Christianity gives Black people a sense of hope and independence.
2   For others, such as Pryce (1979), it encourages hard work, sexual morality, prudent management of finances and strong support of the family and community. In this sense, it reflects the Protestant ethic that Weber saw as essential in the development of capitalism (see Topic 2).

Evangelical churches – both Black and White – have also grown in popularity, in part due to their populist approach and innovative marketing strategies. Members preach the gospel intensely and seek converts in a way that other British Christians do not. The mainly White evangelical churches have developed the 'Alpha course', a movement that has gained two million converts in the UK and ten million worldwide. Other evangelical churches run inspirational radio and TV stations. At worship, their services are filled with popular-style music and videos aimed at the younger generation.

Age

When examining the position of members of ethnic minorities born in Britain, Modood et al. (1994) found that there appears to be an overall decline in the importance of religion for all of the main ethnic groups, and fewer said they observed the various rules and requirements. Even those who said that religion was important wished to interpret their religious traditions and scriptures flexibly. Also, fewer second-generation respondents regularly attended a place of religious worship. The least religiously committed were Sikhs. When asked how they saw themselves, virtually none of the second-generation Punjabis spontaneously said 'Sikh'. However, a decade earlier, Beatrice Drury studied a much larger sample of 16- to 20-year-old Sikh girls and found that, if prompted, all saw their Sikh identity as fundamental (reported in Drury 1991).

This reflects similar trends amongst the majority ethnic group. Aside from a growth in membership of some evangelical, mainly ethnic-minority churches, described above, attendance amongst under 20s in mainstream Christian churches has about halved since 1980. Buddhists, closely followed by Christians, are the group with the smallest percentage of young members (Christian Research 2004). There is also evidence of a general dislike of the church, especially in its institutional form. Peter Brierley (2002) found that 87 per cent of 10 to 14 year olds thought church was boring.

According to Voas and Crockett (2005), younger generations are becoming less and less religious, and it could be that 'believing without belonging' (an idea proposed by Davie (1994) that people still have religious belief but no longer choose to express it formally through church membership) is giving way to no belief at all. Older people are most likely to describe themselves as religious, middle-aged people as spiritual and young people as neither.

But despite their claims to religious indifference, some kind of belief or spirituality appears to be continuing among young people. Recent research by Mayo (2005), Smith (2005) and Rankin (2005) seems to suggest that they are interested in spiritual matters, but that they attribute to the term 'spiritual', a wider variety of meanings, appreciated among themselves, rather than ascribe to those proposed by official religious or spiritual representatives. Rankin (2005) noted the reluctance of young people to identify aspects of their experience as spiritual, but when opportunities were offered for discussion, it became clear that the young people were engaged in the same kinds of soul searching that older people call 'spiritual'.

Young Muslims

Whilst increasing reluctance to demonstrate religiosity was apparent among most young people of all ethnic backgrounds, this trend has become less clear cut in the case of young Muslims. There appears to be a re-emphasis on Islamic identity arising in the wake of perceived injustice. In a PEW poll of 2006, 72 per cent of Muslims of all ages in the UK said they believed that Muslims have a very strong (28 per cent) or fairly strong (44 per cent) sense of Islamic identity, and 77 per cent felt that this sense of identity was increasing.

Some argue that 'Muslim' has become a new ethnicity. According to Samad (2004), 'as South Asian linguistic skills are lost, identification with Pakistan and Bangladesh – countries that young people may only briefly visit – becomes less significant and being Muslim as an identity becomes more important'. Archer (2003) also finds that a strong Muslim identity provides an alternative to the gang and drug cultures of the 'street'. It is a way to resist stereotypes of 'weakness and passivity' and can provide a positive role model as an alternative identity that young Muslims can have pride in.

Though exaggerated by the media, the so-called radicalization of Muslim youth, where it has occurred, is due, according to Choudhury (2007), to a lack of religious literacy and education. He argues that this appears to be a common feature among those drawn to extremist groups. The most vulnerable are those who have been prompted by recent world events to explore their faith for the first time, yet are not in a position to evaluate objectively whether the radical group before them represents an accurate understanding of Islam. Akthar (2005) argued that after 9/11 and the wars in Afghanistan and Iraq, radical Islamic groups were able to exploit the view of a simple dichotomy of oppressors and oppressed – the West versus Islam, which puts the blame for all of the problems faced by Muslims under the same banner. Ironically, according to Hopkins and Kahani-Hopkins (2004), it is also those who are religiously astute as well as academically inclined who have been susceptible to radicalization. They cite how leaders of the banned extremist group Al-Muhajiroun, for example, identify young university students who suffer from a sense of blocked social mobility, as their most important recruitment pool. They suggest that it is this group that believes that they face a discriminatory system preventing them from realizing their potential. Analysis of the 2004 Home Office Citizenship survey showed that for Muslims, perceptions of discrimination, rather than socio-economic status, affect their sense of belonging and attachment to Britain.

However, according to Choudhury (2007) there are also signs of a progressive 'British Muslim' identity forming, partly as a reaction to violent radicalism, which is receptive to Western influences and demonstrates a desire to take a full part in British society.

Young Muslim women

This certainly appears to be the case with regard to young Muslim women, often commented on for their apparent submissiveness and repression, who have actually adapted well to the challenge of maintaining their cultural and religious identity, while at the same time becoming effective, well-integrated members of mainstream society. A number of studies such as that of Butler (1995) have explored this **cultural hybridity**. Recent research shows how veiling and the wearing of traditional dress may actually give Muslim girls greater freedom from patriarchal attitudes experienced by many White girls. (This was discussed further in Topic 6.) Research by Knott and Khoker (1993) and Samad (2006)

suggests that many young South Asian Muslim women draw a distinction between 'religion' and 'culture', in contrast to their parents who, in their view, mistakenly confuse the two. Furthermore, they reject their parents' conformity to cultural traditions whilst at the same time fully embracing their Muslim identity. Dwyer (1999), whose research involved interviewing 35 young Muslim women, aged 13 to 18, found that, for them, their Muslim identity is a source used to resist parental opinion and challenge family prohibitions. They are able to use what is actually in the Muslim texts rather than the culturally biased, received wisdoms, to challenge their parents' attempts to restrict their behaviour. For example, by showing themselves to be 'good Muslims', they gained greater freedom to pursue other interests. Individuals were able to argue that not only should they be able to dress in a style which was both 'Western' and 'Islamic', but that they should have greater freedoms to go out, or to go on to higher education and be fully involved in the choice of marriage partner. Woodhead (2007) goes as far as to suggest that many young Muslim women have developed, as she puts it, 'a careful and often lavish attention to style, mixed with a very deliberate nod to faith', which she terms 'Muslim chic', creatively asserting their Muslim identity, whilst at the same, making a commitment to a British national identity.

Social class

Churches

Recent research by the Christian charity Tearfund (Ashworth and Farthing 2007) demonstrates that churchgoing is associated with those of higher social classes. For both sexes, professionals and senior and middle management have an above-average frequency of churchgoers, whilst skilled, semi-skilled and unskilled manual have the lowest proportion. Many of those dependent on the state, through sickness, unemployment or old age, are open to attending, but often are unable to do so.

The Church of England has always been seen as middle or upper class, having had a close relationship with the monarchy and state. The monarch, members of parliament and other dignitaries are frequently seen at religious ceremonies such as Remembrance Day services. This was more tolerated in the past as working-class membership went hand in hand with **deference** to the middle classes generally, and the adoption of middle-class cultural standards was expected as a mark of decency and respectability. The middle classes went to church and so 'decent' working-class people did too. The greater decline in working-class attendance may, therefore, reflect changes in the relationship between the classes, where deference is no longer expected or given.

In addition, the middle classes tend to be more geographically mobile and this can have an impact on churchgoing. Research for *Religious Trends* showed that while churchgoing is in decline, there are pockets of growth in prosperous areas: 9.6 per cent of people in wealthier areas went to church compared to 5.9 per cent in the poorest areas. According to Brierley (1999), the church offers people new to an area an opportunity to become part of the community. The 'flip side' was that working-class people in poorer areas felt alienated from a church they perceived to be middle class.

Sects

Many sects require members to donate their 'worldly goods'. The middle class tend to be rather more willing to renounce theirs, than the working classes who have never experienced such a lifestyle. On the other hand, some sects appeal to the underprivileged, offering a theodicy of ultimate salvation in a world they experience as offering few rewards. This could explain the appeal of world-rejecting sects to some members of ethnic minorities or young social 'drop-outs'.

Relative deprivation can also explain the appeal of Islamic fundamentalism to those who have been upwardly mobile. Bruce (2002) argues that a sense of a weakening community due to the modernizing influence of Western morality, leaves some feeling relatively deprived. A return to traditional principles is an attempt to reclaim the past and redress the balance.

Cults

The composition of New Age cults is overwhelmingly middle class. As Bruce (1995) argues, spiritual growth appeals mainly to those whose more pressing material needs have been satisfied but who feel there may be more to life. Bruce further maintains that New Age cults appeal specifically to 'university-educated middle classes working in the "expressive professions": social workers, counsellors, actors, writers, artists, and others whose education and work cause them to have an articulate interest in human potential'.

The appeal of NRMs and NAMs

For sociologists, one of the most interesting questions is why people join or support NRMs.

Spiritual void

Since the decline in the importance of established religion, people have been seeking alternative belief systems to explain the world and its difficulties. In addition, as postmodernists argue, there is also an increased cynicism about the ability of science to provide solutions to these problems.

Drane (1999) argues that Western societies are turning against modern institutions and belief systems. Modern rationality is increasingly being blamed for disasters such as the World Wars, the Holocaust, numerous other bloody conflicts, weapons of mass destruction, the depletion of the ozone layer, potentially dangerous genetically modified crops and global warming. People have lost faith in

institutions such as the medical profession, which is now seen as more likely to misdiagnose or even cause illness through new diseases, such as MRSA or CDiff (clostridium difficile), rather than improve the health and welfare of those they treat. Churches are considered to have done little to fill the spiritual void left by wholesale adoption of modern belief systems.

In the absence of either **grand narrative** (religion or science), people may seek to acquire a personal rationale. This can involve a process of 'spiritual shopping', trying out the various alternatives until they find a belief system that makes sense to them. People in the New Age are free to choose whatever fulfils them and have access to a huge range of spiritual and therapeutic products.

Pragmatic motives

Motivations for affiliation with world-affirming groups can be very practical – financial success and a happier life, for example. These **pragmatic motives** are not the sort that many religious people would recognize and this is probably one of the main reasons why the religious nature of many NRMs is questioned.

Marginality

Weber (1920/1963) pointed out how those marginalized by society may find status and/or a legitimizing explanation for their situation through a theodicy that offers ultimate salvation. This could explain the appeal of world-rejecting sects to some members of ethnic minorities or young social 'drop-outs'.

Relative deprivation

People may be attracted to an NRM because it offers something lacking in the social experience of the seeker – whether spiritual or emotional fulfilment. This could explain the appeal of NRMs to certain members of the middle class, who feel their lives lack spiritual meaning.

The appeal to the young of world-rejecting movements

Many young people are no longer children but lack adult commitments, such as having their own children. Being unattached is an outcome of the increasing gap between childhood and adulthood which, as Wallis (1984) has argued, has been further extended by the gradual lengthening of education and wider accessibility of higher education. It is to these unattached groups that world-rejecting movements appeal. They try to provide some certainty to a community of people who face similar problems and difficulties. What seems to be particularly appealing is the offer of radical and immediate solutions to social and personal problems.

Barker, in her famous study *The Making of a Moonie* (1984), found that most members of the Unification Church (the 'Moonies') came from happy and secure middle-class homes, with parents whose jobs involved some sort of commitment to public service, such as doctors, social workers or teachers. She argued that the sect offered a **surrogate** family in which members could find support and comfort beyond the family, while fulfilling their desire to serve a community, in the same way as their parents did in the wider society. High patterns of drop-out from NRMs suggest that the need they fulfil is temporary.

The appeal of world-affirming movements

World-affirming groups appeal to those who are likely to have finished education, are married, have children and a mortgage. There are two issues in the modern world that add to the appeal of world-affirming movements:

1   As Weber suggested, the modern world is one in which rationality dominates – that is, one in which magical, unpredictable and ecstatic experiences are uncommon.
2   There is tremendous pressure (e.g. through advertising) to become materially, emotionally and sexually successful.

According to Bird (1999), world-affirming sects simultaneously do three things that address these issues:

1   They provide a spiritual component in an increasingly rationalized world.
2   They provide techniques and knowledge to help people become wealthy, powerful and successful.

3   They provide techniques and knowledge which allow people to work on themselves to bring about personal growth.

In some ways, there are common issues that motivate both the young and old. They both live in societies where there is great pressure to succeed and hence great fear of failure. Religious movements can provide both groups with a means to deal with the fear of failure by providing techniques that lead to personal success.

Furthermore, New Age and other world-affirming movements, in particular, fit with the tendency within modern society towards greater individualism, a focus on self-improvement and personal indulgence. As Bruce 2002 suggests, people today feel more empowered to change what they are not personally happy about, by spending money upon themselves in ways which would, in relatively recent times past, have seemed selfish. Gym memberships, health spas, counselling, alternative therapies, as well as the rapidly growing number of tourism centres (e.g. yoga retreats) focusing on wellbeing and personal growth, are evidence of this trend.

Key terms

Ambiguities uncertain issues, having more than one meaning.

Assimilate blend in and integrate.

Charismatic movements religious movements that believe that some individuals have gifts of the Holy Spirit, such as healing powers and the ability to speak in tongues.

Conversionist religious groups whose aim is to convert people to their faith.

Cultural hybridity to mix and match different cultural influences.

Deference respect to those defined as superior

Empowerment to be given greater power and recognition.

Evangelical goals the aim of converting others to your faith.

Grand narrative belief system, such as religion or science, that claims to explain the world.

Inclusive all encompassing.

Introversionist sect world-rejecting sect.

Monotheism belief in one god.

Nation of Islam Black, radical, American Islamic organization.

Patriarchal male-dominated.

Pentecostal movement various fundamentalist Christian congregations whose members seek to be filled with the Holy Spirit (emulating the experience of the Apostles at Pentecost).

Pragmatic motives desire to acquire personally beneficial practical outcomes.

Religious dogma rules and regulations, commandments and formal requirements of a particular religion.

Rites customary religious practices, e.g. baptism.

Surrogate replacement.

Check your understanding

1   Check your understanding
2   How do feminists view the role of religion?
3   What evidence is there for women's greater religiosity?
4   What explanations have been given for women's religiosity?
5   What reasons are given for women's greater involvement in NRMs?
6   Give two reasons why immigrants to the UK have placed a greater emphasis on religion than the indigenous population.
7   What role does Pentecostalism play for African-Caribbean believers?
8   What in general appears to be the trend in terms of the religiosity of young people of all ethnic groups?
9   How does the work of Rankin and others question such trends?
10 Why have many second-generation Asians chosen to hold on to their religious identity?
11 What is the relationship between churchgoing and social class and why does it exist?
12 Give three reasons for the appeal of NRMs and NAMs.
13 What is the relationship between age, social attachment and the appeal of NRMs?

Activities

Research idea

Conduct a short survey among your peers to identify any relationships between religious beliefs and behaviour and gender, ethnicity, and social class.

Web.task

Find the results of he Home Office Citizenship Survey at **www.homeoffice.gov.uk /rds/pdfs04/hors274.pdf** How was the survey carried out? Choose any one aspect of the findings and summarise them as a report for the rest of your class.

An eye on the exam — Religion and social position

The two ways need to be stated clearly, probably at the beginning of paragraphs

This term refers to the extent to which an individual or group are religious. It can refer to belief or participation in any type of religious organization

Aim to write for about 15 minutes, spending a roughly equal amount on each of the two ways

(a) Identify and explain two ways in which religiosity is influenced by age. **(17 marks)**

Each of the two ways need to be discussed in depth, using sociological concepts, examples and studies if possible

You can refer to any age group

The relationship between gender and religious belief and participation needs to be described in some detail, using sociological concepts and studies

Remember that 'religious' can be measured in many different ways

(b) Outline and evaluate the reasons why women appear to be more religious than men. **(33 marks)**

The reasons for women's greater religious belief and participation need to be weighed up against each other

Aim to write at least two sides of the answer book in about 30 minutes

Grade booster — Getting top marks in this question

Writers such as Miller and Hoffman, Greeley and Woodhead are likely to figure in good answers. There may also be discussion of why women's religiosity should be greater than men's, bearing in mind the feminist criticism of some organized religion as patriarchal. The best answers will differentiate between types of religious organization, for example between women's participation in churches and new religious movements. A key evaluative point centres on the links between age, gender, social class and ethnicity when attempting to explain the relationship between social position and religiosity.

TOPIC 4

The strength of religion in society

Getting you thinking

Left: The Baitul Futuh mosque, the largest in Western Europe, built in 2003 in the south-west London suburb of Morden

Centre: a former church now housing a carpet warehouse

Right: a former cinema in Woolwich, London, now being used as an evangelical church

Variation between groups

According to the 2004 Home Office Citizenship Survey:

- Only 10 per cent of 16 to 24 year olds say they 'belong to a religion'. The equivalent for those aged 25 to 49 is 43 per cent, and for the over 50s it is 47 per cent.
- 19 per cent of women are frequent or regular churchgoers, compared with 11 per cent of men. Congregations generally reflect a 2:1 split. Among those declaring no religious affiliation the split is 2:3.
- 16 per cent of the middle classes attend church compared with 12 per cent of the working class, yet of the non-attenders, more members of the middle class are non-believers.
- Minority-ethnic groups are generally more religious than Whites. Whites ranked religion as the 10th most important indicator of their identity, compared with Asian and Black respondents, who cited it as second and third respectively.

1   How do the photographs above challenge or support the view that religion in the contemporary UK is declining in significance?

2   What types of religion in Britain appear to be declining and which thriving?

3   Suggest reasons why the variations in religiosity outlined above exist.

4   What may the implications of these patterns be for the future religiosity of British society?

It is difficult to make conclusive statements about religious commitment. The complexity of operationalizing – defining and measuring – religious belief and religious activity (see Topic 1) has long haunted sociologists, particularly those concerned with judging whether or not religion is in decline in the modern world – the process known as **secularization**. This topic outlines some of the problems faced by sociologists in assessing this process and also looks at the actual evidence for and against secularization.

In order to judge whether secularization is or is not taking place, sociologists need to define and measure key concepts, such as religion and religious belief, as well as secularization itself. This is by no means straightforward.

Whether you adopt a substantive definition of religion, which requires a belief in a supernatural force, or whether you consider that religion can be defined merely in terms of societal effect – i.e. you adopt a functional definition – will have an impact upon whether or not you believe secularization is occurring.

As Wilson (1982) has pointed out, those who define religion in substantive terms are more likely to argue that religious belief has declined as people accept other more rational explanations of the world. But those who see religion in functional terms are more likely to reject this view. If the functions of religion are essential to the smooth running of society, they argue, even though religion may change, these functions still need to be fulfilled. What we call religion must simply remain in some form or another to fulfil them.

Furthermore, as the figures in the 'Getting you thinking' opposite illustrate, patterns of religious commitment vary between groups. If certain ethnic groups are religious, but only constitute a small percentage of the population, it may be said that they have little impact on the society as a whole. But, if they are confined to a particular geographical region, then that area may appear to be much more religious and the impact of religion stronger there. If women are more religious than men, they may have more influence on young children. Though the young are generally less religiously affiliated – that is, they tend not to be members of religious organizations – how can we know whether they express religious beliefs privately at home?

Defining secularization

Wilson (1966) provides the following 'classic' definition of secularization: 'the process whereby religious thinking, practices and institutions lose social significance'. This seems a general enough catch-all statement, and is one that has been widely adopted, but problems occur straight away. What exactly is 'religious thinking'? What is meant by 'significance'? How can you measure them?

Measuring religious belief and practice

There is no clear definition of the boundaries of religious belief. Is a belief in fate or luck a religious belief? What about belief in ghosts or guardian angels? If they are, then an awful lot of people share such beliefs and may be termed 'religious'. *Most Haunted* is a British paranormal television programme based on investigating purported paranormal activity. Since 2002, it has been a popular show on satellite and cable channels, primarily for the UK market. Live shows every Halloween attract millions of viewers. It has a dedicated website and significant DVD sales.

There are also problems in measuring religious commitment. In the UK, 33 per cent of people say religion is very important personally (Pew Global Attitudes Project 2002). Does this mean, for example, that for a third of the population, religion has a significant impact upon behaviour? Furthermore, is such religiously influenced behaviour increasing or decreasing?

Church attendance

Declining church attendance has been used as a common indicator of secularization occurring in the UK – Sunday attendance having halved between 1967 and 2006.

However, does this necessarily indicate a reduction in the religiosity of society? Hamilton (2001) points out that the notion of an 'age of faith' in the past is an illusion partly created as a result of concentrating on the religious behaviour of the elite, about which we have more information than the vast majority of ordinary people. This may mean that the past was no more or less religious than the present, as the spiritual life of most people went unrecorded.

Until relatively recently, the religious sentiments of the religious minority restricted non-religious behaviour on Sundays. Before trading laws were relaxed in 1994, options were limited and the decision to attend church was unchallenged by the availability of significantly fewer alternatives. Nowadays, people may still believe, but have a lot more options on a Sunday. Greater levels of personal freedom and individualism may be causing people to see churches as inappropriate these days because they think that religion is a private matter. On the other hand, those who attend church may do so for reasons other than religion: to appear respectable or to make new friends or perhaps to get their child into a denominational school with a good academic reputation.

Is secularization best measured through church attendance anyway? There has undoubtedly been a decline in attendance, at least among Christians in Britain, but Britain is now a multicultural and multifaith society. To assume secularization on the basis of an analysis of the fortunes of Christianity is to dismiss the importance of other major world faiths supported in Britain. Also, at the global level, some social changes are enhancing the importance of religion. Many young Muslims have returned to Islam having been politicized by the widespread perception that Islam is under attack globally.

Glock and Stark (1968) argue that not enough attention has been paid to the detail of defining religion and religiosity, and that, because of this, the secularization thesis cannot be accurately tested. Indeed, the same empirical evidence can be used by different researchers to 'prove' both that secularization 'is' or 'is not' occurring. Martin (1978) has actually advocated the removal of the term 'secularization' from the sociological vocabulary, instead supporting the careful and detailed study of the ways in which the role of religion has changed at different times and different places.

However, despite the difficulties, a large body of sociological literature has emerged involving a debate between two groups of writers on opposite sides of the discussion who have sought to engage with the evidence on some level.

What is the evidence for secularization?

Church attendance and membership

It is likely that declining attendance is, at least to some extent, reflecting a decline in the significance of religion for many people. The growth in evangelical or non-Christian religious practice, and increased membership of New Religious movements have not countered the millions lost from the established churches.

However, the fall in numbers of those in the Christian community is not as rapid as the fall in church attenders. Figures from the 2001 census suggest that the proportion of the population who claim affiliation to Christianity remains high, at 72 per cent, though down from 76 per cent in 1980. Meanwhile, Sunday attendance has fallen from 1.2 million to 850 000 in the same period.

Table 1.5 Percentage of all churchgoers by age group 1979–98			
Age	1979	1989	1998
Under 15	26	25	19
15 to 29	20	17	15
30 to 64	36	39	41
65 and over	18	19	25

Source: Brierley, P. (ed.) (2000)

Age bias

Brierley also points out that the gross figures of decline hide a trend even more worrying for the future of organized Christianity in Britain: age bias. For each of his three English surveys (1979, 1989, 1999), he estimates the age profile of the various groups of denominations. With the exception of the Pentecostal churches, he notes the increasing percentage of the congregations in the older age groups being matched by the declining percentages of younger people – see Table 1.5. This could mean that as congregations age, and fewer and fewer young people join them, they could eventually die out altogether.

Reduced moral influence

Davies (2004) suggests that the UK population in the 21st century is no longer guided by the kinds of collective moral codes and community emphasis once promoted by the church, Sunday schools and voluntary youth and community organizations. He points to the beginning of the 20th century as a turning point, when **individualism** progressively took over, particularly from the late 1950s onwards as the family and working-class community changed. Moral judgements, he argues, became more about minimizing personal harm than taking on board the thoughts and feelings of the wider, generally Christian community. Davies suggests that this is the reason for the increasing acceptance of divorce, illegitimacy, and homosexuality and dramatic increases in crime rates.

Furthermore, as Terry Sanderson (1999), a spokesman for the National Secular Society, put it, the church even seems to be losing its 'core business', that is, to 'hatch, match and dispatch' (i.e. baptize, marry and bury people):

- Weddings now only make up approximately 40 per cent of marriages compared with about 75 per cent 30 years ago (Brierley 2001).
- In the early 1930s, seven out of ten of all children were baptized into the Church of England. More than a third were still christened in the early 1980s. Latest figures (Church of England 2005) show that the proportion has fallen to 1 in 7.
- The Church of England carried out 207 300 funerals in 2005, down from 232 550 funerals in 2000, when figures were first collected, as increasing numbers opt for 'celebration-of-life' ceremonies rather than church services.

Lower status of clergy

As the number of clergy has fallen, their pay and status have declined. As Bruce (2001) states, the number of

clergy is a useful indicator of the social power and popularity of religion. In 1900, there were over 45 000 clerics in Britain; this had declined to just over 34 000 in 2000, despite the fact that the population had almost doubled. In a patriarchal society, the very fact that women are now being ordained may in itself reduce the perceived status of the clergy.

Societal aspects of secularization

Bryan Wilson (1966) and others – notably, Bruce (1996) and Wallis (1984) – cite other evidence for secularization in addition to statistics. They argue that secularization is a development rooted in modernity and focus on three key processes: **rationalization**, **disengagement**, and **religious pluralism**.

Desacrilization and rationalization

This is the idea that the sacred has little or no place in contemporary Western society – the world is no longer seen as being in the control of supernatural forces. Instead, humans are viewed as in control of their own destiny, and with the advent of biotechnology, humans have the opportunity to 'play God'. Our consciousness has been secularized. This growth of **rational** or scientific thinking is seen as a clear indicator of secularization. This approach is particularly associated with Weber, who saw **desacrilization** as the 'disenchantment of the world' – the world losing its mystery and magic. It is suggested that rational thinking in the form of science has replaced religious influence in our lives, because scientific progress has resulted in higher living standards. Moreover, science has produced convincing explanations for phenomena that were once the province of religion, such as how the world was created.

Further, Berger (1973) has suggested that Christianity has ultimately been its own gravedigger. Protestantism focused attention on this life, work and the pursuit of prosperity, rather than on the domain of God and the afterlife.

Disengagement

The disengagement, or separation, of the church from wider society is an important aspect of secularization. The church is no longer involved in important areas of social life, such as politics, and has become disengaged from wider society.

People are now more concerned with their material standard of living, rather than with spiritual welfare, and are more likely to take moral direction from a variety of sources other than the church. Steve Bruce (1995) uses the term 'social differentiation' in pointing out that the church now has much less opportunity to involve itself in non-religious spheres. It has, therefore, become differentiated and assigned to more specialized roles. Religious faith and morality become less and less significant in the culture and institutions of modern societies: Hamilton (2001) has suggested that churches themselves have secularized in an attempt to compromise with those who have rejected more traditional beliefs. For example, he argues the Church of England no longer supports ideas of the Virgin Birth, Hell or even God as a real external force.

Religious pluralism

Bruce (1996) suggests that industrialization has fragmented society into a marketplace of religions and other community organizations. Wilson (1966) argues that, as a result, religion no longer acts as a unifying force in society as social life becomes more fragmented. He points to the **ecumenical movement** as an attempt by institutionalized religion to reverse secularization because such unification only occurs when religious influence is weak. In particular, the growth in the number of sects, cults and NRMs has also been seen by Wilson as evidence of secularization. He argues that sects are 'the last outpost of religion in a secular society' and are a symptom of religion's decline. Competition between religions is seen to undermine their credibility as they compete for 'spiritual shoppers' (see p. 187). Bruce (2002) also interprets the growth of sects as evidence of secularization, as they further undermine the authority of the established church on central issues of moral concern. Religious pluralism is therefore seen as evidence of religion's weakening influence. The established church, along with NRMs and new denominations in the UK, simply lacks credibility.

Religion in the USA: the Religious Economy Theory

On the other hand, the situation in the USA would seem to suggest that religious pluralism may, in fact, be responsible for the increasing appeal of religion there. In the USA, 40 per cent of the adult population regularly attend church. About 5 per cent of the US television audience regularly tune in to religious TV and 20 million watch some religious programming every week.

Scharf (1970), however, suggests American churches have developed in a secular way. They echo the American dream and religion has been subordinated to the American way of life. Churches place little emphasis on theology (belief) but stress the values of democracy, freedom, attainment and success. As Scharf notes: 'Being American includes being religious, and finding in religion a sanction for the American values of individualism and self-improvement.'

Warner (1993) puts the popularity of religion in the US down to the fundamental separation of religion from the influence of the state. The 18th-century American founders distinguished a series of principles of religious liberty, which included equality of faiths and separation of church and state. These principles encouraged religious pluralism without any centralizing influences. In the American context, the different religious traditions compete with each other equally for members. Religion has become a commodity to sell like any other product.

There can be greater specialization as the huge number of denominations (320 000 in 2007) tailor their product to meet market demand. Many advertise their unique characteristics in much the same way as schools in the UK market themselves. The result of competition in the US is a religious economy that results in more participants by expanding the base of participation, rather than a struggle for the loyalty of a fixed number of participants. This, it is suggested, is why there is a contrast between church attendance in Europe and the USA. In Europe, beliefs have not been compromised so much and the churches are empty. In the USA, the church has adapted itself to a changing society and the churches are full because they work to attract customers, free of interference from the church/state apparatus.

Focus on research

Lyon (2000) Jesus in Disneyland

Lyon (2000) argues that the centrality of consumerism to postmodern life means that people choose what to believe in, perhaps as readily as they choose what to wear. However, rather than declining, he sees traditional religious beliefs as merely relocating to the sphere of consumption. Furthermore, because many sources of identity, particularly work and nation, are becoming less significant, religion can become an important source of identity for individuals. However, in the postmodern world, people are less willing to accept an externally imposed narrative or story to put their lives in context, so they personalize the stories available to them from a much broader range of cultural sources. To support his arguments, he cites the example of a harvest day crusade held at Disneyland, California, where Christian evangelists and gospel singers preached and performed. Whereas this might once have been seen as an inappropriate, perhaps irreverent venue, religion here was being practised in a fantasy world, adapting, according to Lyon, to postmodernity and becoming part of it. People are therefore said to be seeking credible ways of expressing faith in contemporary modes outside the walls of conventional churches. Bruce (2002), however, sees this as evidence of secularization, rather than continuing religious vitality, as in his view, such arrangements have little impact upon the way people live their lives.

Lyon, D. (2000) *Jesus in Disneyland: Religion in Postmodern Times*, Cambridge: Polity Press

Explain how the harvest day crusade at Disneyland illustrates Lyon's argument.

Focus on research

Heelas *et al.* (2004)
The Kendal project

Kendal, a town of 28 000 people in the Lake District, has a church-attendance rate slightly above the national average, and is also something of a centre for alternative spirituality, offering the team from Lancaster University an ideal place to explore some of the key questions in current religious studies debates.

The researchers' book begins with the claim made by some commentators that traditional forms of religion appear to be declining, while new forms of alternative spirituality are growing.

The focus of the study was, therefore, on the two main types of sacred groupings:

● the 'congregational domain' (the various church congregations)
● the 'holistic milieu' (a range of activities involving the mind, body and spirit – such as yoga, tai chi, healing and self-discovery).

Between 2000 and 2002, questionnaires and interviews were conducted with members of each grouping – 26 congregations and 62 groups with a spiritual dimension, as well as a doorstep survey of over 100 households.

The researchers found that involvement in church and chapel – at 7.9 per cent of the population – still outweighs that in alternative spirituality, where only 1.6 per cent are estimated to be committed practitioners. However, alternative spirituality is catching up fast, as church congregations are in general decline (down from 11 per cent of the population in 1980) while the holistic milieu is growing. Furthermore, those churches that emphasized individuals 'in the living of their unique lives' were thriving, compared with those that subordinate all individuality to a higher good, e.g. 'the Almighty', which were contracting.

The writers see this as evidence of a 'spiritual revolution', whether Christian or alternative. What people are seeking are forms of religiosity that make sense to them, rather than those which demand that they subordinate their personal truth to some higher authority. In other words, we are witnessing a **'subjectivization'** of the sacred.

While the study reaffirmed an overall decline in total numbers involved in sacred activities, the growth in the holistic milieu, primarily by women practitioners (80 per cent), seems to reflect the 'subjective turn of modern culture', whereby people see themselves more as unique individuals with hidden depths. This is part of a general process of perceiving individuals as consumers who can express their own individuality through what they buy, or buy into. The findings also suggest that the sociology of spirituality ought to take gender more seriously.

However, the age profile of the holistic milieu was very uneven, with 83 per cent being over 40 and many who were ex-hippies who had maintained their affiliation with alternative spiritualities since the 1960s. Many in the holistic milieu also worked in people-centred, caring jobs, where personal wellbeing is a major concern. Given the relatively small number in such jobs and the other demographic and cultural factors, this would suggest that the rate of growth of the holistic milieu is likely to slow down. Nonetheless, on the basis of the Kendal research, the writers predict that holistic milieu activity will exceed church attendance within the next 20 to 30 years.

Adapted from Heelas, P., Woodhead, W., Seel, B., Tusting, K. and Szerszynski, B. (2004) *The Spiritual Revolution: Why religion is giving way to spirituality*, Oxford: Blackwell

1 What problems might the researchers have encountered when conducting a 'doorstep survey' about religious and spiritual belief and behaviour?

2 What do the researchers mean by:
   (a) 'spiritual revolution'?
   (b) subjectivization?

Evidence against secularization in the UK

While established religion may appear to be in decline in Western countries, such as Britain, the growth of their immigrant populations is causing an increase in religiosity in certain localities and regions of the UK. Islam is the fastest-growing religion in Britain and non-Trinitarian church membership has mushroomed.

However, in relation to the non-immigrant population, Grace Davie (1994) has characterized the situation in Britain as 'believing without belonging' – that is, people may admit to private religious beliefs but are less inclined to join religious groups or to attend religious services on a regular basis. Recent research by Day (2007) has cast doubt on this interpretation, suggesting religion is used as a 'public marker of identity', not necessarily highlighting an affiliation to a particular faith but to a community of other people like themselves rather than what they saw as 'others'.

In relation to church attendance, it could in fact be argued that this reflects 'belonging without believing'. That is, people may attend church for social or emotional reasons rather than religious commitment.

Vicarious religion

Davie also compares the UK with other European countries, such as those of Scandinavia. She suggests that religion is not practised overtly by the majority, but that most engage with religion on a **vicarious** level. In this sense, religion involves rituals and practices performed by an active minority on behalf of a much larger number, who (implicitly at least) not only understand, but also clearly approve of what the minority is doing.

Interruptions in 'normality'

One way to unravel what is happening is to observe societies when 'normal' ways of living are, for one reason or another, suspended and something far more expressive comes to the fore. Tragedy provides some examples. For example, the death of Princess Diana in Paris in a car crash in 1997 drew large numbers of British people to church. This shows that well-intentioned gestures of individual mourning are inadequate in themselves to mark the end of particular lives; there is the additional need for public ritual or worship in the established church.

The Princess Diana example is simply a larger-scale version of what goes on in the life-cycles of ordinary people. People expect that they will have the right to the services of the church at critical moments in their lives, such as birth, marriage and death. Churches must exist in order to meet such demands. So churches do not belong exclusively to those who use them regularly. European populations continue to see such churches as public utilities maintained for the common good.

Religious belief

Despite very low levels of church attendance and membership, surveys show that there seems to be a survival of some religious belief. According to the 1998 British Social Attitudes survey, 21 per cent of those surveyed agreed to the statement 'I know God exists and I have no doubt about it', whereas only 10 per cent said that they did not believe in God at all. However, there may be a moral connotation attached to such surveys, such that people feel more inclined to answer 'yes', whether or not they actually believe in God.

Individuation

A number of sociologists, notably Bellah (1987), have argued that, while institutional religion is in decline, this is only one form of religion, and that other aspects of religion continue in a variety of forms in modern society. Individuation is the idea of religion as 'finding oneself' through an individual search for meaning. Rather than uncritically accepting institutionalized religion, many have embarked on what might be called 'spiritual journeys' in search of themselves. Therefore, the importance of religion has not declined, but its form of expression may have changed.

Other criticisms of the secularization thesis

There is evidence that people prefer 'religious' explanations for random events, e.g. the early death of loved ones. Many people still subscribe to the concept of 'luck' or 'fate', as evidenced by the growth of gambling opportunities, such as the National Lottery and the relaxation of gambling laws.

There can be little doubt that religion plays less of a political role than it did in earlier centuries. However, national debates about issues such as the age of homosexual consent, the family, abortion and so on are given a moral dimension by the contribution of religious leaders. The media still shows a great interest in issues such as women priests, while religious programmes like *Songs of Praise* still attract large audiences (7 to 8 million viewers). Some sociologists, notably Parsons (1965), have argued that disengagement is probably a good thing because it means that the churches can focus more effectively on their central role of providing moral goals for society to achieve.

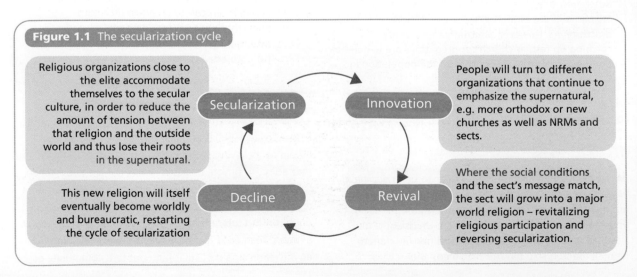

Figure 1.1 The secularization cycle

Religious organizations close to the elite accommodate themselves to the secular culture, in order to reduce the amount of tension between that religion and the outside world and thus lose their roots in the supernatural.

Secularization

Innovation

People will turn to different organizations that continue to emphasize the supernatural, e.g. more orthodox or new churches as well as NRMs and sects.

This new religion will itself eventually become worldly and bureaucratic, restarting the cycle of secularization

Decline

Revival

Where the social conditions and the sect's message match, the sect will grow into a major world religion – revitalizing religious participation and reversing secularization.

According to Hamilton (2001), decline in religious practices may be part of a more general decline in organizational membership and increased privatization. For example, fewer people join trade unions or political parties. It may be that they still 'believe', but are more committed to spending their time with family or on individual priorities.

Thompson (1996) suggests that the influence of the new Christian evangelical churches is underestimated. In the absence of mass political campaigning, church-inspired campaigns have a high media profile, especially in the USA. Many New Right policies on abortion, media violence and single parents are, he argues, influenced by the evangelical churches.

The secularization cycle

According to Stark and Bainbridge (1985), secularization is not an end to religion in itself but part of a dynamic cycle of secularization, innovation and religious revival (see Fig. 1.1).

From Stark and Bainbridge's perspective, Mormonism is the latest in a long series of world religions arising from sects that flourish where conventional religion has become too weak.

Stark and Bainbridge argue that religion can never disappear nor seriously decline. They see religion as meeting the fundamental needs of individuals. Whilst the privileged may have most of what they desire, individuals sometimes want rewards which are so great that the possibility of gaining them can only be contemplated alongside a belief in the supernatural – for instance, answers to our most fundamental questions, or a life after death. Only religion can answer these questions. The need for **religious compensators** is a constant whenever, wherever, and for whom, desired rewards are not obtainable. The less privileged, relatively lacking in rewards in life, may find that the increasingly secularized religions of the more privileged provide insufficient compensation and so seek alternatives, innovating as described above.

Religious pluralism as religious revival?

Rather than being seen as indicative of a weakening influence of religion on society, studies by Greeley (1972) and G.K. Nelson (1986) argue that the growth of NRMs indicate that society is undergoing a religious revival. Nelson argues that, in the 1980s, institutional religion lost contact with the spiritual needs of society because it had become too ritualized and predictable. In this sense, Nelson agrees with Wilson that established religion is undergoing secularization. The young, in particular, are 'turned-off' by such religion. However, Nelson argues that a religious revival is underway, and is being helped by the success of evangelical churches. These churches offer a more spontaneous religion, which is less reliant on ritual and consequently more attractive to the young.

But Bruce (1996) and Wallis (1984) point out that neither NRMs nor those churches that have increased their membership have recruited anywhere near the numbers of those lost from the established churches. Brierley (1999) estimates that the growth of non-Trinitarian churches of

half a million members, amounts to about only one-sixth of those lost to the main churches.

The secularization myth? A global perspective

Many writers have pointed out that secularization has tended to be seen in terms of the decline of organized established churches in Western industrialized countries. However, if one looks at the world globally, then religion is as overwhelming and dominant a force as ever. Berger (1997), one of the foremost advocates of secularization during the 1960s, has formally retracted his earlier claims, 'the world today with some exceptions is as furiously religious as it ever was and in some places more so than ever'. Religious revival among Christians in the USA, Jews in Israel and Muslims throughout the world has gone unexplained by proponents of the secularization thesis.

The postmodernist view

Postmodernists, too, see the development of New Age beliefs, what Heelas *et al.* (2004) call a **'holistic milieu'**, as a rejection of science and modernity in the postmodern age. The true extent of New Age beliefs cannot be known, but the number of internet sites feeding such interests indicates that they are widespread. This new explosion of spirituality doesn't at first seem to detract from the secularization thesis because these private beliefs don't impact upon the way society runs. However, as postmodernists argue, consumption is the way society runs now, or is at least a very significant factor, so this is precisely where we should look to find openings for religious activity.

Secularization: an over-generalization?

As far as the UK is concerned, it is fairly obvious that profound changes are occurring in institutional religion. However, whether these changes can be described as secularization is difficult to ascertain. Religious participation through organized religion has declined, but the extent and nature of continuing belief still proves difficult to determine. Further, increased globalization has meant that **religio-political events** elsewhere have global significance and this is bound to have an impact upon religious influence in Britain.

Bauman (1997) and Giddens (2001), for example, argue that religion is becoming more important in the late modern/postmodern world. According to Giddens:

<< *Religious symbols and practices are not only residues from the past: a revival of religious or more broadly spiritual concerns seems fairly widespread ... not only has religion failed to disappear; we see all around us the creation of new forms of religious sensibility and spiritual endeavour.* >>

Check your understanding

1 According to Wilson, how does the definition of religion affect the way secularization is seen?

2 Why is generalizing about secularization in relation to members of British society as a whole problematic?

3 Why, according to Hamilton, is the notion of an 'age of faith' an illusion?

4 Why is a focus on church attendance as an indicator of declining religiosity essentially flawed?

5 What evidence on religious participation does Wilson give to support the secularization thesis?

6 What is the significance of the changing age profile for the future of religion in Britain?

7 What indicators are there of a reduced status of the clergy?

8 What, according to Wilson, is the significance of rationalization and disengagement for the secularization thesis?

9 How does Bruce argue that religious pluralism is evidence of secularization?

10 Why is the USA so 'religious' relative to the UK?

11 How does Davie counter the view that religion in Britain is declining in significance?

12 How do Stark and Bainbridge explain the cycle of secularization, innovation and revival?

13 Why do they argue that religion can never truly disappear?

14 In what ways does a more global perspective demonstrate that secularization is a myth?

15 How do postmodernists view the secularization thesis?

Activities

Research ideas

1 Conduct a survey to discover the extent of belief in a range of supernatural and spiritual phenomena among students at your school or college. To what extent do your results indicate widespread 'religious belief'? Would your conclusions be different if you used different criteria for measuring 'religious belief'?

Web.tasks

1 Look at the website of the Keep Sunday Special Campaign at www.keepsundayspecial.net

   Summarize the main objections Christian groups have to the secularization of Sunday.

   Evaluate their arguments.

2 Explore the website of the 'Mind, Body and Spirit' organization at www.mindbodyspirit.co.uk

   What do you think the success of these exhibitions tells us about secularization?

Key terms

Desacrilization where sacred explanations give way to scientific rational explanations.

Disengagement where the religious institutions become less engaged in wider aspects of social life.

Ecumenical movement where churches come together in joint worship, each seeing the other as having something to offer.

Holistic milieu a range of activities involving the mind, body and spirit, such as yoga, tai chi, healing and self-discovery.

Individualism putting the interests of the individual before the interests of the state or social group.

Rational based on reason, logic and science.

Rationalization the use of reason and science to replace spiritual and religious thinking.

Religio-political events instances of religion coming into conflict with governments, with national and sometimes international consequences.

Religious compensators aspects of religion that provide temporary answers to fundamental queries about the nature of existence and satisfy universal needs.

Religious pluralism where a variety of religions co-exist, all of which are considered to have equal validity.

Secularization thesis belief in the declining influence of religion in society.

Subjectivization the increasing relevance of the self and personal experiences as a dominant feature of religion.

Vicarious religion religious practices of a socially approved of minority who symbolically represent the religious adherence of the majority.

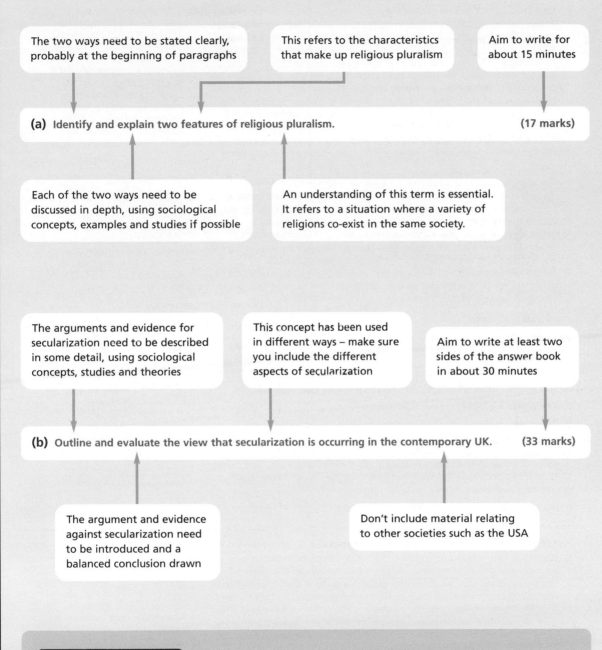

An eye on the exam   The strength of religion in society

The two ways need to be stated clearly, probably at the beginning of paragraphs

This refers to the characteristics that make up religious pluralism

Aim to write for about 15 minutes

(a) Identify and explain two features of religious pluralism.   **(17 marks)**

Each of the two ways need to be discussed in depth, using sociological concepts, examples and studies if possible

An understanding of this term is essential. It refers to a situation where a variety of religions co-exist in the same society.

The arguments and evidence for secularization need to be described in some detail, using sociological concepts, studies and theories

This concept has been used in different ways – make sure you include the different aspects of secularization

Aim to write at least two sides of the answer book in about 30 minutes

(b) Outline and evaluate the view that secularization is occurring in the contemporary UK.   **(33 marks)**

The argument and evidence against secularization need to be introduced and a balanced conclusion drawn

Don't include material relating to other societies such as the USA

Grade booster   Getting top marks in this question

Start with a definition of secularization that identifies some of its main aspects – don't forget to consider the problems of measuring these. Good answers will cover changes in religious belief and participation as well as the impact of disengagement, desacrilization and religious pluralism. Evaluation will need to challenge the way these changes have been interpreted as evidence of secularization and emphasize how religiosity has become privatised and diverse. The idea of 'believing without belonging' and the postmodernist perspective on contemporary religion might be used to help evaluation. Any conclusions will depend on how religion is defined – see Topic 1.

(a) a. Identify and explain two features of fundamentalism.
(17 marks)

One feature of fundamentalism is a complete belief in sacred texts. These might include the bible in the case of Christianity or the Quran for Moslems. Most Christians do not believe that very word of the bible is true, they see it as a general guide to values and morals and as a source of stories and fables that help put across those morals. But fundamentalist Christians believe that it is all true and cannot be questioned. This means that they believe that the world was created in six days and therefore that the theory of evolution is wrong. This has caused fundamentalist Christians to come into conflict with scientists and teachers. In America fundamentalist Christian groups have demanded that creationist accounts of the origin of the world are taught in preference to scientific theories such as the 'big bang' view.

Another feature is a conservative approach to norms and values. They favour traditional arrangements in terms of families, gender roles and sexuality for example and find quotes from sacred texts to justify their beliefs. Fundamentalist Moslems believe in very traditional gender roles with women covering themselves with a hijab (although Watson argues that this can actually be liberating for women as it stops men from staring at them). Christian fundamentalists in the USA have put pressure on politicians to make abortion harder to get and to support traditional nuclear families. Many of George W. Bush's policies reflected these views.

> The first feature is identified clearly and concisely at the start of the paragraph, letting the examiner know exactly what is going to be explained. Contemporary examples are used to illustrate the point. Providing examples is always a helpful aid to explanation.

> The second feature is also identified straight away and explained clearly using examples. These are up to date and reflect very good knowledge and understanding although the points could be developed a little more. The reference to Watson is redundant as evaluation is not asked for.

(b) b. Outline and evaluate Marxist views of the role of religion in society. (33 marks)

Marxism is a sociological perspective that focuses on class conflict. Marxists believe that society is divided into two classes – a ruling class and a lower class and that these two groups are always in conflict because the ruling class exploits the working class. The ruling class try to convince the working class that their domination is justified and this is where religion comes in.

Marx believed that the role of religion was to convince the working class that they should be in their low social position. In this way religion was an ideological device that helped spread the ideas of the ruling class. One way religion did this was to make it appear that the ruling class deserved their position of dominance and that they should not be challenged. For example some religious beliefs in the past suggested that kings and queens were chosen by God. People's place in the old Hindu caste system was fixed at birth and could only be changed in a future life. Another way in which religion controls people is by suggesting that there is not much point in changing society because it is God's will that it is the way it is. Rewards will come in heaven after death. Marx described religion as being like the drug opium – lulling people into a passive, dreamlike state. A more recent example is the growth of fundamentalist beliefs that justify traditional arrangements which Marxists believe always work in the interests of the ruling class.

> It is a good idea to briefly summarize the Marxist perspective referred to in the question and it is linked to religion in the final sentence, leading the reader on to the next paragraph. A promising start.

> The main points of the Marxist view of religion are included and the key concept of 'ideology' is used. Examples are also provided to illustrate points although it might have been better to break this paragraph up so that the separate points could have stood out rather more.

Some more recent Marxists (called neo-Marxists) have argued that religion can sometimes be a more positive force in society when there are no alternative ways of achieving social change. Example might be South Africa under apartheid where the church was quite a radical force and in Latin America where opposition political movements were not allowed and the Catholic Church had quite a radical influence.

This updates and develops the Marxist view, showing sensitivity to the fact that there is not just one Marxist position.

Functionalist views of religion are much more positive about its effects. Durkheim argues that religion brings people together and acts as a unifying influence. Malinowski shows how religion can help social order by helping people come to terms with difficult events in life such as death. Weber showed how religion can cause social change and is not just about class conflict and ideology.

Functionalism is introduced very suddenly. It is relevant as it can be used to criticise Marxist views by offering an alternative interpretation of the role of religion. But an introductory sentence is needed to make that point clear. As the paragraph continues, various writers are introduced but their views are not adequately developed in terms of their links to the Marxist perspective.

In conclusion, Marxism is quite an old-fashioned view that is difficult to apply to the world today where there is religious pluralism. Many religious beliefs and groups exist and people can be 'spiritual shoppers', choosing whichever beliefs suit them. Also, there are lots of signs that secularization is occurring and religion is becoming less important – how can it have an ideological purpose when many people do not believe in it?

Good evaluative points are raised in the conclusion in relation to contemporary trends in religion. But they deserve more explanation _ it would probably have been better to discuss them before the conclusion.

An examiner comments

This answer begins clearly and successfully identifies various aspects of the Marxist position on religion, using examples to help explain the key points. The use of neo-Marxism demonstrates an understanding that not all Marxists share exactly the same view. But the later evaluative part of the answer lacks detail and depth. Good points are raised but not developed. A few extra sentences, for example at the beginning of the penultimate paragraph, could have really made the knowledge included relate to the question more directly.

Chapter 6 Summary

Functionalism

- Socialization
- Social integration
- Civil religion
- Preventing anomie
- Coming to terms with life-changing events

Marxism

- Religion as ideology
- Legitimating social inequality
- Disguising exploitation
- Social control

Weberianism

- Religion can cause social change
- Protestant ethic and spirit of capitalism
- Charismatic leaders

Postmodern views

- 'Spiritual shopping'
- Fundamentalism – an attempt to restore certainty in an unstable world

The role of religion in society

Religion and religious organizations

Religion

The strength of religion in society

Evidence for and against secularization

- Religious belief and attendance
- Rationalization
- Disengagement
- Religious pluralism

Defining and measuring religion

- Functional and substantive definitions
- Belief
- Participation
- Clothing and symbols

Religious organizations

- Churches
- Denominations
- New religious movements
- New Age movements
- Fundamentalism

Religion and social position

Gender

- Feminism – is religion patriarchal?
- Women's greater religiosity
- Women and NRMs
- Women and fundamentalism

Ethnicity

- Religion and ethnic identity
- Differences in styles of worship

Age

- Younger people less religious
- Young Muslims

Social class

- Churchgoing associated with higher social classes
- Some sects appeal to underprivileged
- New Age movements predominantly middle class
- Spiritual void

Appeal of NRMs

- Pragmatic motives
- Marginality
- Relative deprivation

Youth and culture

OCR specification			Coverage
Key concepts and the social construction of youth			
Key concepts	• Youth • Youth subcultures • Spectacular youth subcultures	• Youth culture • Peer group	Concepts explained in Topic 1 and referred to throughout chapter.
Social construction of youth, including the role of:	• The media • Schooling • Globalization	• Consumption • Demographic trends • The economy	Covered in Topic 1.
The role of youth culture/subcultures in society			
Sociological explanations	• Functionalism • Feminism	• Marxism • Postmodern views	Covered in Topic 2.
Issues related to gender			Covered in Topic 2.
Issues related to ethnicity			Covered in Topic 2.
Youth and deviance			
Key concepts, patterns and trends	• Delinquency • Crime • Moral panics	• Deviance • Labelling • Patterns and trends in youth deviance according to social class, gender and ethnicity	Key concepts and patterns explained in Topic 3.
Sociological explanations of the patterns and trends	• Functionalism • Labelling theory	• Marxism	Covered in Topic 3.
The experience of youth in education			
The experience of schooling by:	• Class • Ethnicity	• Gender	Covered in Topic 4
Patterns and trends in subject choice			Covered in Topic 4
Pro- and anti-school subcultures			Covered in Topic 4
Pro- and anti-education subcultures			Covered in Topic 4

TOPIC 1

The social construction of youth

Getting you thinking

1 **What do you think attracts young people to become part of the groups pictured in the first two photos above?**

2 **Look at the young people in the third photograph (below). What attracts them to a night out in the town centre?**

Young people are attracted to particular styles and activities for many reasons. They might identify with the values represented by a group – like New Age Travellers – young males might want to emphasize their toughness and masculinity or they might want to get together with many other young people to socialize in city centres at night. Whatever their choices it does seem that young people often have specific lifestyles and identities that are rather different from those of older generations.

Youth culture: a natural or social creation?

Ageing is a physical and natural process which happens to everyone and has always happened. However, childhood, youth, adulthood and old age are associated with different behaviour, tastes and lifestyles. Different societies – and even the same societies over different historical periods – have divided ageing into different stages. These stages have then had different meanings attached to them. For example:

- Nowadays, childhood is seen as a period of innocence, although it was once seen as a period of potential evil.
- Old age, now seen as a period of dependence, was once viewed as a time of wisdom.
- The typical image of youth is characterized by two overlapping images of enjoyment and bad behaviour.

These age categories are not 'natural', but created by society – that is, they are **social constructions**.

Around 50 to 60 years ago, for the first time, a **youth culture** appeared to be emerging – young people appeared to be developing their own values, customs, tastes, clothes, music and language.

During the 1960s the appearance of a number of youth cultures such as mods, skinheads and hippies caused sociologists to rethink the idea of youth culture – after all, it is difficult to say that all young people share a culture when there are so many differences between them, for example of gender, ethnicity and class. Sociologists began using the term **youth subculture** to describe different groups which, to some extent, shared the values and norms of wider society and of wider young people but also developed some of their own. More recently sociologists have seen the need to distinguish between youth subcultures based, say, on gender and class, with those associated with specialised styles of clothing, music and rebellious behaviour designed to provoke and shock. These groups – like punks and Goths – have often been the subject of media outrage. Some sociologists now refer to them as **spectacular youth subcultures**.

The origins of youth culture

The modern concept of youth culture developed in the early 1950s, although, as we shall see later, the idea of youth as a phase in life has a longer history. There is no single reason for the development of youth culture in Britain; rather, it came about as a result of a number of different social changes occurring at the same time. These developments included:

- the increasing economic power of young people
- the increasing diversity of society
- the impact of American culture
- the development and specialization of the media
- the emergence of 'rock and roll' music
- the lengthening of the period of transition between childhood and adulthood
- an increase in the birth rate.

Increasing economic power of young people

The 1950s were a period of rapid economic growth in Britain. With much of the housing and industry destroyed during the Second World War (1939–45), a huge amount of reconstruction occurred. This, in turn, led to a high demand for workers and, as employers competed for their services, wages rose. The first person to realize the impact this was having on young people was Abrams (1959), who analysed the increased economic power of the 'teenage

consumer'. He demonstrated that real earnings of young people increased by over 50 per cent between 1938 and 1958, double the increase of adult earnings over the same period. Abrams also researched spending patterns and concluded that, by the late 1950s, young people were the age group spending the highest proportion of their income on leisure activities and music, clothes and cosmetics. This increase in economic power created the conditions for the emerging youth culture to develop. For the first time, young people had significant amounts of money to spend.

Social change

The Second World War marked the beginning of a powerful change in British society. In sociological terms, it was the beginning of the decline in modernity and the move towards late modernity (see pp. 20–1 and 199–200 for discussions of modernity and late modernity). Before 1939, Britain was characterized by a rigid class structure and, although this continued into the 1950s, cracks were beginning to show. Changes in the economy and an opening-up of the educational system coincided with new ideas about equal opportunities and individual expression. These ideas did not fully flower until the 1960s and 1970s, but the 1950s saw them emerging. The result was that rigid ideas of superior and inferior social classes and of hierarchy began to be challenged. It was in this 'social space' of challenge and change that new forms of cultural expression emerged. Cinema, art, literature and theatre began to explore new ideas. Amongst the many new ideas was that young people were a distinctive group with new values and ideas about their place in society.

The impact of American culture

Today, the dominance of American culture is simply taken for granted in Britain. **Globalization** has made brands such as Coca-Cola and Nike internationally known. It is difficult for people living in the 21st century to imagine a world which is not dominated by US products. Yet it was not until the Second World War that American products and culture came to Britain (at least, on such a large scale). With the changing culture and the growth in affluence of the 1950s, there was a ready market for American goods and culture, which included rock and roll music and other products aimed at the new 'teenage market'.

Growth and specialization of the media

The next element in the mixture of factors which led to the development of youth culture in Britain was the growth and specialization of the media. Compared to today, the media of the 1950s were tiny in number and variety. However, the 1950s saw an explosion of different sorts of media. These included:

- the emergence of television to rival the cinema as the most common form of leisure activity
- the diversification and specialization of magazines, as they sought new audiences – for example, The New Musical Express (NME) was started in this period.

This media explosion was only possible because of the growth in social diversity and an increase in spending power that persuaded companies (very often American) to spend large amounts of money advertising in the new media. As a high-spending and newly discovered group, young people became the target for advertisers and hence the commercial media competed to attract this market.

The emergence of new musical forms

The early 1950s saw the arrival in Britain of a new harder-edged style of singing and guitar playing, which had developed in the USA out of blues and country music. The new style of music challenged accepted 'crooning' styles and carried with it a barely disguised sexual orientation. Its development from Black blues music also added the issue of race. For many younger people looking for a distinctive cultural identity and a break from their parental culture, rock and roll provided the answer. For the American companies and the new media, rock and roll provided a useful commercial opportunity.

Longer transition from childhood to adulthood

Transition refers to the movement from being economically and socially dependent on parents towards independence. The length of transition increased over the 20th century as the average period spent in education increased. During the 20th century, the typical age of leaving education (and hence dependency) increased from 12 years of age to 18 or even 21. This means that typical adult responsibilities were taken on increasingly later in life, leaving young people with a number of years where they were physically mature but without the responsibilities of adulthood.

Increase in the birth rate

The final factor that combined to generate youth culture was the dramatic increase in the birth rate soon after the end of the 1939–45 War. The armed forces had conscripted millions of young British men (and women), and hundreds of thousands had been sent abroad. Many couples were separated for a period of up to six years. For others, their first sexual experiences might have been delayed for some years. The result was that when the men were released from the armed forces in 1945/46, there was a huge increase in the birth rate. Although many of the children born at this time were not 'teenagers' until the end of the 1950s, they did ensure that youth culture continued and grew as a cultural form.

The key characteristics of youth culture

So far we have described the emergence of youth culture without actually saying what marks it off as a separate culture. Abercrombie *et al.* (2000) have suggested that it has three distinguishing features: leisure, style and peer group. It is useful to add a fourth feature: **consumption**.

Leisure

Until relatively recently, most adult cultures – or at least adult male cultures – were based on work. Studies by sociologists of male life from the 1950s to the 1970s constantly return to the importance of work in social life. Income, political attitudes, awareness of social position and general social identity were all tied up with occupation. This did not weaken until the 1980s, when leisure and consumption patterns began to rival work as important elements of male adult lives. But the move towards leisure as a defining characteristic of young people's culture began much earlier in the 1950s and has subsequently continued.

To some extent, this has been linked to the increased length of time that young people spend in education, which we discussed earlier. Young people are unlikely to experience work until a later age, so that it is not atypical for people to delay entry into the workforce until 21. As a consequence, young people have fewer financial responsibilities and are less likely to be 'tied in' to the discipline of employment, with its requirements to attend work for a set number of hours each day, to have limited holiday opportunities and to dress in the way required by the employer.

The importance of style

The importance of image is a key element of youth culture, with style being perhaps the core component. Style is composed of two main elements:

- how one appears to others
- how one sounds to others.

Appearance is related to clothes, hairstyle and make-up. These give clues as to the interests and musical likings of the person. How one sounds is equally important and this is demonstrated by use of **argot** (special language). The combination of these elements will give strong clues as to musical allegiance, leisure choices and even social class. Once again, youth culture predated the changes in the wider culture, where style has become more important to a range of age groups.

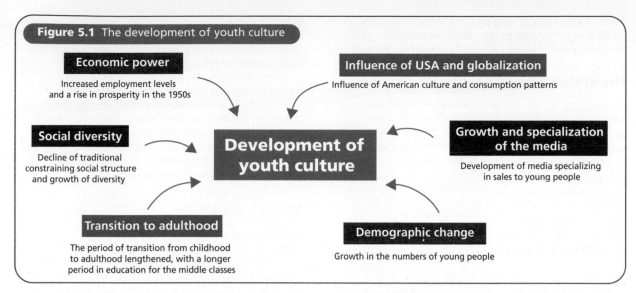

Figure 5.1 The development of youth culture

Economic power
Increased employment levels and a rise in prosperity in the 1950s

Influence of USA and globalization
Influence of American culture and consumption patterns

Social diversity
Decline of traditional constraining social structure and growth of diversity

Development of youth culture

Growth and specialization of the media
Development of media specializing in sales to young people

Transition to adulthood
The period of transition from childhood to adulthood lengthened, with a longer period in education for the middle classes

Demographic change
Growth in the numbers of young people

The importance of the peer group

The term **peer group** refers to a group of people of a particular age who share similar interests and attitudes. Young people have strong affiliation to peer groups, which partially replace or complement the relationships provided by the family. Functionalist sociologists (see Topic 2) argue that the peer group provides a bridge between childhood and adulthood.

Consumption

Youth culture is based upon consumption. As we have already seen, this is a period in life where money can be spent on nonessential items. Youth culture is closely linked with specific styles of clothing, cosmetics, recorded music and a range of other items which serve to demonstrate membership of a particular form of youth culture.

Images of youth

Earlier we said that youth culture emerged in the early 1950s; however, ideas of youth or 'adolescence' as a distinct phase in people's lives (as opposed to a distinct youth culture) has a much longer history. Certainly, ideas about youth (although very different from today's concept) existed when Shakespeare was writing in the early 17th century. This history also illustrates the double-edged image

of youth that persists today. According to Aries (1962), modern ideas of youth began to emerge in the 19th century. At this point, the more affluent middle classes began to expand the length of their children's education with the hope that they would emerge with a more mature view of the world and ready to take on adult responsibilities. As the 19th century progressed, the length of this maturation period lengthened and these affluent young people became more separated from the adult world.

According to Pearson (1983), by the late 19th century, middle-class youth were joined by working-class young people who were reluctant to enter regular employment, preferring to 'get by' in rather different ways including petty theft. Two different **discourses** (way of thinking and acting) towards young people began to emerge, seeing youth as either 'trouble' or a time of fun and enjoyment, or indeed both. These two discourses have run along together for the last 150 years. As Hebdige puts it:

> << The two image clusters, the bleak portrayal of juvenile offenders and the exuberant cameos of teenage life, reverberate, alternate and sometimes they get crossed.>> (Hebdige 1988)

When youth culture emerged in the 1950s, it fitted into these existing attitudes towards young people and so is viewed suspiciously by adults as both a time of crime and of fun and enjoyment.

Two images of 1960s youth: mods and rockers fighting on the beach (right) and a poster for the hit film Summer Holiday (below). How do these photographs illustrate the two discourses about youth?

Key terms

Argot the use of special terms for everyday items, only understood by the members of that culture.

Consumption a term used to describe the process of buying goods, usually for status and pleasure reasons.

Discourse way of thinking about a particular group or issue.

Globalization describes the fact that political, economic and social forces now operate across the world rather than in national boundaries.

Peer group a group of people of similar age and interests.

Social construction something that is created by society.

Spectacular youth subculture youth subculture associated with specialised styles of clothing, music and, often, rebellious behaviour

Transition the process of moving from childhood to adulthood.

Youth culture a set of values and behaviour shared by young people that is distinctive from the culture held by the older generations.

Youth subculture groups of young people that, to some extent, share the values and norms of wider society and of wider young people but also develop some of their own.

Activities

Research idea

Interview two adults, such as your parents, and, if possible, older adults such as grandparents, about the music and stars of their youth. What clothes did they wear? Were there any ways of expressing themselves (argot) they can recall? How did their parents react to their behaviour? What are their views on current youth culture?

Web.tasks

Summaries of sociological research projects on the changing nature of youth culture in Newcastle, Bristol and Leeds can be found at:
www.ncl.ac.uk/youthnightlife/home.htm

Browse the reports and find out the methods used and the key findings.

Check your understanding

1   Explain how the age group 'youth' is socially constructed.

2   Give two examples of how the same 'age' has changed its meaning over time.

3   What is the relationship between the increase in young people's income and the development of youth culture?

4   Explain the social changes identified in the text. How did they impact on youth culture?

5   How did the development of rock and roll music influence youth culture?

6   Explain why leisure has become more important to young people since the 1950s.

7   In what ways are the following important to youth culture:

   (a) style?

   (b) consumption?

8   Identify the two dominant images of youth.

The social construction of youth

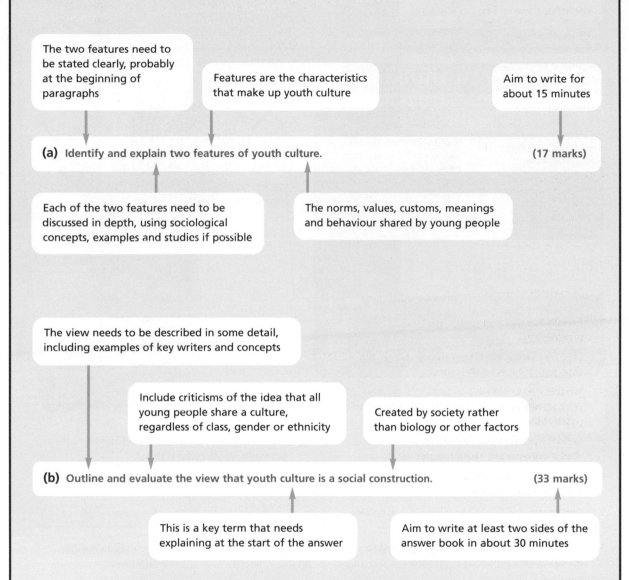

The two features need to be stated clearly, probably at the beginning of paragraphs

Features are the characteristics that make up youth culture

Aim to write for about 15 minutes

(a) Identify and explain two features of youth culture. (17 marks)

Each of the two features need to be discussed in depth, using sociological concepts, examples and studies if possible

The norms, values, customs, meanings and behaviour shared by young people

The view needs to be described in some detail, including examples of key writers and concepts

Include criticisms of the idea that all young people share a culture, regardless of class, gender or ethnicity

Created by society rather than biology or other factors

(b) Outline and evaluate the view that youth culture is a social construction. (33 marks)

This is a key term that needs explaining at the start of the answer

Aim to write at least two sides of the answer book in about 30 minutes

Grade booster Getting top marks in this question

Two key terms need to be dealt with right at the start of the answer: the ideas of social construction and youth culture. Social construction suggests that social influences are the key factors in creating youth culture although youth is an age category so may appear to be biologically determined. The idea of youth culture implies that young people share norms, values, rituals and so on. You will need to explain how youth culture emerged as a result of a combination of social factors. These include the economy, education, music, globalization and demographic factors. Evaluation should consist of a discussion of whether it is possible to generalise in this way about young people regardless of their gender, ethnicity or class. The concept of subculture is likely to appear.

TOPIC 2

Youth culture and youth subcultures

Getting you thinking

1. **What names would you give to the youth cultural styles pictured here? When were they most popular? Are they still popular?**

2. **Identify as many youth cultures as you can.**

3. **Take one of these and try to work out what attracts young people to this particular style.**

4. **How many of your friends would identify with a particular youth cultural style?**

5. **To what extent do you think youth cultural styles are important to young people?**

In Topic 1, we saw how youth culture developed in the 1950s as a result of a number of different social changes occurring together. However, sociologists are interested in looking beyond this to see if there are any general theoretical explanations for the development of youth culture.

Four major theoretical schools have provided competing overall explanations for the nature and existence of youth culture. These are:

- functionalist
- conflict
- late modern
- postmodern.

Because these approaches cover such wide ground, we have divided them into two topics. In this topic, we are going to explore functionalist and conflict (or Marxist-derived) approaches. Later, we move on to look at countercultures, late-modern and postmodern theories. In

both topics, we will choose various youth subcultural styles that sociologists have studied and use them as examples of the theories. We will also include discussion on 'race' and gender issues where they are relevant. However, you must remember that both topics are closely related and, in order to gain a full understanding, you need to combine the insights of both topics.

The functionalist approach: youth as transition

Functionalist theories are based on the idea that if something exists in society, then it must be there for a purpose. Their argument is simple: youth culture undoubtedly exists and it must, therefore, serve some purpose. This approach to understanding social phenomena has a long history in sociology. It can be traced back as early as the end of the 19th century in the work of Emile Durkheim and then, in a more sophisticated form, in the writings of Talcott Parsons in the middle of the 20th century.

Parsons argued that in most traditional societies, young people go through a 'rite of passage', a ceremony marking the move from childhood into adulthood. In contemporary societies, these ceremonies have largely fallen into disuse, though a few remnants remain, such as the Jewish bar mitzvah and 18th-birthday celebrations. According to Parsons, youth culture has taken over this 'rite of passage' role, extending it over a number of years, but still essentially acting as form of transition from childhood to adulthood. Young people, he suggests, have to find a way of moving from the secure, cosy world of the family into the competitive adult world of work, where individual talent and sharp competition with others bring the financial rewards. The role of youth culture smooths this path by providing a link between the conflicting values of the home (childhood) and work (adulthood).

Eisenstadt (1956) took Parson's general ideas a little further. According to him, most young people need to find a way to distinguish themselves from their parents. They need to move from the **ascribed** position of being the child of a particular adult, to the **achieved** position of being an adult person in one's own right. However, breaking away from the home and family is difficult and emotionally stressful. Youth culture provides a mechanism for coping with this period of stress by providing a peer group of like-minded people of a similar age who adopt the same styles of dress and attitudes.

This serves the twin purposes of setting young people apart from their parents and providing them with a model of how to behave during this potentially stressful period. According to Eisenstadt, therefore, youth culture is a method of helping young people make the transition from childhood to adulthood. As this is the sole purpose of youth culture, the actual style and the content of the youth culture is of absolutely no importance. Eisenstadt further argues that any differences in the backgrounds of young people and between the various forms of youth cultures are unimportant. The important point to him is that all youth need some kind of transition mechanism, and it is unimportant what cultural form it takes.

Age: the new social division

A development of functionalist youth culture was the argument put forward by Roszak (1970) amongst others that a new division in society was emerging between young people and the older generations – a 'generation gap'. The values, interests and behaviour of youth was the replacement for divisions based on class, gender and race. Roszak argued that age cut across all these, making them outdated and irrelevant. This approach became extremely influential, Murdoch and McCron (1976), for example, argued that youth culture was 'a generation in itself', the advanced guard of a whole new culture which would radically change society, eliminating the out-dated divisions of social class. (These sorts of analyses have also been used to explore the nature of countercultures – see Topic 3, p. 199.)

Youth culture or youth subcultures?

Those who subscribed to the functionalist school and those that argued that youth formed the most significant division in society all used the term 'youth culture' in their analyses. A **culture** refers to a set of values and beliefs that provide clear guidelines on how to act in different situations. Cultures are complete in themselves, providing a 'world view'. Most tribal societies have only one culture shared by all their members. However, in modern, complex societies, although there is one main culture which most people share, within that there are numerous variations that tend to be known as **subcultures**.

If we apply this distinction to youth, we come to the heart of a major debate between sociologists. Can we say there is one youth culture, shared by all young people and highly distinctive from the adult culture, or are there, rather, a series of different youth subcultures reflecting social divisions of class, ethnicity and gender? Functionalist writers argue that there is essentially only one youth culture – or at least any variations are of little or no importance. Other writers, however, argue that the variations in youth that functionalists ignore are actually very important indeed. For example, according to the subcultural conflict models, there is no one, single youth culture, but instead, a variety of youth subcultures. So, while functionalists see no importance in analysing the content of youth culture, the conflict approach (along with the postmodern approach, discussed in Topic 3) argues that understanding the content and style of youth subcultures is crucial for an understanding of modern youth. They suggest that the idea of a division of age replacing class is simply not true.

The Marxist approach: subculture as solution

In Britain in the 1970s, conflict theories based on Marxism were very influential. Conflict theories are derived from the Marxist theory that modern, capitalist societies are based on the exploitation of the population, but especially the working class, by a small ruling class. Because of this exploitation, the working class and the ruling class are routinely in conflict. The ruling class, according to conflict theorists, use a variety of mechanisms to control the working class. The obvious form of control is the criminal justice system and the police. However, a much more important method is by controlling the very values of society, so that capitalism and inequality seem 'natural'. This concept of controlling values is known as **hegemony** and is achieved through control of the mass media and of the values taught in schools.

It was within this academic tradition that a group of sociologists from what was Birmingham University's Centre for Contemporary Cultural Studies (CCCS), began to study youth subcultures. Writers such as Hall and Jefferson (1976), argued that working-class young people (particularly those who had done poorly at school) formed the weakest point in the ruling class's control of society, as unlike adults they were not tied into capitalist society through jobs and family commitments. This partly explains the reason why there is so much control of young people by the police and the other control agencies. This set of views became known as the 'critical cultural studies approach'.

We saw earlier that, for functionalist writers, youth culture is a means of helping young people in the transition from childhood to adulthood, and that they viewed it as essentially positive. However, for conflict theorists, youth culture is a form of **resistance** against capitalism and, as such, is hostile to the dominant culture. Young people cause 'trouble' because they are engaging in class conflict, whether or not they are aware of this. Youth culture is an **inarticulate** means of resolving the problems faced by each generation of working-class youth. These problems consist of being offered a life of routine and low-paid employment, or perhaps no employment at all, just like their parents before them. Working-class youth cultures are a response to this bleak future – a way of expressing their anger and resistance.

However, if working-class youth face the same futures over generations, why do the forms or 'style' of youth culture alter over time? After all, expressing their opposition to their futures could be achieved in the same way by each generation. The answer to this, according to the CCCS, was that each generation of young people encounter the same problems, but in very different circumstances. For example, the 16-year-old growing up in the 1950s will have had a different experience of life compared to a 16-year-old today, with different cultural expectations, media output, leisure possibilities, drug availability and so on. Yet underneath these cultural differences, similar inequalities in jobs and life in general remain.

The outcome of all this is that youth subcultures alter over time and place in response to these wider changes.

Resistance through style

The problem for the critical cultural studies writers was how to prove their ideas were true. Their answer was to analyse the style and content of youth subcultures in the belief that these would demonstrate that they contained 'symbols of resistance' to capitalism. They therefore undertook what is known as **semiotic analysis**. Semiotics refers to the study of signs – symbols that communicate something – to find out what they mean. The cultural studies analysts therefore began to **decode** the meaning of the choice of clothes, haircut, hair colour, music, argot and ritual forms of behaviour of a range of youth subcultures in order to demonstrate how they were really expressions of opposition to capitalism.

The outcome was a series of studies of working-class youth subcultures, each of which explored in great detail the clothes worn, the music listened to, and the general form of slang language used. The aim of this research was to uncover the real, underlying meaning of the content of the subcultures.

Examples of working-class subculture

Teddy boys

Hall and Jefferson (1976) researched Teddy Boys, a 1950s working-class youth subculture. The rise of Teddy Boys in the early 1950s coincided with the expansion of employment and the general rise in affluence as a result of the major resurgence of industry after the Second World

War. However, according to Fyvel (1961), the Teddy Boys were drawn from those youths who had been excluded from this – they had lost out in the education system and missed out on the affluence. Like generations of young people after them, they had nowhere to go and in their case, took over local cafes which they used as bases for hanging around. The Teddy Boys' trademarks were their Edwardian style jackets, suede shoes and bootlace ties. Hall and Jefferson then analysed the symbolic meaning of each of these articles of clothing. He suggested that the bootlace ties were from characters in Western films who had to live off their wits – the sort of characters whom working-class lads could aspire towards. Furthermore, the jackets and shoes were a subversion of the Edwardian Dandy style which had become popular with the upper middle class. Their use by the working-class Teddy Boys showed contempt for the class system by usurping the clothing style of their supposed 'social superiors'.

Skinheads

Phil Cohen (1972) conducted a similar semiotic study of skinheads. Skinheads (both male and female) wore an exaggerated version of traditional working-class male clothes, comprising cropped hair, braces, half-mast jeans and Doc. Marten boots. Their drug of preference was alcohol. Their clothes represented both a 'caricature and reassertion of solid, male, working-class toughness'. This reassertion of values was a response to a number of factors linked to the decline in working-class inner-city communities, which were threatened by the decline in the large-scale manufacturing and dock work that had traditionally provided the economic basis for the inner-city communities. They were also an attempt to deal with the large-scale immigration into these areas by poorer Asians (particularly from Pakistan), whom the White working class perceived as destroying their communities and taking their jobs. Skinhead subculture was therefore wrapped in racism. Much of the activity of the skinheads was involved in reclaiming territory, and this was often played out through football violence, which allowed groups to claim ownership of a club and the area around it.

Punk

Dick Hebdige (1979) studied Punk subculture. He suggests that a process of 'bricolage' (the reuse of ordinary objects in a different way to create challenging new meanings) occurred in Punk subculture. Punk emerged in the 1970s as a response to the dominance of the media, fashion and music industries. It had various routes: on the one hand, working-class young people disenchanted with their economic and social situation, and on the other side, art college students attracted by its creativity and energy. Punk attempted to undermine and disrupt existing styles, with the Punks seeing themselves outside existing cultures and class structures. Hebdige (1979) coined the term the 'blank generation' to describe this, saying that the only thing that Punks had in common was their rejection of anything orderly, restrained and sacred. Punk was one of the few 'resistance' subcultures that did have political elements to it. The lyrics of bands such as The Clash were about experiences of life on estates, unemployment benefit and 'White riots'. In many ways, Punk was the complete opposite of skinhead subculture and yet, at the same time, significant elements of it dealt with problems of

Focus on research

Iain Borden
Skateboarding subculture

Iain Borden claims a certain 'outlaw' status for skateboarders as figures standing apart from and against the 'rule of the commodity' (the reduction of everything to profit-making). In particular, skateboarders reject the control of urban streets by profit-making leisure industries and the repressive legislation which supports this, such as laws of trespass and antisocial behaviour. He argues that skateboarders are a 'countercultural'/'subcultural' group, primarily consisting of 'youth', who seek to reclaim the city space. Skateboarding is a collective act of resistance:

《 *Skateboarding, like other subcultures, attempts to separate itself from groups such as the family, to be oppositional, appropriative of the city, irrational in organization, ambiguous in constitution, independently creative of its marginal or 'sub' status'.* 》

Adapted from: Borden, I. (2001) *Skateboarding, Space and the City: Architecture and the Body*, Oxford: Berg

1   What is the nature of skateboarding subculture?

2   In what ways can skateboarding be a form of 'resistance'?

unemployment and the drabness of working-class life. Punk style was a deliberate attempt at a do-it-yourself culture, which cost very little and was based on subverting the normal use and meanings of items. Clothes were ripped and drawn from a variety of sources, hair shaped in unusual ways and bodies pierced. Safety pins changed from household objects to body-piercing ornaments; bin liners became clothes; bondage gear was removed from the bedroom to everyday use. Hebdige's point was that, unlike the analyses of Jefferson and Cohen, youth

subculture did not have to look to the past to be **oppositional**, but could be innovative too.

Race, conflict and subcultural style

By the 1960s, there were significant enough numbers of young people of African-Caribbean origin in Britain to forge their own distinctive youth subcultures. Sociologists were accused of ethnocentrism – ignoring these Black subcultures in favour of focusing on the spectacular subcultures favoured by some White youth. Hebdige (1979) suggests that the first subcultural style was that of Rude Boys. In Jamaica, 'Rudies' formed a subculture based on looking cool, dealing in cannabis and pimping. The image of coolness was transferred to the UK along with ska music and, like any other youth subculture, a degree of minor offending. Overlapping with the Rude Boys' subculture was the Rastafarian Movement. The Rastafarian Movement developed in Jamaica, but sees Ethiopia as the Holy Land and the last Ethiopian Emperor, Haile Selassie (or Ras Tafari) as their leader. Rastafarianism sees Babylon (or White colonial capitalism) as evil, and salvation coming from an eventual move back to Ethiopia. Marijuana plays a key role in the religion, as it allows the user to enter into an altered, apparently higher, state of consciousness.

Rastafarianism and the Rude Boy culture of Jamaica provided a cultural context for a generation of Black youths that was distinctive from White culture, according to Sivanandan (1981). He argues that the distinctive Black youth cultures emerged in Britain as a result of the experiences of a second generation of Black young people, who were born and raised in Britain, and yet were socially and economically marginalized by the wider White society on the basis of 'race'. Sivanandan suggests that the Black subcultures were a continuation of a colonial struggle transposed to Britain. Whilst working-class White youths expressed their opposition through forming subcultures such as the skinheads, Sivanandan argued that the 'Black' youth subcultures were different styles, but driven by the same sense of opposition to capitalist and racist society.

The response of the media to these Black subcultural forms was different from their treatment of White subcultures. There were some attempts to exploit them by the music and leisure industries, but the media generally opted to represent Black youth subcultures as threatening and criminal. In particular, as Hall *et al.* (1978) pointed out, young Black men were closely linked in the media with street crime.

Magic!

A related, though distinctive version of a critical sociological approach to youth cultures is provided by Brake (1984).

Brake is sympathetic to the idea that youth subcultures are a form of resistance to capitalism, but he also notes that they do nothing to alter the power and economic differences in society that create the problems for working-class youth in the first place. In terms of actually challenging capitalism, they are therefore pointless. Nevertheless, according to Brake, they do provide a 'magical' solution for working-class youth's plight.

By using the term 'magical', Brake means that whilst they appear to provide a way out for each generation through new forms of subculture, in fact this is merely an illusion (as most magic tricks are). Each generation uses this trick to convince themselves they are different and are not going to become like their parents. However, in reality, the same economic and social structures that have constrained their parents' behaviour eventually constrains them too. They form relationships, get jobs, have kids and so on. But the magic trick keeps each working-class generation believing they are different.

Brake also explored middle-class youth subcultures and suggested that these are significantly different from those of working-class youth. Brake argues that middle-class youth subcultures are more all-encompassing than working-class ones and are more likely to be 'countercultural'. By this he means that they can provide complete cultural alternatives (for example political or religious) to the existing mainstream culture.

Criticisms of the critical cultural studies approach

The cultural studies analyses of working-class youth subcultures were immensely influential, but have been strongly criticized:

- Stan Cohen (1972) argued that these writers wanted to find forms of resistance in the style and argot of the working-class subcultures and were biased in their analyses. They therefore interpreted argot and style in a way that supported their political beliefs. Cohen pointed out that there were various different ways of interpreting the symbols, most of which were not supportive of the critical cultural studies approach.
- This approach completely ignored middle-class youth subcultures. This could be because, according to this approach, there really should not be any, as middle-class youth do not face the same problems.
- Critical cultural writers credit working-class youth with an amazing ability to create complete, highly sophisticated subcultures based on a complex set of symbols. Cohen suggests this is very naive, ignoring as it does the role of the media and other commercial interests in developing and exploiting young people.
- A final criticism came from McRobbie (1991), who argues that critical youth cultural writers have largely ignored girls' subcultures. She argues that these are very different in content and style, and do not fit the theoretical framework of the conflict approach.

Feminism and girl subcultures

What sociologists, particularly feminists, most commonly state when exploring youth subcultures is that females are largely missing. Indeed, the term '**invisible girl**' is often used. McRobbie and Garber (1976) comment that the place of young women in youth culture reflects their general position in society. Although they are present in all youth subcultures, they are pushed to the margins of this largely male social activity. McRobbie argues that the range of possibilities open to females in subcultures is much more limited than that of the males. According to her, youth cultures let males have 'temporary flights' away from the responsibilities and constraints imposed upon male adults in society, but females are denied this possibility because of greater parental control and the constraints imposed by

other females concerning appropriate sexual conduct. This is linked to ideas about the 'natural' place of women being in the home rather than hanging around in the streets.

According to McRobbie, this results in girls engaging in 'bedroom culture', where they meet their friends and chat. This is a place, in the home, which is regarded as safe and appropriate for females.

Although McRobbie's study was completed in the 1970s, more recent research confirms the continuing existence of bedroom culture. However, the nature of the bedroom environment has changed. Lincoln (2004) found that boyfriends were sometimes allowed into bedrooms and that access to the internet and TV meant that there were more external influences beyond the immediate friendship group.

More recent evidence about the marginalization of females in subcultures is provided by Thornton (1995). She studied the dance music scene of the 1990s and discovered that, although females were more likely to go 'clubbing' than boys, they were often accorded less status than males because they were associated with a taste for mainstream pop music.

Reddington (2003) takes a more positive view of the role of females in subcultures. She suggests that the active participation of girls in subcultures has actually been ignored by many sociologists. She focuses on the punk subculture of the 1970s to make her point. Women like Vivienne Westwood played a key role in punk fashion and punk bands often featured women as equal members (e.g. The Adverts) or were made up entirely of female members (e.g. The Slits). Female journalists such as Julie Burchill were also important in publicizing and supporting the movement.

Now we will continue our exploration of youth subcultures by discussing two other theoretical approaches: late-modern and postmodern. These two approaches share the belief that the importance of social class and employment has declined as an influence on youth culture. Instead, youth subcultures stretch across class lines and are more concerned with individuals expressing themselves in various ways. The idea of resistance is completely dropped.

Late modernity: consumerism and countercultures

In recent years, sociologists have argued that the traditional social structure associated with capitalism and industrial societies has been swept away. Social class, for example, which was an extremely important determinant of life in the 1950s, has declined considerably. Certainly inequalities still exist, but they are experienced and perceived in different ways by people now. The decline in the importance of social class is just one of many social and economic changes taking place. In order to help us understand these changes, sociologists have suggested using the term **modernity** for the more traditional industrial social and economic arrangements which began to decline in the second part of the 20th century and **late modernity** for society since then. Late modernity is characterized by choice and a stress on the individual. Work as a central focus of most people's lives and identity has increasingly been replaced by leisure and consumption (what you buy).

This shift from modernity to late modernity has very important implications for youth. In particular, it points the direction of youth subcultural studies away from resistance in two very different directions:

1 towards the exploration of self and new social arrangements, which has led to countercultures or new social movements
2 towards the development of youth lifestyles based on consumerism and leisure.

Countercultures

The term 'counterculture' is used to describe subcultures that present proposals as to how society ought to be organized that contrast with – or run counter to – the current arrangements. The term was developed by writers such as Marcuse (1964) and Roszak (1970). The rise of youth countercultures was possibly one of the first indications of the arrival of late modernity.

The first large-scale counterculture in Britain was that of the hippies who sought to withdraw from the organized, technological and bureaucratic lifestyle predominating by the 1960s. Their general beliefs were that love should replace violence and that people should be free to express themselves artistically, musically and socially. Most political movements demand a change in society, but hippies argued first for a change in the way people thought. Changes in society would then follow. The counterculture emerged in the 1960s in San Francisco, where ideas had developed on the use of drugs to liberate the mind.

The 1970s saw the decline of hippies, and counterculture appeared to shrink to its base of the student population, which, at that time, was undergoing a massive expansion. However, the 1980s saw the emergence of new concerns centred less on personal development and more on concerns about the way society was developing and the effects of technological change on society, the physical environment and the animal world (McKay 1996). A wide range of very different groups began to emerge that had few specific interests in common, but that shared a broad philosophy opposed to materialism, urbanism, consumerism and capitalism. McKay describes the New Age counterculture as a 'loose network of loose networks'. It was composed of New Age travellers, eco-warriors and animal liberation activists, amongst others.

The key point about all these countercultures was that, although they were critical of existing social arrangements, their supporters were drawn from a wide range of society and the central themes were the exploration of new directions and new ideas of self. The notion of working-class resistance did not come into it.

Consumerism and leisure

So far, the youth subcultures we have explored have been portrayed as being in some ways critical of existing social arrangements. This is true whether they are setting out specifically to criticize society, such as the hippies or the eco-warriors, or whether they are 'inarticulate' in their opposition, such as punks and skinheads. Coleman (1980), however, has argued that this approach relies too heavily

on exploring the relatively few 'spectacular' youth cultures that have hit the headlines and have been used by the leisure and fashion industries as images. Other sociologists, such as Muncie (1984), have argued that young people on the whole are actually very conformist. Though they may follow the fashion, it does not mean that they 'buy into' the meanings that sociologists suggest underpin the subcultures. You can, for example, have 'locks' but not be a Rastafarian. The major interests of young people reflect and correspond to those of the dominant value system, they do not oppose it. In fact, in a national study of young people's attitudes (Roberts 1997), the overwhelming majority were conformist in attitude. What young people want, according to these analyses, is to enjoy the new leisure industries that have emerged in the last 30 years. City centres have become places where young people go out at weekends, engage in drinking, meeting others and generally seeking to enjoy what the leisure industry has to offer. Chatterton and Hollands' (2001) study of nightlife in Newcastle also finds that there is a considerable amount of conservatism in what appears to be irresponsible, drunken nights out at the weekend. They argue that the idea of 'going out' was not to get drunk, to find a sexual partner or to fight, but simply reflected the more obvious desire to go out with friends and enjoy oneself. There is no intention of confronting society – instead, going out provided social space away from education or work, where young people could 'construct their identities'.

According to Roberts (1997) the gender patterns, too, have remained conservative, with male and female youth exhibiting the broader society's attitudes towards expectations of appropriate behaviour for the different sexes.

The shift from modernity to late modernity has, therefore, opened up 'spaces' where very different forms of youth subcultures can exist.

Postmodern youth subcultures

During the 1990s postmodernist approaches began to emerge as a useful way of analysing a range of social issues. **Postmodernism** challenged sociology in a profound way by arguing that most of the social phenomena that sociologists seek to understand are actually impossible to understand through rational analysis. According to postmodernists such as Bauman (1993) there is no coherent, structured social world that can be understood by rational inquiry. They suggest instead that the world is totally complex and confusing. At first, this might seem to herald the end of sociology, but modified forms of postmodernism were successfully adopted by sociologists, and one of the areas most intensively studied was that of youth subculture.

This postmodernist approach introduced new questions and innovative research methods to the study of youth subculture. In terms of research, for example, Widdicombe and Wooffitt (1995) encouraged young people to talk about their experiences and views of the world. The researchers refused to impose a framework on the conversations they held with the young people (unlike the approach of the Centre for Contemporary Cultural Studies – see p. 231) and argued that youth subcultures did not have fixed meanings or any real independent existence. They suggested instead that young people used the notion of a youth subculture in many different ways. There was, therefore, no one meaning of youth culture or subculture. The anarchy of punk, the oppositional attitudes of working-class youth or the countercultural ideas of the middle-class youth were, in fact, merely meanings 'imposed' upon young people's activities by sociologists.

The analysis of youth subculture moved away from notions of opposition or counterculture and started to stress the way that subculture was as much about style as anything else. Roberts (1997) argued that young people pick up styles and fashions from those available in the media and others around them and there is no underlying opposition or real meaning.

Other writers such as Maffesoli (1998) suggested that youth subcultures as such had ceased to exist for young people, and instead were being replaced by fluid and open movements or '**neo-tribes**'. He uses this term to describe a wide range of groupings, all of which share a commitment to 'the communal ethic', which 'has the simplest of foundations: warmth, companionship – physical contact with one another' (Maffesoli 1998). These neo-tribes, he argues, tend to be based on networks that have developed through the choice to be together for 'elective sociality' (based simply on the desire to be together), rather than for any particular collective purpose.

These sorts of approaches offered explanations for the emergence of a wide range of rapidly changing 'subcultures', such as those associated with raves and clubbing. However, as well as being highly critical of sociologists, postmodern approaches also raised a question that had not previously been discussed adequately by sociologists: whether youth culture emanated from young people themselves or was the creation of the mass media and commercial interests.

Postmodern perspectives on youth culture and the media industry

Functionalist writers had no interest in the basis of youth culture, seeing it as merely a form of transition into adulthood. Critical sociologists, however, were convinced that youth subcultures were generated by young people themselves in their attempts to resist capitalism. Others, such as Coté and Allahar (1996), oppose this view, seeing youth subcultures as products of media manipulation. According to this view, young people are the 'dupes' of commercial interests, and youth subcultures are essentially the products of an industry which wishes to make profit.

>> *What lies at the heart of all this activity, however, is the fact that these media can sell young people some element of an identity they have been taught to crave ... leisure industries such as music, fashion and cosmetics have a largely uncritical army of consumers awaiting the next craze or fad.*>> (Coté and Allahar 1996, p. 149)

In a similar vein, Giroux (1998) argues that the large multinational media and fashion companies are exploiting the multiplicity of social divisions in contemporary society and seeking to make profit out of them. Giroux argues that differences of religion, 'race', locality and gender are simply marketing categories that are being encouraged as new and growing markets to sell music and clothes to.

Postmodern approaches throw a different light on this debate. Kahane (1997) suggests that contemporary youth subcultures are a genuine attempt to construct new and original subcultures from the enormous choice of music, style and language available to young people, based on 'symbols of freedom, spontaneity, adventurism and **eclecticism**'. Thornton (1995) suggests that youth culture is actually a complex mixture of both. On the one hand, youth cultures can be manufactured by commercial interests and then taken up by young people and refashioned in a way never imagined by the music/fashion industry; on the other hand, 'genuine' youth cultures can be generated by young people and then taken over by commercial interests.

Globalization and hybridized youth subcultures

An important element of postmodernist thinking about youth subcultures is that of **globalization**. Writers such as Luke and Luke (2000) argue that in the modern cultural world, influences derive from films, music and other media that are global in nature, not just national or local. They suggest the idea of a '**hybridized**' youth culture, whereby young people take elements from the global youth cultures featured in the media, and then adapt these according to local values and ideas. So, young people in Japan place a Japanese perspective on international music and styles, and young people in Britain place a British cultural perspective on the same music. Even more specific, Muslim young people in Britain will place a different perspective on this than African-Caribbean youth.

Postmodernity and 'race'

This takes us into postmodern debates on 'race' and youth subcultures. The Rude Boy and Rastafarianism subcultures which we discussed earlier were regarded by Sivanandan as 'oppositional'. He claimed to have found a meaning underpinning ethnic minority youth subcultures. Postmodern analyses present a rather different image.

The first step towards a postmodern approach can be found in the work of Gilroy (1987), who argued that we can understand all ethnic-minority youth subcultures through diasporas (patterns of dispersal) created by the postcolonial migrations. People who have left their place of origin have links there, but also must adapt to their new environment. For Gilroy, all ethnic-minority youth subcultures are, therefore, a mix of their cultural origins and of their present circumstances. Although, at first, this seems the same argument as we saw earlier, what Gilroy is arguing is that the ethnic minority subcultures are very flexible and open, taking elements from a range of influences and constantly changing. This moved sociologists into applying the notions of hybridity to ethnic-minority youth subcultures.

Cashmore (1997) gives a good example of hybridity in his analysis of 'gangsta' rap. This began in the 1960s in Jamaica and then, in the 1970s, became popular in the Black neighbourhoods of New York. By the mid 1980s, it had been taken up in Los Angeles and from there was promoted world wide. But there are numerous variations of the original rap, which has constantly changed in response to genuinely creative ideas, as well as to the demands of the international music industry. Rap has also crossed the

Focus on research

Andy Bennett
Subcultures or neo-tribes?

Bennett set out to see if the claims of the postmodernist sociologist Michel Maffesoli that youth subcultures had been replaced by 'neo-tribes' were true. Bennett researched clubs in Newcastle and found no evidence for youth subcultures. Instead, loose, fluid and relatively short-term youth groupings occurred, which were drawn from a range of social backgrounds. Unlike traditional working-class subcultures which were clearly definable, these new neo-tribes are based around fashion and lifestyle, but without the shared values. Individuals mixed and matched fashion influences and didn't feel they belonged to any definable group. Bennett suggests that youth identity is now very fluid and doesn't involve fixed commitments or norms and values, as claimed by traditional youth subcultural theorists.

Bennett, A. (1999) 'Subcultures or neo-tribes: rethinking the relationship between youth, style and musical taste', *Sociology*, 33(3), pp. 599–617

1 **What are the differences between a 'neo-tribe' and a subculture?**

2 **Explain Bennett's conclusions about youth identity in your own words.**

barriers of race and has been taken up enthusiastically by White youth. Youth subcultures therefore draw upon

---

Figure 5.2 Summary of late-modern and postmodern approaches to youth culture

Late modernity and postmodernity

AGREE on the following changes to society:

- Decline in traditional hierarchy, such as social class
- Growth of individualism
- Importance of the media and its presentation of 'reality'
- Leisure and consumption replace work as a key component of society

Late modernity
A range of fast-changing youth styles occur, but also some more long-lasting subcultures and countercultures. The media are extremely influential, as are large commercial leisure organizations.

Postmodernity
No subcultures, but instead a rapidly changing and ever-increasing range of fashions, styles and 'looks'. These are partly genuine innovation by young people, partly manipulation. The individual and the expression of individuality are core experiences.

but they INTERPRET these changes differently:

different global elements and then adapt them to local or relevant ethnic circumstances.

Key terms

Ascribed social position fixed at birth, such as son or daughter.

Achieved social position chosen or earned, such as A-level student.

Culture a complete-in-itself set of values and guide to behaviour.

Decode the process of uncovering hidden meanings.

Eclectic drawn from a wide variety of sources.

Ethnocentrism focusing on your own cultural group and considering it to be 'normal'

Globalization refers to international nature of trade and the media.

Hegemony a complete set of ideas and values which provide an explanation for the social world; the term is usually associated with Marxist or conflict theorists, who argue that the ruling class 'imposes' hegemony on society to explain why they should be in control.

Hybridization the linking of local and global cultures to form youth subcultures.

Inarticulate unable to express clearly.

Invisible girl a phrase often used to emphasize the way that youth cultures appear to be dominated by males.

Late modernity the period since the 1970s where the structures of modernity have been replaced by individual values and a stress on leisure.

Neo-tribes temporary groups coming together when they wish and then parting. An alternative to the idea of more static and long-lasting subcultures.

Modernity the traditional set of social and economic relationships dominated by industry and social class.

Oppositional subcultural values opposed to the dominant hegemony of the ruling class.

Postmodernism an alternative to late modernity; describes the rejection of rational ways of explaining action and a stress on emotions.

Resistance a term used by conflict theorists to refer to a subculture being critical of capitalism and protective of working-class interests.

Semiotic (semiotic analysis) the analysis of signs and symbols in order to uncover the hidden meanings.

Subculture a set of distinctive values existing within a broader culture.

Check your understanding

1. Explain what is meant by a 'rite of passage'.

2. What is the purpose of youth culture according to functionalists?

3. According to Roszak what has the division of age replaced?

4. What is meant by the terms 'oppositional' and 'semiotic'?

5. Why is the term 'invisible girls' used?

6. Identify and explain any one criticism made by Cohen of the critical cultural studies approach.

7. What ideas are shared by both late-modern and postmodern sociologists?

8. How did the concerns of countercultural movements change during the 1980s?

9. According to Chatterton and Hollands, what do young people seek when they go out?

10. How do sociologists such as Coleman and Muncie criticize the view that youth subcultures are a way of resisting society?

11. Explain Maffesoli's view of 'neo-tribes'.

12. How do postmodern sociologists attack the view that youth culture is simply the result of manipulation by the media, fashion and music industries?

13. How can the idea of 'hybridity' help us to understand the link between race and youth culture?

Activities

Research idea

Observe groups of students around your school, college or local town. Observe clothes, hair styles, use of language and behaviour. Is it possible to categorize people into clear styles? If not, why not?

Web.tasks

Go to the archives of the web discussion pages of 'Subcultural Styles' at

www.jiscmail.ac.uk /archives/subculturalstyles.html

Here, academics and other interested people ask and answer questions on youth culture.

Browse the archives for some fascinating stuff!

The two ways need to be stated clearly, probably at the beginning of paragraphs

You can refer to any subculture, either emphasizing the marginal role of women or the view of those such as Reddington who believe women can play a central role in some youth subcultures

Aim to write for about 15 minutes, spending a roughly equal amount on each of the two ways

(a) Identify and explain two ways in which young women are involved in youth subcultures. (17 marks)

Each of the two ways need to be discussed in depth, using sociological concepts, examples and studies if possible

Each of the two ways need to be discussed in depth, using sociological concepts, examples and studies if possible

The view needs to be described in some detail, using sociological concepts, studies and theories

This idea will need to be explained. The resistance is symbolic

(b) Outline and evaluate the view that youth subcultures are a form of resistance to capitalism. (33 marks)

You need to use other theories about the origin of youth culture and subcultures to criticise the view in the question

Aim to write at least two sides of the answer book in about 30 minutes

Grade booster Getting top marks in this question

Use an introduction to explain the key concepts of youth subculture and resistance to capitalism. This second concept should be linked to the Marxist perspective. There should be a detailed description of the view of subcultures as resistance that originated in the Birmingham University Centre for Contemporary Cultural Studies, including examples of the kind of analysis that led them to these conclusions. The concept of hegemony will be helpful. Evaluation will need to include criticisms of the CCCS view such as their failure to take into account girls and 'ordinary' young people as well as alternative interpretations of youth subcultures.

Youth and crime

Getting you thinking

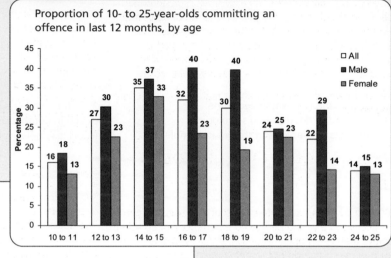

Proportion of 10- to 25-year-olds committing an offence in last 12 months, by age

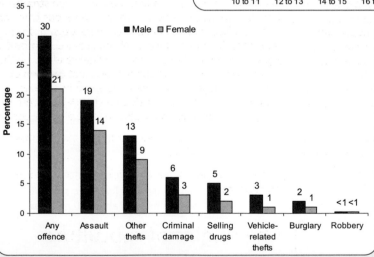

Proportion of 10- to 25-year-olds committing an offence in last 12 months

Masculinities

In *Masculinities and Crime*, Messerschmidt applies an analysis of masculinities to an understanding of youth crime. There are different masculinities depending upon class, location and ethnic background.

So, White middle-class youth may construct masculinity in terms of a future of office work, career, economic and status success. Working-class White youths may construct masculinity in terms of physical aggression and hostility to other groups considered 'inferior' to them. Masculinity for certain ethnic-minority males may find expression in the street gang and crime in order to achieve the status they feel is lacking. Therefore, crime or violence provides a way of 'doing masculinity' when other resources are not available.

Adapted from Muncie, J. (2004) *Youth and Crime*, London: Sage, p. 130

1   Summarize the patterns and trends in the two bar charts.

2   How does the work of Messerschmidt help us understand the relationship betwen gender and youth offending?

Crimes and anti-social behaviour committed by young people has come to be known as delinquency. Concern about delinquency is not new. Pearson (1983) shows that concern about the behaviour of 'hooligans' has been expressed since the Victorian era. Often the more spectacular activities of some young people have caused outrage in the media and this has fuelled great concern in society, with pressure to 'clamp down' on these 'trouble makers'. The banning of 'hoodies' by the Bluewater shopping mall is just one recent example of this sort of concern. Back in the 1960s Stan Cohen (1972) examined the social reaction to scuffles between mods and rockers in some British seaside towns at Bank Holiday times. He identified a huge overreaction by the press who exaggerated the conflict to a massive extent, causing widespread public concern. He called the resulting concern a moral panic and the youth groups responsible for these moral panics folk devils. Effectively the media was playing a large part in creating fear of young people among older generations, labelling them as troublemakers and as a social problem.

But what do we actually know about real patterns of crime among young people?

Patterns and trends in youth crime

It is difficult to get an accurate picture of the extent of youth crime. Many more young people admit offences when asked in surveys than ever appear in official statistics. This is because many people do not report crimes, considering them too trivial or, in the case of violence, a private matter. Even when crimes are reported, detection rates are low. But even bearing these problems in mind, it does seem that young people are more likely than adults to offend. The peak age of offending in 2007 was 17 years for males and 15 years for females (NACRO, 2009). Young people are also the most likely group to become victims of crime.

The picture over time shows that between the early 1990s until 2003, youth offending fell by 27 per cent although it has increased since then. As no self-report studies indicate significant increases in youth offending since 2003, it seems likely that the recent increase is more to do with

changes in the reporting and recording of offences rather than any change in actual offending.

Gender

During 2007, 74 per cent of all young people convicted, warned or reprimanded for an offence were male. Despite concern about 'girl gangs', there is no evidence that female youth offending is increasing at any faster rate than that of males. It appears that the kind of hegemonic masculinity described by writers such as Connell (2002) is still having an effect on rates of offending.

Ethnicity

'During 2007-8, while Black or Black British young people made up three per cent of the general 10-17 population, they accounted for seven per cent of those coming to the attention of the youth justice system, 14 per cent of those receiving a custodial sentence and almost one in three of those given a sentence of long-term detention.' (NACRO, 2009) There has long been concern about discrimination in the justice system but these patterns may equally be the result of poverty and social exclusion and/or the formation of subcultures within minority ethnic groups.

Social class

While there are few statistics directly linking youth crime to social class, the association between offending, poverty and social exclusion is well established. Pitts' (2008) research on gangs shows that there are often stronger links between young people's involvement in serious crime and living in disadvantaged areas than there are with their individual, family or educational characteristics. In fact, living in poverty is likely to have a negative effect on these other aspects. It may also be the case that the kind of deviance engaged in by middle-class youths such as cannabis smoking is less likely to be labelled as worthy of attention by the police and other agents of social control.

We will now move on to look at the reasons for these patterns in more detail.

These explanations focus on one key concept, that of **subculture**.

The origins of subculture

Subcultural approaches to explaining youth offending are drawn from two traditions. Initially, these two traditions were quite separate, but over time they have become increasingly intertwined, as we shall see. The first of these two traditions is the environmental school, which emerged from studies by sociologists at the University of Chicago in the early to mid 20th century. The second tradition derives from strain theory, first devised by Robert Merton in the 1930s.

Subculture and the University of Chicago

This approach developed as a result of massive social change in American cities in the early 20th century. Sociologists went out into the streets and observed or hung around with gangs in the streets or just observed what was happening amongst deviant groups. A huge

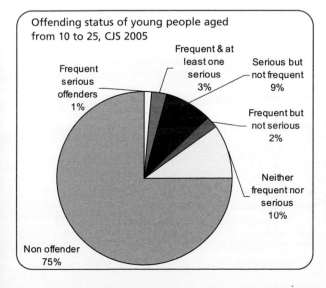

Offending status of young people aged from 10 to 25, CJS 2005

- Frequent serious offenders 1%
- Frequent & at least one serious 3%
- Serious but not frequent 9%
- Frequent but not serious 2%
- Neither frequent nor serious 10%
- Non offender 75%

number of books were published including Thrasher's *The Gang* (1927) and Whyte's *Street Corner Society* (1955). What emerged from these studies was that these deviant groups had clear norms and values of their own (or subcultures) which they used to justify their deviant behaviour.

Functionalist approaches

Subculture and strain theory

First writing in the 1930s, Merton argued that the offending committed by young people was the result of a poor fit or a **strain** between the socially accepted goals of society and the socially approved means of obtaining those desired goals. This resulting strain led to deviance.

Merton argued that all societies set their members certain socially approved goals and approved ways of achieving these goals. For example, a socially approved goal is have a job and the means to achieving the job is to work hard at school and college, do well in exams, and be awarded the position on merit.

However, if the majority of the population are unable to achieve the socially set goals, because the approved means simply are not available to them (for example, if education is so expensive that only a few affluent people can attend school), then a significant proportion of the population will become disenchanted with the society and seek out alternative (often deviant) ways of behaving. Merton used the term **anomie** to describe the situation where it is difficult for people to achieve the approved goals. In a situation of anomie, people get frustrated and develop a number of responses to deal with the situation:

- carrying on conforming regardless
- seeking new ways of achieving the goals, including crime (innovation)
- simply 'going through the motions', knowing it is pointless (ritualism)
- turning to drugs or alcohol in despair (retreatism)
- rejecting the traditional means and goals, and turning to political, religious or social rebellion.

Merton has been criticized for his belief that there are common goals that people share; critics argue that there are numerous goals in society and equally numerous means of achieving them.

Status frustration

Writing in the mid 1950s, Albert Cohen (1955) drew from both Merton and the Chicago School. He was particularly interested in the fact that a very high proportion of offending by young people does not benefit them financially, but consists of vandalism or violence. The first thing that Cohen noted was that the overwhelming majority of young people committing offences or engaging in antisocial behaviour, were from working-class backgrounds. Cohen suggested the answer lies in **status frustration**, that is, a sense of personal failure and inadequacy. According to Cohen, this comes from the experience of school. Working-class boys are more likely to fail at school and consequently feel humiliated. In an attempt to gain status, they develop subcultures which

'invert' traditional middle-class values such as obedience, politeness and obeying the law. Instead, they behave badly and engage in a variety of antisocial behaviour. Within the values of their subculture, this behaviour provides them with status.

Cohen has been criticized quite heavily for constructing a theory of subculture that is much more applicable to males than to females.

Illegitimate opportunity structure: illegitimate subcultures

Merton's ideas also influence the work of Cloward and Ohlin (1960), who agreed that a mismatch between socially approved goals and means could lead to offending. However, they suggested that Merton had failed to appreciate that there was a parallel illegal set of goals and means to the legal one, which they called the '**illegitimate opportunity structure**'. By this they meant that, for some groups in society, an illegal career was possible. A recent example of this is described in Dick Hobbs' book *Bad Business* (1998). Hobbs interviewed successful professional criminals and demonstrated how it is possible to have a career in crime, given the right connections and 'qualities'.

According to Cloward and Ohlin, the illegal opportunity structure had three possible subcultures:

- Criminal – In this adaptation, there is a thriving local criminal subculture, with successful role models. Young offenders can 'work their way up the ladder' in the criminal hierarchy.
- Conflict – Here, there is no local criminal subculture to provide a career opportunity. Groups brought up in this sort of environment are likely to turn to violence, usually against other similar groups. Cloward and Ohlin give the example of violent gang 'warfare'.
- Retreatist – This occurs where the individual has no opportunity or ability to engage in either of the other two subcultures. The result is a retreat into the subculture of alcohol or drugs.

This explanation is useful and, as Hobbs' work shows, for some people there really is a criminal opportunity structure. But the approach shares some of the weaknesses of Merton's original theory. First, it is difficult to accept that such a neat distinction into three clear categories occurs in real life. Second, there is no discussion whatsoever about female deviance. The explanation is implicitly about males.

Focal concerns: subculture as normal working-class values

Walter Miller (1962) developed a rather different approach to explaining subculture and offending. He suggested that antisocial behaviour was simply an extreme development of normal working-class male values.

Miller suggested that working-class males have six 'focal concerns' which are likely to lead to delinquency:

- trouble – 'I don't go looking for trouble, but ...'
- toughness – a belief that being physically stronger than others (and being able to show it) is good
- smartness – that a person both looks good, but is also witty and has a 'sharp repartee'
- excitement – that it is important to search out thrills

Focus on research

Carl Nightingale
On the Edge

Although Merton and Cloward and Ohlin's writings are quite dated, it would be wrong to think that they are irrelevant. In America, there is still a strong tradition which uses their original ideas.

In *On the Edge* (1993), Carl Nightingale studied young Black youth in an inner-city area of Philadelphia. Nightingale noted the way that the youths in his study were avid television devotees, spending many hours watching television and eagerly identifying with the successful characters, both real and fictional. They desperately wanted to be successful like the media celebrities, yet as Black inner-city youths, they were excluded economically, racially and politically from participating in the mainstream US culture. Rather than reacting to this by turning against the dominant culture, they desperately wanted to be successful. For them, this meant having the 'right' clothes, music, cars, etc. – in particular by possessing articles with high-status trade names or logos. The only way to afford this was breaking the law. For Nightingale, the only way to understand the subculture is also to understand that it emerges from a real desire to be part of the mainstream US culture.

1   How does Nightingale argue that youth crime can result from a 'real desire to be part of the mainstream US culture'?

● fate – that the individual has little chance to overcome the wider fate that awaits them
● autonomy – that it is important not to be pushed around by others.

According to Miller, then, young lower-class males are pushed towards crime by the implicit values of working-class male culture. However, Box (1981) has argued that these values could equally apply to males right across the class structure.

Subterranean values: subculture as normal

Matza (1964) has suggested that, in explaining youth offending, we should think less about the notion of subculture and more about subterranean values. According to him, everyone has some deviant values, but they are kept in check most of the time.

All young people crave thrills and excitement and all break rules if it is to their advantage, but most of the time they control these desires and conform. For the majority of young people (and older ones too), these subterranean values only emerge on holiday or a drunken night out. On occasions such as these, most behave badly. But when they do emerge, people will then use excuses to explain why the excesses were justified. Matza called these excuses techniques of neutralization. The difference between a persistent offender and a law-abiding young person may simply be how often and in what circumstances the subterranean values emerge and are then justified by the techniques of neutralization. Matza is not denying that some groups, or subcultures, are more likely to express subterranean values, but these groups are not completely different from other young people (see Fig. 5.5)

Figure 5.5 Matza: techniques of neutralization

Denial of responsibility – The offender denies that it was their fault: 'it wasn't me, it was the alcohol/drugs'.

Denial of victim – The offender claims that in this particular case the victim was in the wrong – for example in a rape case where the woman was dressed in a way that 'led him on'.

Denial of injury – The offender claims that the victim was not really hurt or harmed by the crime. Often used to justify theft from a company as opposed to stealing from individuals.

Condemnation of condemners – The offender feels a sense of unfairness of being picked on for something others have done and not been punished for.

Appeal to higher loyalties – The offender claims that the rule or law had to be ignored because more important issues were at stake. The offender was, for example, 'standing up for his family/community/race'.

Labelling theory

The opening of this Topic outlined the way in which some young people can become labelled as deviant. Some labelling theorists take this view further. They argue that once an individual or group has become labelled, they will be affected by all the negative responses they get from others outside their group. This will lead them to change their self-image and to begin to live up the image others have of them. This process is known as a **self-fulfilling prophecy** – a prediction that makes itself become true. So, if young people wearing 'hoodies' are thrown out of shopping centres, they may become angry and aggrieved about the society that they feel is rejecting them. This could well lead to their becoming aggressive and anti-social. This process is known as **deviance amplification**. Back in the 1970s, Jock Young (1971) showed how police clampdowns on young marijuana smokers in the Notting Hill area of London caused these 'hippies' to go further underground and to associate more with those selling harder drugs – their initial deviance was amplified by the reaction of the forces of social control.

Labelling theory has been criticised for making the process of deviance amplification appear inevitable when in reality, people may respond in different ways to their labelling. Also, for ignoring the reasons why people may commit deviant acts in the first place.

Marxist subcultural theories

In Topic 2, we explored the contribution of Marxist or conflict approaches to youth subcultures. The same approaches are used by Marxist writers to explain youth crime. Young working-class males commit crime as a form of resistance to capitalism (for a full discussion, see p. 230–233).

Left realism and youth subculture

Left-realist approaches to crime emerged from Marxist approaches. Marxist analyses of youth offending saw it as an act of resistance against capitalism. Left realists, such as Lea and Young (1984), however, argue that youth crime harms the working-class people in the neighbourhood in which it takes place.

Lea and Young suggest that youth offending is the result of two linked factors:

1 Young inner-city males (and in particular, ethnic-minority males) feel relatively deprived, as they see affluence all around them, but are unable to gain access to the wealth.
2 They feel socially and politically marginalized, in the sense that they have little status in society and few ways to change the society around them, which they believe causes their poor social and economic situation. The result is that a subculture develops which provides them with status and justifies criminal acts.

Contemporary approaches to subculture

Postmodernity: subculture and emotion

Postmodern ideas relating to youth culture were discussed in Topic 2, so you may wish to turn there for a more detailed examination of their ideas. Here, we will simply explore their relationship to youth offending subcultures.

The approaches we have looked at so far seek to explain youth offending by looking for some rational reason why the subculture might have developed. Recent postmodern approaches reject this form of explanation.

Instead, they argue that emotions are an important and ignored drive for behaviour that includes youth offending. Two forms of emotion-based explanation are suggested for behaviour which transgresses the accepted boundaries.

● Katz, (1988) argues that crime is **seductive** – young males get drawn into it, not because of any process of rejection, but because quite simply it is thrilling. That is why so much of youth offending is not for financial gain. There is simple pleasure in spraying a 'tag' on a wall or vandalizing a public building. Once a young person has tried this activity, they are drawn (or 'seduced') into repeating the process.
● Lyng (1990) argues that young males like to engage in **edgework**, which he defines as placing oneself in situations of potential harm by flirting with danger. There is no rational explanation for this desire to take risks – attempts to do so fail because they impose a rational explanation on a non-rational emotion. Like Katz, Lyng suggests simply that the rush or pleasure of experiencing danger is something that young males seek. An example of this is the practice of stealing cars and driving them dangerously.

Subculture and gender

Masculinity

Subcultural theories are overwhelmingly about male offending. If you read back through the various explanations in this topic, they are clearly about the behaviour of males.

Collison (1996) points out that if instead of seeing all these explanations as alternatives and instead look at what they all share, we can see that it is the idea of 'being a male'. Amongst a host of other aspects, **masculinity** includes:

● physical toughness
● the ability to take risks and court danger
● looking smart
● maintaining 'face' in the presence of others
● owning status objects.

Collison suggests that exploring the nature of masculinity is the key to understanding youth subcultures. This would involve a broad exploration of how boys are socialized by parents, the education system and the media.

Feminist subcultural explanations

Females are much less likely to engage in **antisocial behaviour** than males as we have seen in Figure 5.4 on p. 204. This has been reflected in the lack of research into female subcultures linked to offending. The majority of studies have actually indicated that female subcultures are far more likely to be restraining girls from offending. McRobbie and Garber (1976) argue that some females are involved in antisocial behaviour, but that within subcultures they tend to be marginalized through the dominance of males. However, McRobbie (1991) has also pointed out that it is actually more difficult for girls to enter youth subcultures, as there is more parental control on their behaviour. They are less likely to be allowed out in the evening and are usually required to explain where they have been. Frith (1983) has argued that **girls' culture** is more likely to be that of the bedroom, where girls can meet, listen to music, chat, compare sexual notes and practise dancing skills.

However, these sociological views are somewhat dated according to Chatterton and Hollands (2001), who studied young people's experience of 'nights out' in Newcastle. Their research suggests that for females aged over 16, the growth of city nightlife, changing attitudes to women's behaviour and increased self-confidence have all combined to change female social behaviour. They are now more likely have a public social life, using clubs, bars and pubs almost as much as young males.

Activities

Research idea

Devise a questionnaire for a sample of young people to test out some of the theories covered here. Avoid asking whether or not anyone has actually committed a crime. Questions might cover:

- strain theory – to what extent the sample share the ambitions of material success and the extent to which they accept the formal means to achieve these goals
- focal concerns – whether working-class members of the sample share similar 'focal concerns' to those identified by Miller
- techniques of neutralization – whether the sample have ever used any of the techniques identified by Matza
- seduction – whether those in the sample believe that deviance can be thrilling and exciting
- gender – whether male members of the sample are more tolerant of deviance than female.
- labelling – have your sample ever felt labelled. What effect did it have on them?

Check your understanding

1. How is the banning of 'hoodies' by a shopping mall an example of labelling?
2. Summarize changes in youth crime since 1990.
3. What is the relationship between ethnicity, social class and youth crime?
4. What is 'anomie'?
5. Give three examples of normal working-class behaviour that can lead to crime.
6. How does school failure lead to subculture, according to Albert Cohen?
7. What are 'techniques of neutralization' and how do they undermine some subcultural arguments?
8. How does the idea of a self-fulfilling prophecy help our understanding of delinquency?
9. How can crime be 'seductive'?
10. Why is the idea of 'masculinity' relevant to understanding offending behaviour?

Web.tasks

Go to: **http://www.nacro.org.uk/data/files/nacro-2009070900-280.pdf**.

This is a summary of information about youth offending from the charity NACRO. Read it and write two newspaper reports based on the information. One should present a balanced picture of youth crime in Britain. The other should be an exaggerated and sensational account designed to provoke a moral panic.

Key terms

Anomie a society overstresses achieving socially approved goals, but does not provide the means for the bulk of the population to achieve these goals.

Antisocial behaviour a wide range of more minor crimes.

Edgework doing dangerous or socially disapproved acts for the thrill of it.

Delinquency term commonly used to describe the crime and anti-social behaviour of young people.

Deviance amplification becoming more committed to deviant behaviour because of the reaction of the forces of social control

Folk devils term used to describe subcultures which become negatively labelled by the media

Girls' culture socializing with female friends at home, usually in the bedroom.

Illegal opportunity structure an alternative, illegal way of life to which certain groups in society have access.

Labelling treating a person or group on the basis of stereotypes

Masculinity values traditionally associated with males.

Moral panic great public concern created by media exaggeration

Seductive the pleasure of committing antisocial acts.

Self-fulfilling prophecy a prediction that makes itself become true

Status frustration according to Cohen, when young people feel that they are looked down upon by society.

Strain when the values of a society are difficult to achieve.

Subculture a distinctive set of values which provides an alternative to those of the mainstream culture.

The two patterns or trends need to be stated clearly, probably at the beginning of paragraphs

These could be changes or similarities over time, or relationships between crime rates and different social factors

Aim to write for about 15 minutes

(a) Identify and explain two patterns or trends in rates of youth crime. **(17 marks)**

Each of the two patterns or trends need to be discussed in depth, using sociological concepts, examples and studies if possible

Sociological explanations need to be described in some detail, using concepts, studies and theories

Avoid a discussion of crime in general or of subcultural style

(b) Outline and evaluate sociological explanations of youth crime. **(33 marks)**

The different explanations need to be compared with each other, evaluated and a balanced conclusion drawn

Aim to write at least two sides of the answer book in about 30 minutes

Grade booster　Getting top marks in this question

An introduction could provide the 'big picture' by summarising the main theories that provide these sociological explanations. They could include functionalism, labelling, Marxism, left realism and postmodernism. A key concept running through your answer is likely to be subculture. Each of the main explanations needs to be summarised with examples of studies provided where possible, for example A. Cohen (functionalism), Young (labelling), Sivanandan (Marxism), Katz (postmodernism). The explanations can be compared and evaluated as your answer progresses or in a separate section.

TOPIC 4

The experience of youth in education

Getting you thinking

ITEM A

Young money – the three marketeers

<< Despite being fresh out of Torquay Boys' Grammar, Adrian Bougourd, 18, Will Rushmer, 19, and Ryan Hayward, 18, beat the other five teams on the Channel 4 fantasy share game show, Show Me The Money, at the end of the 10-week series. The youngest contestants have made a profit of over £55000 on an imaginary £100000 lump sum in only eight weeks.

The teenagers, who have all recently started university, with 11 A-level A grades between them, are not new to stocks and shares. They started taking an interest in the stock market last year when their school entered the ProShare national investment programme. That competition for school pupils ended in May, and was won by a group of girls from Haberdashers' Aske's School, who were still doing GCSEs at the time.

Both Will, who is studying economics at Warwick, and Ryan are hoping for a career in the City, in either fund management or investment banking, once they have finished their degrees. Adrian, who is studying finance, accounting and management at Nottingham University, is toying with the idea of financial journalism. The Three Freshers, as they called themselves for the show, are just one of thousands of investment clubs in the UK. The number of investment groups increased by 3800 last year, pushing the total to more than 9000, according to ProShare, which promotes share ownership.>>

The Times, 11 November 2000

ITEM B

Do teenagers deliberately fail exams to stay cool?

A poll of 4000 Tyneside teenagers says peer pressure stops many pupils from studying or taking part in lessons.

Researchers say that members of an antischool subculture known as 'charvers' reject school as uncool and refuse to do GCSE course work, meaning they fail their exams. They say the situation could be the same across other UK cities, although the groups might have different names. The charvers typically wear fake designer and sports gear and are usually from poor backgrounds.

Researchers questioned teenagers aged between 15 and 17. They found the charvers' attitude was that school was uncool but college was OK, and that most expected to resit their GCSEs at further education colleges.

The research was by Lynne Howe, director of the South Tyneside Excellence in Cities programme. She said: 'For some youngsters – those known as charvers – being cool and well-thought of among their peers is the most important thing.

'These youngsters were largely from a deprived population but they didn't lack confidence or self-esteem. They deliberately fail their GCSEs because their social standing outside school is more important than any qualification.

'They were scared of being called names, physical threats and damage to the family home and property if they were seen doing homework or answering questions in class, but they consider college cool.'

The former teacher said the teenagers identified five different groups in school, including charvers, radgys (more aggressive than charvers), divvies (impressionable hangers-on to the charvers), goths (wear dark clothes but often work hard) and freaks, who work hard and are considered 'normal' by teachers.

Nearly a third of the 15-year-olds said they had been picked on for doing well at school, while the same proportion admitted teasing others who participated in lessons. More than 90 per cent of bright pupils said they wanted to go to university, but only one in four said they were doing their best at school.

Some said they would rather fail their GCSEs and take resits at college, hoping to get into higher education later, than risk being targeted by bullies while still at school.

Adapted from Leonard, M. (2000) 'Back to the future: the domestic division of labour', *Sociology Review*, 10(2)

1 Explain what is meant by 'antischool subcultures' (item B)

2 Suggest two ways in which the writer considers educational achievement is affected by peer group membership

3 Identify three reasons 'charvers' give for deliberately underperforming at school (item B)

4 Identify and explain two ways in which the proschool subculture described in Item A differs from the antischool subcultures referred to in Item B.

You probably don't need to be told that students respond to their schooling in different ways. In secondary schools in particular, usually by year 9, different groups emerge with very different attitudes. At one extreme, there are those groups of students who accept the rules and the authority of teachers without question, while at the other extreme, there are those who appear to devote all their attention to rule-breaking and avoiding work. You are probably familiar with this behaviour from your own experiences in education. Sociologists are particularly interested in these groups – or subcultures. Why do they form, and what effect do they have on their members, other pupils, teachers and schools?

The significance of educational experiences for youth

There are four major influences on the attitudes and behaviour of young people – the home, the school, the peer group and the media. These cannot really be separated from each other, as we see throughout this unit. Each has an impact on the other – we have seen examples of this in all the topics so far. In this topic, we will focus on the links between peer groups and the school. In particular, we will examine the way in which issues of social class, gender and ethnicity are played out in the formation of peer groups in the school setting. As you will see, these three forms of social division impact heavily on the development of peer groups and their members' attitudes to school, as well as to life in general.

Social class and the experience of schooling

Early studies of peer groups

The first studies of peer groups in schools took place during the 1960s and concentrated mainly on White, working-class youths. Hargreaves (1967) and Lacey (1970) studied single-sex boys' schools. Both found that working-class boys developed antischool subcultures, partly a result of being labelled by teachers as potential or actual troublemakers and partly because working-class boys were more likely to be consigned to lower streams in these schools. Unable to achieve status in terms of the mainstream values of the school, these pupils substitute their own set of delinquent values by which they can achieve success in the eyes of their peers. They do this by, for example, not respecting teachers, messing about, arriving late, having fights, building up a reputation with the opposite sex, and so on.

Perhaps the best known study into White youths at school during this period was by Willis (1977), who identified two school subcultures. The first, composed of working-class, school 'failures' – the 'lads' – aimed to 'have a laff' by rejecting the values of the school. The second group was more conformist, accepting the values and aims of the school. This group was referred to by the 'lads' as 'ear'oles'.

Willis' analysis showed that these 'lads' shared a subculture which contained elements of traditional working-class values of 'masculinity'. These were: physicality, toughness, collectivism, territoriality, hedonism/having fun and opposition to authority.

Willis' central argument is that working-class youths at school adopt these values because they can see that they are likely to be school failures. By adopting these, they reject the school and its values, but of course, they also guarantee their own failure.

Writers such as Hargreaves, Lacey and Willis refer to the pro- and antischool cultures as coherent groups, sharing their own uniform set of values. But for a number of writers following them, this was too simplistic.

Later studies of peer groups

Ball (1981) conducted a similar study on a mixed-sex comprehensive school and, whilst generally agreeing with the earlier studies, found there were more complex attitudes to school. Working-class boys did not necessarily reject school – they could also be indifferent to it. So, social class did not necessarily determine attitudes, but was one factor amongst others.

Phil Brown (1987) also criticizes the polarized image of working-class youth that Willis, Hargreaves and Lacey all put forward. Based on his survey of students in a South Wales comprehensive school, Brown argues that the majority of working-class males and females simply want to 'get by'. Brown suggests three different ways working-class students approach 'being in school and becoming adult':

1 The 'getting in' approach – Members of this group were usually low academic achievers (the 'rems'). They wanted to get into working-class culture and a working-class job. They also wanted to leave school at the earliest opportunity.
2 The 'getting out' approach or the 'swots' – Members of this group wanted middle-class jobs and the associated comfortable lifestyle.
3 The third approach – 'getting on' – was taken by the majority of the working-class students who 'neither simply accept nor reject school, but comply with it'.

Brown's view is that the differences between the 'rems' (equivalent to Willis' 'lads') and the ordinary students are quite subtle. The ordinary kids are just as likely to be influenced by outside conflicts, social activities and youth subcultural interests as the rems. It is simply that the ordinary students (the vast majority at the school) never let these develop into full-blown opposition to the school.

Economic influences and opposition to school

In our exploration of working-class experiences of school, we saw that sociological studies found that divisions emerged between the students in terms of their attitudes and behaviour in the classroom, leading to the conclusion that social class does interact with the experience of school to produce different subcultures. The studies differ, however, in the extent to which opposition to school was demonstrated. The explanation for these differences might possibly lie in the wider economy. Riseborough (1993) has suggested that the lads in Willis' study were only able to 'have a laff' because at the time of the study, it was easy to find unskilled work. By the time of Brown's study, these jobs were difficult to find and so the same attitude to school was not really possible. Riseborough found the young people in his study had an awareness of the economic situation which did influence their behaviour. Knowing that there were not many jobs available for unskilled workers made them concentrate more on learning work-related skills.

Schooling and masculinity

The relationship between social class and school subcultures is only one of a number of relationships which sociologists have explored. A second area of research is the way that school interacts with notions of **masculinity**. By masculinity, we mean the use of appropriate attitudes and behaviour that males use to demonstrate to both themselves and to others that they are 'male'. One of the most influential writers on the concept of masculinity is Connell (1995), who argues that the view of what constitutes masculinity changes over time. The dominant view of masculinity at any one time is known as **hegemonic masculinity**. For Connell, there are always competing versions of masculinity striving to become the dominant or hegemonic one. There is always tremendous pressure on males to conform to this hegemonic masculinity. An example of this comes from Haywood (2003), who studied how pupils use language to 'regulate masculinity'. His middle-class sample of hard-working A-level students were referred to as 'wankers', 'bum bandits', 'gays' and 'poofs' – even to their faces. Their 'crime' was not to engage in more 'typical' male behaviour of taking their studies lightly and enjoying an active social life.

But it is not just males who engage in the process of defining and shaping masculinity; women too have an important role in deciding which form of masculinity is dominant. The refusal of women over the last 40 years to accept patriarchy unquestioningly has had an impact on what is currently viewed as hegemonic masculinity. Though it is true too that females play an ambiguous role in 'liberating' males, as Mac an Ghaill's study shows, they also like 'masculine' males. Mac an Ghaill's study (1994) illustrates the complexity of subcultural responses by examining the relationship between schooling, work, masculinity and sexuality. Like the other writers in this tradition, he identifies a range of school subcultures. However, unlike the earlier studies, he also includes middle-class (male) students and also looked at a separate small group of homosexual students.

Working-class youths and masculinity

The 'macho lads'

This group was hostile to school authority and learning, not unlike the lads in Willis' study. However, the economic context which helped to create the 'lads' of Willis' study had changed by the time of this study and the attitudes they had seemed to come from an earlier time. Mac an Ghaill suggested that these youths were facing some degree of crisis, as their masculinity had traditionally been demonstrated in their manual labour. Yet it is precisely this area of employment which was contracting rapidly at the time of the study (and has continued to do so). Nevertheless, few expressed total contempt for school as Willis' 'lads' had done.

The academic achievers

This group were from mostly skilled manual working-class backgrounds and adopted a more traditional upwardly mobile route via academic success. However, they had to develop ways of coping with the stereotyping and accusations of effeminacy from the 'macho lads'. They would do this either by confusing those who bullied them, by deliberately behaving in an effeminate way, or simply by having the confidence to cope with the jibes.

The 'new enterprisers'

Mac an Ghaill suggested that this was a new form of proschool subculture, embracing the 'new **vocationalism**' of the 1980s and 1990s. They rejected the traditional academic curriculum, which they saw as a waste of time, but accepted the new vocational ethos, with the help and support of the new breed of teachers and their industrial contacts. In studying subjects such as business studies and computing, they were able to achieve **upward mobility** and employment by exploiting school–industry links to their advantage.

Middle-class youths and masculinity

'Real Englishmen'

These were a small group of middle-class pupils, usually from a liberal professional background (their parents were typically university lecturers, or writers, or they had jobs in the media). They rejected what teachers had to offer, seeing their own culture and knowledge as superior. They also saw the motivations of the 'achievers' and 'enterprisers' as shallow. Whilst their own values did not fit with doing well at school, they did, however, aspire to university and a professional career. They resolved this dilemma by achieving academic success in a way that appeared effortless (whether it was or not).

Gay students

Mac an Ghaill also studied a number of individual gay students from different educational institutions in the same area. These students did not have a subculture as such, because of their small numbers in each institution. However, they were fully aware of assumptions regarding sexual normality in schools, which took for granted the naturalness of heterosexual relationships and the two-parent nuclear family.

Mac an Ghaill's work can be criticized, however, because it was based on only 11 heterosexual students from one Midland school and a similar small number of homosexual students from other local educational institutions.

'Real men don't work hard'

Sociologists such as Mac an Ghaill (1994) and Haywood (1993) describe the dominant hegemonic masculinity that, in an educational context, is characterized by rejecting academic work as '**feminine**'. The dominance of hegemonic masculinity is achieved through a process of peer pressure to conform to what is perceived to be normal for a boy. For example, if boys want to avoid the verbal and physical abuse attached to being labelled as 'feminine' or 'gay', then they must avoid academic work, or at least appear to avoid academic work.

The result of all this is that working hard at school (or most importantly, appearing to work hard) and achieving educational success actually runs counter to an important form of masculinity.

Female subcultures

In Mac an Ghaill's study, although girls disliked the masculinity of the '**macho** males', many still sought boyfriends with this attitude. Some working-class girls, in particular, even saw work as a potential marriage market. More upwardly mobile girls saw careers more in terms of independence and achievement.

Griffin (1985) studied young, White working-class women during their first two years in employment. Rather than forming a large anti-authority grouping, they created small friendship groups. Their deviance was defined by their sexual behaviour rather than 'trouble-making'. Most importantly, there was not the same continuity between the school's culture and that of their future workplace as there had been for the lads in Willis' study. Instead, there were three possible routes for the girls, which they could follow all at the same time:

1 the labour market – securing a job
2 the marriage market – acquiring a permanent male partner
3 the sexual market – having sexual relationships, whilst at the same time maintaining their reputation, so as to not damage marriage prospects.

Lads and ladettes

Carolyn Jackson (2006) investigated the idea of '**laddishness**' in schools. Laddishness refers to a specific form of masculine behaviour based on humour, popularity, sportiness, hardness and not being seen to make an effort at school. Jackson found evidence of laddish behaviour among both boys and girls. Girls sometimes made deliberate efforts to avoid being seen as a 'swot'. They rejected the 'good girl' model in favour of a 'feisty and sassy' image that did not sit well with homework and academic effort. Teachers found them more difficult to manage than boys.

Boys felt under more pressure to do well than girls but both genders felt it was important to be seen to be clever. However, to be seen to work hard was 'uncool' so the trick was to succeed in tests without appearing to do any work. Some pupils responded by doing little at school but catching up at home. Others even hid the fact that they were revising or doing homework from their friends. This balancing act was difficult to achieve.

Jackson argues that much laddish behaviour can be seen as an attempt to avoid revealing weakness and failure in an education system based on tests and exam results.

Ethnic subcultures

The third element which impacts on the experience of education is ethnicity. This is a complex subject, as various ethnic groupings are responded to differently by teachers and the different groupings may also have very different experiences of racism, economic opportunity and cultural values in the wider society.

The experience of Black males

According to Sewell (2000), the culture of the streets is anti-educational. It is a culture that puts style and instant gratification ahead of the values of school and college. According to Sewell, males of African-Caribbean origin see educational success as 'feminine'. The way for them to get respect is through the credibility of the street, or as Sewell puts it, to be a 'street hood'. Success in the schoolroom marks the Black youth out from his peers or classmates and is likely to make him the target of ridicule or bullying (as we saw earlier). Sewell argues that educational failure becomes a badge to wear with pride.

Mac an Ghaill (1988) also studied the specific effects of ethnicity in an earlier study to the one mentioned above. He found that young male students of African-Caribbean origin responded very strongly to the way they were labelled by teachers, by developing subcultures based strongly on masculine images. The names they gave themselves indicate the nature of their groups – 'The Warriors' and 'The Rasta-Heads'.

O'Donnell and Sharpe's (2000) study of the impact of race and masculinity on schooling, supports the findings of Sewell and those of Mac an Ghaill (in both his studies). They found that the dominant form of masculinity amongst male students from an African-Caribbean background was of being 'macho'. O'Donnell and Sharpe suggest that the only way to understand this construction of masculinity is to see it as a reaction to a range of influences including racism and poor economic prospects. There are many parallels with their attitudes to school and those of the White youths studied by Willis 20 years earlier. However, the economic situation had improved for the White youths, so that their form of masculinity and opposition to school was no longer common, but in the case of the Black youths, the economic prospects remained poor and so opposition to school was still a relevant response.

The experience of Black females

In an investigation of three classes of 5- to 6-year-olds in a multi-ethnic, inner-city primary school, Connolly (1998) found that negative stereotypes are not just confined to boys. Like Black boys, girls were perceived by teachers as potentially disruptive but likely to be good at sports. The teachers in one school tended to 'underplay the Black girls' educational achievements and focus on their social behaviour'. Like their Black male counterparts, they were quite likely to be disciplined and punished, even though their behaviour did not always seem to justify it.

Other studies, such as that by Mirza (1992), point out that females from African-Caribbean backgrounds resent negative labelling and racism in schools – and, in particular, the fact that many teachers expect them to fail. Like males, they develop resistance to schooling. However, they do not form totally antischool subcultures – they realize that these lead to educational failure. Instead, they adopt strategies that enable them to get what they need from the system, that allow them to maintain a **positive self-image**, obtain the qualifications they desire and, above all, prove their teachers wrong.

Mirza found that the Black girls in her study, whilst rarely encountering open racism, were held back by the well-meaning but misguided behaviour of most of the teachers. The teachers' 'help' was often patronizing and counterproductive, curtailing both career and educational opportunities that should have been available to the Black girls. For example, the girls were entered for fewer subjects to 'take the pressure off', or they were given ill-informed, often stereotypical, careers advice. The girls, therefore, had to look for alternative strategies to get by, some of which hindered their progress, such as not asking for help. Alternatively, they helped each other out with academic work, but were seen to resist the school's values by refusing to conform through their dress, appearance and behaviour.

The experience of Asian youths

Connolly (1998) also examined the treatment of South Asian male and female school students. He found that teachers tended to see South Asian boys as immature rather than as troublemakers. Their behaviour was **feminized** and as such was seen as unthreatening. Consequently, much of their bad behaviour went unnoticed by teachers and was not punished to the same extent as that of Black youths. At the same time, the South Asian boys had difficulty in gaining status as males, which made it more difficult for them to enjoy school and feel confident. However, teachers did have high expectations of their academic potential and they were often praised and encouraged. South Asian girls were seen as even more obedient than the South Asian boys, even though their behaviour, in reality, showed a similar mix of work, avoidance of work and disruptiveness, and was largely indistinguishable from their female peers. Expectations regarding their academic potential were high and it was felt that they needed little help when compared with other groups. These judgements were more likely to be related to the perception that they were largely quiet, passive, obedient and helpful, rather than being related to academic outcomes.

O'Donnell and Sharpe came to very similar conclusions regarding the problems faced by Asian youths. Whereas Black youths were admired by many White youths for their 'macho' behaviour, Asian youths were viewed as falling into one of three categories, which O'Donnell and Sharpe call the 'weakling', the 'warrior' and the 'patriarch':

- Weakling refers to the traditional view of Asian youths as conformist and trouble avoiders.
- Warriors refers to the growing numbers of Asian youths who have taken this image and have set out to cultivate a tougher new edge.

- Patriarch refers to the **cultural tendency** to accept the power of the family, particularly the family males in determining behaviour.

O'Donnell and Sharpe say this crude categorizing of Asian youths fails to appreciate the way that they have successfully 'negotiated' new masculine identities, taking elements from the various cultures surrounding them. They also point out that Asian males and females have been particularly successful in education. Interestingly, the only Asian group which has performed poorly, those from Bangladeshi backgrounds, were those most likely to have been involved in violence and had developed a clear 'macho' image.

Subject choice

Girls are now achieving better academic results than boys at school, yet relatively few choose science or science-related subjects. Males dominate in maths, science and technology, with consequent implications for future career choices. For example, 60 per cent of working women are clustered in only 10 per cent of occupations. The same is true in vocational subjects, with male students comprising 95 per cent of students studying engineering-based subjects and female students forming 90 per cent of those studying health and care. Mac an Ghaill refers to the '**remasculinization**' of the vocational curriculum.

Our discussions on the role of gender and masculinity are relevant here. Sociologists such as Skelton (2001) show that a **hidden curriculum** exists that helps to perpetuate gender difference by influencing subject choices. This refers to the belief amongst teachers and students about the appropriate behaviour for the various sexes. Included is the belief that certain subjects are regarded as more appropriate for the different sexes. Teachers may make assumptions about the abilities and interests of students and encourage them accordingly.

Peer groups are important too. If a pupil's same-sex friends all choose or reject a subject, the individual may find it hard to be different and so subjects can become stereotyped as 'feminine' or 'masculine'.

However, things have changed since the original sociological studies in these areas in the 1970s and 1980s. Spender (1982), for example, found that female students expected to cease paid work in order to become housewives and mothers and then to work part time. Today, aspirations are higher and women do look for future careers, according to Arnot et al. (1999). Riddell (1992), however, argues that girls still carry competing ideas for their futures, influenced partly by choosing subjects useful for future employment, and partly by future ideas of motherhood and domesticity, which remain important parts of their identity as women.

Focus on research

Gender and subject choice

The 10 most popular A-level subjects for females and males in order of popularity (2007/8)

Females	Males
1 English	1 Mathematics
2 Psychology	2 General Studies
3 General Studies	3 English
4 Biology	4 History
5 Art and Design	5 Biology
6 Mathematics	6 Physics
7 History	7 Chemistry
8 Sociology	8 Business Studies
9 Chemistry	9 Geography
10 Media/Film/TV Studies	10 P.E.

Source: Department for Children,
Families and Schools

1 Can you identify any patterns in the subjects preferred by males and females?

2 Use your sociological knowledge to explain the gender differences in subject preference shown above.

Check your understanding

1 How, according to Hargreaves, did 'low-stream failures' respond to their label?

2 What subcultures did Mac an Ghaill suggest existed?

3 What sorts of subjects do female school students tend to choose?

4 Give three examples of the ways in which the experience of female subcultures is said to be different from that of male subcultures.

5 Explain in your own words the relationship between GCSE achievement and ethnicity.

6 Why, despite their generally positive identification with school, do Black girls remain disadvantaged in the education system?

7 How, according to Connolly, do teachers' perceptions of South Asian pupil subcultures affect their experience of schooling?

8 Give two examples of ways in which the hidden curriculum may encourage school pupils to make gender-stereotyped subject choices.

Key terms

Cultural tendency process whereby the values of a society stress the normality of a particular form of behaviour.

Feminine stereotypical ideas about women being soft and caring.

Feminized suitable for women.

Hegemonic masculinity the socially accepted idea of what a male should be.

Hidden curriculum ideas and values passed on at school that are not formally taught.

Laddishness type of behaviour adopted by some pupils emphasizing hardness, popularity, humour and the avoidance of schoolwork.

Macho/masculine common ideas about men being tough and strong.

Positive self-image feeling good about yourself.

Remasculinization making something male-orientated again.

Upwardly mobile moving up in the social classes.

Vocationalism skills-based subjects.

Activities

Research idea

● Conduct a participant observational survey of your school or college to identify pro- and antischool subcultures. (Use Mac an Ghaill's categories as well as some of your own.)

● Select a sample of male and female A-level students in your school or college. Design a questionnaire to find out what have been the key influences on their A-level subject choice. Analyse the results – do they tell you anything about the relationship between gender and subject choice?

Web.tasks

Go to the website of Women into Science and Engineering at **www.wisecampaign.org.uk**.

What are the aims of this organization and how is it trying to encourage girls into non-traditional subjects and careers? Do you think WISE is needed?

An eye on the exam — The experience of youth in education

The two reasons need to be stated clearly, probably at the beginning of paragraphs

Use example of particular subjects to illustrate your points

Aim to write for about 15 minutes

(a) Identify and explain two reasons why girls may select different school subjects to boys. **(17 marks)**

Each of the two reasons need to be discussed in depth, using sociological concepts, examples and studies if possible

The reasons need to be described in some detail, using sociological concepts, studies and theories

Avoid generalizing – bear in mind gender, class and ethnic differences between pupils

Aim to write at least two sides of the answer book in about 30 minutes

(b) Outline and evaluate the reasons why some pupils may join anti-school subcultures. **(33 marks)**

Each of the reasons needs to be evaluated, with a balanced conclusion drawn

These are groups of pupils who share an active dislike and rejection of their education

Grade booster — Getting top marks in this question

Use an introduction to provide a clear explanation of the idea of anti-school subcultures. Then you need to describe some key studies that provide reasons for their formation. These might include Willis, Mac an Ghaill, Jackson and Sewell. Make sure your answer includes references to social class, gender and ethnicity in its discussion of subcultures. Evaluative points might include the fact that some of these studies were conducted more than ten years ago (more than 20 in the case of Willis), that a focus on anti-school cultures might cause sociologists to ignore the majority of pupils and that students may have exaggerated their deviance to sociological researchers.

(a) Identify and explain two features of a moral panic *(17 marks)*

A moral panic is when the media exaggerate something like youth crime or youth subcultures. They did this in the 1960s at the time of the mods and rockers and Stan Cohen wrote about it in 'Folk Devils and Moral Panics'. He said that the mods and rockers became folk devils.

Defining moral panic is a good idea and should lead directly to the identification of two features. The example here does not really develop the idea of what a moral panic actually is, it just defines some relevant research.

One feature of a moral panic is media exaggeration. The tabloid press want to sell as many copies as they can and so make stories appear more sensational than they really are. In the 1960s mods and rockers were two youth subcultures. The mods rode scooters and liked ska and Black American music. The rockers rode motor bikes, wore leather and liked rock and roll music. Sometimes the mods and rockers would meet at coastal holiday resorts like Clacton and there would be conflict. When newspapers reported these conflicts they used sensational language and photographs.

Good idea to start the paragraph with a clear identification of the first feature. Explanation of the feature is limited because too much time is spent describing the mods and rockers.

Another feature of a moral panic is a reaction by politicians and the public who perceive the youth culture as a threat to the morals and values of society. There are calls for harsher and longer sentences and the youth group is often seen as a sign that society is in decline. When the media covered a lot of stories about the dangers of 'hoodies' young people wearing hoodies were actually banned from a shopping centre.

$\frac{16}{17}$

Again, the feature is identified clearly at the beginning of the paragraph although explanation could be more detailed. The example introduced at the end of the answer is a good contemporary one but there is no time to develop it.

(b) Outline and evaluate the view that youth culture exists in the contemporary UK. *(33 marks)*

The term youth culture suggests that all young people will share common values, norms, customs, traditions and so on. The idea that young people did share a culture grew after the Second World War due to a variety of factors which will be explained later. Today, sociologists tend to see youth as divided into a number of different cultures according to factors like class, gender and ethnicity. This answer will deal with the view that youth culture still exists and then go on to evaluate that view.

This introduction does well to define the key term in the question and to explain to the reader how the question will be addressed.

In the 1950s and 60s many people believed that a youth culture existed. Before this point in time young people had often moved straight from being dependent children to marriage and the responsibilities of adulthood. Various factors caused youth culture to develop. Abrams found that young people had more disposable income and they began to spend their money on items such as clothes and records. There were also lots of new ideas in society, with people more free to act in their own way. Companies started to make products aimed at teenagers such as records, magazines and clothes. At the same time the media was growing rapidly and they began to advertise these products and to make programmes aimed at teenagers. The increase in the time children spent in education meant that there was a longer gap between childhood and adulthood.

This is a sociologically accurate and detailed paragraph explaining the origins of the idea of youth culture. But there are two problems: the actual features of youth culture are not described and the material relates to the 1950s and 60s when the question specifically asks about contemporary Britain. Background material can be helpful but this is too much.

Functionalists believe that youth culture has a function. Eisenstadt argued that changing from childhood where status is ascribed to the adult world where status is achieved is very difficult and youth culture helps this change by providing support and role models from the peer group.

There are many examples of different types of youth culture and subcultures in the contemporary UK so it is difficult to argue that one youth culture exists. For example many types of youth subculture exist such as punks and Goths – no one culture is dominant. Maffesoli argues that youth subcultures have actually been replaced by neo-tribes. Also, many subcultures are associated with social class, the Birmingham CCCS argue that subcultures relate to wider social class groups, for example skinheads are a working-class group. Gender is also important in dividing youth culture. McRobbie researched young girls and found that they were more controlled than boys and are 'invisible' in subcultures. Instead they develop a 'bedroom culture' where they meet their friends and chat. However, Reddington argues that girls were a central part of the punk movement. There are also ethnic differences in subcultures. For example 'rude boys', 'gangsta rap' and Rastafarians, as described by Hebdidge.

It is difficult to say that one youth culture exists in Britain because so many subcultures exist. However, as Muncie says, most young people are 'ordinary' and not in any subculture anyway. Young people's lives and experiences are very different according to their gender, race and class. Life is very different for someone at private school with lots of money compared to someone brought up on a council estate in poverty. But young people do still share certain things like the experience of school and finding a job.

25/33

Again, fine as background but how does it relate to the question?

Suddenly the answer switches into top gear and hits the question head on. The problem is that there is now not enough time to develop any of the very good points raised. These issues of subcultures and class, gender and ethnic divisions should have taken up the main part of the answer.

This is a balanced conclusion that tries to see both sides of the argument and apply them specifically to Britain today. Excellent points are made but, again, it would have helped to explain these in more depth.

An examiner comments

This answer shows the need to plan answers carefully based on the exact wording of the question. Too much time is spent near the start of the answer on issues which are really only relevant as background. By the time the key points are addressed time is running short so they cannot be developed in the detail they deserve. This is a shame because the final two paragraphs show excellent knowledge, application and evaluation skills. If the whole answer had taken the form of developing the points raised in these paragraphs, full marks could well have been achieved.

Chapter 7 Summary

Social construction of youth

- Increasing economic power
- Social change
- Globalization
- Growth and specialization of media
- Lengthened period of transition to adulthood
- Demographic changes

Youth culture and youth subcultures

Functionalist
- One youth culture
- Eases transition to adulthood

Marxist
- Many youth subcultures
- Represent working-class resistance

Feminist
- Invisible girls
- Bedroom culture

Late-modern
- Subcultures along social-class lines
- Decline of spectacular subcultures
- Importance of media

Postmodern
- Subcultures replaced by fast-changing styles
- Term 'neo-tribes' becomes popular

Ethnicity
- Black subcultures resist racism
- Growth of hybridized subcultures

Youth and culture

The experience of youth in education

Class
- Working-class youths more likely to join anti-school subcultures
- Willis – working-class youths 'help' their own failure

Gender
- Affects subject choice
- Girls more able to combine study and leisure
- Part of hegemonic masculinity is to appear not to study
- 'Laddishness' in both boys and girls a response to fear of failure

Ethnicity
- African Caribbean youths exhibit attributes of masculinity
- Asian youths more likely to study and be successful

Youth and deviance

Patterns and trends
- Youth crime associated with males in disadvantaged areas
- Problems in getting reliable data

Functionalism
- Subculture and strain theory
- Status frustration
- Illegitimate opportunities
- Focal concerns

Marxism
- Crime as resistance to capitalism

Labelling theory
- Folk devils and moral panics
- Self-fulfilling prophecy

Postmodernism
- Seductions of crime
- Edgework

Preparing for the AS exams

TOPIC 1

Preparing for the OCR AS-level exams

What will I study?

You study two units of work and sit two exams, one for each unit. The topics studied in each unit are shown in table 8.1. In the first unit you learn about socialization, culture and identity and sociological research methods. A few weeks before the exam you will be give a summary of a piece of sociological research. This will form the basis of the exam question about research methods. In the second unit you study at least one topic from Family, Health, Religion and Youth and answer two, two-part structured essay questions, chosen from the same or different topics.

How will I be assessed?

The knowledge, understanding and skills that you develop in studying the AS-level Sociology course are assessed in terms of two assessment objectives. Each of these is worth approximately half of the total marks available.

Assessment Objective 1 (AO1): knowledge and understanding

To meet this objective successfully, you have to show that you know and understand the topic on which you are answering a question (e.g. on the Sociology of the Family,

Table 8.1 Unit content and forms of assessment

Unit code	Topics	Form of assessment
G671	**Exploring socialization, culture and identity** This topic also includes sociological research methods	Written examination paper of one and a half hours, some of which is based on a pre-released summary of a piece of sociological research
G672	**Culture and socialization** You have to study at least one topic from Family, Health, Religion and Youth	Written examination paper of one and a half hours

or Religion). This knowledge and understanding covers the full range of relevant sociological material, including concepts, theories, perspectives, the findings of sociological studies, relevant facts (e.g. from official sources) and sociological methods.

AO1 also includes assessment of the quality of your written communication. In other words, you need to be able to express yourself clearly in writing. Obviously, if you don't do so, the examiner will have difficulty in deciding whether you actually know and understand the material that you are using in your answers.

Assessment Objective 2 (AO2): analysis, evaluation and application

While it is probably obvious that you need to know some sociological material, you also need to be able to use and discuss it in ways that actually answer the question. For example, you need to be able to interpret what the question is about, select relevant material (e.g. theories, studies) from what you know, and apply it to the question appropriately. Similarly, you need to be able to analyse arguments logically, showing in detail how their ideas fit together. You also need to be able to evaluate sociological material and issues. This involves being able to weigh up strengths and weaknesses, advantages and disadvantages, evidence and arguments, to reach an appropriate conclusion.

How can I do well in the exams?

Timing

Using the limited time you have in an exam to good effect is crucial to exam success. There is nothing more dispiriting than knowing a great deal, having all the skills required, but underachieving because you run out of time and are unable to complete a question worth a large number of marks.

Work out your timings in advance so you know at exactly what time you should be moving from one question to the next. Both of the AS papers are worth 100 marks and you are given 90 minutes to complete each. This means that you have just less than a minute per mark. Allocate time a little more generously for the longer answers that are worth a significant proportion of the marks available and require more detail and analysis.

Style of questioning

It is important to familiarise yourself with the way questions are asked well before you sit the two exams. Each chapter of this book includes examples of questions in the style of OCR AS-level exams. Past papers are available from the OCR website (www.ocr.org.uk).

Unit G671: Exploring socialization, culture and identity

This exam involves pre-release material. Some weeks before the exam you will be given a summary of a sociological study that will provide the basis for the final question in the exam. This is the question that tests your knowledge and skills in the area of sociological research methods. You will need to use some of your revision time to familiarise yourself with this material in detail although you are not allowed to take it into the exam with you. In the actual exam you are given a fresh copy of the summary, along with the questions you have to answer.

The first question is worth eight marks and asks you to define a particular concept using examples. There is a list of possible concepts in the specification. Make sure your definition is simple and clear. Try to use two examples to illustrate your understanding of the concept but avoid going into too much detail – you should only spend five or six minutes on this question.

Question 2 asks you to 'outline and explain' two things, usually aspects of socialization. There are 16 marks allocated so make sure you do not spend more than 15 minutes on it. To help answer this question it is worth knowing how each agent of socialization can influence the construction of different identities, for example different gender, ethnic or social class identities. You can separate the two parts of your answer by leaving a line between them.

The third question always asks you to 'explain and briefly evaluate' an aspect of culture, socialization or identity. It is worth 24 marks so should take around 20 minutes to answer. Your explanation is likely to use examples, sociological concepts, studies and, possibly, theories. Four of the 24 marks available are allocated for evaluation so you need to make one or more critical points about the issue in question.

The final question is worth by far the most marks – 52 – just over half the total marks for the paper. Aim to spend half of your exam time on this, around 45 minutes. This question is based on the pre-release material and tests your knowledge and skills in the area of sociological research methods. It will probably ask you to 'explain and evaluate'

Table 8.2	Key command words in AS-exam questions
Define	State the meaning of something.
Identify	Show that you can recognize an argument, example, idea, fact, viewpoint, etc.
Outline	Provide an overview of the key points.
Explain	Show your knowledge and understanding by applying them in a way that is relevant to the question. Often you will need to give reasons or causes for social changes, trends or relationships.
Evaluate	Weigh up the arguments and/or the evidence for and against something (possible a theory, method, argument or viewpoint) and draw an appropriate conclusion.

the use of a particular method or combination of methods used by the sociologist or sociologists in the research summarised in the pre-release material. Your task is to explain the reasons for their choice and to assess the success of that approach. As you have had access to the study in advance, a high level of detail is expected. Good knowledge of the concepts of validity, reliability, representativeness and generalisability is also important as these concepts will certainly be among the tools you use to do your explaining and evaluating. Make sure the points you make about methods refer to the research context and are not too general.

Unit G672: Topics in socialization, culture and identity

In this exam there are two questions on each of four topics: Family, Health, Religion and Youth. Each question is divided into two parts – (a) and (b). You have to answer two complete questions in 90 minutes, which can be chosen from the same or from different topics.

Part (a) of the questions is worth 17 marks and is always phrased as 'identify and explain two …'. Examples of what these 'two' might be include 'reasons', 'ways' and 'features'. Aim to spend about 15 minutes on these questions. You will need to be careful that the two points you identify are distinct and that you are able to explain them in reasonable depth using examples, sociological concepts and, if appropriate, theories and studies.

Part (b) is more of an essay-style question. It is worth 33 marks and is always phrased as 'outline and evaluate'. You

will probably be asked to outline and evaluate a particular view or perspective. Aim to spend about 30 minutes on these questions. Make a brief plan in advance. Your answer could start with an introduction where you identify the sociological context of the question and explain any key sociological terms in the question. Then move on to outline the view in the question by explaining its key points and using examples. Try to include sociological concepts and some references to studies. The next stage would be to evaluate the viewpoint: what are its strengths and weaknesses? How has it been criticized? Finally, aim to draw a balanced conclusion.

Exam tips

- Read the whole question very carefully before you begin your first answer. This will give you an understanding of which aspects of the topic are covered.
- After reading the question, make a brief plan for your answers to the longer questions before you begin any writing. As you write your other answers, you may well remember things that you will wish to slot into these answers. Stick to your plan and refer back to it throughout.
- Start each point on a separate line. You can add extra points if you want – you won't be penalized for giving wrong ones, but you will be rewarded for correct ones.
- If you find yourself using the same information in more than one answer, check carefully that you are answering the question set. The examiner is unlikely to be asking the same question twice.
- Particularly in the longer, higher-mark questions, you should refer to appropriate theories, perspectives, studies and evidence to support and inform your answer. Where possible, bring in examples of recent events to illustrate the points you are making.
- Finally, make sure that you answer the question that the examiner has set, rather than the one that you wished had been set! This is a serious point – many candidates fail to achieve good marks because they have failed to stick to the question. No question is likely to ask you simply to write everything you know about a certain topic and yet this is what some students do.

How can I find out more?

The specification, examiners' reports, past papers, mark schemes and other guidance material are available from the OCR website at www.ocr.org.uk.

BIBLIOGRAPHY

Abbott, D. (1998) *Culture and Identity*, London: Hodder and Stoughton

Abercrombie, N., Ward, A., Soothill, K., Urry, J. and Walby, S. (2000) *Contemporary British Society* (3rd edition), Cambridge: Polity Press.

Abrams, M. (1959) *The Teenage Consumer*, London: Routledge and Kegan Paul

Acheson, Sir Donald (1998) *Independent Inquiry into Inequalities in Health: Report*, London: The Stationery Office

Ahmed, L. (1992) *Women and Gender in Islam: Historical Roots of a Modern Debate*, New Haven and London: Yale University Press

Akinti, P. (2003) 'Captivate Us', Guardian 21 Feb

Akthar, T. (2005) '(Re)turn to religion and radical Islam', in T. Abbass (2005) *Muslim Britain: Communities under Pressure*, London: Zed Books

Alcock, P. (2006) *Understanding Poverty*, Palgrave MacMillan

Aldridge, A. (2000) *Religion in the Contemporary World: A Sociological Introduction*, Cambridge: Polity Press

Alford, R.R. (1975) *Health Care Politics: Ideological and interest group barriers to reform*, Chicago: The University of Chicago Press

Ali, S. (2002) 'Interethnic families', *Sociology Review*, 12(1)

Allan, G. (1985) *Family Life: Domestic roles and social organization*, London: Blackwell

Althusser, L. (1971) 'Ideology and ideological state apparatuses', in *Lenin and Philosophy and Other Essays*, London: New Left Books

Anderson, M. (1971) 'Family, Household and the Industrial Revolution', in M. Anderson (ed.) *The Sociology of the Family*, Harmondsworth: Penguin

Anderson, P. and Kitchin, R.M. (2000) 'Disability, space and sexuality: Access to family planning services', *Social Science and Medicine,* 51

Annandale, E. (1998) *The Sociology of Health and Illness*, Cambridge: Polity Press

Antle, B.J. (2000) 'Seeking strengths in young people with physical disabilities', *Dissertation Abstracts International, Humanities and Social Sciences,* 60

Anwar, M. (1981) *Between Two Cultures: A Study of Relationships Between Generations in the Asian Community*, London: CRE

Arber, S. and Ginn, J. (1993) 'Class, caring and the life course' in S. Arber and M.E. Vandrow (eds) *Ageing, Independence and the Life Course*, London: Jessica Kingsley

Archer, L. (2003) Race*, Masculinity and Schooling: Muslim boys and education*, Maidenhead: Open University Press

Aries, P. (1962) Centuries of Childhood, London: Random House

Armstrong, K. (1993) *The End of Silence: Women and the Priesthood*, London: Fourth Estate

Arnot, M., David, D. and Weiner, G. (1999) *Closing the Gender Gap,* Cambridge: Polity Press

Ashworth, J. H. and Farthing, I. (2007) *Churchgoing in the UK: A research report on church attendance in the UK*, Middlesex: Tearfund

Aune, K., Sharma, S. and Vincett, G. (eds) (2008) *Women and Religion in the West: Challenging Secularization*, Aldershot: Ashgate

Badawi, L. (1994) 'Islam', in J. Holm and J. Bowker (eds), *Women in Religion*, London: Pinter

Bainbridge, W.S. (1978) *Satan's Power,* Berkley: University of California Press

Ball, S. (1981) *Beachside Comprehensive: a case study of secondary schooling,* Cambridge: Cambridge University Press

Barber, B. (1963) 'Some problems in the sociology of professions', Daedalus, 92(4)

Barker E. (1984) *The Making of a Moonie*, Oxford: Blackwell

Barnett, S. and Curry, A. (1994) *The Battle for the BBC: a British Broadcasting Conspiracy?*, London: Aurum

Barrett, M. and McIntosh, M. (1982) *The Anti-social Family*, London: Verso

Bates, S. (2006) 'Devout Poles show Britain how to keep the faith', *The Guardian*, 23 December, pp.12–13

Bauman, Z. (1990) *Thinking Sociologically*, Oxford: Blackwell

Bauman, Z. (1992) *Intimations of Postmodernity*, London: Routledge

Bauman, Z. (1993) *Postmodern Ethics*, Blackwell: Oxford

Bauman, Z. (1997) *Postmodernity and Its Discontents*, Cambridge: Polity Press

Baumeister, R. (1986) *Identity: Cultural Change and the Struggle for Self*, Oxford University Press

Beck, U. (1992) *Risk Society: Towards a New Modernity*, London: Sage

Beck, U. and Beck-Gernsheim, E. (1995) *The Normal Chaos of Love*, Cambridge: Polity Press

Becker, H. (1950) *Through Values to Social Interpretation: Essays on Social Contexts, Actions, Types and Prospects*, California: Duke University Press

Becker, H. (1963) *Outsiders: Studies in the Sociology of Deviance*, London: Macmillan

Beckford, J.A. (1985) *Cult Controversies,* London: Routledge

Beckford, R. (2000) 'Dread and Pentecostal: A political theology for the Black church in Britain', London: SPCK

Bellah, R.N. (1970) 'Civil religion in America', in *Beyond Belief: Essays in Religion in a Post-traditional World'*, New York: Harper & Row

Bellah, R.N. (1987) 'Introduction: America's Cultural Conversation', in R.N. Bellah, R. Madsen, R., W.M. Sullivan, A. Swidler and S.M. Tipton (eds) *Individualism and Commitment in American Life: Readings on the Themes of Habits of the Heart*, New York: Harper & Row

Bennett, A. (2004) 'Rap and Hip Hop: community and identity', in S. Whiteley, A. Bennett and S. Hawkins (eds) *Music, Space and Place,* Aldershot: Ashgate

Bennett, T. and Holloway, K. (2004) 'Gang membership, drugs and crime in the UK', *British Journal of Criminology* 44(3), pp. 305–23

Bennett, T. and Holloway, K. (2005) *Understanding Drugs Alcohol and Crime*, Milton Keynes: Open University Press

Benston, M. (1972) 'The political economy of women's liberation', in N. Glazer-Malbin and H.Y. Waehrer (eds) *Women in a Man-Made World*, Chicago: Rand McNally

Berger, A.L. (1997) *Children of Job: American Second Generation Witnesses to the Holocaust*, New York: NY State University Press

Berger, P. (1967) *The Sacred Canopy: Elements of a Sociological Theory of Religion*, New York: Anchor Books

Berger, P. (1971) *A Rumour of Angels*, Harmondsworth: Penguin

Berger, P. (1973) *The Social Reality of Religion*, Harmondsworth: Penguin

Bernard, J. (1982, originally 1972) *The Future of Marriage*, Yale: Yale University Press

Bernardes, J. (1997) *Family Studies: An Introduction*, London: Routledge

Berthoud, R. (2000) 'Family formation in multi-cultural Britain: three patterns of diversity', Working Paper of the Institute for Social and Economic Research, Colchester: University of Essex

Berthoud, R. (2003) Lecture at ATSS Conference 2004, based on research conducted in 2003

Best, S. (2005) *Understanding Social Divisions*, London: Sage

Bhatti, G., (1999) *Asian Children at Home and at School: An Ethnographic Study*, London, Routledge

Billington, R., Hockey, J. and Strawbridge, S. (1998) *Exploring Self and Society*, Basingstoke: Macmillan

Bilton, T., Bonnett, K., Jones, P., Lawson, T., Skinner, D., Stanworth, M. and Webster, A. (2002) *Introductory Sociology* (4th edn), Basingstoke: Macmillan

Bird, J. (1999) *Investigating Religion*, London: HarperCollins

Bittman, M. and Pixley, J. (1997) *The Double Life of the Family*, St Leonards, NSW: Allen & Unwin

Blackburn, C. (1991) *Poverty and Health: Working with Families*, Milton Keynes, Open University Press

Blackman, S. (1997) 'An ethnographic study of youth underclass' in R. McDonald (ed.) *Youth, the Underclass and Social Exclusion*, London: Routledge

Blaxter, M. (1990) *Health and Lifestyles*, London: Tavistock

Bourgois, P. (2003) *In Search of Respect* (2nd edn), Cambridge: Cambridge University Press

Box, S. (1981) *Deviance, Reality and Society* (2nd edn), Eastbourne: Holt Rheinhart Wilson

Bradley, H. (1996) *Fractured Identities: Changing Patterns of Inequality*, Cambridge: Polity Press

Brah, A. (1993) 'Race and culture in the gendering of labour markets: South Asian young women and the labour market', *New Community*, 19(3)

Brake, M. (1984) *The Sociology of Youth and Youth Subcultures,* London: Routledge

Brannen, J. (2003) 'The age of bean-pole families', Sociology Review, September

Brierley, P. (2002) *Reaching and Keeping Tweenagers*, London: Christian Research

Brierley, P. (2006) *Pulling Out of the Nose Dive: A Contemporary Picture of Churchgoing; What the 2005 English Church Census Reveals*, London: Christian Research

Brierley, P. (ed.) (1979, 1989, 1999, 2000, 2001) *Christian Research Association, UK Christian Handbook, Religious Trends* 1979, 1989, 1999, 2000, 2001, London: HarperCollins

Brookes-Gunn, J. and Kirsch, B. (1984) 'Life events and the boundaries of midlife for women', in G. Baruch and J. Brookes-Gunn (eds) *Women in Midlife*, New York: Plenum Press

Brown, C. (1979) *Understanding Society*, Harlow: Longman

Brown, C.G. (2001) *The Death of Christian Britain: Understanding Secularization 1800–2000*, London: Routledge

Brown, D. (1994) 'An ordinary sexual life? A review of the normaliation principle as it applies to the sexual options of people with learning disabilities', *Disability and Society,* 9(2)

Brown, G.W., Harris, T.O. and Hepworth, C. (1995) 'Loss, humiliation and entrapment among women developing depression', *Psychological Medicine*, 25, pp. 7–21

Brown, P. (1987) *Schooling Ordinary Kids: Inequality, unemployment and the new vocationalism,* London: Tavistock

Bruce, S. (1995) *Religion in Modern Britain*, Oxford: Oxford University Press

Bruce, S. (1996) *Religion in the Modern World: From Cathedrals to Cults*, Oxford: Oxford University Press

Bruce, S. (2001) 'The social process of secularisation' in R.K. Fenn (2004) *The Blackwell Companion to the Sociology of Religion*, Oxford: Blackwell

Bruce, S. (2002) *God is Dead: Secularization in the West*, Oxford: Blackwell

Bullock, K. and Tilley, N. (2002) *Shootings, Gangs and Violent Incidents in Manchester*, London: Home Office

Burchill, J. (2001) *The Guardian*, Saturday 18 August

Burghes, L. (1997) *Fathers and Fatherhood in Britain*, London: Policy Studies Institute

Burghes, L. and Brown, M. (1995) *Single Lone Mothers: Problems, prospects and policies*, York: Family Policy Studies Centre with the support of the Joseph Rowntree Foundation

Busfield, J. (1988) 'Mental illness as a social product or social construct: a contradiction in feminists' arguments?', *Sociology of Health and Illness*, 10, pp. 521–42

Butler, C. (1995) 'Religion and gender: young Muslim women in Britain', *Sociology Review*, 4(3), Oxford: Philip Allan

Campbell, A. (1984) *The Girls in the Gang,* Oxford: Blackwell

Campbell, A. and Muncer, S. (1989) 'Them and Us: a comparison of the cultural context of American gangs and British subcultures', *Deviant Behavior,* 10, pp. 271–88

Campbell, B. (2000) *The Independent*, 20 November 2000

Cant, S. and Sharma, U. (2002) 'The state and complementary medicine: a changing relationship?', in S. Nettleton and U. Gustafsson (eds) *The Sociology of Health and Illness, A Reader*, Cambridge: Polity

Caplan, L. (ed.) (1987) *Studies in Religious Fundamentalism*, London: Macmillan

Cashmore, E. (1997) *The Black Culture Industry*, London: Routledge

Chamberlain, M. and Goulborne, H. (1999) *Caribbean Families in Britain and the Trans-Atlantic World*, Basingstoke: Macmillan

Chapman, T. (2004) *Gender and Domestic Life: Changing Practices in Families and Households*, Basingstoke: Palgrave Macmillan

Charlesworth, S. (2000) *A Phenomenology of Working Class Experience*, Cambridge: Cambridge University Press

Chatterton, P. and Hollands, R.G. (2001) *Changing Our 'Toon': Youth, nightlife and urban change in Newcastle*, Newcastle: University of Newcastle

Cheal, D. (2002) *Sociology of Family Life*, Basingstoke: Palgrave

Chesler, P. (1972) *Women and Madness*, New York: Doubleday

Choudhury, T. (2007) *The Role of Muslim Identity Politics in Radicalization (a study in progress)*, London: Department for Communities and Local Government

Christian Research (2004) 'Home Office Citizenship Survey', *Quadrant*, September 2004: 4

Christian Research (2006) 'Three new churches a week', press release, London: Christian Research, 23 February

Clarke, J and Critcher, C., (1995*) The Devil Makes Work: Leisure in Capitalist Britain*, Basingstoke, Palgrave MacMillan

Clarke, J.N. (1992) 'Cancer, heart disease and AIDS: What do the media tell us about these diseases?', *Health Communication*, 4(2)

Cloward, R. and Ohlin, L. (1960) *Delinquency and Opportunity*, London: Collier Macmillan

Cohen, A. (1955) *Delinquent Boys*, New York: The Free Press

Cohen, P. (1972) 'Subcultural conflict and working-class community', *Working Papers in Cultural Studies* 2, University of Birmingham: Centre for Contemporary Cultural Studies

Cohen, R. and Kennedy, P. (2000) *Global Sociology*, Basingstoke: Macmillan

Cohen, S. (2003, originally 1972) *Folk Devils and Moral Panics,* Oxford: Martin Roberston

Coleman, J.C. (1980) *The Nature of Adolescence*, London: Methuen

Collier, R. (2002)'Masculinities', *Sociology*, 36(3), pp.737–42

Collison, M. (1996) 'In search of the high life: drugs, crime, masculinities and consumption', *British Journal of Criminology* 36(3)

Connell, R. (1995) *Masculinities*, Cambridge: Polity Press.

Connell, R.W. (2002) *Gender*, Cambridge: Blackwell

Connolly, P. (1998) *Racism, Gender Identities and Young Children*, London: Routledge

Cote, J. (2000) *Arrested Adulthood: The Changing Nature of Maturity and Identity*, New York University Press

Coté, J. and Allahar, A.L. (1996) *Generation on Hold: Coming of age in the late twentieth century*, London: New York University Press

Coward, R. (1989) The Whole Truth; The Myth of Alternative Health, London: Faber

Crawford, M. (1977), 'You are dangerous for your health', *International Journal of Health Services*, 7(7)

Cumberbatch, G. and Negrine, R. (1992) *Images of Disability on Television*, London: Routledge

Cunningham, H. (2006) *The Invention of Childhood*, London: BBC Books

Daly, M. (1973) *Beyond God the Father*, Boston, MA: Beacon Press

Daly, M. (1978) *Gyn/Ecology: The Meta-ethics of Radical Feminism*, Boston, MA: Beacon Press

Davey Smith, G., Shipley, M.J. and Rose, G. (1990) 'The magnitude and causes of socio-economic differentials in mortality: further evidence from the Whitehall study', *Journal of Epidemiology and Community Health*, 44, pp. 265–70

Davidman, L. (1991) *Religion in a Rootless World: Women turn to Orthodox Judaism*, Berkeley: University of California Press

Davie, G. (1994) *Religion in Britain 1945–1990, Believing Without Belonging*, Oxford: Blackwell

Davie, G. (1995) 'Competing fundamentalisms', *Sociology Review*, 4(4), Oxford: Philip Allan

Davies, C. (2004) *The Strange Death of Moral Britain*, Edison, NJ: Transaction Publishers

Davis, M. (1990) *City of Quartz*, London: Verso

Day, A. (2007) 'Believing in belonging: religion returns to sociology mainstream', *Network*, British Sociological Association, Summer 2007

de Beauvoir, S. (1953) *The Second Sex*, London: Jonathan Cape

De'Ath, E. and Slater, D. (eds) (1992) *Parenting Threads: Caring for children when couples part*, Stepfamily Publications

Decker, S. (2001) 'The impact of organizational features on gangs activities and relationships', in M.W. Klein, H.J. Kerner, C.L. Maxson and E.G.M. Weitekamp (eds) *The Eurogang Paradox: Street Gangs and Youth Groups in the US and Europe*, London: Kluwer Academic Publishers

Delphy, C. (1984) *Close to Home*, London: Hutchinson

Denscombe M. (2001) *Sociology Update 2001*, Leicester: Olympus Books

Dennis, N. and Erdos, G. (2000) *Families Without Fatherhood* (3rd edn), London: Civitas

Department of Health (2003) *NHS Patient Survey Programme: GP Survey 2003*, London: DoH

Department of Health (2007) *Health Survey for England*, London: DoH

Dex, S. (2003) *Families and Work in the Twenty-first Century*, York: Joseph Rowntree Foundation

Dobson, B., Beardsworth, A., Keil, T. And Walker, R. (1994) *Diet, Choice and Poverty: Social, Cultural and Nutritional Aspects of Food Consumption among Low-income Families*, London, Family Policy Studies Centre

Doyal, L. (1979) *The Political Economy of Health*, London: Pluto

Drane, J. (1999) *What is the New Age Saying to the Church?,* London: Marshal Pickering

Drury, B. (1991) 'Sikh girls and the maintenance of an ethnic culture', *New Community*, 17(3), pp. 387–99

Dryden, C. (1999) *Being Married Doing Gender*, London: Routledge

Duncombe, J. and Marsden, D. (1995) 'Women's "triple shift": paid employment, domestic labour and "emotion work"', *Sociology Review* 4(4)

Dunne, G A. (ed.) (1997) *Lesbian Lifestyles: Women's Work and the Politics of Sexuality*, Basingstoke: Macmillan

Durkheim, E. (1893, reprinted 1960) *The Division of Labour in Society*, Glencoe: Free Press

Durkheim, E. (1897/1952) *Suicide: a Study in Sociology*, London: Routledge

Durkheim, E. (1912, reprinted 1961) *The Elementary Forms of Religious Life*, London: Allen & Unwin

Durkin, K. (1995) *Developmental Social Psychology, from Infancy to Old Age*, Oxford: Blackwell

Dwyer, C. (1999) 'Contradictions of community: questions of identity for young British Muslim women', *Environment and Planning A,* 31(1), p. 53–68

Eisenberg, L. (1977) 'Disease and illness: distinction between professional and popular ideas of sickness', *Culture, Medicine and Psychiatry*, 1, pp. 9–23

Eisenstadt, S.N. (1956) *From Generation to Generation*, London: Routledge

El Sadaawi, N. (1980) *The Hidden Face of Eve: Women in the Arab World*, London: Zed Books

Elias, N. (1978) *The Civilising Process*, Oxford: Blackwell

ESRC Society Today (2006) 'Pentecostals overtake Methodists in England', press release, Swindon: Economic and Social Research Council, 19 December

Evans, J. and Chandler, J. (2006) 'To buy or not to buy: family dynamics and children's consumption', *Sociological Research Online*, 11(2)

Fenn, R.K. (ed.) (2004) 'Feminism and the sociology of religion: from gender blindness to gendered difference', in *The Blackwell Companion to the Sociology of Religion*, London: Blackwell

Festinger, L., Riecken, H., and Schachter, S. (1956) *When Prophecy Fails*, Minneapolis: University of Minnesota Press

Finkelstein, V. (1980) Attitudes and Disabled People: Issues for Discussion, New York: World Rehabilitation Fund

Fletcher, R. (1988*) The Shaking of the Foundations: Family and Society*, London: Routledge

Flouri, E. and Buchanan, A. (2002) 'Father involvement in childhood and trouble with the police in adolescence: Findings from the 1958 British birth cohort', *Journal of Interpersonal Violence*, 17, pp.689-701

Flowers, A. (1998) *The Fantasy Factory: An insider's view of the phone sex industry*, Philadelphia: University of Pennsylvania Press

Ford, R. and Millar, J. (eds) (1998) *Private Lives and Public Costs: Lone parents and the state*, London: Policy Studies Institute

Foster, J. (1990) *Villains: Crime and Community in the Inner City*, London: Routledge

Foucault, M. (1965) *Madness and Civilization*, New York: Random House

Foucault, M. (1976) *The Birth of the Clinic*, London: Tavistock

Fox Harding, L. (1996) *Family, State and Social Policy*, Basingstoke: Macmillan

Frazer, J.G. (1922, originally 1890) *The Golden Bough*, London: Macmillan

Friedson, E. (1965) 'Disability as social deviance', in M.B. Sussman (ed.) *Sociology of Disability and Rehabilitation*, Washington, DC: American Sociological Association

Fulcher, J. and Scott, J. (2007) *Sociology* (3rd edn), Oxford: Oxford University Press

Fyvel, T.R. (1961) *The Insecure Offender,* London: Chatto & Windus

Gardner F., Collishaw S., Maughan B. and Scott J. (2009) Has P*arenting Changed Over Recent Decades? Can changes in parenting explain time trends in adolescent problem behaviour?* York: Joseph Rowntree Foundation for the Nuffield Foundation

Gershuny, J. (2000) *Children and the Family Today*, University of Essex with the Future Foundation for Abbey National

Giddens, A. (1991) *Modernity and Self-Identity: Self and Society in the Late Modern Age*, Cambridge, Polity Press

Giddens, A. (2006) *Sociology* (5th edn), Oxford: Polity Press

Gilroy, P. (1987) *There Ain't No Black in the Union Jack*, London: Hutchinson

Gilroy, P., *The Black Atlantic: Modernity and Double Consciousness*, London: Verso, 1992

Giroux, H.A. (1998). 'Teenage sexuality, body politics, and the pedagogy of display'. In J.S. Epstein (ed.) *Youth Culture: Identity in a postmodern world,* Oxford: Blackwell

Glaser, B. and Strauss, A. (1967) *The Discovery of Grounded Theory*, Chicago: Aldine

Glasner, P. (1977) *The Sociology of Secularisation*, London: Routledge & Kegan Paul

Glendinning, A. and Bruce, S. (2006) 'New ways of believing or belonging: is religion giving way to spirituality?' *British Journal of Sociology*, 57(3), pp.399–414

Glock, C.Y. and Stark, R. (1969) 'Dimensions in religious commitment', in R. Robertson (ed.) (1969) *The Sociology of Religion*, Harmondsworth: Penguin

Goffman, E. (1961) Asylums, Harmondsworth: Penguin

Goffman, E. (1963) *Stigma: Notes on the Management of Spoiled Identity*, New York: Prentice Hall

Goffman, E. (2004, originally 1959) *The Presentation of Self in Everyday Life*, Harmondsworth: Penguin

Goody, J. (1961) 'Religion and ritual: the definitional problem', *British Journal of Sociology*, 12, pp.142-64

Gottman, J.S. (1990) 'Children of gay and lesbian parents', in F.W. Bozett and M.B. Sussman (eds) *Homosexuality and Family Relations*, New York: Harrington Press

Gove, W.R. (1982) 'The current status of the labeling theory of mental illness', in W.R. Gove (ed.) *Deviance and Mental Illness* (pp. 273–300), Beverly Hills, CA: Sage Publications

Graham, H. (2002) 'Inequality in Men and Women's Health', in S. Nettleton and U. Gustafsson (eds) *The Sociology of Health and Illness, A Reader*, Cambridge: Polity

Gramsci, A. (1971) *Selections from the Prison Notebooks*, London: Lawrence and Wishart

Gray, A (2006) 'The time economy of parenting', *Sociological Research Online*, 11(3)

Greeley, A. (1972) *Unsecular Man*, New York: Schocken Books, Inc

Greeley, A. (1992) *Sociology and Religion: A Collection of Readings*, New York: HarperCollins Publishers

Grieshaber, S. (1977) 'Mealtime rituals: power and resistance in the construction of mealtime rules', *British Journal of Sociology*, 48(4)

Griffin, C. (1985) *Typical Girls: Young Women from School to the Job Market*, London: Routledge & Kegan Paul

Griffin, C., *Representations of Youth: the Study of Youth and Adolescence in Britain and America*, Polity Press 1993

Gross, R.M. (1994) 'Buddhism', in J. Holm and J. Bowker (eds) *Women in Religion*, London: Pinter

Guibernau, M. and Goldblatt, D. (2000) 'Identity and nation', in K.Woodward (ed.) *Questioning Identity: Gender, Class, Nation*, London: Routledge/Open University Press

Hadden, J. and Bromley, D. (1993) *Religion and the Social Order: The Handbook on Cults and Sects in America*, Greenwich, CT: JAI Press

Haddon, J.K. and Long, T.E. (eds) (1993) *Religion and Religiosity in America*, New York: Crossroad Publishing Company

Hakim, C. (1996) *Key Issues in Women's Work*, London: Athlone

Halevy, E. (1927) *A History of the English People in 1815*, London: Unwin

Hall, S. (1985) 'Religious ideologies and social movements in Jamaica', in R. Bocock and K. Thompson (eds) *Religion and Ideology*, Manchester: Manchester University Press

Hall, S. and Jefferson, S. (eds) (1993) *Resistance through Rituals: Youth Subcultures in Post-war Britain*, London: Routledge

Ham, C. (1999) *Health Policy in Britain*, Basingstoke: Palgrave

Hamilton, M. (2001) *The Sociology of Religion* (2nd edn) London: Routledge

Hanson, E. (1997) *Decadence and Catholicism*, Cambridge, Mass: Harvard University Press

Hardey, M. (1998) *The Social Context of Health*, Buckingham: Open University Press

Hardill, I., Green, A., Dudlestone, A. and Owen, D.W. (1997) 'Who decides what? Decision making in dual career households', *Work, Employment and Society*, 11(2)

Harding, S. (1986) *The Science Question in Feminism*, Ithaca & London: Cornell University Press

Harding, S. (1987) *Feminism and Methodology*, Bloomington, IN & Buckingham: Indiana University Press & Open University Press

Hargreaves, D.H. (1967) *Social Relations in a Secondary School*, London: Routledge & Kegan Paul

Hart, N. (1976) *When Marriage Ends*, London: Tavistock

Hayward, K.J. (2004) *City Limits: Crime, consumer culture and the urban experience*, London: Glasshouse Press

Haywood, C. (2003) *Men and Masculinities: Theory, research and social practice*, Buckingham: Open University Press

Heath, S. (2004) 'Transforming friendship', *Sociology Review*, 14(1), September 2004

Hebdige, D. (1979) *Subculture: The meaning of style*, London: Methuen

Hebdige, D. (1988) *On Hiding in the Light*, London: Comedia

Heelas, P. (1996) *The New Age Movement*, Cambridge: Polity Press

Heelas, P., Woodhead, W., Seel, B., Tusting, K. and Szerszynski, B. (2004) *The Spiritual Revolution: Why Religion Is Giving Way to Spirituality*, Oxford: Blackwell

Hennink, M. *et al.* (1999) 'Young Asian women and relationships: traditional or transitional', *Ethnic and Racial Studies*, 22(5)

Herberg, W. (1960) *Protestant – Catholic – Jew* (revised edn), New York: Anchor Books

Hockey, J. and James, A. (1993) *Growing Up and Growing Old*, London: Sage

Holden, A. (2002) *Jehovah's Witnesses: Portrait of a Contemporary Religious Movement*, London/New York: Routledge

Holm, J. and Bowker, J. (eds) (1994) *Women in Religion*, London: Pinter

Hook, S. (1990) *Convictions*, New York: Prometheus Books

Hopkins, N. and Kahani-Hopkins, V. (2004) 'Identity construction and political activity: beyond rational actor theory', *British Journal of Social Psychology*, 43(3), pp.339–56

Hough, J.M. and Roberts, J.V (2004) *Juvenile Delinquency in England*, Oxford: Polity Press

Humphreys, L. (1975) *Tearoom Trade: Impersonal sex in public places*, New York: Aldine De Gruyter

Humphries, S. (1981) *Hooligans or Rebels: An oral history of working class childhood and youth, 1889–1939*, Oxford: Blackwell

Hunt, S. (2001) 'Dying to be thin', *Sociology Review*

Hunt, S. & Lightly, N., A healthy alternative? A sociology of 'fringe' medicine, Sociology Review, February 1999

Hunt, S. (2005) *Religion and Everyday Life*, London: Routledge

Hunter, J.D. (1987) *Evangelism: The Coming Generation*, Chicago: University of Chicago Press

Illich, I (1975) *Medical Nemesis*, Marion Boyars: London

Illsley, R. (1986) 'Occupational class, selection and the production of inequalities in health', *Quarterly Journal of Social Affairs*, 2(2), pp. 151–64

Innocenti Report (2007), *Child Well-Being in Rich Countries*

Jackson, C. (2006) *Lads and Ladettes in School: Gender and a Fear of Failure*, Milton Keynes: Open University Press

Jacobson (1998) *Islam in Transition: Religion and identity among British Pakistani Youth*, London: Routledge

Jefferis, B., Power, C. and Hertzman, C. (2002) 'Birth weight, childhood socioeconomic environment, and cognitive development in the 1958 British birth cohort study', *British Medical Journal*, 325, p.305

Johal S. (1998) 'Brimful of Brasia', *Sociology Review*, 8(1), Oxford: Philip Allan

Johnson, J. and Bytheway, B. (1993) 'Ageism: concept and definition', in J.Johnson and R.Slater (eds) *Ageing and Later Life*, London: Sage

Jones G. and Wallace, C. (1992) *Youth, Family and Citizenship*, Milton Keynes: Open University Press

Jordan, B. (1992) *Trapped in Poverty: Labour Market Decisions in Low Income Households*, London: Routledge

Jowell, R., Curtice, J., Park, A., Brook, L. and Ahrendt, A. (eds) (1995) *British Social Attitudes: the 12th Report*, Aldershot: Dartmouth

Kahane, R. with Rapoport, T. (1997) *The Origins of Postmodern Youth: Informal youth movements in a comparative perspective*, Berlin; New York: Walter de Gruyter

Kallianes, V. and Rubenfeld, P. (1997) 'Disabled women and reproductive rights', *Disability and Society,* 12(2)

Katz, J. (1988) *Seductions of Crime: Moral and sensual attractions in doing evil*, New York: Basic Books

Katz, J. (2000) 'The gang myth', in S. Karstedt and K.D. Bussman (eds) *Social Dynamics of Crime and Control,* Oxford: Hart

Kaur-Singh, K. (1994) 'Sikhism', in J. Holm and J. Bowker (eds) *Women in Religion*, London: Pinter

Kautsky, K. (1953) *Foundations of Christianity*, New York: Russell

Kellner, D. (1999) 'Theorizing/Resisting McDonaldization: A Multiperspectivist Approach' in B. Smart (ed) Resisting McDonaldisation, London: Sage

Kempson, E. (1996) *Life on a Low Income*, York, Joseph Rowntree Foundation

Kepel, G. (1994) *The Revenge of God: The Resurgence of Islam, Christianity and Judaism in the Modern World*, Cambridge: Polity Press

Kidd, W. (2002) *Culture and Identity*, Palgrave: Basingstoke

Kiernan, K. (2007) quoted in '"Marriage still the best way to play happy, healthy families", says study', Polly Curtis, *The Guardian*, 5 October 2007

Kilkey, M. (2005) 'New Labour and reconciling work and family life; making it fathers' business', *Social Policy and Society*, 5(2), pp.167–75

Knott, K. and Khokher, S. (1993) 'Religious and ethnic identity among young Muslim women in Bradford', *New Community,* 19(4), p.593–610

Krause, I.B. (1989) 'Sinking heart: a Punjabi communication of distress', *Social Science and Medicine*, 29, pp. 563–75

Lacey, C. (1970) *Hightown Grammar,* Manchester: Manchester University Press

Lader, D., Short, S. and Gershuny, J. (2006) *The Time Use Survey, 2005*, London: Office for National Statistics

Laidler, K. and Hunt, G. (2001) 'Accomplishing femininity among the girls in the gang', *British Journal of Criminology,* 41, p. 658

Langone, M.D. and Martin, P. (1993) 'Deprogramming, exit counselling, and ethics: clarifying the confusion', *Cult Observer*, 10(4)

Laslett, P. (1972) 'Mean household size in England since the sixteenth century', in P. Laslett (ed.) *Household and Family in Past Time*, Cambridge: Cambridge University Press

Lea, J. and Young, J. (1984) *What is to be done about Law and Order?* Harmondsworth: Penguin

Leach, E. (1988) *Culture and Communication*, Cambridge: Cambridge University Press

Lees, S. (1986) *Losing Out: Sexuality and Adolescent Girls*, London: Hutchinson

Leighton, G. (1992) 'Wives' paid and unpaid work and husbands' unemployment', *Sociology Review*, 1(3)

Lenin (1965) *Collected Works*, Vol. 10, Moscow: Progress Publishers

Levine, E. (1980) 'Deprogramming without tears', *Society*, 17 (March), pp.34–8

Lewis, J. (2007) *Families and Labour's Family Policies*, posted on www.lse.ac.uk/collections/pressAndIn formationOffice/newsAndEvents/arch ives/2007/BlairsLegacyJune07.htm

Lincoln, S. (2004) "Teenage girls, 'bedroom culture': codes versus zones" in Bennett, A. and Kahn-Harris, K. (eds) *After Subculture: Critical Studies in Contemporary Youth Culture*. Basingstoke: Palgrave

Link, B. and Phelan, J. (1995) 'Social conditions as fundamental cause of disease', *Journal of Health and Social Behaviour*, pp. 80–94

Longmore, F. (1987) 'Screening stereotypes: images of disabled people in TV and motion pictures', in A. Gartner and T. Foe (eds) *Images of the Disabled, Disabling Images*, New York: Praeger

Luke, A. and Luke, C. (2000) 'A situated perspective on cultural globalisation', in N. Burbules and C. Torres (eds) *Globalisation and Education,* New York: Routledge

Lupton, D. (1994) *Medicine as Culture: Illness, Disease and the Body in Western Societies*, London: Sage

Lyng, S. (1990) 'Edgework: a social psychological analysis of voluntary risk-taking', *American Journal of Sociology*, 95(4), pp.851–6

Lyon, D. (2000) *Jesus in Disneyland: Religion in Postmodern Times*, Cambridge: Polity Press

Lyotard, J-F. (1984) *The Post-Modern Condition: A Report on Knowledge*, Manchester: University of Manchester Press

Mac an Ghaill , M. (1991) 'Young, gifted and Black: methodological reflections of a teacher/researcher', in G.Walford (1991) *Doing Educational Research*, London: Taylor & Francis

Mac an Ghaill, M. (1988) *Young, Gifted and Black*, Milton Keynes: Open University Press

Mac an Ghaill, M. (1994) *The Making of Men: masculinities, sexualities and schooling*, Milton Keynes: Open University Press

Mac an Ghaill, M. (ed.) (1996) *Understanding Masculinities: Social Relations and Cultural Arenas*, Buckingham: Open University Press

MacGuire, M.B. (1981) *Religion: The Social Context*, California: Wadsworth Publishing

MacIntyre, S. (1993) 'Gender differences in the perceptions of common cold symptoms', *Social Science and Medicine*, 36(1), pp. 15–20

Maduro, O. (1982) *Religion and Social Conflicts*, New York: Orbis Books

Maffesoli, M. (1998) 'The future and postmodern youth', in J.S. Epstein (ed.) *Youth Culture: Identity in a postmodern world*, Oxford: Blackwell

Malinowski, B. (1954) *Magic, Science and Religion and Other Essays*, New York: Anchor Books

Marcuse, H. (1964) *One Dimensional Man,* London: Routledge and Keegan Paul

Mares, D. (2001) 'Gangstas or Lager Louts? Working class street gangs in Manchester', in M.W. Klein, H.J. Kerner, C.L. Maxson and E.G.M. Weitekamp (eds) *The Eurogang Paradox: Street Gangs and Youth Groups in the US and Europe,* London: Kluwer Academic

Margo, J. & Dixon, M., *Freedom's Orphans: Raising youth in a changing world*, IPPR, 2006

Marsh, I. and Keating, M. (2006) *Sociology: Making Sense of Society* (3rd edn), Harlow: Pearson Education

265

BIBLIOGRAPHY

Marshall , G. (1998) *Oxford Dictionary of Sociology*, Oxford University Press

Marshall, G. (1982) *In Search of the Spirit of Capitalism: Max Weber and the Protestant Ethic Thesis*, London: Hutchison

Marshall, G., Newby, H., Rose, D. and Vogler, C. (1988) *Social Class in Modern Britain*, London: Hutchinson

Martin, D. (1969) *The Religious and the Secular*. London: Routledge & Keegan Paul

Martin, D. (1978) *A General Theory of Secularisation*, Blackwell: Oxford

Marx, K. (1844) *Selected Writings* (2000 edn), Oxford: Oxford University Press

Marx, K. (1845) 'The German Ideology', extract in T. Bottomore and M. Rubel (eds, 1963 edn) *Karl Marx: Selected Writings in Sociology and Social Philosophy*, Harmondsworth: Penguin

Marx, K. (1848) *The Communist Manifesto* (2002 edn), Harmondsworth: Penguin

Marx, K. and Engels, F. (1957) *On Religion*, Moscow: Progress Publishers

Marx, K. and Engels, F. (1974) *The German Ideology* (2nd edn), London: Lawrence & Wishart

Marx, K. and Engels, F. (1975) 'On the history of early Christianity', in *Collected Works of Karl Marx and Frederick Engels,* Vol. 27, Moscow: Progress Publishers

Matza, D. (1964) *Delinquency and Drift*, New York: Wiley

Mayo, R. (2005) *'Nazareth Project: second draft Monday February 14th 2005', unpublished paper.*

McAllister, F. with Clarke, L. (1998) *Choosing Childlessness*, York: Family Policy Studies Centre and Joseph Rowntree Foundation

McKay, G. (1996) *Senseless Acts of Beauty: Cultures of Resistance since the Sixties*, London: Verso

McKeown, T. (1979 *The Role of Medicine: Dream, Mirage or Nemesis*, Oxford: Blackwell

McKinlay, J. (1984) *Issues in the Political Economy of Health Care*, London, Tavistock

McNamara, R.P. (1994) *The Times Square Hustler: Male prostitution in New York City*, Westport: Praeger

McRobbie, A. (1991) 'Romantic individualism and the teenage girl' in A. McRobbie (ed.) *Feminism and Youth Culture*, Basingstoke: Macmillan

McRobbie, A. and Garber, J. (1976) 'Girls and subcultures', in S. Hall, and T. Jefferson, *Resistance through Rituals*, London: Hutchinson

McRobbie, A. and Nava, M. (1984) *Gender and Generation*, London: Macmillan

Mead, M. (1928) *Coming of Age in Samoa*, New York: Morrow

Merton, R.K. (1938/1968) *Social Theory and Social Structure*, New York: The Free Press

Metcalf, H., Modood, T. and Virdee, S. (1996) *Asian Self-Employment*, London: Policy Studies Institute

Miller, A.S. and Hoffman, J.P. (1995) 'Risk and religion: an explanation of gender differences in religiosity', *Journal for the Scientific Study of Religion*, 34, pp. 63–75

Miller, W.B. (1962) 'Lower class culture as a generating milieu of gang delinquency', in M.E. Wolfgang, L. Savitz and N. Johnston (eds) *The Sociology of Crime and Delinquency*, New York: Wiley

Miller, W.B. (1975) *Violence by Youth Gangs and Youth Groups as a Crime Problem in Major American Cities*, Washington: Government Printing Office

Mirrlees-Black, C. (1999) 'Domestic violence: findings from a new British Crime Survey self-completion questionnaire', Home Office Research Study 191

Mirza, H. (1992) *Young, Female and Black*, London: Routledge

Mirza, H. and Reay, D. (2000) 'Spaces and places of Black educational desire: rethinking Black supplementary schools as a new social movement', *Sociology,* 34, pp.521–44

Mirza, H. (2008), Religious Extremism and British Muslims, *Sociology Review*, 17(4)

Mirza, M., Senthilkumaran, A., & Ja'far, Z. (2007) *Living Apart Together: British Muslims and the Paradox of Multiculturalism*, London: Policy Exchange

Mitchell, R., Shaw, M and Dorling, D. (2000) *Inequalities in Life and Death: What if Britain were more equal?* Bristol: The Policy Press

Modood, T. (2005) *Multicultural Politics: Racism, Ethnicity and Muslims in Britain*, Minneapolis: University of Minnesota Press

Modood, T., Beishon, S. and Virdee, S. (1994) *Changing Ethnic Identities*, London: Policy Studies Institute

Modood, T., Berthoud, R., *et al.* (1997) *Ethnic Minorities in Britain*, London: PSI

Moore. S. (2004) 'Hanging around: the politics of the busstop', *Youth and Policy*, 82, pp. 47–59

Morgan, D.H.J. (1996) *Family Connections: An Introduction to Family Studies*, Brighton: Polity

Morgan, P. (2000) *Marriage-Lite: the Rise of Cohabitation and its Consequences*, London: Civitas

Morris, D. (1968) *The Naked Ape*, London: Corgi

Morrow, V. (1998) *Understanding Families: Children's Perspectives*, York: National Children's Bureau in association with the Joseph Rowntree Foundation

Mort, F. (1996) *Cultures of Consumption: Masculinities and Social Space in Late Twentieth-Century Britain,* London: Routledge

Moser, K., Goldblatt, P., Fox, J. and Jones, D. (1990) 'Unemployment and mortality', in P. Goldblatt (ed.) *Longitudinal Study: Mortality and Social Organisation*, London: HMSO

Mount, F. (2004) *Mind the Gap: The New Class Divide in Britain*, London: Short Books

Muncie, J. (1984) *The Trouble with Kids Today: Youth and Crime in Post-War Britain*, London: Hutchinson

Muncie, J. (2004) *Youth and Crime*, London: Sage

Murdock, G. and McCron, R. (1976) 'Consciousness of class and consciousness of generation', in S. Hall and T. Jefferson (eds) *Resistance through Rituals,* London: Hutchinson

Murdock, G.P. (1949) *Social Structure*, New York: Macmillan

Murphy, M. (2006) *Household and Family: Past, Present and Future,* taken from presentation made to ESRC/BSPS/ONS Public Policy Seminar 'Changing Household and Family Structure Including Complex Living Arrangements', 18 May 2006

Murphy, M. (2007) quoted in '"Marriage still the best way to play happy, healthy families", says study', Polly Curtis, *The Guardian*, 5 October 2007

Murray, C. (1994) *Underclass: The Crisis Deepens*, London: IEA

Myers, J. (1975) 'Life events, social integration and psychiatric symptomatology', *Journal of Health and Social Behaviour*, 16, pp. 121–7

NACRO (2009) *Youth Crime Briefing: Some Facts about Children and Young People who Offend*

Navarro, V. (1977) *Medicine under Capitalism*, London: Martin Robertson

Nazroo, J. (1999) 'Uncovering gender differences in the use of marital violence: the effect of methodology' in G. Allan (ed.) *The Sociology of the Family: A Reader*, Oxford: Blackwell

Nazroo, J.Y. (2001) *Ethnicity, Class and Social Health*, London: PSI

Nelson, G.K. (1986) 'Religion', in M. Haralambos (ed.) *Developments in Sociology*, Vol. 2, Ormskirk: Causeway Press

Nettleton, J. (2006) *The Sociology of Health and Illness, 2nd edition*, Cambridge: Polity

Niebuhr, H.R. (1929) *The Social Sources of Denominationalism*, New York: The World Publishing Company

O'Beirne, M. (2004) *Religion in England and Wales: Findings from the 2001 Home Office Citizenship Survey*, Home Office Research Study 274, London: HMSO

O'Brien, M. and Jones, D. (1996) 'Revisiting family and kinship', *Sociology Review*, February 1996

O'Brien, R., Hunt, K, & Hart, G. (2005) 'It's caveman stuff, but that is to a certain extent how guys still operate', *Social Science and Medicine*, 61 (3): 503-16.

O'Connor, J. (1973) *The Fiscal Crisis of the State*, Basingstoke: Macmillan

O'Donnell, M. and Sharpe, S. (2000) *Youth, Ethnicity and Class in Contemporary Britain*, London: Routledge

Oakley, A. (1982) *Subject Women*, London: Fontana

Oakley, A. (1986) 'Feminism, motherhood and medicine – Who cares?', in J. Mitchell and A. Oakley (eds) *What is Feminism?* Oxford: Blackwell

Office for National Statistics (2004) *Mental health of children and young people in Great Britain*, Basingstoke: Palgrave Macmillan

Office for National Statistics (2007) *Focus on Religion* HYPERLINK "http://www.statistics.gov.uk/focuson/religion/" http://www.statistics.gov.uk/focuson/religion/ accessed 28/03/2010

Oliver, M. (1990) *The Politics of Disablement*, Basingstoke: Macmillan

Oliver, M. (1996) *Understanding Disability*, London: Macmillan

Olney, M.F. and Kim, A. (2001) 'Beyond adjustment: integration of cognitive disability into identity', *Disability and Society*, 16

O'Toole, R. (1984) *Religion: Classic Sociological Approaches*, Toronto: McGraw Hill

Palmer, S. (2007) *Toxic Childhood: How the modern world is damaging our children and what we can do about it*, London: Orion

Parkin, F. (1972) *Class Inequality and Political Order*, St. Albans: Paladin

Parry, N and Parry, J. (1976) *The Rise of the Medical Profession*, Croom Helm, London

Parsons, T. (1955) 'The social structure of the family', in T. Parsons and R.F. Bales (eds) *Family, Socialization and Interaction Process*, New York: The Free Press

Parsons, T. (1965) 'Religious perspectives in sociology and social psychology', in W.A. Lessa and E.Z. Vogt (eds) *Reader in Comparative Religion: An Anthropological Approach* (2nd edn), New York: Harper & Row

Parsons, T. (1965) 'The normal American family', in S.M. Farber (ed.) *Man and Civilization: the Family's Search for Survival*, New York: McGraw Hill

Parsons, T. (1975) 'The sick role and the role of the physician reconsidered', *Millbank Memorial Fund Quarterly: Health and Society*, 53, pp 257–78

Pearson, G. (1983) *Hooligan: A History of Respectable Fears*. Basingstoke: Macmillan

Pew Global Attitudes Project (2002) www.pewglobal.org

Pew Global Attitudes Survey (2006) *The Great Divide: How Westerners and Muslims View Each Other*, Washington, DC: Pew Research Center

Phillips, M. (1997) *All Must Have Prizes*, London: Little Brown

Phillipson, C. and Downs, M. (1999) *The Futures of Old Age*, London: Sage

Pilcher , J. (1996) *Age and Generation in Modern Britain*, Oxford University Press

Pilgrim, D. and Rogers, A. (1999) *A Sociology of Mental Health and Illness* (2nd edn), Buckingham: Open University Press

Pitts, J. (2008) *Reluctant Gangsters*. Cullompton: Willan

Platt, L., Ethnicity and Family: *Relationships Within and Between Ethnic Groups*, Institute for Social and Economic Research, 2009

Plummer, K. (2000) *Documents of Life*, Thousand Oaks, CA: Sage

Postman, N. (1982) *The Disappearance of Childhood*, New York: Delacorte Press

Pryce K. (1979) *Endless Pressure*, Harmondsworth: Penguin

Pudney, S. (2002) *The Road to Ruin? Sequences of initiation into drug use and offending by young people in Britain,* Home Office Research Study 253 HYPERLINK "http://www.homeoffice.gov.uk/rds/pdfs2/hors253.pdf" www.homeoffice.gov.uk/rds/pdfs2/hors253.pdf

Pugh, A. (2002) *From 'Compensation' to 'Childhood Wonder': Why Parents Buy,* Working Paper No 39. University of California Berkeley: Centre for Working Families

Putnam, R. (2000) *Bowling Alone*, New York: Simon and Schuster

Rankin, P. (2005) *Buried Spirituality*, Salisbury: Sarum College Press

Rapoport, R.N., Fogarty, M.P. and Rapoport, R. (eds) (1982) *Families in Britain*, London: Routledge

Reddington, H. (2003) "'Lady punks' in bands: a subculturette?' in Muggleton, D. and Weinzierl, R. (eds) *The Post-Subcultures Reader*. Oxford: Berg

Reynolds, T., Callender, C. and Edwards, R. (2003) *Caring and Counting: The impact of mothers' employment on family relationships*, Bristol: The Policy Press

Rich , A. (1984) 'Compulsory heterosexuality and lesbian existence', in A. Snitow *et al.* (eds) *Desire: The Politics of Sexuality*, London: Virago

Riddell, S. (1992) *Polities and the Gender of the Curriculum,* London: Routledge

Riseborough, G. (1993) 'The gobbo barmy army: one day in the life of YTS boys', in I. Bates (ed.) *Youth and Inequality*, Milton Keynes: Open University Press

Ritchie, J. and Lewis, J. (eds) (2003) *Qualitative Research Practice A Guide for Social Science Students and Researchers*, London: Sage Publications

Robbins, T. (1988) *Cults, Converts, and Charisma*, London: Sage

Roberts, K. (1997) 'Same activities, different meanings: British youth cultures in the 1990s', *Leisure Studies,* 16, pp. 1–15

Roberts, K. (2001) *Class in Modern Britain,* Basingstoke: Palgrave Macmillan

Rodgers, B. and Pryor, J. (1998), *Divorce and separation: The outcomes for children*, York: Joseph Rowntree Foundation

Rosenhan, D.L. (1973/1982) 'On being sane in insane places', *Science*, 179, pp. 250–8; also in M. Bulmer (ed.) (1982) *Social Research Ethics*, London: Holmes and Meier

Rosenhan, D.L. (1973/1982) 'On being sane in insane places', *Science*, 179, pp. 250–8; also in M. Bulmer (ed.) (1982) *Social Research Ethics*, London: Holmes & Meier

Ross, N., Hill, M., Sweeting, H. and Cunningham-Burley, S. (2006) *Grandparents and Teen Grandchildren: Exploring Intergenerational Relationships*, Edinburgh: Centre for Research on Families and Relationships

Roszak, T. (1970) *The Making of a Counter Culture*, London: Faber & Faber

Samad, Y. (2006) 'Muslims in Britain today', *Sociology Review*, 15(4)

Sanders, W.B. (1994) *Gangbangs and Drive-Bys: Grounded Culture and Juvenile Gang Violence*, New York: Aldine De Gruyter

Sanderson, T. (1999) 'UK Church offers atheists 'baby blessing'', BBC News online article, 14 July

Savage, J. (2007) *Tenage: The Creation of Youth Culture*, London: Chatto & Windus

Savage, M. (1995) 'The middle classes in modern Britain', *Sociology Review*, 5(2), Oxford: Philip Allan

Scambler, G. and Hopkins, A. (1986) 'Being epileptic; coming to terms with stigma', *Sociology of Health and Illness*, 8, pp. 26–43

Scharf, B. (1970) *The Sociological Study of Religion*, London: Hutchinson

Scheff, T. (1966) *Being Mentally Ill: A Sociological Theory*, Chicago: Aldine

Schudsen, R. (1994) 'Culture and integration of national societies', in D. Crane (ed.) *The Sociology of Culture*, Oxford, Blackwell

Sclater, S.D. (2000) *Access to Sociology: Families*, London: Hodder Arnold

Scott, R.A. (1969) *The Making of Blind Men*, New Brunswick, Transaction Publishers

Scott, J. (1991) *Who Rules Britain?* Cambridge: Polity Press

Scott, S. (2003) 'Symbolic interactionism and shyness', *Sociology Review*, 12(4)

Self, A. and Zealey, L. (eds) (2007) *Social Trends 37*, Basingstoke: Office for National Statistics/Palgrave Macmillan

Sewell, T. (2000) 'Identifying the pastoral needs of African-Caribbean students: A case of "critical antiracism"', *Education and Social Justice*, 3(1)

Shakespeare, T. and Watson, N. (1997) 'Defending the social model', in L. Barton and M. Oliver (eds) *Disability Studies: Past, Present and Future*, Leeds: The Disability Press

Sharpe, S. (1994) *Just Like a Girl* (2nd edn), Harmondsworth: Penguin

Shaw, M., Dorling, D., Gordon, D. and Davey Smith, G. (1999) *The Widening Gap*, Bristol: Policy Press

Shilling, C. (2003) *The Body and Social Theory* (2nd edn), London: Sage

Shiner, L. (1967) 'The concept of secularization in empirical research', *Journal for the Scientific Study of Religion*, 6, pp.207–20

Shropshire, S. and McFarquhar, M. (2002) *Developing Multi-Agency Strategies to Address the Street Gang Culture and Reduce Gun Violence among Young People Briefing No. 4,* Manchester: Shropshire & McFarquhar Consultancy Group

Simon, R.J. and Nadell, P.S. (1995) 'In the same voice or is it different? Gender and the clergy', *Sociology of Religion*, 56(1)

Singh Ghumann, P.A. (1999) *Asian Adolescents in the West*, Leicester: BPS Books

Sivananden, A. (1981) 'From resistance to rebellion', *Journal of Race and Class*, 23(2/3)

Skelton, C. (2001) *Schooling the Boys: Masculinites and Primary Education*, Buckingham: Open University Press

Smart, C. and Stevens, P. (2000) *Cohabitation Breakdown*, London: The Family Policy Studies Centre

Smith, C. (2005) Soul Searching: The religious and spiritual lives of American teenagers, Oxford: Oxford University Press

Smith, J. (2001) *Moralities, Sex, Money and Power in the 21st Century*, London: Allen Lane

Sontag, S. (1978) 'The double standard of ageing', in V. Carver and P.Liddiard (eds) *An Ageing Population*, London: Hodder & Stoughton

Southwold, M. (1978) 'Buddhism and the definition of religion', *Man* (NS), 13, pp.362–79

Spender, D. (1982) *Invisible Women,* London: Writers & Readers

Sproston, K. and Mindell, J. (2006) *Health Survey for England 2004: the health of ethnic minorities*, Leeds: The Information Centre

Stanko, E. (2000) 'The day to count: a snapshot of the impact of domestic violence in the UK', *Criminal Justice*, 1(2)

Stark, R. and Bainbridge, W. (1985) *The Future of Religion: Secularisation, Revival and Cult Formation*, Berkeley: California University Press

Statham, J. (1986) *Daughters and Sons: Experiences of Non-Sexist Childraising*, Oxford: Blackwell

Steel, E. and Kidd, W. (2001) *The Family*, Basingstoke: Palgrave

Stopes-Roe, M. and Cochrane, R. (1990) *Citizens of this Country: the Asian British*, Clevedon: Multilingual Matters

Swingewood, A. (2000) *A Short History of Sociological Thought*, Basingstoke: Macmillan

Szasz, T. (1973 first published 1962) *The Myth of Mental Illness*, London: Paladin

Taylor, P. (1997) *Investigating Culture and Identity*, London: Collins Educational

Taylor, S. (1999) 'Postmodernism: a challenge to sociology', 'S' Magazine, 4

Thompson, D. (1996) *The End of Time: Faith and Fear in the Shadow of the Millennium*, London: Sinclair Stevenson

Thompson, I. (1986) *Sociology in Focus: Religion*, Harlow: Longman

Thornes, B. and Collard, J. (1979) *Who divorces?*, London: Routledge & Kegan Paul

Thornton, S. (1995) *Club Cultures: Music, media and subcultural capital*, Cambridge: Polity

Thrasher, F. (1927) *The Gang,* Chicago: University of Chicago Press

Tizard, B. and Hughes, M. (1991) 'Reflections on young people learning', in G. Walford (ed.) *Doing Educational Research*, London: Routledge

Tizard, B. and Phoenix , A. (1993) *Black, White or Mixed Race: Race and Racism in the Lives of Young People of Mixed Parentage*, London: Routledge

Troeltsch, E. (1931/1976) *The Social Teachings of the Christian Churches*, Chicago: University of Chicago Press

Tudor-Hart, J. (1971) *The Inverse Care Law*, Lancet, Vol 1 pp.405-12

Tunnell, K.D. (1998) 'Honesty, secrecy, and deception in the sociology of crime: confessions and reflections from the backstage', in J. Ferrell and M.S. Hamm (eds), *Ethnography at the Edge*, Boston: Northeastern University Press

Turner, B. (1983) *Religion and Social Theory*, London: Sage

Tylor, E.B. (1903, originally 1871) *Primitive Culture,* London: Murray

Virdee, S. (1997) 'Racial harassment', in T. Modood, R. Berthoud, J. Lakey, J. Nazroo, P. Smith, S. Virdee and S. Beishon (eds) *Ethnic Minorities in Britain: Diversity and Disadvantage*, London: PSI

Voas, D. and Crockett, A. (2005) 'Religion in Britain: neither believing nor belonging', *Sociology*, 39(1), pp.11–28

Waitzkin, H. (1979) 'Medicine, superstructure and micropolitics', *Social Science and Medicine*, 13a, pp. 601–9

Walker, A. and Aune, K. (eds) (2003) *On Revival: A Critical Examination*, Carlisle: Paternoster Press

Wallis, R. (1984) *The Elementary Forms of New Religious Life*, London: Routledge

Walter, N. (1999) *The New Feminism*, London: Virago

Warin, J., Solomon, Y., Lewis, C. and Langford, W. (1999) *Fathers, Work and Family Life*, York: Joseph Rowntree Foundation

Warner, R.S. (1993) 'Work in progress toward a new paradigm for the sociological study of religion in the United States', *American Journal of Sociology*, 98(5), pp.1044–93

Waters, M. (1995) *The Death of Class*, London: Sage

Watson, H. (1994) 'Women and the veil: personal responses to global process', in A. Ahmed and H. Donnan (eds) *Islam, Globalisation and Postmodernity*, London: Routledge

Watson, N. (1998) 'Enabling identity: disability, self and citizenship', in Shakespeare, T. (ed.) *The Disability Reader: Social Science Perspectives*, London, Cassell

Weber, M. (1905/1958) *The Protestant Ethic and the Spirit of Capitalism*, London: Unwin

Weber, M. (1920/1963) *The Sociology of Religion*, Boston, Mass: Beacon Press

Wertz, R.W. and Wertz, D.C. (1981) 'Notes on the decline of midwives and the rise of medical obstetricians', in P. Conrad and R. Kerns (eds) *The Sociology of Health and Illness: Critical Perspectives*, New York: St Martin's Press

Whyte, W.F. (1943) *Street Corner Society: The social structure of an Italian slum*, Chicago: University of Chicago Press.

Widdicombe, S. and Wooffitt, R. (1995) *The Language of Youth Subcultures,* Hemel Hempstead: Harvester

Wilkinson, H. (1994) *No Turning Back: Generations and the Genderquake*, London: Demos

Wilkinson, R. and Pickett, K. (2010), *The Spirit Level: Why Equality is Better for Everyone*, Penguin Books

Wilkinson, R.G. (1996) *Unhealthy Societies: The Afflictions of Inequality*, London: Routledge

Williams, W.M. (1956) *The Sociology of an English Village: Gosforth*, London: Routledge & Kegan Paul

Willis, P. (1977) *Learning to Labour*, Aldershot: Ashgate

Wilson, B. (1982) *Religion in Sociological Perspective*, Oxford: Oxford University Press

Wilson, B.R. (1966) *Religion in a Secular Society*, London: B.A. Watts

Witz, A. (1992) *Professions and Patriarchy*, London: Routledge

Woodhead, L. (2004) 'Feminism and the sociology of religion: from gender blindness to gendered difference', in R.K. Fenn (ed.) *The Blackwell Companion to the Sociology of Religion,* London: Blackwell

Woodhead, L. (2005) *Christianity: A Very Short Introduction*, Oxford: OUP

Woodhead, L. (2007) cited in R. Pigott, 'Lifting the veil on religion and identity', *The Edge*, Spring 2007, pp.16–20

Woodhead, L. and Heelas, P. (2000) *Religion in Modern Times: An Interpretive Anthology*, Oxford: Blackwell

Yinger, M. (1970) *The Scientific Study of Religion,* London: Routledge

Young, J. (1971) *The Drugtakers*. London: McGibbon and Kee

Young, M. and Willmott, P. (1957) *Family and Kinship in East London*, Harmondsworth: Penguin

Young, M. and Willmott, P. (1973) *The Symmetrical Family*, Harmondsworth: Penguin

Zachary, G.P. (1999) 'This singing sensation from Liverpool longs to be in Hong Kong', *Wall Street Journal*, pp. 1, 10

Zaretsky, E. (1976) *Capitalism, the Family and Personal Life*, London: Pluto Press

INDEX

Sociology AS for OCR

INDEX

NOTES

Acknowledgements

William Collins' dream of knowledge for all began with the publication of his first book in 1819. A self-educated mill worker, he not only enriched millions of lives but also founded a flourishing publishing house. Today, staying true to this spirit, Collins books are packed with inspiration, innovation and practical expertise. They place you at the centre of the world of possibility and give you exactly what you need to explore it.

Collins. Do More.

Published by Collins
An imprint of HarperCollins*Publishers* Limited
77-85 Fulham Palace Rd
Hammersmith
London
W68JB

Browse the complete Collins catalogue
at www.collinseducation.com

©HarperCollinsPublishers 2010

Reprint 10 9 8 7 6 5 4 3 2 1

ISBN 978-0-00-735373-6

British Cataloguing in Publication Data.
A cataloguing record for this publication is available from the British Library.

Commissioned by Charlie Evans
Consultant editor Peter Langley
Production by Simon Moore
Cover design by Occulus Design and Communications
Internal design by Ken Vail Graphic Design
Figures typeset by Liz Gordon
Cartoons by Oxford Designers and Illustrators